88 - 00551

United States Foreign Policy

United States Foreign Policy
Choices and Tradeoffs

Miroslav Nincic
New York University

A Division of Congressional Quarterly Inc.
1414 22nd Street N.W., Washington, D.C. 20037

Figure 7-1 from Charles Kindleberger, *World in Depression* (University of
California Press), Figure 8. Copyright © 1973 by Charles Kindleberger.

Figure 10-1 from *Historical Maps on File*. Copyright © 1983 by Martin
Greenwald Associates. Reprinted with permission of Facts on File, Inc., New
York.

Library of Congress Cataloging-in-Publication Data

Nincic, Miroslav.
    United States foreign policy: choices and tradeoffs/Miroslav Nincic.
        p. cm.
    Includes index.
    ISBN 0-87187-449-0
    1. United States—Foreign relations—1945-   I. Title.
JN1417.N56 1988   87-33417
327.73—dc19   CIP

To Jacqueline

Contents

s e c t i o n   t h r e e

Friends and Adversaries

s e c t i o n   f o u r
War and Peace

s e c t i o n   f i v e
National Prosperity and International Welfare

s e c t i o n   s i x
Conclusions

Tables and Figures

Tables

Figures

Preface

World affairs are becoming more and more complicated, and the external challenges facing the United States have less-apparent solutions than they once seemed to have. If ever there was a time when countries could be easily divided into friends and foes, it has long since passed. If ever the ends and means of foreign policy were linked in an obvious and simple fashion, this too is no more. Ideology is no longer a predictable measure of rivalry, and national interests are too complex to yield simple clues to friendship and enmity. Military force, as evidenced in ventures from Vietnam to the Persian Gulf, has proven a much less effective way of imposing the national will than it was once thought to be. Politics and economics have become increasingly intertwined, and more international interactions have become more politicized than ever before. Ethical distinctions, which had seemed so clear in the world of earlier decades, have become blurred to all but the most dogmatic eyes.

This book is built around a central assumption: that the conduct of foreign policy is the business of confronting dilemmas which often have no optimal solution, that it is in essence a matter of making appropriate compromises and establishing workable tradeoffs. The dilemmas are of three sorts. There is, first of all, a need to choose between goals that are mutually irreconcilable, or between means of pursuing them that are largely incompatible. This may be termed the dilemma of effective choice, and it is a permanent part of the making of foreign policy. Second, there is a need to translate a variety of differing individual, group, and institutional preferences into a national foreign policy—a challenge called in this book the dilemma of aggregation. Finally, policy cannot be divorced from the values on which a society rests, and the conduct of U.S. foreign policy should be brought into line with the principles that stand at the core of the nation's political system. This may be referred to as the dilemma of political principle.

The book seeks to establish a factual and conceptual foundation that will help the student of U.S. foreign policy come to intellectual grips with these dilemmas. It will begin by providing an overview of the mechanisms by which foreign policy is made and of the problems which they occasionally create. The book will then explore the more general issues of international conflict and cooperation, especially as they concern the United States, and specific contemporary issues such as the use of military force for political ends, the danger of nuclear war, the goals and future outlook of arms control, and the problems of constructing an acceptable international economic order. Finally, the ethical challenges that pervade the conduct of U.S. foreign policy will be addressed.

Ole Holsti, Robert Jervis, and Martin W. Sampson III offered valuable comments on the structure of the book, and Steven Chan, Richard Herrmann, Donna Klick, and Bruce Russett critiqued the entire manuscript. I have benefited from their conscientious and wise suggestions. Joanne D. Daniels, the director of CQ Press, was consistently encouraging and helpful. Kerry Kern efficiently ushered the manuscript through production, and Robert Feldmesser helped streamline the prose.

The Challenges
and the Setting

The Foreign Policy Challenge

To MANY PEOPLE foreign relations are simply a matter of morality versus immorality. The world consists of peaceful nations and aggressive nations, cooperative nations and recalcitrant nations, friendly nations and enemy nations—in short, good guys and bad guys. Politicians along with the mass media often reinforce these conceptions, depicting "our" people as heroes, with all the qualities one admires, and "theirs" as villains who would stop at nothing to make their evil empire prevail. The task of foreign policy is to ensure that the good guys win in the end.

In reality matters are not that clear-cut. Countries that are usually friendly to the United States may occasionally act in ways that run counter to U.S. interests, and normally hostile nations sometimes help the United States (and, hostile though they may be, the United States may in turn do them a favor). A nation that is cooperative in one set of circumstances may be quite uncooperative in other circumstances. Some citizens may want the government to behave abroad in ways that others regard as improper or perhaps outrageous. Very frequently, people find that their own moral principles conflict with other, equally important moral principles—as when a very commendable goal can be reached only by distasteful or even repugnant means—and in such situations it is all but impossible for a government to avoid actions that are objectionable on some level. And perhaps most common of all are instances in which it is extremely difficult even to decide what the "moral" course of action is, because situations are so complex and the consequences of a nation's actions so unpredictable.

The making of foreign policy—the determination of a nation's behavior in its relations with other nations—is thus an agonizing affair. Because of the problems just described, it can be thought of as a continuous effort to resolve dilemmas—making tradeoffs between needs that are barely if at all compatible, dealing with problems whose solutions yield undesirable consequences, and simultaneously pursuing goals among which one cannot establish satisfactory priorities. Overlaying this process is the ever-present realization that mistakes can place in jeopardy the lives of individual people or the very existence of a nation. In the case of the United States, this realization is intensified by the fact that this country has more power to harm or to benefit the rest of the world than does any other country. Though our first concern is often to ask how the government's foreign policy will affect our individual interests or those of the nation as a whole, it is reasonable to suggest that exceptionally powerful nations should also be judged by their impact on persons residing outside their borders. In other words, and more than in most areas of domestic policy, the manner in which the dilemmas of U.S foreign policy are resolved have consequences of global proportions.

Toward the end of this chapter, three specific types of foreign policy dilemmas will be described, but before that can be done, the main elements that go into the making of foreign policy must be set forth.

The Objectives of Foreign Policy

A natural starting point in trying to understand any nation's foreign policy is to ask what its goals are: What does it wish to achieve by the activities which its government directs toward other nations? Some isolationists claim that most U.S. national objectives can be pursued domestically and that the less America has to do with other nations, the better. Other, more sophisticated observers recognize that the international environment affects the United States in many profound ways and that it can be ignored only at grave peril to the nation's goals. If the nation wishes to achieve much that it considers important, it can do so only by interacting with other countries: by encouraging foreign behavior that furthers its goals and discouraging activities by which they may be frustrated. The nature and meaning of U.S. foreign policy can be understood only by first grasping the aims and objectives by which it is guided.

Foreign policy goals are often shrouded in rhetoric. The aims of a government's external behavior are professed to be lofty (security, human welfare, democracy), and its means peaceful and enlightened, by those who formulate and implement it. Similarly, some of the harshest domestic criticisms of a nation's foreign policy are linked to the interests of political challengers, and the alternatives they propose may be couched in oratory that is just as inflated and self-serving. Thus, we must first strip away the layers of rhetoric if we are to examine the essence of foreign policy dispassionately and with analytical rigor.

The United States is in certain ways similar to other nations and in other ways significantly different. Accordingly, some of its objectives are of the kind that virtually all nations pursue, while others, because they are rooted in its own conditions and beliefs, are more specifically U.S. objectives. The two most prominent among the universal foreign policy goals are national *security* and national *prosperity*. More specifically U.S. goals would include such external *ideological* objectives as the defense abroad of those political principles that the United States espouses at home. These objectives will be briefly discussed in this chapter and dealt with more extensively throughout this book.

National Security

Most people would agree that the principal task of U.S. foreign policy is to preserve and enhance national security. Security refers to the absence of threats to those things we most value; in the case of *national* security, the absence of threats to the things we most cherish as a nation. Although some threats to these values may be rooted in domestic sources, the sort of threats we most often have in mind come from outside our borders and spring from external coercion and aggression. What are the principal values that can be thus threatened?

To begin with, and perhaps most fundamentally, they are the lives and physical well-being of Americans and the institutions and norms that they have chosen to live by. It is against these that the threats we usually fear most are directed. Indeed, the image of invading foreign armies wreaking vast human destruction and inflicting an unwelcome system of political and economic organization is one that is typically associated with threats to national security.

However, the United States has been subjected to this kind of danger less than have most other countries. Almost alone among the nations of the world, the United States has never (with the exception of brief skirmishes with British troops during the War of 1812) been the victim of direct foreign aggression. It has fought a war of national independence against a colonial master, but never a war against a foreign invader. Due to a combination of its insular geographic position and its obvious strength, no foreign armies have crossed its borders or alighted on its shores. Most European countries (on both sides of the Cold War divide) have suffered directly from the ravages of intense fighting, both in World War I and in World War II. Many Europeans have seen their cities destroyed, have lived where armies were fighting within earshot, or have experienced foreign military occupation. Nations that did not fall victim to hostile foreign troops on their territory have suffered devastation of another kind: by enemy airplanes, buzz bombs (as in the case of Great Britain), or even (in the Japanese case) atomic weapons. Numerous developing countries have also been victims of external aggression and conflict. By contrast, and although U.S. lives have been lost in battles on distant shores, Americans have had the unusual historical fortune not to have experienced war in the streets of their cities, the bombardment of their industries, or the indignities of foreign occupation.

Moreover, the United States has been for many decades the most powerful nation on earth and, because of this, one might assume that it would not be alarmed about its security—yet clearly it is. To some extent, this might be an instance of what Karl Deutsch has called the "Parkinson's Law of national security," according to which a nation's feeling of insecurity expands in direct proportion to its power. The more powerful a nation, according to Deutsch, the higher its level of aspiration in world affairs and hence the greater the scope of its objectives that could be threatened by others.[1] To some extent, too, the current sense of insecurity has much to do with the existence of nuclear weaponry. Although an invasion of the United States by foreign troops is as unlikely now as it ever was, the march of military technology has made invasions unnecessary: the development of atomic and thermonuclear weapons and of the means of delivering them across great distances has changed the nature of external threats, and traditional military calculations have had to be revised.

Despite some confusion on this score, it is important to bear in mind that national security is not coextensive with military policy. The latter deals with the choice of weapons and strategies needed to meet national objectives by military means. Its purpose is to prepare the country to fend off foreign onslaughts, to deny an enemy all hope of military victory, or to threaten an adversary with a retaliation so devastating as to make aggression an unwise course of action. It may also be used to coerce other nations into behaving in a certain way. Military policy is a necessary, but plainly very limited, tool of national security. What it does not do, and is not designed to do, is eliminate or lessen the causes of rivalry or enmity with other nations so as to make aggression unlikely at the outset. It is in a nation's interest to convince an adversary that aggressive objectives cannot be successfully achieved; it is even more in its interest to have as few adversaries as possible. In fact, it can be argued that when military competition makes rivalries more bitter, and when it makes conflicts of interest appear even greater than otherwise, armed force undermines the very need by which it is justified.

This is certainly a problem: insufficient military power may render a nation vulnerable to foreign aggression or pressure, but too vigorous a pursuit of armed might can heighten international tension, complicate the resolution of differences with other countries, and thus, ultimately, make the nation *less* secure.

National Prosperity

A distinction is frequently made in international relations between "high" politics, which concerns matters of national security and major diplomacy, and "low" politics, which involves mainly economic matters (for example, trade policy). The implication is that the former is somehow grander and more vital than the latter. This is often disputed, and in fact most nations, including the United States, devote as much of their foreign policy efforts to dealing with matters of low politics as with high politics.[2] There is an obvious overlap between national security and national prosperity: the massive material abundance of the United States could, in principle, fall victim to coercive threats from abroad, no less than the security of its population or of its political institutions.

As an illustration, U.S. dependence on foreign sources of oil and other raw materials increased rapidly during the decades after World War II, and by the mid-1970s, this led to concern that hostile foreign nations might try to deny the United States access to these natural resources. When a number of petroleum-producing Arab nations withheld their oil from the United States during the winter of 1973-1974, because of U.S. support for Israel in the 1973 Middle East war, responsible U.S. statesmen openly discussed the possibility of military intervention to secure the nation's external oil supplies. Plainly, the economic consequences of a long-term denial of natural resources could be very serious, and this realization has influenced the nation's foreign policy. Since the late 1970s, the United States has made efforts to acquire allies and to establish a military presence in the Persian Gulf and Southwest Asia. In the summer of 1987, the United States made highly visible moves to increase its naval force in the Persian Gulf, in order to protect oil tankers from attacks by Iran and ensure the continued flow of oil to the industrialized West—although the desire to thwart what were believed to be Soviet ambitions in the area was an important consideration as well.

On the other hand, at some point prosperity and security come into conflict. An excessive emphasis on military growth might put too large a portion of the economy into the defense sector. Defense production might drain investment away from sectors of considerably greater civilian benefit, decreasing overall productivity growth and increasing inflation. Moreover, it is generally understood that military production generates less employment than most other forms of economic activity, thus exacerbating problems of jobless-ness.[3]

The United States is not only the wealthiest country on earth but it is also economically more self-sufficient than most other nations. Although it does import a number of important raw materials, it has many others in abundance. It generates virtually all of its technology domestically. It produces much of what it consumes at home, and so it does not depend as extensively on imports as many other countries. Thanks to a large domestic market, many products can be profitably manufactured even in the absence of significant export sales. As a rule, therefore, economic matters are regarded in the United States as being outside the context of national security. But self-reliance is a relative notion in the contemporary world, and, the nation's privileged position notwithstanding, much of America's growth and prosperity depends on economic developments abroad.

Despite its relative self-sufficiency, foreign trade amounts to approximately one-sixth of the U.S. gross domestic product (see Table 1-1), and both imports and exports have substantial implications for the nation's economic well-being. Imports almost certainly benefit American consumers. For example, the fact that we can choose to buy Japanese, German, or French automobiles increases our options as car buyers. This is true of many other products as well. Also, competition from other countries helps keep domestic manufacturers on their toes, as it forces them to match the prices and quality of

Table 1-1   Foreign Trade as a Proportion of Gross Domestic Product in Selected Countries

Country	Trade as a percentage of GDP
United States	15
France	39
United Kingdom	41
Uruguay	25
Kenya	43
Poland	33

Source: United Nations Conference on Trade and Development, *Handbook of International Trade and Development Statistics, 1985 Supplement* (New York: United Nations, 1985), 416.

their foreign challengers. On the other hand, there are predictable sources of opposition to imports. Domestic producers of automobiles, textiles, or color television sets, who fear they will be driven out of business by foreign competitors, find it hard to appreciate the virtues of international economic competition, and they often petition the political authorities for barriers against imports.

The benefits of exporting are less controversial. The more we sell abroad, the more money the nation earns and the more jobs are generated at home. Currently, approximately one out of every six jobs in the United States is created by production for export, and approximately one out of every three acres of agricultural land is devoted to production for foreign needs. This may be less than for many other nations, but it still means that America's prosperity is very much dependent on the willingness of other countries to buy its goods.

There are other ways in which our prosperity is linked to the international economic environment. U.S. firms have traditionally been major investors abroad. Mining and oil companies have acquired access to foreign sources of raw materials and energy, and manufacturing companies have benefited from cheaper foreign labor and, by producing their goods abroad, have often made them less expensive to U.S. consumers. Profits realized abroad by U.S. multinational corporations have contributed to their solvency and healthy operation at home.

It might suit a notion of "natural order" if economic issues were dealt with in the economic realm, while political matters were relegated to the political realm. Indeed, it has been the wish of classical liberal theorists that the two should not interfere with each other. But this is not the way the world works:

economic interests and political purposes are inextricably connected, and this is revealed in the foreign policies of all nations, not least the United States. For example, U.S. political power has often been used to open the door of foreign markets to American exports—in the Far East, for instance. When foreign governments have sought to expropriate the assets of American corporations, or even to limit their freedom of action, these corporations have called on the U.S. government for help. And when domestic producers feel threatened by foreign competition, the U.S. government sometimes engages in political arm-twisting to induce foreign nations to limit their sales to the United States. Thus, international economic issues often become intensely politicized, and foreign policy is often infused with economic content, as later chapters in this book will demonstrate.

Ideological Goals

Neither security nor prosperity are uniquely U.S. goals. They are as much the foreign policy objectives of France or the Soviet Union, of Paraguay or Bulgaria, of Egypt or Italy. But in addition to these universal objectives, some nations also seek to achieve less tangible ideological aims through their foreign policy. They wish to promote abroad the political or spiritual values to which they adhere at home, and to see their own institutions and practices replicated in other countries. Of course, not all countries have a sense of ideological mission, and most are probably unwilling to run real risks or to accept major national sacrifices for the sake of promoting their values outside their national borders. A few nations, on the other hand—Ayatollah Khomeini's Iran or Colonel Qaddafi's Libya are examples—have displayed near fanaticism in promoting their beliefs beyond their own frontiers. The United States and the Soviet Union occupy somewhat of a middle ground in this respect. They appear to share a sense of national exceptionalism and self-righteousness, a feeling of historical mission, and a clearly articulated set of ideological principles viewed as a model for other societies. But they also share a basic prudence in promoting their values when this might bring them into conflict with each other, and they sometimes seem willing to subordinate external ideological goals to their pragmatic geostrategic interests.

Yet ideological goals are considered important by both superpowers and have provided the justification for activities ranging from the acquisition of nuclear weapons to the establishment of foreign aid programs. They have inspired the ethos, if not always the substance, of U.S. foreign policy. In 1918, President Woodrow Wilson proclaimed: "The world must be made safe for democracy. Its peace must be planted upon the tested foundations of political liberty." [4] Again referring to the promotion of democratic ideals, President Lyndon B. Johnson said, in 1964, "Our cause has been the cause of all mankind." [5] During the past several decades, few U.S. presidents have failed to associate the country's foreign policy with elevated ideological goals, and U.S. military interventions, from Vietnam to Grenada, have claimed largely ideological justifications. Democracy, not just for ourselves but for others as well, has been central to the nation's professed sense of global purpose. Foreign aid, it is often said, is meant to alleviate poverty and thus to make it less likely that nondemocratic movements will take root in developing societies; military interventions are explained by the need to defend democracy abroad; arms sales are justified by the goal of strengthening democratic forces, and so forth.

All of this may seem quite reasonable, but there are problems that cannot be ignored. In particular, the way democracy is defined when applied to other nations is sometimes troubling. Two conceptions of the political acceptability of other governments have traditionally guided U.S. foreign policy. The first is rooted in the belief that the only meaningful ideological distinction is that between democracy and communism. From this point of view, a nation that is strongly anticommunist is at least potentially democratic and thus worthy of U.S. political, economic, and at times military support. According to the second perspective, this notion is much too simplistic: equally ruthless dictatorships can be found at both the right and the left extremes of the political spectrum, and there is little to choose between them. The actual existence of democratic institutions and practices—not merely the mouthing of anticommunist slogans— is what should qualify a nation for support by the United States.

On the whole, the first perspective has dominated postwar U.S. policy, particularly when the goal of promoting democracy abroad has clashed with other, seemingly more pressing, foreign policy objectives. Indeed, many of the regimes whose friendship we consider useful can be termed democratic only by the greatest stretch of political imagination. Occasionally, governments to whose support we are pledged cannot be considered democratic by any reasonable standard at all. In such cases, officials may contrive shades of political oppressiveness to differentiate governments to which the United States is bound in different degrees. For example, one member of the Reagan administration made a distinction between "authoritarian" regimes (mainly dictatorships of the right) and "totalitarian" regimes (essentially dictatorships of the left).[6] The implication was that the former are less undemocratic than the latter, but such distinctions are not entirely convincing. Censorship or political imprisonment is similarly experienced by its victims whether imposed by the right or the left, and torture is perhaps even more frequently practiced by "authoritarian" than "totalitarian" regimes in the Third World. It remains a major challenge to the U.S. sense of national purpose to decide which values can be appropriately promoted in other countries and how this mission can be made congruent with other external goals.

The Instruments of Foreign Policy

If nations wish to achieve foreign policy goals, they must have the means of doing so in a complex and sometimes hostile world. External objectives are pursued in a world of many nations, each of which has its own values, perceptions, and external needs. These may or may not be compatible with those of the United States: moves that enhance U.S. security might diminish that of its rivals and adversaries and perhaps even of its friends; U.S. access to foreign markets could preclude such access by other countries; and so forth. Of course, nations often achieve their goals in cooperation with other countries, a cooperation that can be either explicit or tacit (the two superpowers have tacitly cooperated, for instance, to prevent the Republic of South Africa from acquiring nuclear weapons). At other times, there is a mixture of cooperative and competitive elements in a relationship; for example, most Western democracies agreed in the 1970s that they should cooperate to ensure access to the oil of the Persian Gulf, but that did not stop several of them from seeking to wrest preferential deals from the oil-exporting countries of the region. Still, the element of competition and the presence of incompatible goals frequently define the nature of international relations and set the rules of foreign policy.

Though foreign policy sometimes involves efforts to coordinate the pursuit of one nation's goals with those of other countries, it frequently implies the pursuit of external objectives even when these do not mesh with, or run directly counter to, the goals of other nations. One nation may try to get others to modify their objectives, to alter their goals so as to make them compatible with its own, but if this is not possible, the nation's aims may be pursued at the expense of other nations. Consequently, the major instruments of foreign policy are those of *power* and *influence*.

There are several ways to try to make nations change their behavior: by offering them rewards, by convincing them that the desired behavior is in their own interest as well, or by inflicting various punishments should they fail to act in the desired fashion. A useful spectrum along which these methods can be ranked is according to their level of coerciveness. At one extreme would be the means of inflicting, or threatening to inflict, physical pain on other societies; these are the instruments of force, particularly of military force. To some minds, this is the obvious way in which international power is exercised. In the United States, the role assigned to military force has varied over time; for example, the nation's foreign policy posture was much more militarized in the early 1980s than in the mid-1970s. At the other extreme would be the means of inducement and persuasion, usually achieved via *aid* and *diplomacy*. Between these two extremes lie some of the least well understood but increasingly common instruments of foreign policy. Their degree of coerciveness exceeds that of normal diplomacy but falls short of military force. Among these methods are economic sanctions and the practice of external subversion of other nations through the informal and clandestine penetration of their political systems. Let us examine each of these instruments of foreign policy more closely.

Military Force

Military force is the first thing that comes to most minds when the issue of national power arises; power and weaponry are often considered nearly synonymous. They may be thought of either in absolute terms (how much do we have?) or in relative terms (how much more than other countries do we have?).

The United States has used military power rather frequently. It has been employed in the fashion of a colonizing nation, as in the Spanish-American War, by which virtual control of Cuba was acquired; in defense of allies and political democracy, as in the two world wars; in an ill-conceived and unsuccessful defense of "credibility," as in Vietnam; to remove disagreeable foreign governments from power, as in Grenada; and for other reasons as well. But military force is not merely, and perhaps not even principally, a matter of its physical use, for it can be employed even in the absence of bombing, shooting, and the like. To illustrate this vital point, we need to distinguish between the various uses to which military force can be put. Perhaps the most helpful categorization has been made by the political scientist Robert Art, who has proposed four major functions.[7]

The first function is *defense*: fending off foreign aggression or mitigating its consequences by countering the aggressor's military force with one's own. In this category were, for example, Belgian efforts in World War I to ward off the German invasion, and South Korea's efforts (assisted by the United States and other nations) to repel aggression from North Korea. Although the United States has used its military force in defense of friends and allies, it has not, since the War of 1812, had the occasion to use it for its own direct defense, for reasons already stated. Nations usually describe their military forces as essentially defensive; to put it differently, while defensive weapons are those which one has deployed oneself, offensive weapons are those deployed by one's adversaries. In any event, the notion of defense has been somewhat impaired by the advent of nuclear armaments, since no effective defense against them has been devised to date (more will be said about this in a later chapter).

The second major function of military force is *deterrence*, and the difference between defense and deterrence is fundamental. The purpose of deterrence is to prevent an external assault from occurring. This is done by threatening punishment through retaliation against an aggressor. A nation says, in effect, "Do not try to hurt me, because, if you do, the pain I will make you suffer will outweigh any advantage you may expect from your assault." Deterrence is meant to avoid unpleasantness, whereas defense is designed to deal with unpleasantness when it has occurred. If defense becomes necessary, then plainly deterrence has failed. The amount of military force needed for defense may differ from that required by deterrence. France's decision to acquire a modest nuclear arsenal did not spring from a belief that it could successfully defend itself against the much more powerful Soviet Union; rather, it was based on the conviction that the threat of nuclear retaliation, even on a small scale, would dissuade the Kremlin from attempting aggression. There are, however, ways in which defense and deterrence may overlap. Most obviously, an aggressor who realizes that his victim's defensive capacities are very great may be deterred by the anticipated difficulties and costs of a successful aggression. For example, the Soviet Union is a much more impressive military power than is the People's Republic of China; yet even if it wished to invade China, recognition of China's defensive abilities would probably deter it from making the attempt.

Just as nuclear weaponry has limited the defensive possibilities of military force, it has enhanced its deterrent function. As the massive destructiveness of nuclear weapons became evident, and as it became clear that there were no effective defenses against them, it was also often understood that these were not weapons that could be used as normal instruments of warfare. As one nuclear strategist pointed out as early as 1946: "Thus far, the chief purpose of our military establishment has been to win wars. From now on, its chief purpose must be to avert them. It can have almost no other useful purpose." [8]

The third function of military force is what Art calls *compellence*. This refers to the actual or threatened application of military force to stop another nation from doing something it is doing or (less frequently) to force it to do something it would otherwise not do. When the United States began bombing Hanoi in the late 1960s, the purpose was to force it to stop assisting the communist-led revolution in South Vietnam. When the Soviet Union invaded Czechoslovakia in 1968, the aim was to force the country off the track of expanding liberalization and to prevent it from trying to usher in what the Czechs called "socialism with a human face." As is true of defense, it is not usually thought that compellence can rely on nuclear weapons. Yet the only actual use of such weapons to date had compellence as its primary purpose, for the aim of the nuclear bombing of Hiroshima and Nagasaki by the United States in 1945 was to force Japan to surrender in World War II. The use of nuclear weapons for compellence seems possible only if one country is their sole possessor (as the United States indeed was at the time) or, at least, if neither the victim nor its allies are in any position to retaliate. The first condition is obviously not true any more, and the second can no longer be safely assumed. Thus, although conventional forces could theoretically be used for any of the three purposes mentioned so far, the enormous destructiveness of nuclear weapons implies that they are presently suited only for deterrence.

Nevertheless, weapons technology does not stand still, and even nuclear weapons have become increasingly diversified. They differ not only in explosive yield but also in degree of "dirtiness" (the amount of radioactivity they produce) and in the accuracy with which they can be delivered. These developments have led some observers to believe that certain types of nuclear weapons could be used in much the same way as conventional weapons, after all. Others disagree vehemently, and the matter of whether the functions of nuclear weapons can now include more than just deterrence has become one of the most hotly debated questions of strategic doctrine. Obviously, its implications are enormous (they will be further discussed in Chapter 12).

The fourth function that Art assigns to military force is what he calls *swaggering*, and it is somewhat less important for our purposes. Swaggering involves the acquisition of military power for purposes of national prestige and perhaps simply to intimidate other countries by brandishing one's might. While this is not an insignificant objective, its practical implications for foreign policy are not as great as those of the other missions of armed force.

These functions notwithstanding, it should be reiterated that military strength does not necessarily enhance national security and that its acquisition, beyond certain levels, can imperil other national objectives (such as increased welfare and prosperity). The problem, as yet not adequately resolved, has been to find the proper balance between desiderata that are at least partly incompatible.

Diplomacy and Bribery

Diplomacy is the process of communicating, persuading, and negotiating.[9] Used by itself, it is a noncoercive tool of foreign policy, located at the opposite end from military force on the spectrum of foreign policy instruments. Both military force and diplomacy have a history virtually as long as that of political organization, but they have been employed in very different circumstances. The use of military force implies that the goals of the parties are virtually irreconcilable; diplomacy, on the other hand, can be effective whenever goals are at least partially compatible or complementary. Fortunately, all nations, including the United States, conduct most of their foreign affairs via diplomacy. Examples of recent diplomatic successes are the agreements on arms control between the United States and the Soviet Union, the negotiations leading to the Camp David accord between Egypt and Israel, and the arrangements by which a number of western industrialized nations agreed not to flood the U.S. market with goods that would seriously threaten the livelihood of American producers. The improvements in U.S. relations with the Kremlin in the 1970s and the reestablishing of cordial relations with China since 1972 are other examples. Failures include the inability to create better relations with many developing nations, the deterioration of U.S.-Soviet relations in the early 1980s, and the difficulty in generating a truly strong sense of common purpose with several West European nations.

Communication is the essence and foundation of diplomacy, and how much more than communication diplomacy requires depends on the extent to which two countries' goals are compatible. Among the chief functions of U.S. diplomacy are to explain the nation's purposes and policies and to point out the links that bind its national interest with that of other countries. This is essentially a matter of diplomatic persuasion, but at times even this may be unnecessary. Where there is basic agreement on objectives at the outset, the main purpose of diplomacy will typically be to harmonize, and perhaps coordinate, national efforts in the pursuit of the common aims. In a situation of such fundamental goal convergence, diplomatic efforts would consist largely of an exchange of information among the cooperating parties. Each would wish to learn what the others are doing, what to expect from them in the form of co-operation, and any other information required for policy coordination. Conversely, each would influence the behavior of the others in a desirable direction by providing them with appropriate information.

When nations have at least partially competitive goals, diplomacy becomes more a matter of bargaining and negotiation. Communication is still essential: each party wants to have a clear understanding of the other's objectives and bargaining positions. But whenever there is some element of goal incompatibility, the amount of leverage that each party can exert over the other will determine the outcome of the negotiation. If they are negotiating on more than one issue, leverage can be acquired by making tradeoffs across the issues. One party might yield on a matter to which it did not assign high priority in order to get a concession on something which it considered more important.

Often, however, diplomatic leverage will be associated with a variety of inducements—that is to say, with *bribery*. The term *bribery* does not have attractive connotations, yet it is a very frequently employed instrument of foreign policy. It means that a payment of some sort will be made in exchange for desired behavior; it embodies the "you-scratch-my-back-and-I-will-scratch-yours" principle in international relations. Obviously, it is most extensively used by nations that are in a good position to offer inducements, and the United States is particularly well endowed in this regard. Everyone understands, for instance, that foreign economic aid is not so much an unrequited gift to development as a pragmatic tool of external policy.[10] The Philippines long enjoyed U.S. economic aid, largely in exchange for the use of its territory for military bases; both Egypt and Israel were offered very substantial economic inducements to make them more forthcoming during the Camp David negotiations (sponsored by President Jimmy Carter). Offering gifts for good behavior is not coercion; it does not involve making the recipient worse off, but the possibility of making him better off.

Frequently, leverage will be acquired not by dangling carrots but by brandishing sticks; this is more apt to be so the more incompatible the goals are. When this is the case, diplomacy will be used in conjunction with instruments of foreign policy that are further up the spectrum of coerciveness. Threats of military force can be used to induce cooperation, a practice known as "gunboat diplomacy." But frequently the means of applying pressure will be somewhat less coercive than that, and these other means are worth considering in some detail.

The Middle Ground

There are many foreign policy instruments that are more coercive than diplomacy, or diplomacy associated with bribery, but less coercive than military force. Much of U.S. foreign policy activity occupies this middle ground. One reason may be that advances in the technology of military destruction, particularly, the acquisition of large nuclear arsenals by both superpowers (who are frequently on opposite sides of international disputes), have made excessive reliance on military force an overly risky business. At the same time, America's international objectives are as pressing as they ever were and will not simply be abandoned when diplomacy (even coupled with inducements) does not work. Another reason may be that the United States has developed other tools for influencing the behavior of foreign nations and has thus broadened the range of its policy options. Two significant examples of this are economic sanctions and informal penetration (or, more bluntly, subversion).

ECONOMIC SANCTIONS. This practice involves withholding an economic advantage from another country in pursuit of some political goal.[11] The sanctioning country may refuse to export its goods to the other country or to allow imports from it. Recently, the United States has wielded this instrument of external pressure against the Soviet Union and, following the repression of the Solidarity movement, against Poland as well. Nicaragua has been the target of a U.S. economic boycott, as have Cuba and, to a certain extent, Vietnam, Angola, Mozambique, Iran, and Libya. From a U.S. point of view, there is much that seems to commend economic sanctions as a tool of foreign policy. The United States has at its disposal considerable economic power, a condition necessary to the effective use of this instrument; and, as already pointed out, since the possible costs of a military confrontation between the superpowers are so great, economic coercion is a less perilous way of pursuing the East-West rivalry.

Sometimes economic sanctions are designed to pressure a foreign government into abandoning policies that the United States finds objectionable; for instance, the sanctions against Nicaragua were at first designed to force that country's government to withdraw its military support of El Salvador's leftist rebels. At times, this may indeed work—U.S. economic pressure against Poland may have been responsible for some of the liberalization introduced by the Warsaw government in 1983—but cases of success are rare. Few governments are willing to bow to foreign economic pressure. Sanctions have been especially unsuccessful when their goal has been to make another country alter its policies in a fundamental way. Often, however, their real purpose is to engineer the ousting of an unpalatable government, rather than to make it change its behavior. The idea is that, by imposing economic hardship on another country, sufficient discontent will be created to lead to the government's removal by internal forces. The sanctions against Cuba, for example, were probably motivated more by the hope of causing Castro's downfall than by the expectation that he could be made to reform. One possible instance of the successful application of economic pressure for this purpose was the ouster of Chile's Marxist president, Salvador Allende, in 1973, which was probably encouraged by economic dislocations created by the United States. More often, however, such outside pressure causes a people to rally around its leaders, even if these leaders would otherwise have been quite unpopular. Yet we cannot conclude that economic sanctions are ineffective because they rarely cause objectionable policies to be altered or objectionable leaders to be removed, for these may not be the most significant functions of sanctions.

Frequently, their purpose is to deter future misbehavior rather than to modify present behavior. If the unwanted policies are punished with sufficient severity, they may not be repeated in the future, even if currently objectionable activities are not abandoned. Also, the example of the punishment may discourage other countries from engaging in the same kind of activities. If deterrence is indeed their chief intent, the record of economic sanctions may be more favorable. For example, an additional purpose of the sanctions against Cuba was to dissuade other Latin American nations from following in Cuba's footsteps. When the Carter administration imposed economic sanctions against the U.S.S.R. following the invasion of Afghanistan, it probably did not believe that the Soviet Union would be pressured into withdrawing its troops: the more plausible intention was to deter future instances of Soviet aggression. Indeed the policy may have been successful in discouraging a Soviet invasion of Poland to suppress the Solidarity movement.

But economic sanctions present problems as well. To begin with, it is hard to hurt a nation with which one has economic relations without also hurting oneself. If the United States reduces foreign aid to a country, the United States itself might suffer from a consequent reduction in trade or investments. This prospect might provoke domestic opposition to the sanctions. For instance, U.S. farmers have opposed the imposition of grain embargoes against the Soviet Union. Furthermore, it is hard to contain the effects of economic sanctions; by trying to hurt an adversary, a nation may also hurt others toward which it bears no ill will. Sanctions against South Africa, to induce it to alter its racist policies, may well also injure other African nations that trade extensively with that country. Thus, this is a foreign policy instrument that deserves mixed reviews.

INFORMAL PENETRATION. All the instruments of foreign policy discussed so far have involved fairly overt government-to-government relations. Diplomacy is based on communication between the official representatives of countries; although it may be secret from the public's point of view, it is quite overt as far as the governments in question are concerned. When inducements such as foreign aid are used, this involves both the donor and the recipient governments. And plainly, military force is deliberately applied (and countered) by governmental armies. Indeed, it is often difficult to conceive of foreign policy in anything other than government-to-government terms.

There are occasions, however, when foreign policy goals are pursued not by exerting official pressure on another government from the outside, but rather by acting on it from within—by gaining access to elements of its society and by using this access to influence the policies or stability of the government.

Sometimes, though not always, this is done in a clandestine, or covert, fashion; and since the goal is to exert pressure on the government or to bring about its downfall, there is definitely a coercive dimension to it. Such "Trojan-horse" tactics do not usually come in for much praise but, whether ethically appealing or not, they are common in contemporary international politics.

The best-known type of informal penetration is *propaganda*. Governments often try to exert pressure on other countries by influencing their public opinion.[12] The purpose may simply be to portray one's own nation or its policies in a favorable light, so as to create a mood of public sympathy in the other country; but propaganda may go further, by attempting to malign the other government and to rouse internal public opinion against it. While propaganda pervades international politics, it is most extensively employed by those nations with the greatest external interests and the greatest resources for its use—especially the United States and the Soviet Union.

Several U.S. governmental agencies perform propaganda functions. The United States Information Agency (USIA), for example, has a major role in conveying favorable (and for the most part accurate) information about the United States abroad. It also promotes the circulation of American newspapers, periodical literature, and films abroad, organizes lectures by prominent U.S. citizens in foreign countries, and subsidizes the translation of American books. The objective behind these activities is to explain U.S. policies to people in other nations, to project a favorable image of American life and institutions, and to counter hostile and inaccurate propaganda. Radio Free Europe and Radio Liberty are quasi-governmental organizations that specialize in transmitting information favorable to the United States and its policies to the Soviet Union and Eastern Europe.

The Central Intelligence Agency (CIA) is also active in propaganda, but its functions (like those of the Soviet Union's security agency, the KGB) go considerably beyond this.[13] In addition to being the nation's premier intelligence agency, it plays the leading role in U.S. informal penetration efforts. One of its major jobs seems to be to obtain access to, or to "penetrate," strategically important parts of other nations' sociopolitical structures and, by dint of this access, to shape those nations' policies. For example, it has tried to influence political parties in other countries—including some of America's friends and allies—by giving them financial assistance. Similarly, by acting in conjunction with the major American labor organization, the AFL-CIO, it has sought to influence or control trade unions in countries ranging from Zaire to Italy, mainly to steer them away from a left-wing orientation.[14]

The most controversial activities of the CIA have been those aimed at the removal of foreign governments (some of them duly elected) from office. It has been reported that the Congo's mildly pro-Soviet prime minister, Patrice Lumumba, was the object of CIA assassination plans (one idea was apparently to use poison injected into his toothpaste). When the popular Iranian prime minister Mohammed Mossadegh nationalized foreign oil companies, the CIA organized a coup in 1953 that removed him from office and replaced him with Reza Shah Pahlavi. When the democratically elected government of Jacobo Arbenz Guzmán in Guatemala nationalized the landholdings of the United Fruit Company, as part of a program of land reform, it was overthrown by an army of mercenaries organized and equipped by the CIA. The CIA was also involved in attempts at blocking the assumption of power by Chile's President Allende; in 1958, it allegedly sponsored an unsuccessful rebellion against the Indonesian leader, Sukarno; and in 1961, it organized the Bay of Pigs invasion, which was intended to get rid of the Castro government in Cuba but which also failed. In the 1980s, it has supervised the attempts by rebels in Nicaragua to unseat, by force, the leftist Sandinista government.

This is a very substantial record, and it has generated heated dispute both within and outside the United States. To begin with, it is contrary to recognized norms of international conduct to meddle in other nations' internal politics, to say nothing of trying to provoke the violent removal of their governments. Subversion as a tool of foreign policy also runs counter to the country's self-image; it is something we tend to associate with communists, the KGB, and the like. There is nothing in democratic theory to suggest that foreign agents should shape a society's political decisions.

On the other hand, covert penetration, even of the most extreme sort, has its defenders. The argument is made that one must fight fire with fire. After all, our adversaries have no qualms about resorting to these tactics; it would therefore be irresponsible for the United States to refrain from using them. Perhaps more importantly, the contention is made that there are no other satisfactory options. If one agrees that there are external objectives that America simply cannot abandon, and if, furthermore, they cannot be successfully pursued by diplomacy, with or without bribery, one is left with the choice of relying on either military force or informal penetration. Since the former is so costly and risky, the latter may be the only course of action left.

Decisions about the use of informal penetration in particular cases depend on several judgments. How important is the national goal that is being pursued? Is it so important that basic principles of international conduct should be sacrificed to its attainment? Had covert CIA activity been able to stop Hitler from assuming power or to remove him from power, most people would agree that it would have been justified, but that is quite different from blocking land reform in Guatemala on behalf of United Fruit. One would also wish to know whether all nonviolent means of pressure have really been exhausted: Has a diplomatic solution been diligently sought? Has the full range of positive inducements been thoughtfully employed? Foreign policy and the pursuit of the national interest rarely involve easy choices, yet these choices have far-reaching implications, which must be recognized and taken into account if the policy is to be effective and consistent with national values.

Foreign Policy and the Political System

The structure of means and ends constitutes an important part of the contours of a nation's external affairs. But foreign policy is also rooted in a domestic setting of values, practices, and institutions, which determine the way in which the policy should be made and implemented. We must therefore consider the link between the nation's foreign policy and its political system.

In the case of the United States, there is general agreement that its external policies must be compatible with democratic government. Although this form of government has several variants, it rests on a set of core principles, of which three are especially relevant to our purposes.[15] The first is that government should, in some explicit way, stem from the consent of the governed; in other words, policy ought to reflect public preferences. This can be ensured in several ways. Those who run the nation's affairs should be freely elected to do so by the public or at least be accountable to people who were. In addition, the public should be in a position to monitor political decisions between elections, to make its preferences known to the authorities, and to expect that these preferences will generally be acted upon. This in turn implies that members of the public must be minimally acquainted with the issues and understand the likely impact of various policies, and that they must have ready access to the information needed for these purposes.

Secondly, democracy assumes that there must be effective limits on political power, even where policy does reflect the preferences of the majority. After all, absolutism may be compatible with the public will (many dictators have been national idols at the time of their rule), but it would nevertheless be politically repugnant. In the United States, the major concern has been to ensure adequate control over executive power. The system of separation of powers, together with a set of checks and balances, was the Founding Fathers' response to this concern. The intention was to force the executive branch to share power with the legislative and judicial branches and, at the same time, to give each branch some control over the others.

Constitutional norms are not the only foundation of political power. It also springs from the control of such resources as knowledge, position, and wealth: if they are concentrated in a narrow and unchanging elite, democracy would be more a matter of form than of substance. Political *pluralism* is often proposed as an antidote to this threat. This means that many different groups, not an omnipotent elite, should both possess the resources that yield power and participate in the making of political decisions—particularly when these decisions affect the groups' own interests. Bargaining between these interest groups, not the unilateral preferences of a single group, should determine policy. For example, a decision on whether or not to impose restrictions on imports from other countries should involve both the businesses that would benefit and those that would suffer; organized labor, since its interests will probably be affected; and any other groups that believe their interests are at stake.

A third defining element of political democracy is a guarantee of basic civil liberties. There must be a significant core of rights that cannot be curtailed, even by a "democratic" procedure. These rights are usually held to include the electoral franchise and freedom to speak, write, and organize for political activity. In the United States, they are enumerated and described in the Bill of Rights.

Together, these three principles form the foundation of political democracy as we understand it, and since the conduct of foreign policy is embedded in the U.S. political system, we should ask how it is related to them. Are the mechanisms of democracy consistent with the making of sound foreign policy decisions? On the other hand, do these decisions, or the way in which they are made, strengthen or weaken democratic institutions? These matters will be discussed throughout this book, but some issues can be raised at the very beginning.

First of all, some observers doubt that the U.S. public is concerned about foreign policy at even the minimal level thought to be necessary. U.S. citizens seem to know remarkably little about their country's foreign affairs. Surveys of public opinion often reveal a startling degree of apathy and ignorance in this area (see Chapter 3), and one may well wonder how a public that knows very little about foreign policy can convey its preferences to the nation's leaders or hold them electorally responsible for policies whose meaning it does not understand.

One could also argue that people are not particularly well informed on matters of domestic policy, either. But there is at least one vital difference between the two policy arenas, and that is that the national constituencies whose interests are affected by domestic policies often do not exist for foreign policy. In the case of, say, national industrial policy or educational policy, it is usually easy to identify the groups whose interests are immediately affected (managers and workers, in the first of these examples, students and teachers in the second). Since these interests create "natural" constituencies for or against the policies, the link between the public and the policy is automatically established. There are identifiable groups to which the government must respond, and, because of this, there is some assurance that the policies will be monitored and the authorities punished or rewarded as a result. It is usually less easy to identify the groups that are directly affected by foreign policy decisions. Economic competition from other countries may threaten the jobs and material security of Americans, and at times U.S. citizens are asked to fight foreign wars. But in general, the public is more likely to be indifferent to matters of foreign policy than to matters of domestic policy, and this inevitably has implications for the accountability of government in its foreign dealings.

A second problem in some eyes comes from an excessive concentration of foreign policy power in the executive branch and in particular in the hands of the president. It is true that the Constitution does vest broad responsibility for the conduct of the nation's foreign affairs in the presidency, but some observers believe that this principle has been taken much further than was initially intended or than is consistent with democratic control of foreign policy. For example, the Constitution empowers the president to make treaties with other nations, but it also provides that these treaties must be ratified (approved) by the Senate. Increasingly, however, external commitments are taking the form of what are called *executive agreements*, entered into by the executive branch and not subject to Senate control. Or, more dramatically, while only Congress can declare war on other countries, any resort to nuclear weapons—that is, to the most destructive form of warfare—would almost surely be made by the president alone. The Manhattan Project, which led to the discovery and development of the atomic bomb and thus profoundly altered the conditions of national security, was authorized solely by the president; most members of Congress did not even learn about it until the atomic bomb was used against the Japanese city of Hiroshima.

Indeed, it has been argued that the United States has, in a manner of speaking, two presidencies: a domestic presidency, subject to a strong measure of congressional control, and a foreign policy presidency, which has much greater freedom of action.[16] Presidents, of course, don't feel that their foreign policy authority is excessive; rather, they argue that Congress interferes too much in the conduct of foreign policy. It may be that the new challenges of the international environment make a greater measure of executive power over foreign affairs necessary. It may also be that the dangers of a so-called "imperial presidency" are overstated. These are not insignificant issues, and they will be discussed at greater length in a later chapter.

A third problem involves the proper balance between national security imperatives, on the one hand, and civil liberties and political rights, on the other. For example, the U.S. government has limited the ability of the press to cover national military involvements abroad; during the invasion of Grenada in 1983, the press was not even allowed near the fighting. The right to travel in other countries has been restricted in the name of national security, and foreign citizens with certain political beliefs have been denied entrance into the United States, thus depriving U.S. citizens of the right to hear those beliefs stated. In the 1960s, the CIA was found to be illegally spying on U.S. citizens, again in the claimed interests of national security. The dilemma is evident. If national security were undermined from abroad, basic rights and liberties might be destroyed by our adversaries. Thus, the long-term survival of democratic principles might at times necessitate their temporary curtailment. Yet, it might be argued, encroachments on civil rights and liberties in order to protect them is a contradiction, and they can surely be damaged in the long run by contriving circumstances in which they need not be respected.

Even this brief survey will make clear the difficulties that are encountered in making democratic principles mesh with foreign policy objectives. It is unlikely that we would want to abandon these objectives; national security, national prosperity, and even external ideological goals are simply too important to us. At the same time, we would not wish to compromise the basic tenets upon which our political system is founded. Making these different demands compatible is a major challenge of U.S. foreign policy.

The Three Dilemmas of Foreign Policy

Everything discussed so far reinforces the statement at the beginning of this chapter that the making of foreign policy is an agonizing task. There are rarely easy choices or clear-cut solutions to the difficulties facing the United States in its relations with other countries. The foreign policy maker must continuously confront three types of dilemmas, representing distinct though overlapping problems.

The first, and conceptually the most straightforward, may be termed the dilemma of *effective choice*. It involves the need to choose among foreign policy objectives that are to some extent incompatible—for it is a fact of political life that many goals can be successfully pursued only at the expense of others—or among foreign policy instruments each of which appears to have both advantages and drawbacks. The United States may, for example, wish to have good relations with both Greece and Turkey, but since these two countries tend to be at loggerheads with each other (over issues such as Cyprus and control of the Aegean Sea), supporting one usually means alienating the other. The needs of the U.S. economy might suggest an expansion of exports to the Soviet Union, but national security interests might suggest that such exports be limited lest they bolster the Soviet economy. During the Reagan administration, there has been a debate over whether the United States should work against apartheid in South Africa through discreet diplomatic pressure (which has been the president's preference) or through more coercive economic sanctions (the preference of many or most members of Congress).

The second dilemma is *aggregation*. This refers to the problems involved in translating the varying interests and preferences of individuals, groups, geographic regions, and so forth into a coherent national foreign policy. The concept of a U.S. foreign policy is an abstraction. In a narrow sense, it is merely the foreign policy chosen by the incumbent administration. But it is, as well, the foreign policy that Congress has agreed to fund; it also corresponds in some way to the expressed preferences of the general public and it reflects the demands of powerful interest groups. In other words, the political actors who participate in the making of foreign policy do not necessarily have identical or even similar interests and aspirations, nor do they always deem the same foreign policy instruments suitable to their pursuit. Yet foreign policy is assumed to represent at least a minimal national consensus. The problems of finding a common denominator among discrepant foreign policy preferences create the dilemma of aggregation. As an illustration, industries for which exports represent a large portion of total sales are likely to be champions of free trade, while those that feel threatened by foreign competition are more inclined to support protectionism. A policy on foreign trade must somehow deal with these opposing interests.

A more subtle question is to what extent should political leaders respond to public preferences that do not stem from an adequate appreciation of the facts. How broad a base of public support is needed, and how much acquaintance with policy problems in order to meet the criterion of democratic participation? The dilemma of aggregation also involves the problem of the roles to be played in the making of foreign policy by the different branches of government—a problem that usually boils down to settling on a proper division of labor between Congress and the president.

The third dilemma, that of *political principle*, refers to the problem of bringing the conduct of foreign policy into line with the values at the heart of the nation's political system. The United States considers itself bound to promote abroad certain ideological goals, principally its understanding of political democracy and of social equity and justice. But the promotion of ideological values can conflict with other external interests. The regime of Ferdinand Marcos, longtime leader of the Philippines, was widely recognized as one of the more unsavory regimes on the world scene. Not only did it relegate the majority of its people to an existence of squalor, not only was it spectacularly corrupt, but it was also (and perhaps understandably in light of its other attributes) very repressive. When the regime did not rule by martial law, it did not hesitate to rig elections. The press was tightly controlled, opposition leaders were frequently jailed, and political assassinations were not uncommon. Yet, despite its repugnant features, the Marcos regime benefited from staunch U.S. support virtually until its final days when, in 1986, it was thrown out on a powerful wave of popular opposition. The reason was to be found in two important military installations located on its territory: the Clark Air Force Base and a naval base at Subic Bay. These facilities were considered so valuable from a geostrategic standpoint that successive U.S. governments sought to gloss over the nature of the Philippines' political system. For example, on a visit to that country in 1981, Vice President Bush declared to President Marcos: "We stand with the Philippines. We love your adherence to democratic principles and procedures. We will not leave you in isolation." [17] Such statements seem hypocritical, but what does the national interest require? Should U.S. security needs override distaste for such regimes, or should oppression be opposed even when this might jeopardize other foreign policy objectives? To a large extent, this overlaps with the dilemma of effective choice, but it is distinguished by the fact that it involves an ethical rather than a practical judgment.

Another aspect of the dilemma of political principle involves the protection of the values on which the U.S. system itself is founded when this appears to conflict with specific foreign policy needs. A number of political thinkers, from Alexis de Tocqueville to Walter Lippmann, have questioned whether democracy is well suited to success in international affairs.[18] The occasional conflict between secrecy—often considered necessary to the effective conduct of foreign policy—and democratic participation in the making of major national decisions has already been alluded to. In a related vein, the dominant role played by the executive branch in the conduct of foreign policy is at times considered inconsistent with the principle of checks and balances, one of the central tenets of political organization in the United States.

These, then, are the principal types of quandaries that U.S. foreign policy must resolve. Each of the problems discussed in this book can be seen as arising from one or more of these dilemmas. Section 2, "The Domestic Politics of Foreign Policy" (Chapters 3-6), will revolve primarily around the dilemmas of aggregation and political principle. Section 3, "Friends and Adversaries" (Chapters 7-10), and Section 4, "War and Peace" (Chapters 11-13), will involve principally the dilemmas of effective choice and political principle; while Section 5, "National Prosperity and International Welfare" (Chapters 14-15), will be concerned with those of effective choice and aggregation. Finally, Section 6, "Conclusions" (Chapter 16), will discuss all three dilemmas.

Notes

1. Karl W. Deutsch, *The Analysis of International Relations* (New York: Prentice-Hall, 1978), 101.
2. See, for example, Richard N. Cooper, "Trade Policy Is Foreign Policy," in *A Reordered World: Emerging International Economic Problems*, ed. Richard N. Cooper (Washington, D.C.: Potomac Associates, 1973), 46-64.
3. On the economic effects of the arms race, see Robert W. DeGrasse, Jr., *Military Expansion, Economic Decline* (Armonk, N.Y.: M. E. Sharp, 1983), and Miroslav Nincic, *The Arms Race: The Political Economy of Military Growth* (New York: Praeger, 1982).
4. Albert Shaw, ed., *President Wilson's State Papers and Addresses* (New York: George A. Duncan, 1918), 38.
5. Lyndon B. Johnson, *Public Papers of the President* (Washington, D.C.: Government Printing Office, 1964), 1134.
6. Jeane Kirkpatrick, "Dictatorships and Double Standards," in Jeane Kirkpatrick, ed., *Dictatorships and Double Standards* (New York: Simon and Schuster, 1982), chap. 1.
7. Robert J. Art, "To What Ends Military Power?" *International Security* 8 (Spring 1980): 3-35.
8. Bernard Brodie, *The Absolute Weapon* (New York: Harcourt, Brace, Jovanovich, 1965), 5.
9. On diplomacy and negotiation, see Harold G. Nicholson, *Diplomacy*, 3d ed. (London: Oxford University Press, 1950); John W. Burton, *Systems, States, Diplomacy, and Rules* (London: Cambridge University Press, 1968), chap. 12; and William I. Zartman, ed., *The Negotiation Process* (Beverly Hills, Calif.: Sage, 1978).
10. For an early statement equating foreign aid with bribery, see Hans J. Morgenthau, "A Political Theory of Foreign Aid," *American Political Science Review* 56 (June 1962): 301-309.

11. Miroslav Nincic and Peter Wallensteen, eds., *Dilemmas of Economic Coercion: Sanctions in World Politics* (New York: Praeger, 1983).
12. A euphemism for propaganda is "public diplomacy." See Kenneth L. Adelman, "Speaking of America: Public Diplomacy in Our Time," *Foreign Affairs* 59 (Spring 1981): 913-936.
13. On the CIA, see Victor Marchetti and John D. Marks, *The CIA and the Cult of Intelligence* (New York: Alfred A. Knopf, 1974); John Stockwell, *In Search of Enemies* (New York: W. W. Norton, 1974); and "Final Report of the Select Committee to Study Governmental Operations with Respect to Intelligence," publication of the U.S. Senate, 94th Cong., 2d sess. (Washington, D.C.: Government Printing Office, 1974), books 1-6.
14. The link between the CIA and U.S. labor unions in activity in developing nations is described in Jonathan Kwitny, *Endless Enemies* (New York: Congdon and Weed, 1984), chap. 20.
15. There is a rich literature on the theory and prerequisites of modern political democracy. Among the contemporary works with applications to the United States are two books by Robert A. Dahl: *A Preface to Democratic Theory* (Chicago: University of Chicago Press, 1956) and *Democracy in the United States: Promise and Performance*, 3d ed. (Chicago: Rand McNally, 1976). See also J. Roland Pennock, *Democratic Political Theory* (Princeton: Princeton University Press, 1979), and Austin Ranney and Willmoore Kendal, "Basic Principles for a Model of Democracy," in *Empirical Democratic Theory*, eds. Charles C. Cnudde and Deane E. Neubauer (Chicago: Markham, 1969), 41-64.
16. Aaron Wildavsky, "The Two Presidencies," *Trans-Action* 4 (December 1966): 7-15.
17. "In Toast to Marcos, Bush Lauds Manila Democracy," *Washington Post*, July 1, 1981.
18. Alexis de Tocqueville, *Democracy in America* (New York: Alfred A. Knopf, 1945), 232-237, and Walter Lippmann, *The Public Philosophy* (Boston: Little, Brown, 1955), chap. 2.

c h a p t e r   t w o

The International
Environment

IN PURSUING its foreign policy objectives and in confronting the various dilemmas that this involves, the United States interacts with an international environment that, while often unpredictable and only partly malleable, presents it with many opportunities and occasionally with threats. The purpose of this chapter is to provide, as a background to later chapters, an overview of this environment—a brief sketch of the international actors toward which foreign policy is directed and of the principal issues by which the United States is linked to, or separated from, other nations. The international environment is, moreover, a product of its own past, and it cannot be adequately understood without an elementary grasp of this history. The previous chapter sought to provide a basic conceptual framework within which to consider U.S. foreign policy; the present chapter seeks to furnish a fundamental factual framework.

From the point of view of the United States, the international system consists of three "worlds," each of which creates a specific set of relationships and issues. The First World is the world of industrial democracies, nations similar to the United States and with which its relations are generally harmonious and cooperative. The Second World is that of the Soviet Union and its allies. It is from this world that the principal threats to U.S. national security are usually believed to come. America's future, and that of the rest of humanity, may well depend on how wisely relationships with the Second World are managed. The Third World consists of the developing nations, which have not attained the levels of development of the industrialized West (and generally not of the Soviet bloc, either). While the United States has tended to view the Third World as an arena within which to pursue its competition with the Soviet Union, the nations in those regions have sought to make issues of international economic redistribution the focus of their dealings with industrialized countries.

Although each of the three worlds is important in its own right, there is no doubt that U.S. foreign affairs are dominated by relations with the Second World: the so-called "superpower competition" or "Cold War," which continuously intrudes on policies toward our allies and largely determines how American interests in the developing world are conceived. Economic conditions in West Germany, religious upheavals in India, elections in Italy, guerrilla movements in Guatemala—all tend to be viewed through the prism of the Cold War. The U.S.-Soviet rivalry is without doubt the principal focus of America's foreign relations.

The Second World: The Politics of Hostility

For most of us, the image conjured up by the Soviet Union is that of a ruthless and sinister foe with which we simply cannot get along. The question of whether this nation, which is both different from and in some ways similar to our own, is inevitably an adversary will be discussed at length in Chapter 8. For now, we need to look back into the past and see how relations between the two countries have evolved.

Before the Bolshevik Revolution

From the eighteenth through the early twentieth centuries, Russia and the United States did not impinge much on each other's existence. They were geographically distant from each other, and each was, in its own way, a rather introverted society. Their external concerns were, for the most part, regional, not global. Nevertheless, the two nations were very aware of each other and occasionally their interests did intersect. At such times, U.S. attitudes toward Russia were rarely dispassionate; periods of surprising affection alternated with periods of intense hostility. These moods swung sharply, and it is instructive to realize that the periods of strong anti-Russian sentiment did not preclude subsequent movements toward more amicable and cooperative moods.

When Catherine the Great, the Russian empress at the time of the War of Independence, refused to give George III of England the 20,000 Russian soldiers he asked for to help crush the rebellious Americans, she was viewed as a champion of the American Revolution—a sort of benevolent Mother of Independence.[1] Yet when Russia divided Poland (a country for which the young nation had considerable sympathy) with Austria and Prussia, attitudes toward the empress shifted from appreciation to anger, and a deep chill engulfed relations between the two countries.

During the Civil War, Tsar Alexander II was correctly considered a supporter of the Union. Just as Lincoln had emancipated the slaves, the tsar had freed the Russian serfs (a couple of years earlier, actually), and he too had to deal with internal rebellion. Moreover, France openly supported secession by the South and Britain remained neutral, so Russia seemed to be the Union's major foreign friend. Relations warmed further when several Russian ships dropped anchor in New York and San Francisco. Although the ships were merely seeking safe anchorage in friendly ports, the Union government interpreted this as a gesture of military support for its cause, made to deter European intervention on behalf of the South. Sentiment ran so deep that, when Russia sold Alaska to the United States for $7,200,000 in 1867, the modest price was interpreted as additional proof of Russia's great affection for America.

But attitudes soured toward the end of the nineteenth century. Tsar Alexander III turned out to be a brutal ruler, unlike his predecessor, and as news of prison camps and anti-Jewish pogroms reached the United States, good will toward Russia eroded. Moreover, a direct kind of rivalry also began intruding on relations between the two countries. At this time, the United States was seeking to expand its commercial access to Asia and had decided that its interests required an "open door" to the rich Chinese province of Manchuria. But Russia was intent on colonizing Manchuria and acquiring exclusive economic access to the region. Mark Twain reflected the state of relations when he observed that, if the Russian regime could be destroyed only with dynamite, "then, thank God for dynamite." [2] Theodore Roosevelt, in a similar frame of mind, described the Russians as "utterly insincere and treacherous," with "no conception of the truth . . . and no regard for others." [3]

Though active dislike had replaced friendship, no one really viewed Russia as a direct threat. The United States was outside the reach of Russia's modest military might, and, in any case, there was no evidence of hostile Russian designs. In fact, the tsar seemed genuinely unhappy about the strained relations and eager to recapture the good will of earlier days. Had events taken a different course, this may well have happened: feelings in the United States tend to shift abruptly, often for reasons that seem minor in retrospect, and the old friendship might well have been rekindled. But the Bolshevik Revolution of 1917 altered the terms in which the United States viewed Russia and cast a new and deep pall on relations. The basis for the animosity now seemed more profound: where Russia had previously been nothing more than annoying, it now emerged as a genuine menace. Although it had been ruthlessly authoritarian and locally expansionistic, at least it had not been considered, as now, an ideological threat—a force striving to overthrow the political and economic system that the United States stood for and claiming, with brash confidence, to have history on its side. Where before policies may have clashed, contrary conceptions of Manifest Destiny now collided.

Rupture and Partial Healing

When the Communists seized power in Russia in the Revolution of 1917, one of the biggest and potentially most powerful of the world's nations adopted a philosophy and a political and economic system that was antithetical to fundamental American beliefs and values. People often refuse to acknowledge that which they fear or dislike, and the reaction in the United States to the Russian Revolution was one of stunned disbelief. In fact, by one count, the *New York Times* predicted the collapse of the Bolshevik regime ninety-one times between November 1917 and November 1919.[4] The hostility toward the new regime also led to extreme steps to weaken it. It is often forgotten that President Woodrow Wilson dispatched more than 10,000 U.S. troops to help combat the Bolsheviks. While one of their missions was to assist 70,000 Czechoslovakian soldiers who were trapped in Russian territory, another major purpose was to help the anti-Bolshevik factions in the civil war that was raging in that country. The last U.S. troops did not leave until 1920, and the intervention still rankles in Soviet memory.

These actions had no effect in weakening the Bolsheviks' grip on power. Rather, it can be argued that the external threat gave the revolution's leaders an excuse to tighten the reins of domestic control. After several rough years, the regime began standing on firmer economic legs, and hopes of its collapse began to evaporate. In any case, U.S. capacity for hostility was not inexhaustible, and by the early 1930s attitudes toward the Bolsheviks had slightly mellowed. There was also a basis of self-interest for improved relations. The United States at the time was weathering the onslaught of the Great Depression: unemployment had reached unprecedented heights, while industrial production and the stock market dropped to previously unimaginable lows. Under the circumstances, the idea of gaining access to Soviet markets was tempting. Exports to so large a country might increase production in the United States and therefore raise incomes and reduce unemployment. In 1933, the Soviet government spoke of placing orders abroad amounting to $1 billion. Consequently, many U.S. businessmen pressed President Franklin D. Roosevelt to reestablish diplomatic relations with the Soviet Union—they had been broken after the revolution—and that was done late in 1933.

Soon, however, the attention of both nations shifted elsewhere: the threat of war began to hover over Europe, and no nation was more disturbed by the rumblings in Nazi Germany than the Soviet Union. Hitler's anti-Bolshevik feelings were loudly proclaimed, and his stated intention to provide Germany with vast new "living space" in the East was a direct threat to the Soviet Union. As Hitler began encroaching on the territory of neighboring nations, the Soviet Union tried unsuccessfully to stimulate a common effort to stop him. When Hitler moved on Austria in 1938, the British and the French adopted a policy of appeasement, in the hope that Nazi appetites could be satisfied. When he followed the seizure of Austria by dismembering and then occupying Czechoslovakia, nothing was done to stop him. At that point, Stalin, the Soviet dictator, became convinced that the capitalist West was actually eager to see Hitler acquire a gateway to the Soviet Union. Faced with this peril, and realizing that Germany could not be stopped by Russian armed force alone, Stalin decided to act on his own to remove the threat. In August 1939, to the shocked disbelief of the West (and even of many Communists), Stalin signed a nonaggression pact with Nazi Germany, by which each country promised to refrain from military action against the other.[5]

But Hitler finally went further than the West was willing to tolerate, and Germany's invasion of Poland in September 1939 triggered World War II. In June 1941, Germany ended its agreement with the Soviet Union and launched a major offensive against its former associate. Britain and the United States decided that, of the two dictators, Stalin was the less immediate threat, and thus began the strained collaboration in which the Soviet Union was their wartime ally.

This was a marriage of convenience preceded by no love or courtship, but once again Americans' feelings toward the Russians turned nearly warm. Most people in the United States regarded Soviet war aims as nonaggressive and felt that the United States should make a real effort to stay on good terms with the Soviets. Even the Soviet political system came to appear less objectionable. Before the war, a majority of Americans had declared that they would prefer fascism to communism; during the war, the proportion favoring fascism dropped to below 10 percent, while more than half the respondents said that communism was the lesser evil.[6]

Still, the wartime collaboration did little to dispel Soviet distrust of the West, a distrust that was rooted in the Western intervention of 1918-1920 and in the West's refusal to make common cause with the Soviet Union against Hitler in the 1930s. During the war, Soviet suspicions were heightened by British and U.S. reluctance to open a second front in central Europe. The Germans had driven deep into Soviet territory, causing enormous human and material devastation, and Stalin pleaded with his allies for an invasion from western Europe in order to relieve the military pressure on his country. By Winston Churchill's own account, in early 1943, the West was engaged with no more than twelve German divisions, the Russians with 185.[7] Roosevelt promised an invasion from western Europe on two occasions, but both times he and Churchill reneged. They believed that it was preferable to invade North Africa and Italy and to gradually encircle and squeeze Germany from those positions. By the time a second front was finally opened in 1944, the Soviet Union had already begun to push the Nazis back, but it lost at least twenty million lives in the process. Stalin was infuriated by the delay. The capitalist nations, he felt, were intent on having Germany and the Soviet Union bleed each other dry, so that they would face a weakened Germany in the short run and a crippled Soviet Union in the long run. The accusation was probably unfair, but the conviction became etched in the Soviet mind.

The Onset of the Cold War

While the course of events before and during World War II persuaded the Soviet Union that the West longed for its demise, Moscow's behavior after the war led the United States to believe that the Soviet Union was duplicitous and

expansionist. Several factors strengthened this perception. At the Yalta conference in 1945 on the future of a liberated Europe, the Soviets had promised to
permit free elections and national self-determination in Eastern Europe. But
Moscow failed to keep its promise. During the war, Soviet troops had been
instrumental in liberating several Eastern and Central European countries, and
in most of these nations Stalin established pro-Soviet coalition governments, in
which the key ministries of defense and the interior were held by Communists.
This control of the instruments of coercion then enabled them to subvert the
democratic process and to turn the countries into Soviet satellites. The United
States was particularly incensed at Soviet behavior in Poland. There, despite
repeated promises to the contrary, all non-Communist forces were excluded
from the government, and Poland was forced into the Soviet orbit. Only
Czechoslovakia briefly maintained a multiparty government, but there, too, in
1948 democratic parties were eliminated and exclusive Communist rule was
established.

Soviet determination to insulate itself with buffer states against its former
enemies (Germany in particular) probably accounted for these moves. But the
concern of its wartime allies was understandably aroused. Stalin's activities in
other regions, especially in Iran and Turkey, were no more reassuring. Fear of
Iranian collaboration with the Nazis had prompted Britain, the United States,
and the U.S.S.R. to occupy Iran in 1941. After the war, only Soviet forces were
not withdrawn. In fact, Moscow was busy promoting an autonomous
Azerbaijani Republic in northern Iran under the dominance of the local
Communist party. The West was furious, and the United States issued an
ultimatum for the Soviet Union to withdraw. It did, but only after it was
promised a joint Iranian-Soviet oil company, subject to ratification by the
Iranian parliament. However, following the withdrawal, the promised oil
company was rejected by the parliament. Once again, the Soviet Union felt
cheated by the West, while the United States was increasingly convinced that
the Soviet Union harbored expansionistic ambitions.

A dispute over Turkey further widened the rift. The Soviet Union
demanded the cession to it of several Turkish regions lying on the Soviet
border, as well as joint control of the Dardanelles Straits, which linked Soviet
ports on the Black Sea to the Mediterranean (and thus to the Indian and
Atlantic oceans). President Harry S Truman rejected the Soviet demands, and,
to demonstrate U.S. determination, he dispatched a naval task force, including
an aircraft carrier, to the area in August 1946. The Soviet Union relented, while
the United States was strengthened in its conviction that toughness was the only
way to deal with the Kremlin. The Cold War mentality was rapidly becoming
entrenched, and it solidified in the Berlin crisis of 1948.

As World War II came to an end, the Allied powers decided that
Germany would be divided into zones of occupation, with the eastern portion
of the country under Soviet control. Berlin, the former capital, was located in
the Soviet zone, but it was to be jointly administered by the U.S.S.R., Britain,

France, and the United States. As relations with the Soviet Union deteriorated, the Western nations decided that Germany should be strengthened economically as a possible bulwark against Moscow. In protest, and also in an attempt to drive the Western powers out of Berlin, the Soviet Union initiated a blockade of the city in 1948, cutting it off from the rest of Germany. The U.S. reaction was firm: President Truman ordered a massive airlift of supplies to Berlin, to demonstrate to its inhabitants and to the world that the city could not be choked off. To reinforce this show of determination, he also sent a fleet of nuclear-capable B-29 bombers to Britain, which meant that the force was within striking distance of the U.S.S.R. The airlift was kept up for eleven months, at the end of which the Soviet Union realized that the blockade was to no avail and called it off.

At this point, the United States was utterly convinced that only firm resolve and military power could deter further Soviet encroachments on Western security interests. This implied that a system of collective defense was needed, and in April 1949 a treaty among the Western nations established the North Atlantic Treaty Organization (NATO). In this treaty, the parties agreed that "an armed attack against one or more of them in Europe or North America shall be considered an attack against them all." The Cold War had now unequivocally begun, and increasingly it took the form of preparations for possible military conflict. In 1949, years before the time predicted by many U.S. experts, the Soviet Union detonated its own nuclear-fission bomb, ending the U.S. monopoly over the most powerful instrument of destruction that had been devised up to then (though it would be exceeded in a few years by the development in both countries of the hydrogen bomb). Since that time, the threat of unprecedented devastation has been the dominant feature of U.S.-Soviet relations.

These events were accompanied by dramatically altered views of the Soviet Union among the U.S. public. In January 1945, nearly 70 percent of the respondents in a national survey said they expected the United States to get along better with the U.S.S.R. after the war than it had before the war. Six months later, 50 percent of the public felt that the Soviet Union was out to dominate as much of the world as possible. By February 1948, more than 70 percent of the respondents said that Moscow was arming "to build herself up to be the ruling power of the world." [8]

Meanwhile, Soviet actions in Europe were hardening the bipolarity of relations. Although Yugoslavia seceded from the bloc in 1948, the Soviet grip on its East European allies was progressively tightening. In 1949, the Council for Mutual Economic Assistance (COMECON) was established by the Soviet Union, Poland, Czechoslovakia, Hungary, Romania, Bulgaria, and Albania (East Germany joined a year later). It arose as a counter to the Marshall Plan, by which the United States had supplied large amounts of economic aid to help the economies of Western Europe recover from the havoc wrought by the war. Its chief function was to coordinate the economic plans of its members; its main effect has been to bind the satellite economies tightly to the Soviet economy. A few years later, the Soviet Union acted to lock its allies in political bonds as well.

Since the end of World War II, the Kremlin had exercised military control of its allies through "dependable" military officers trained in the Soviet Union. This form of control was supplemented in 1952 by the creation of a joint military coordinating committee and a combined general staff headed by a Russian general. In 1955, a further step was taken. That year, West Germany was admitted into NATO. This was what the Soviet Union had feared all along. A nation that had been its enemy in both world wars was now firmly and officially part of a military organization directed against it. In response, the Warsaw Pact—a formal military alliance between the Soviet Union and its East European clients—was founded. It added institutional substance to an organization which had, for all intents and purposes, already existed, but it was also both a concrete and a symbolic manifestation of the political and military bipolarity which the Cold War had brought to Europe (see Figure 2-1).

Figure 2-1   The Political Division of Europe, 1955

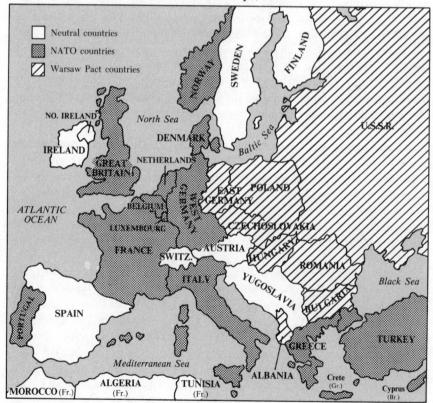

This bipolarity is now a deeply ingrained part of the international environment. It has become accepted as a settled feature of world politics. When Soviet troops crushed a national uprising in Hungary in 1956, which was directed largely against Soviet political repression, the United States did no more than condemn Moscow's action and register sympathy for its victims. When Soviet tanks rolled into Czechoslovakia in 1968 to put an end to the modest liberalization attempted by that country's Communist government, Washington's response was even more tepid; for example, the invasion barely interrupted the talks that led to the opening of the strategic arms limitation talks the following year.

By the late 1940s, alignments outside of Europe also reflected the world's emerging bipolarity, as testified to by the Korean War (see Chapter 4). The United States had become totally convinced of Soviet perfidy and aggressiveness. The U.S.S.R., in turn, was more certain than ever that the West was bent on undermining its security, by trying to deprive it of "friendly" buffer states along its borders, by initiating the development of nuclear weapons, and by indulging in shrill anti-Soviet rhetoric. The Cold War, though it has at times abated, has provided the major focus of the security fears of both countries during the past several decades.

Hostility reached a peak of intensity at the time of the Berlin blockade and the Korean War, then leveled off for a few years. During the early 1950s, ideological diatribes continued but acquired a somewhat stale flavor, and actual behavior was rather cautious and circumspect. But new tensions began forming around 1957.

Prior to that date, the United States did not feel militarily threatened by the Soviet Union, at least not directly, for although the U.S.S.R. had the nuclear bomb, it did not have the means of effectively delivering it to U.S. soil. It lacked an adequate long-range bomber force, military bases near U.S. territory, or intercontinental missiles. All of this changed in 1957, when the Soviet Union launched Sputnik, the first artificial satellite, into orbit. The obvious implication was that if it was capable of placing a satellite into orbit, it could also build missiles capable of reaching targets within the United States. Increased fear was infused into the existing rivalry, which was no longer just a competition between incompatible ideologies but a political struggle in the context of the threat of mutual destruction.

Several disputes further poisoned the climate. In 1958, China, then still a close Soviet ally, began bombing Quemoy and Matsu, two islands off its coast that were still under the control of Taiwan and to whose defense the United States had pledged itself in 1955. In a show of resolve, President Dwight D. Eisenhower ordered the U.S. Seventh Fleet to escort Taiwan's ships to within three miles of the beleaguered islands. Eventually, the Chinese backed down, but U.S. involvement in a shooting war had been a real possibility. Two years later, another crisis erupted. The United States had developed a high-altitude airplane, the U-2, which could take photographs of Soviet territory for intelligence purposes—for example, to see whether intercontinental missiles were being deployed. In May 1960, a U-2 was shot down 1,300 miles inside the Soviet Union. President Eisenhower at first denied that it was a spy plane, claiming that it had simply been engaged in meteorological observations. But, unbeknown to the United States, the pilot had been captured and much of the equipment aboard the downed plane had been retrieved. The Soviet Union was thus in a position to prove that the plane had indeed been on a spy mission and that Eisenhower had lied. Tempers flared, and preparations then being made for a summit conference between Eisenhower and the Soviet leader, Nikita Khrushchev, collapsed.

But the most menacing crisis of this period, and indeed in the entire history of the Cold War, occurred in October 1962. It very nearly plunged humanity into the nuclear abyss, and it caused the two rivals to take a long, hard, and yet ultimately ephemeral look at their relations.

Toward Détente and Back Again

In the fall of 1962, U.S. intelligence discovered that, despite the Kremlin's assurances to the contrary, the Soviet Union was building launch sites for some seventy medium- and intermediate-range missiles in Cuba. This move was probably prompted by America's substantial lead in intercontinental missiles, but it was nevertheless considered unacceptable by Washington. Apart from the obvious military threat that it could present for the United States (because of the reduced warning time of a nuclear attack), the political damage of allowing the Soviet Union to deploy the missiles would have been substantial. Other countries could conclude that the United States had lost its nerve in the face of Soviet nuclear power, and the nation's international credibility and influence might suffer. In addition, President John F. Kennedy was worried about the domestic political cost to himself of not acting decisively—in particular, about the likely assaults from right-wing forces.

Consequently, Kennedy ordered a naval blockade to prevent Soviet missile-bearing ships from reaching Cuba, and demanded dismantlement of the sites that had already been constructed. In addition, the president placed half the Strategic Air Command's nuclear bombers on alert and dispersed them to civilian airfields. The fleet of Polaris submarines, carrying nuclear-tipped missiles, was moved to within striking distance of the Soviet Union. The superpowers were on the brink of a confrontation. Ultimately, the Soviet Union agreed to remove the missiles, but had Khrushchev decided to try to break through the U.S. blockade, a nuclear war might well have occurred. The Soviet leader observed that "the smell of burning pervaded the air," while Kennedy estimated that the odds of a disaster claiming some 100 million lives on both sides was "between one out of three and even." [9]

It was a dangerously close call, but it did have a salutary effect on U.S.-Soviet relations. The near brush with nuclear destruction caused both sides to reassess their relationship and to take some steps, albeit modest ones, to decrease the perils they had created for themselves. The two nations made a tentative move toward arms control by signing the Nuclear Test Ban Treaty in 1963. In the same year, they also established a "hot line," a direct and immediate link between the Kremlin and the White House that was to facilitate rapid communication in any future crises. The tone of Soviet-American relations became less strident, and each side tried to avoid behavior the other might consider unduly provocative.

Thus, and for the second time since the Cold War began, a movement away from hostility was initiated. Its pace, however, was sluggish. The war in Vietnam, which the United States entered in 1964, became a new obstacle to *détente*, as the relaxation of tensions was called. Also, it may be that President Lyndon B. Johnson, who had succeeded Kennedy after the latter's assassination in 1963, did not wish to jeopardize his liberal domestic programs by attracting too much wrath from the political right. Continuing toughness toward the nation's traditional opponents might therefore have been a domestic political necessity. By the same token, it should not be surprising that the first meaningful steps toward détente were taken by a Republican president, Richard Nixon, who assumed office in 1969 and whose domestic conservatism and established anticommunist credentials made him virtually invulnerable to attacks from hard-liners on the right.

Two features distinguished the new approach to superpower relations adopted by President Nixon and his chief foreign policy adviser, Henry Kissinger. The first was an abandonment of the ideological vehemence and self-righteous emotionalism characteristic of the height of the Cold War. From now on, pragmatism would take precedence over ideology in U.S. dealings with the Soviet Union. The second was an emphasis on nonmilitary methods of moderating Soviet behavior. Armed force would not be neglected, but it would be supplemented by less dangerous means of pressure. These modifications were meant to enable the United States to pursue its foreign policy objectives at less peril. As Kissinger pointed out: "Détente is not rooted in agreement on values. . . . To us, détente is a process of managing relations with a potentially hostile country in order to preserve peace while maintaining our vital interests." [10]

According to Kissinger, the aim was to give the Soviet Union a vested interest in the international status quo and a disincentive to challenge the international goals of the United States. To accomplish this, new forms of influence over Soviet behavior were needed. The operative concept was that of *linkage*—that is, to allow progress on issues that were important to Moscow only if there was also progress on issues that the United States considered important. If the Soviet Union wanted the United States to do something, or to desist from action which it found objectionable, some quid pro quo would be asked for. To make this policy work, the administration counted chiefly upon two sorts of leverage.

The first was the evolving U.S. relation with the People's Republic of China. Moscow and Peking had ceased to be friends in the late 1950s and had since become archrivals. Each claimed the mantle of authentic communism, and each accused the other of various forms of treachery and perfidy. The United States and China, on the other hand, were overcoming two decades of intense hostility. This culminated in President Nixon's visit to Peking in 1972, which launched relations between the two countries on a new and more cordial path. Not only was this improvement desired as an end in itself, terminating the awkward situation in which the most powerful nation and the most populous country in the world ignored each other, but it was also seen as an aid in relations with the Soviet Union. The implication was that if Moscow was obstinate and obstructive in its dealings with the United States, America would align itself more closely with the Soviet Union's enemy, China. As Kissinger pointed out, "The hostility between China and the Soviet Union served our purposes best if we maintained closer relations with each side than they did with each other." [11]

Economic cooperation was to be the second form of leverage. Growth rates in the U.S.S.R., which had been very respectable in the postwar period, were slowing down. For the most part, this was due to the Soviet Union's low productivity and to its inability to master such dynamic sectors of economic activity as computers, electronics, and petrochemicals—the very areas in which the United States was most advanced. In addition, the Soviet Union was experiencing serious agricultural problems. Unfavorable weather conditions, bureaucratic ineptitude, and a lack of peasant motivation had led to substantial shortfalls in grain production. By contrast, the United States regularly produced a large surplus of grain beyond the needs of domestic consumers. Thus, the United States was in a position to provide some of the things that the Soviet economy most needed. With this in mind, President Nixon agreed to improve economic cooperation with the U.S.S.R., as long as it did not try to undermine the international interests of the United States.

This new approach soon bore fruit. The tone of relations between the two superpowers lost much of its stridency, and Soviet behavior seemed more circumspect than usual. Cultural, scientific, and commercial contacts expanded somewhat. Most importantly, meaningful steps toward arms control were finally taken. In 1972, the Soviet Union and the United States signed two agreements that together comprised the Strategic Arms Limitation Treaty of 1972 (SALT I). The first, the Anti-Ballistic Missile (ABM) Treaty, limited the number of each side's antiballistic missiles and thus put a stop to what could have emerged as a new aspect of the strategic arms race. The second, the Interim Offensive Arms Agreement, placed a ceiling on the number of intercontinental missiles that either side could deploy. Negotiations for a SALT II treaty were also initiated during this period, and it appeared that agreements would become increasingly comprehensive and ambitious.

Americans' feelings toward the U.S.S.R. were becoming almost affable. Public-opinion surveys registered approval ratings of the Soviet Union that were higher than they had ever been. The United States and the Soviet Union have probably never experienced as cordial peacetime relations as during the détente of the Nixon-Kissinger era. But, once again, the respite was short-lived.

It is not easy to identify exactly when the cordial optimism of détente became transmuted into the bitterness of the late 1970s and early 1980s. However, the seeds of change were probably sown in late 1973, at the time of the Middle East war. Egypt and Syria, two countries friendly to the Soviet Union, had launched a sudden and initially successful attack on Israel, a de facto ally of the United States. Although Israel eventually drove its assailants back, the United States suspected that Moscow had prior knowledge of the attack and felt that it should have alerted the United States. The damage to U.S.-Soviet relations was not immediately felt—in fact, the two countries signed another agreement limiting offensive nuclear weapons in 1974—but the foundations of cooperation were weakened. By this time, the view that the Kremlin had exploited détente for its own purposes was making steady headway within the United States. Expressed through powerful and well-organized lobbies, it exerted an increasingly powerful influence on U.S. policy toward the U.S.S.R. and provided a significant domestic obstacle to further improvements in superpower relations.

Additional problems arose. In 1975, Cuban forces intervened in the civil war raging in Angola. The Cubans fought on the side of the Marxist faction, the MPLA (Popular Movement for the Liberation of Angola, from the initials of its name in Portuguese), while the United States supported (but gave no direct military assistance to) the MPLA's opponents. Two years later, 14,000 Cuban troops and several hundred Soviet military advisers intervened on the other side of the African continent, in Ethiopia, to help that country in its war against Somalia over the disputed Ogaden region, which both countries claimed as their own. To many people in the United States, this smacked of a Soviet effort to establish a foothold in Africa through Cuban proxies. In sum, the Soviet Union was perceived as being dangerously on the prowl, in a way not deemed compatible with the spirit of the new relationship. This provided further ammunition for the opponents of détente within the United States: Senators Henry Jackson (D-Wash.) and Howard Baker (R-Tenn.) suggested, for example, that Soviet behavior in Africa should be considered sufficient grounds for opposing a new SALT agreement.

The Kremlin too was beginning to feel cheated by détente. Washington's use of its "China card" in order to extract concessions from the Soviet Union began to rankle. Furthermore, one of the major benefits that the Soviet Union had expected from improved relations with the United States—namely, more trade and technology—was not forthcoming. Congressional hawks were blocking expanded cooperation in this area in a variety of ways. Senator Jackson, for example, had managed to make improved economic relations contingent on a more liberalized Soviet policy on Jewish emigration—which Moscow considered an intolerable meddling in its internal affairs. Other congressional initiatives further undermined the chances for increased Soviet purchases of U.S. goods and for the transfer of sophisticated technology to the U.S.S.R. In addition to these irritations, President Jimmy Carter, who took office in 1976, made it a point to speak out frequently on behalf of human rights in nondemocratic countries, and of course the Soviet Union received its share of criticism on this score. To the Soviet leaders, this looked not only like interference in their internal affairs but also like a return to the moralistic posturing of the fifties—probably with a view to undermining the regime's legitimacy.

On December 24, 1979, Soviet troops invaded Afghanistan to quell a rebellion by fundamentalist Muslim forces intent on overthrowing the nation's Marxist government (which the Soviet Union had been instrumental in establishing). The reasons for the invasion were fairly evident: fear of a solid phalanx of hostile nations (Iran, Afghanistan, China) on the Soviet Union's southern flank, and fear that Islamic fundamentalism, if successful in Afghanistan as well as in Iran, might spread to the U.S.S.R.'s own Asian regions, perhaps leading to domestic instability. Moreover, by establishing a military presence in Afghanistan, the Soviet Union would be in a better geostrategic position with respect to the oil-rich region of the Persian Gulf, on which much of the West relied for its petroleum.

This was more than the United States was willing to bear, and its response, like that of the rest of the world, was swift, bitter, and vigorous. Economic sanctions were imposed, efforts at arms control were abandoned, and President Carter threatened to meet any Soviet incursion into the Persian Gulf with military force. Détente had crumbled, and the hard-liners felt vindicated. After Ronald Reagan became president in 1981, superpower relations returned to the stridency, intolerance, and surging arms races of earlier decades. While a plateau in hostility seemed to have been reached by the end of President Reagan's first term, there was no authentic movement toward a more cooperative state of relations until 1986.

The First World: Friendship and Its Limits

Observers of the international situation at earlier stages of the history of the United States would have had trouble anticipating the present pattern of its friendships. In the nineteenth century, it had fought wars with Britain and Spain and experienced stormy relations with France. In the twentieth century, Britain and France have consistently been its friends, and relations with Spain are now very good as well. In both World War I and World War II, U.S. participation was largely directed against Germany and Italy, and in World War II, Japan became an adversary as well. Each of these three nations is now considered a valuable ally.

The determinants of friendship between countries will be discussed in Chapter 9, but for now suffice it to say that international friendships and alliances can be formed by two sorts of influences: by positive circumstances, such as similarities of values, trading opportunities, and possibilities for beneficial cultural and other exchanges; and by negative considerations, especially the existence of common rivals and antagonists. While both influences matter, the friends and allies of the United States, at least since World War II, have been shaped mainly by negative concerns—specifically, by the East-West fissure. Because of this, it is important to establish the link between the U.S. postwar commitment to its friends, on the one hand, and the Cold War, on the other. Of course, it ought not be assumed that the West in general, or even the North Atlantic region, is a harmonious family of like-minded countries. Allies do not always see eye-to-eye with each other, even on matters of common security. Moreover, the United States and its industrialized friends are also each others' rivals in certain ways, especially with regard to international trade. Consequently, the historical roots and the present manifestations of opposing interests within the Western alliance must also be understood.

U.S. "Entanglement" in Europe

World War II left a devastated Europe in its wake. A continent that had prided itself on its industrial might, technological drive, and high standards of living lay shattered in the rubble of history's most destructive conflict. In February 1947, less than half of Britain's factories were operating. Despite a valiant effort at economic recovery, France's iron and steel production had reached only half of its prewar level in 1946. In Germany, cigarettes were replacing money as the prevailing unit of exchange. From the U.S. point of view, the implications were disturbing in several respects. To begin with, an economically weak Europe could not provide an effective bulwark against the emerging Soviet threat—yet it was felt that the first line of defense should indeed be established in Western Europe. Second, this area was in many ways the cradle of modern democracy, and its geostrategic significance was enormous as well. Third, it was feared that economic disarray could lead to the collapse of democracy from within. In several European nations, local Communists had played a major role in the resistance against the Nazis and the Fascists, and so they emerged from the war with newly found respectability. The French Communist party claimed the support of 25 percent of that country's electorate; in Italy, approximately one-third of the electorate supported the Communists. Economic despair, it was feared, would further bolster the political fortunes of national Communist movements; this, in turn, could spell disaster in the global ideological and military rivalry. Finally, a destitute Europe did not bode well for U.S. economic interests. The United States had come out of the war economically unscathed (in fact, growth had been rapid during the wartime years), but continued prosperity depended on a sound international economy and on external markets capable of absorbing U.S. goods. The most promising markets were those of Western Europe, but they would not realize their promise unless the region's economy showed renewed vigor.

The United States adopted two courses of action. On the one hand, recognizing that there was not very much that could be done if the Europeans did not work with each other in launching their own economic recovery, U.S. leaders urged them to strengthen their cooperation. Indeed, a common European effort was made a condition of further help. In 1948, by way of response, seventeen nations established the Organization for European Economic Cooperation (OEEC), whose purpose was to promote recovery through cooperation, the common assessment of needs, and a mutual reduction of trade barriers. As a second course of action, the United States provided an infusion of economic assistance: $17 billion for the European Recovery Program, more commonly known as the Marshall Plan, after Secretary of State George Marshall, who first proposed the program.

The assistance fell on fertile soil. By 1950, Europe had exceeded its prewar production by 25 percent; by 1952, the corresponding figure was 200 percent. The specter of economic collapse had vanished, and, at a moderate price, the United States had managed both to strengthen Western security and to bolster its own prosperity by ensuring itself of vigorous trading partners. The Marshall Plan has surely been one of the most glittering success stories in the history of U.S. foreign policy.

Nevertheless, purely economic solutions were not enough to deal with the military dimension of the Soviet threat. Following the termination of hostilities in 1945, the U.S. public was eager for a speedy demobilization, and the nation's armed forces were drastically reduced. At the same time, the Soviet Union was intent on establishing a permanent military presence in those portions of Eastern and Central Europe that its forces had occupied at the end of the war. Whether its troops were a direct threat to Western Europe or simply a defensive presence—a first line of its own defense and a force designed to impose political discipline within the satellite nations—is open to debate. But the situation was not reassuring from the West's perspective, and, as the saber-rattling and shrill invective of the period gained amplitude, tangible evidence of Western readiness for a common defense was deemed necessary.

In March 1949, at almost the same time that the OEEC was established, five European nations (Britain, France, Belgium, the Netherlands, and Luxembourg) signed the Treaty of Brussels, creating a military alliance ostensibly directed against a revival of the German threat but actually concerned primarily with the Soviet Union. Plainly, however, no defensive alliance against the Soviet bloc could be credible if it did not include active U.S. assistance and participation. The Europeans realized this, and so did the U.S. administration. The idea of U.S. military support for European defense also had congressional support and was generally endorsed by the U.S. public. The outcome, already mentioned, was the NATO treaty, by which the United States and eleven other signatory nations created a permanent organization for military planning and political consultation, with the major purpose of providing the U.S. allies with the military assurance they wanted. At this time, the West had approximately a dozen modestly equipped divisions in Central Europe, facing twice that number of Soviet divisions. The counterweight of a U.S. military presence was needed for two purposes: to establish a *forward defense* in Central Europe, capable of repelling Soviet forces before they could penetrate too deeply westward, and, more importantly, to deter those forces from attempting aggression by making it obvious that an attack would automatically trigger a response from the United States. U.S. troops stationed along the principal routes of anticipated Soviet attack would therefore serve as a "tripwire" that would ensure retaliation. In addition, the possession by the United States not only of the atomic bomb but also of the means of delivering it to Soviet territory was to provide the credibility of deterrence that the Europeans required.

For the first time in its history, the United States had undertaken a major military commitment in peacetime. The principle of avoiding "entangling alliances," which George Washington had advocated in his farewell address and which had been a cornerstone of the nation's foreign policy, was sacrificed on the altar of Western security. The military and economic future of the United States was now thoroughly entwined with that of Western Europe. Other nations are also considered friends and allies, but the United States has not linked its fate quite so closely to that of any other region.

Bipolarity in Europe thus took root in the late 1940s. Although Yugoslavia seceded from the bloc in 1948, the Soviet grip on its East European allies was progressively tightening and, at the height of Stalin's domestic terror and external bluster, the Soviet threat appeared very genuine. Yet those decades of mutual fear and political bitterness have faded from Europe's memory, and, despite a lingering distrust and major ideological differences, there is much that historically unites the eastern and western regions of the continent. Consequently, the United States and its European partners do not always agree on the specifics of Western policy toward the Eastern bloc.

Limits to Partnership

Because of their geographical location, the European allies of the United States are particularly vulnerable to Soviet military pressure, and they have made persistent efforts to secure a firm U.S. military commitment to their defense. Yet to many American eyes, Europeans have often seemed less concerned about the Soviet peril than the U.S. government has been, and less inclined to place a dire interpretation on the Kremlin's external activities. In the late 1970s and 1980s, they failed to get very exercised about the invasion of Afghanistan or about Soviet aid to the Marxist government in Nicaragua. They have agreed to become major importers of Soviet natural gas, they trade quite extensively with the Soviet Union, and they have frequently taken the position that the United States was insufficiently forthcoming in arms-control talks. Occasionally, these divergent views are a source of bewilderment and resentment for both political leaders and the general public in the United States.

European attitudes and behavior spring from a reasonable assessment of the continent's interests and security needs. To begin with, although the military requirements of security are understood, Europeans appear to have a healthy appreciation of the limitations of military force as well. More precisely, they tend to be equally concerned with the role that the overall tone of relations plays in preserving security. Thus, when the United States becomes aroused over some instance of Soviet misbehavior—for example, the invasion of Afghanistan—the European response is often moderate by comparison. It is also true that the West European nations have been more willing than the United States to establish commercial links with the Eastern bloc. Apart from the purely economic advantages that the West Europeans derive from these transactions, they are also often seen as a means of reducing tension. The idea is that, if the Soviet bloc is even partially economically bound to the West, its general posture will probably be less pugnacious and menacing. An economically dependent neighbor is not as likely to be a militarily dangerous neighbor.

This notion has not been applied solely to the Soviet Union; economic interdependence was also viewed as a way of reducing future threats from Germany after World War II. In 1952, six European nations founded the European Coal and Steel Community (ECSC). It included France, Germany, Italy, Belgium, the Netherlands, and Luxembourg, but it was principally established with the first two of those countries in mind. France and Germany were traditional enemies: they had fought each other not only in both world wars but in the nineteenth century as well. Coal and steel were the two main ingredients of postwar industrial production, each of them essential to heavy industry, but neither of these two countries had both. France had substantial iron reserves, while Germany was rich in coal. Through the ECSC, each was to furnish what the other lacked, and consequently the heavy industries of the two traditional enemies would be interwoven to the point where, it was believed, Germany could no longer represent a threat to the other members. It seemed reasonable to Europeans to extend this concept to the Soviet Union.

The Western bloc is therefore not monolithic, and this fact partially defines the environment within which U.S. foreign policy operates. Indeed, there are areas where the allies of the United States are also its rivals. In the immediate postwar years, Western Europe and Japan relied heavily on U.S. assistance to set them on the road to prosperity. By the 1960s, these nations had not only recovered but, in many significant ways, they had become economic competitors of the United States. The problems arising out of this commercial rivalry frequently seem to dominate relations within the Western alliance.

The outstanding illustration has stemmed from the economic activity of Japan. In the 1950s, the designation "Made in Japan" was synonymous with cheap, imitative, and even shoddy products. By the 1970s, a dramatic change had occurred: Japan began displacing the United States in such crucial areas as steel, electrical consumer goods, and automobiles. The competition has been particularly bitter in automobiles, as U.S. consumers became increasingly drawn to the well-designed, reliable, and fuel-efficient Hondas, Toyotas, and Nissans. The U.S. automobile industry suffered as a result. In 1980, more than 200,000 workers were laid off, the industry lost $4 billion, and one company, Chrysler, managed to survive only with an infusion of federal assistance. During that same year, Japanese automobiles constituted 21 percent of sales in the U.S. market, and there was every indication that this presence would be expanded further. The United States exerted various forms of diplomatic pressure to persuade Japan to adopt "voluntary" restraints on its automobile exports. This was achieved, but at the price of Japanese resentment, since that country did not feel it should have to bear the costs of Detroit's inability to provide U.S. consumers with the type of car they wanted. By the mid-1980s, South Korea was also becoming an important actor in the U.S. automobile market, providing competition to domestic producers from another Asian ally.

Western Europe has also emerged as a significant economic rival, with similar consequences. For example, a number of European nations (as well as Japan and a few Third World countries) have been increasing their sales of steel in the United States. U.S. steel producers have felt threatened and have lobbied the government for protection—on the whole successfully. A *trigger-price* mechanism was introduced in the late 1970s, setting minimum import prices below which Europeans could not sell their steel in U.S. markets if they wished to avoid stiff import duties. Also, diplomatic arm-twisting has led the European Common Market (an outgrowth of the ECSC, established in 1957 and now including twelve European nations) to accept restraints on the amount of steel shipped to the United States.

The obvious question that grows out of this discussion is: How should we best manage our relations with nations whose basic and long-term interests coincide with ours, but whose short-term goals and perceptions are at odds with our own? Also, how is the United States to reconcile its international security objectives with its national economic goals in dealing with its allies? These questions are part of what was referred to in Chapter 1 as the dilemma of effective choice.

The Third World: Politics and Equity

The First and Second worlds are actually a rather small, though important, part of the international system. It is within the Third World that the majority of mankind resides. Many Third World nations have only recently become full-fledged members of the community of nations, so the starting point in any consideration of their role in international affairs must be an examination of their colonial roots.[12]

Approximately two-thirds of the population of the non-European world lives in countries that were, at one time or another, the colonial possession of a European power. Spain and Portugal were the first major colonizers, and they were soon joined by Britain, France, Holland, and, at a somewhat later date, Germany. Colonialism experienced its first peak in the late eighteenth century, but it then witnessed major setbacks as countries in North, Central, and South America managed to free themselves from their European overlords. Toward the end of the next century, however, the world experienced a second bout of imperial expansion. The industrial revolution called for new sources of raw materials, while the balance of power that had been achieved in Europe meant that successful new conquests could only be undertaken elsewhere. Much of this second wave of colonial growth, which lasted from the 1870s until the beginning of World War I, was directed at Africa: in 1870, only one-tenth of Africa was under European control; thirty years later, only one-tenth remained independent. But much of the force behind colonialism had spent itself by the end of the war and the foundations for eventual independence were, to some extent, laid in the period after World War I. The crumbling of the colonial world began in earnest after World War II, and within a single generation, more than seventy nations acquired independence. The spirit in much of the Third World was a combination of fervent nationalism and heady optimism. Jawaharlal Nehru of India captured the mood by declaring, "For too long have we been petitioners in Western courts and chancelleries . . . that story must now belong to the past. We propose to stand on our own two legs . . . we do not intend to be the plaything of others." [13]

Part of the optimism that surrounded the attainment of colonial independence was linked to economic expectations. The poverty of Third World nations was, for the most part, attributed to colonialism and the exploitation by which most of these nations felt that they had been victimized. With independence, it was assumed, meaningful growth would finally get under way and the legacy of poverty would be rapidly left behind. In addition, many of the problems that had afflicted Third World societies were thought to have resulted from the fact that they had been the passive victims of the power politics practiced by the developed nations. Now they would have as little as possible to do with great-power politics; instead, grouped within their own *nonaligned movement*, as they called it—that is, detached from both superpower blocs—they would be in a position to attend to their own international interests.

However, many of the expectations of the Third World have been disappointed. Although it has some rather prosperous members, who have become part of the global middle class, most remain poor and are struggling to share in the material prosperity enjoyed by the members of the other two worlds. There has consequently been a call, launched by developing nations of a different ideological stripe, for a redistribution of the world's wealth. As the richest country on earth, the United States has been a central target of this call.

Moreover, the Third World has not found it as easy as it had initially imagined to steer clear of the international politics of the major powers. In particular, the U.S.-Soviet rivalry has persistently insinuated itself into U.S. policy toward the developing areas. Not only has the East-West competition frequently shaped U.S. attitudes toward issues in these regions, but events there have also had a major impact on the Cold War.

Thus, there are two dimensions to U.S. relations with the Third World: an East-West dimension, which the United States has frequently imposed on its dealings with developing nations, and a North-South, or economic-redistributive, dimension, which the Third World itself more typically emphasizes.

Impact of the Cold War

Although both the Cold War and détente originated in Europe, subsequent shifts in the superpowers' relations have been strongly influenced by their competition in developing regions. As already described, Soviet behavior toward Iran and Turkey amplified U.S. fears of Soviet militarism and expansionism, confirmed the worst suspicions of those within the United States who had never believed the wartime alliance could be extended into peacetime, and weakened the position of those who had argued against overstating the Soviet threat. And it was in Korea that U.S. troops were dispatched for the first time to combat a Soviet ally.

Despite U.S. edginess about Moscow's external forays, Stalin did not seem very interested in the Third World (with the exception of countries directly contiguous to the Soviet Union). Even though the postwar disintegration of colonial empires created many newly independent states, and therefore seemed to open up opportunities for expanding the Soviet sphere of influence, such opportunities were rarely acted upon in Stalin's time. These nations were not militarily or economically weighty enough to interest someone obsessed with calculations of raw international power. In any case, he seems to have felt that most of the new nationalist leaders—such as Nehru and Gandhi in India and Sukarno in Indonesia—were essentially "bourgeois" politicians and "imperialist lackeys" and, as such, unlikely to be of much use to Moscow.

After Stalin's death, in 1953, the Kremlin's attitude toward the Third World changed. Khrushchev, the new Soviet leader, had a far less narrow view of the new nations and a better sense of their possible role in the East-West competition. Although most of these countries espoused nonalignment, the Kremlin now embraced them as a "zone of peace" and recognized the legitimacy of even non-Marxist nationalist movements. Moreover, Khrushchev explained that developing nations, even if not formally part of the Soviet bloc, could "draw on its achievements in building an independent national economy and in raising their people's living standards. Today they need not go begging to their former oppressors for modern equipment. They can get it in the Socialist countries, free from any political or military obligations." [14]

In 1955, the Soviet Union began discussing a contribution to the construction of the Aswan High Dam in Egypt, which was to harness the power of the lower Nile River and enlarge the country's area of arable land. It also offered to build a large steel mill in India, and it extended economic assistance to Syria, Indonesia, and Afghanistan. Several African nations became beneficiaries of the Kremlin's largess as well.

Now the Third World began to play an important part in the superpowers' rivalry, even though it was still not as crucial as Europe. Like the Soviet Union, the United States had showed no taste for assistance to Third World countries in the immediate postwar years. But by the mid-1950s, aid suggested itself as a way of gaining friends and clients in the developing world—that is, as a form of bribery. Moreover, the stakes were increasing as the number of independent Third World nations grew. Accordingly, in the early 1950s, the United States initiated programs of economic and military assistance, directing them initially at nations bordering the U.S.S.R. and the People's Republic of China and at certain countries in the Middle East. U.S. foreign aid grew throughout the decade. It reached its heyday in the 1960s with the Alliance for Progress, a vast program of economic aid for Latin American countries. Although couched in lofty terms of unselfish beneficence, this program was permeated with Cold War concerns. It was prompted particularly by the fear that poverty and despair in these countries could lead to the emergence of more regimes like that of Cuba, where Fidel Castro had, in 1959, established a state explicitly associated with the Soviet Union.

But economic assistance was not the only means of pursuing the Cold War in the Third World; military coercion played a role as well. Mention has already been made of the CIA-aided army of mercenaries that was dispatched to Guatemala in 1954 to remove the apparently leftist Arbenz government (see Chapter 1). Four years later, 14,000 U.S. troops landed in Lebanon to quell a purportedly Communist-led rebellion. In 1965, President Johnson sent more than 20,000 U.S. Marines into the Dominican Republic to remove the government of Juan Bosch, who enjoyed a limited amount of Communist support.

The most dramatic confrontation of the Cold War occurred in October 1962 over the presence of Soviet missiles in Cuba. Never before or since has a developing country played so dramatic a role in superpower relations. Still, the crisis had an instructive side. The glimpse it provided into the nuclear abyss jarred both Moscow and Washington into a more constructive frame of mind, setting them on the road that led to the détente of the late 1960s and early 1970s. For once, this road was relatively free of clashes in the developing world. During détente, the Third World was simply not much of an issue in superpower relations—and indeed, an absence of competitive imbroglios in the developing regions may be a precondition for improvements in those relations. The two sides seemed to act upon this assumption in signing the Basic Principles Agreement (BPA) of 1972.

This document was conceived by President Nixon and Leonid Brezhnev, the Soviet leader at that time, as part of a general guide to better U.S.-Soviet relations. It stated that ideological and social differences should be the object of peaceful negotiations and that "both sides recognize that efforts to obtain unilateral advantages at the expense of the other, directly or indirectly, are inconsistent with these objectives." This provision was particularly interesting for its implication that neither side should expand its sphere of influence to the other's detriment, and it was taken to refer particularly to the Third World. Interesting or not, the agreement was very vague, and it was interpreted by each side in the fashion most consistent with its own interests.

The BPA did not clearly specify which forms of competition were acceptable and which were not. Did it obligate Moscow to warn the United States that Egypt was planning to attack Israel in 1973? (Would the United States have done as much had the roles been reversed?) Was indirect Soviet intervention in Angola and Ethiopia consistent with the terms of the agreement? In each of these cases, the United States contended that the Soviet Union had reneged on an obligation and had thus demonstrated again that it could not be trusted to keep promises. Relations deteriorated once more, and they reached a nadir upon the Soviet invasion of Afghanistan in December 1979. This was, by any standard, an act of naked aggression—an attempt by the Soviet Union to coercively rid itself of an unwelcome government on its southern flank—and it set U.S.-Soviet relations back to the condition of earlier decades.

Clearly, then, alterations in relations between the superpowers are very much influenced by their competition in the Third World. Both countries have tended to view the Third World as another arena within which to pursue their rivalry. But developing nations have, for the most part, objected to being pawns of superpower relations, and they have even found it difficult to get very absorbed with Cold War issues. Their own poverty, and their desire to bridge the economic gap that separates them from the industrialized world, weigh much more heavily on them. Regional security matters, mainly rivalries with their neighbors, are often a major concern to developing countries. But at the level of global issues, accelerated economic development and a greater measure of international equality are their dominant foreign policy objectives.

The Problem of Global Inequality

Some Third World nations are doing well economically. South Korea, Singapore, Taiwan, and several other countries have developed rapidly in recent decades. Their average citizen earns several thousand dollars a year, they export sophisticated manufactured goods, and they are leaving the developing world for the ranks of the relatively affluent. But these are the exception. For the most part, the nations of the Third World are characterized by a squalid daily existence for their people and a gloomy future outlook. Theirs is a world of poverty. Even in nations where there is an opulent economic elite, the majority of the population may hover precariously close to the margin of subsistence. Caloric intake for citizens of the developing nations is about half that of the average U.S. citizen, and their life expectancy is about twenty years lower. Their annual income is one-twentieth to one-fiftieth that of the typical U.S. citizen. Nor are conditions likely to improve significantly in the coming decades. Perhaps the ordinary people in these countries do not compare their lot to that of people in the United States—the differences may be too vast for such comparisons to be meaningful—but their political leaders do draw the contrasts.

Several circumstances have made international economic disparities a serious issue for the developed countries in general and for the United States in particular. To begin with, by most measures the disparities are not being reduced. Although many developing countries have made substantial increases in their gross national product (GNP), population expansion has in most cases kept abreast with or even outrun this growth. The result is that GNP per capita (GNP divided by population) has grown very slowly, if at all. Furthermore, even if GNP per capita were growing at the same rate in the developing countries as in the already developed countries, the gap between them could still be widening, because of the vastly different starting points. Take, for example, the average U.S. citizen, with an annual income of $16,000, and the average citizen of Zambia, with an annual income of $700. If both figures increased by 5 percent a year, then after one year, the American's income would have grown by $800, the Zambian's by $35. The gap was previously $15,300; now, despite identical growth rates, it is $16,065. Therefore, if the gaps are really to be narrowed, the Third World will have to grow quite a bit faster than the industrialized world. All of this makes the persistence of disparities, and maybe ever greater future disparities, entirely conceivable. The developing world's frustration is easy to understand, particularly since its predicament is contrary to what was expected a few decades ago.

Many former colonies had blamed their economic plight on a lack of political independence. As Kwame Nkrumah, Ghana's first leader, liked to proclaim, "Seek ye first the political kingdom." Once this was achieved, all good things would follow, including economic development. But the waves of decolonization of the 1950s and 1960s were generally not followed by surges of economic growth. The resulting dashed expectations have magnified the political salience of calls for the international redistribution of wealth—for now, the industrialized countries, the United States among them, are often blamed for the Third World's problems. In the 1960s and 1970s, a growing number of scholars from Latin America, Africa, and even the United States and Europe, have argued that these problems are rooted in the economic bonds between the Third World and the First World. These authors are known as *dependency* theorists, because they attribute international inequality and Third World poverty to the continuing economic dependence of the less-developed countries (LDCs) on the wealthy nations—a relationship sometimes referred to as *neo-colonialism*. As Nkrumah later wrote: "The essence of neo-colonialism is that the State which is subject to it is, in theory, independent and has all the outward trappings of international sovereignty. In reality its economic system and thus its internal policy is directed from outside." [15]

There are several ways in which developing nations are thought to suffer from their economic relationships with the wealthy nations. LDCs have historically been exporters of primary commodities (mainly foodstuffs or minerals) to the developed countries, and importers of manufactured goods from them. According to the dependency theorists, the prices of primary commodities tend to rise more slowly than the prices of manufactured goods, and consequently, LDCs are less and less able to buy what they need from abroad out of what they earn from their exports. Dependency theorists also maintain that the penetration of the LDC economies by investments from wealthy nations contributes to international inequality. These investments, which are usually undertaken by multinational corporations, are said to be inherently exploitative, because more money is taken out of the country through repatriated profits than was originally invested. Furthermore, since the investments are designed to serve the corporations' interests, they may well add to the economic problems (for instance, distorted consumption patterns) of the host country. Whatever people in the wealthy nations may think of these charges, they are widely believed in developing nations, and LDC demands for a restructured international economic order are thus driven by a sense of righteous indignation. The United States, whose economy is the wealthiest and biggest in the First World, is the butt of much of this resentment.

The LDCs have organized themselves in pursuit of their demands for a re-formed world economy. In 1964, the United Nations Conference on Trade and Development (UNCTAD) was founded on the initiative of a group of seventy-seven developing countries. UNCTAD, which now has more than 120 members, has, ever since its first meeting, suggested ways of restructuring international economic relations to promote the LDCs' aspirations. The organization's image became, in the eyes of one observer, "that of a class organization with member states who are engaged in a class struggle." [16] Developed countries have been unenthusiastic, but Third World nations have pressed on with their demands.

In 1974, at a special session of the United Nations General Assembly, the LDCs called for a "new international economic order" (NIEO), which was to include a number of significant changes in economic relations between rich and poor countries. First, foreign aid was to be expanded; the goal was for it to amount to 0.7 percent of the wealthy nations' GNPs. (That may not seem like very much, but it is approximately three times what U.S. economic assistance usually amounts to.) Second, LDCs were to receive preferential treatment in trade; for example, lower tariffs would be imposed on their exports to developed countries than on the exports of non-LDCs, and they would not have to reciprocate with lower tariffs of their own when importing goods from wealthy countries. Finally, the LDCs were to have a greater say in the decisions made by the major international financial institutions. At present, the World Bank (which grants assistance to LDCs) and the International Monetary Fund (which helps countries having balance-of-payments difficulties) have systems of weighted voting, under which the wealthier countries, which contribute the largest share of the two institutions' resources, have a larger voice in their decisions. Under the NIEO, more of this decision-making power would be shifted to the LDCs.

Although not really radical, the proposals were far-reaching and ambitious. They will be discussed in greater detail in Chapter 15, but it may be noted here that they were considerably more than even the most generous developed nations would assent to. Although recognizing that some changes might be called for, the United States has generally opposed most of the NIEO provisions, considering some of them impractical or unnecessary, others as damaging to U.S. economic interests. Typically, liberals have been more sympathetic to the Third World's desires than conservatives, but no U.S. administration has seriously embraced the proposed reforms. Nor have most of the other industrialized nations. The upshot has been that, in addition to the East-West line of fissure in international affairs, a North-South cleavage has opened as well and is now a part of America's international environment.

Notes

1. Actually, Russia did welcome American independence, but it seems that this was less out of sympathy with the American cause than out of classical balance-of-power considerations: the United States was simply viewed as a useful counterweight to Britain and France. See, for example, Frank A. Golder, "Catherine II and the American Revolution," *American Historical Review* 21, no. 2 (October 1915): 92-96.
2. Walter Lefeber, *America, Russia, and the Cold War: 1945-1975* (New York: John Wiley and Sons, 1976), 2.
3. H. F. Pringle, *Theodore Roosevelt* (New York: Macmillan, 1931), 385.
4. *New Republic*, August 4, 1920.
5. Stalin proceeded to benefit from the agreement by invading Finland and occupying the Baltic states of Latvia, Lithuania, and Estonia. Russian-German relations in the interwar period are dealt with in Gerald Freund, *Unholy Alliance: Russian-German Treaty of Berlin* (New York: Harcourt & Brace, 1957), and Gustav Hilger and Alfred G. Meyer, *The Incompatible Allies: German-Soviet Relations, 1918-1941* (New York: Hafner, 1971).
6. Gabriel Almond, *The American People and Foreign Policy* (New York: Harcourt, Brace, 1950), 93.
7. Winston Churchill, *The Hinges of Fate* (New York: Bantam, 1950), 663-679.
8. Almond, *The American People*, 95.
9. Both quoted in Graham T. Allison, *The Essence of Decision* (Boston: Little, Brown, 1971), 1.
10. Quoted in John G. Stoessinger, *Nations in Darkness*, 3d ed. (New York: Random House, 1981), 187.
11. Henry A. Kissinger, *White House Years* (Boston: Little, Brown, 1979), 195.

12. Among the good treatments of colonialism and its consequences are Benjamin J. Cohen, *The Question of Imperialism* (New York: Basic Books, 1973); Parker T. Moon, *Imperialism and World Politics* (New York: Macmillan, 1926); and Hugh Seton-Watson, *The New Imperialism* (Chester Springs, Pa.: Dufour, 1961).
13. Quoted in David Kimche, *The Afro-Asian Movement* (New York: Halsted, 1973), 21.
14. Quoted in Robert S. Walters, *American and Soviet Aid: A Comparative Analysis* (Pittsburgh: University of Pittsburgh Press, 1970), 30.
15. Kwame Nkrumah, *Neo-Colonialism: The Last Stage of Imperialism* (New York: International Publishers, 1965), ix.
16. Branislav Gosovic, *UNCTAD: Conflict and Compromise* (Leiden: Sijthoff, 1972), 332.

The Domestic Politics
of Foreign Policy

c h a p t e r   t h r e e

Directions and Effects
of Public Opinion

SINCE DEMOCRACY implies that, in some way, "the people rule," the peoples' views and preferences should be embodied in a democratic nation's policies. But what exactly does that mean? Plainly, it does not mean that governments must never act without previously commissioning and studying a public-opinion survey, for that would make the conduct of government impossible, and, in any case, the public would soon become exasperated with the claims made on its time and interest. On the other hand, there is a minimum level of popular involvement without which a democratic political system cannot operate. Just how much involvement is appropriate will depend on several considerations. First, it depends on the complexity of the matter at hand; some problems, like monetary policy, are too esoteric to allow for much public participation. Second, it depends on the nature of the issue; for example, national security sometimes requires secrecy or an immediate decision, neither of which is compatible with public debate. Most fundamentally, perhaps, it depends on the degree of public interest in and acquaintance with the issue, since there is little point in pressing involvement on people who do not care enough, or know enough, to want to become involved. Let us address this last matter first, to see what implications it has for the public's role in foreign policy with regard to both the directions in which the public may wish to drive the nation's external affairs and the impact it can hope to have.

Political Animals and Prehistoric Monsters

As we observe our friends, neighbors, and co-workers, most of us come to realize that they are not avidly concerned with politics and policy. They rarely

57

launch into a discussion of international issues. They do not devour the pages of major newspapers for the latest information on current events or spend much of their time (if any at all) trying to influence the actions of government. In short, the typical U.S. citizen is not a political animal (and neither is the typical citizen of most other countries). Not more than 50 percent of the adult population in this country can correctly identify their representative in Congress,[1] and it appears that about 40 percent of the population are unaware that U.S. presidents are limited to two terms in office.[2] This is a greater level of ignorance than might be expected. Information generally presented in elementary civics classes, or conveyed regularly by the mass media, seems to escape very many people.

This is certainly the situation in matters of foreign policy. For example, in the early 1980s events in Central America were regularly reported on in the media and they concerned the president and his advisers intensely. In Nicaragua, the Marxist Sandinista government was accused by the Reagan administration of fomenting revolution elsewhere in the region, particularly in neighboring El Salvador. The administration undertook a military buildup in Honduras, from which a U.S. intervention could be launched. It also supported anti-Sandinista insurgents in Nicaragua (the so-called "contras"), and it provided substantial assistance to the beleaguered government of El Salvador. These developments were widely and prominently covered in the newspapers and on television. Yet in 1984, only 32 percent of the respondents in a national survey knew that El Salvador was a nation with which the U.S. had friendly relations, and 56 percent thought that the antigovernment rebels in Nicaragua—whom the United States had largely organized and financed—were either enemies or not friendly to the United States.[3]

Other examples of the surprising degree of public ignorance can be presented. According to a survey taken in 1964, only 58 percent of the U.S. public knew that the United States was a member of NATO, while 38 percent thought that the Soviet Union—the nation against which the alliance is directed—was a member![4] During the 1970s, the SALT negotiations were the major setting within which the United States and the Soviet Union discussed the control of nuclear weapons, and they were an important focus of domestic political debate. Yet, in a Roper poll taken in 1979, only 34 percent of the respondents could correctly identify the two nations involved in the negotiations. Even after they were told, only 58 percent knew that the talks concerned long-range weapons, 27 percent simply had no idea what they were about, and the others were evenly divided among those who thought the talks dealt with troop reductions in Europe, U.S.-Soviet trade, and halting arms transfers to developing countries.[5]

The picture which these statistics paint is not flattering. It depicts a public which neither knows nor cares much about the major external problems that confront the country. This is not a recent phenomenon. Alexis de Tocqueville, one of the most perceptive students of U.S. political character, noted in the early nineteenth century that Americans were far more concerned with private and material values than with matters of public interest or with philosophical questions.[6] Most issues of general national policy might seem too distant from the daily concerns of a people that seeks fulfillment primarily in private pursuits and material gratification. One would expect this distance to appear even greater with regard to foreign affairs, where the consequences of governmental activity appear less immediate than those of domestic policy and harder to connect to the individual's personal concerns. Most people understand how they would be affected by a tax increase, but few know or care how a shift in relations with New Zealand, or a reduction in aid to Peru, might affect their daily existence.

Thus, when the U.S. public is stirred by major national problems, it is more likely to happen in issues of domestic than of foreign policy. In particular, Americans are interested in economic matters. When asked what they consider to be the most important problem facing the country, well over half of survey respondents usually select "pocketbook" issues; far fewer choose issues of foreign policy. In 1980—a year marked by the Soviet invasion of Afghanistan and the Iranian seizure of American hostages—only 44 percent of the public identified foreign policy problems as those that worried them most, while approximately the same proportion (43 percent) chose unemployment or inflation.[7] And that was probably a high-water mark in public concern with external affairs. In a more typical year, about 10 to 20 percent of the public say they are worried most about some international problem and 60 to 70 percent put inflation, unemployment, or some other economic issue at the top of their list. As a whole, then, the U.S. public is neither enlightened about nor concerned with foreign affairs.

But the public is not an undifferentiated mass. There are many people who do care about external problems and are reasonably well informed about the issues. In an influential model of U.S. public opinion on foreign policy, James Rosenau has depicted the public as a pyramid with three tiers.[8] At the pyramid's base is the *mass public,* in its middle section the *attentive public,* and at its apex a small group of *opinion makers.* Opinion makers are those who, by virtue of their leadership positions in society, mold the opinions of others. They constitute an elite that enjoys access to the means of mass communication and is eager to convey foreign policy information and its own ideas to the rest of society. It includes prominent journalists, professors, business leaders, and the like. But opinion makers are, in a way, proximate policy makers, whereas when we speak of public opinion, we have in mind ordinary Americans rather than political leaders. These are the people who are located at the first two levels of the pyramid.

The mass public comprises, by Rosenau's estimate, between 75 and 90 percent of the adult population. It generally knows almost nothing about foreign policy and is not interested in knowing more. Its response to issues is "less one of intellect and more one of emotion, less one of opinion and more one of mood." And while the dominant mood is "indifference and passivity," it sometimes swings "from one extreme to another—from tolerance to intolerance, optimism to pessimism, idealism to cynicism, withdrawal to intervention." It is a moody and uninformed public, whose lethargy is punctuated by lurches between extremes. The attentive public, on the other hand, is relatively sophisticated: it knows more, cares more, and its opinions show "greater structure and depth." Because of these qualities, the attentive public "tends to offset the irrational impact of mass moods and to fill the vacuum which exists when indifference is the prevailing mood." It is therefore a force of relative moderation and it compels a measure of political accountability for foreign policy, but its ranks are quite limited: between about one-quarter and one-tenth of the population. Perhaps the attentive public is no larger in other societies, and perhaps it is natural and well for people to care more about their personal affairs, but the implications for foreign policy nevertheless cannot be ignored.

One inference that has been drawn from the mass public's size and the nature of its opinions is that the overall foreign policy mood of the nation will be volatile, for if beliefs are not anchored by coherent thought and sufficient information, they are less likely to be stable and consistent. Thus, the national mood could swing abruptly from indifference to angry belligerence, and this can weaken the government's capacity to mobilize the nation when it is faced with a threat, while also impeding its ability to reduce tensions when threats subside. George Kennan, a historian and an experienced U.S. diplomat, has expressed this lament:

> Democracy is . . . similar to one of those prehistoric monsters with a body as long as this room and a brain the size of a pin: he lies there in his primeval mud and pays little attention to his environment: he is slow to wrath—in fact, you practically have to whack his tail off to make him aware that his interests are being disturbed; but once he grasps this, he lays about him with such blind determination that he not only destroys his adversary but largely wrecks his native habitat.[9]

One may question how far decision makers can allow themselves to be guided by either uninterested attitudes or intemperate moods and, under the circumstances, it may be reasoned that it is the government's duty to lead rather than to follow its public. On the other hand, even if most Americans know little about the issues, their views could still be connected to their perceived interests, and that may be a sufficient basis for democratic control. People who do not know much about economics, and may have no understanding of budgetary deficits and monetary supply, may nevertheless recognize inflation when they see it, conclude that it is bad for them, and want their government to control it. Thus, it is not certain that public *accountability* need always imply full public *understanding* of the issues. Often, it may be enough for the people to know what they want and to be able to determine whether or not the government is providing it. As long as their desires are not mutually incompatible, and assuming (which is often not the case) that people do know what they want, a measure of democratic control over policy decisions may still be attainable. In addition to inquiring about the extent of the public's knowledge or ignorance, then, it is also necessary to ask what the U.S. citizenry wants in foreign affairs. This will yield not only a broader basis for understanding the likely impact of the public on policy, but also an indication of the directions that the public would like policy to take. Since national security and relations with the Soviet Union are such a central part of U.S. foreign policy, it makes sense to begin an exploration of this question with the public's views and preferences in those areas. Afterwards, attitudes on relations with U.S. allies and friends and with the Third World will be examined.

Public Opinion on Foreign Policy Issues

The historical circumstances described in the previous chapter explain the concern which the superpowers have with each other and the misgivings of the U.S. government about Soviet intentions and credibility. But how does the American public fit into this picture? Do its concerns mirror those of the government?

National Security and the Soviet Union

Kennan's judgment that citizens of a democracy are "slow to wrath" suggests that, for the most part, the public is not sufficiently alert to external threats, that complacency will be the norm. Observers on the political right are even more likely to feel that U.S. society is not as wary of the Soviets as it should be. Norman Podhoretz, a conservative author and columnist, has bemoaned what he views as a "culture of appeasement" that permeates the nation.[10] But these descriptions do not appear to be accurate: the U.S. public, on the whole, is neither naively complacent about the outside world nor unwilling to incur costs and risks for the nation's defense.

To begin with, Americans are firm believers in military preparedness. When asked to list the major factors in U.S. greatness, 80 percent of the respondents in one survey mentioned military strength.[11] They also generally support military spending, although without automatically endorsing whatever level of expenditure the government proposes. During the late 1960s and early 1970s, public support for large defense outlays declined, partly because of disillusionment with the war in Vietnam and partly because U.S. relations with Moscow were improving. But when these relations deteriorated, and when it became evident that the Soviet Union had made large strides in increasing its military power, support for higher defense spending rose. Thus, it seems that people in the United States do want an adequate defense, but they also recognize that changing circumstances change the nation's defense needs, and they do not necessarily accept the government's estimate of those needs.

Furthermore, the public is not at all naively trusting, at least not where the Soviet Union is concerned. The average American disapproves of and distrusts the U.S.S.R., and Soviet domestic and foreign policies. The history of U.S.-Soviet relations, and the socialization to which Americans are subjected make it unlikely that attitudes could be much different. The Soviet Union is generally viewed as a menacing country, it elicits pronounced "we-they" feelings, and an atmosphere of brutality and deceitfulness surrounds the Soviet government in the eyes of U.S. citizens. Certainly, most Americans would have grave doubts about the patriotism of a neighbor who expressed admiration for the U.S.S.R. or, say, took to driving a Soviet-made automobile.

In 1982, respondents to a national survey were asked to express how warmly they felt about twenty-four countries by rating their feelings toward each on a "feeling thermometer." The Soviet Union came out last with a chilly 26-degree temperature rating (as opposed to 74 degrees for Canada and 68 degrees for Great Britain). Admittedly, 1982 was a bad year for Soviet-American relations, and public attitudes toward the Soviet Union do shift as the tone of relations changes. Still, they fluctuate only within a band ranging from cool to frigid. For example, in 1986 the Soviet Union received a thermometer rating of 31 degrees, which placed it next to last among the rated countries (just before Iran).[12] Other surveys revealed similar results. In 1953, at the height of the Cold War, a mere 3 percent of Americans expressed a favorable opinion of the U.S.S.R. This was an all-time low in polling history, but the figure has never been very high. Even in 1972, when détente was in full swing, only 40 percent of the public said they had a favorable opinion of Russia (see Figure 3-1).

Figure 3-1   U.S. Public Approval of the Soviet Union

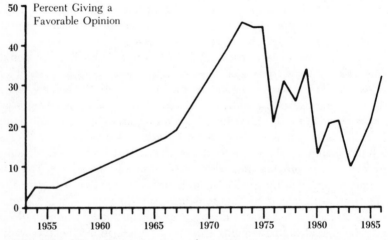

Source: Gallup Poll and Roper Organization surveys of respective years.

This disapproval is associated with a good deal of distrust: most people in the United States do not believe that the Kremlin will live up to its obligations and promises. Typically, for instance, at least two-thirds of those surveyed doubt that the Soviets would comply with the terms of an arms control agreement or of an agreement to reduce tensions between the two countries (see Table 3-1). In sum, the U.S. government can be confident that its public expects an assertive policy toward the Kremlin and will not be pleased with a position of military inferiority.

But this does not imply an endorsement of saber-rattling or of indiscriminate confrontation. Despite their feelings toward the U.S.S.R. and their support for a strong defense, most people in the United States do not endorse unbridled militarism or a pugnacious "high-noon" posture in dealing with Moscow. Indeed, the U.S. public, far from being a prehistoric monster wildly lashing out when jarred by events, may at times be less immoderate than the U.S. government. Consider, for example, the situation in 1982. That was a troubled year for U.S.-Soviet relations. Arms control negotiations were at a standstill, while both sides were engaged in energetic programs of military growth. The administration of President Ronald Reagan was accusing the Soviet Union of subversion in Central America and of abetting international terrorism. The president taunted the Soviet leaders with the failures of their system; the year before he had declared that they were prepared to "commit any crime, to lie, to cheat" in pursuit of their international objectives; he also denounced their country as "the focus of evil in the modern world." [13] The Kremlin responded with invective of its own. In short, relations had sunk to perhaps their lowest level in three decades. The public approval rating of the Soviet Union had fallen to 21 percent, about half the level of ten years before. Yet most

Table 3-1 Trust of U.S. Public in Soviets

Can the Soviet Union be trusted not to build more nuclear weapons?		*Can the Soviet Union be trusted to relax U.S.-Soviet tensions?*	
Answer	Percentage of responses	Answer	Percentage of responses
Very likely	6	Cannot be trusted	66
Fairly likely	27	Can be trusted	24
Not at all likely	60	Not sure	10
No opinion	7		

Sources: Responses concerning nuclear weapons from *Gallup Report,* April 1981, 8; responses concerning U.S.-Soviet tensions from a survey made by NBC News/Associated Press, October 16-17, 1978, as reported in Everett Carll Ladd, "The Freeze Framework," *Public Opinion* 5 (August/September 1982): 36.

Americans were not swept up in a wave of belligerence. Rather, they wanted better relations and believed that they could be achieved. A majority of those questioned in 1982 favored arms control talks, cultural and educational exchanges, and joint efforts to solve energy problems. Likewise, a majority opposed grain embargoes and prohibitions against scientific exchanges.[14] By 1984, the idea of pursuing peaceful cooperation became even more popular: 90 percent of the public wanted arms control negotiations, and over 80 percent wished to expand academic and cultural exchanges with the Soviet Union.[15]

The public also disapproved of President Reagan's seemingly implacable hostility toward Moscow. When it appeared that he had no interest in decreasing tensions, most Americans frowned on his attitude. But when steps were taken to improve relations in 1984, the public seemed to pat the president on the back. By May 1984, toward the end of Reagan's first term, when relations between the two countries had degenerated in just about every way, only 38 percent of Americans approved his handling of those relations.[16] But endorsement of the president's policy toward Moscow increased sharply when he took steps toward fence-mending and arms control. In September 1984, Soviet Foreign Minister Andrei Gromyko attended the United Nations General Assembly session in New York and had his first constructive talk with U.S. Secretary of State George Shultz. A trip to Washington was also arranged, where Gromyko and President Reagan conferred and decided in principle to reopen arms control negotiations. A poll conducted the following month found that now 48 percent of the respondents approved of the way their president was dealing with the Kremlin. In January 1985, high-level U.S. and Soviet delegations met in Geneva to discuss the conduct of the new arms control talks. The atmosphere was cordial, and there appeared the first signs of a thaw in the five-year chill which had engulfed U.S.-Soviet relations. Approval of the president's Soviet policy rose to its highest level—60 percent.[17] These shifts are revealing. Not only do they show a public distaste for belligerence and an endorsement of cooperation, but they also indicate that the public does not blindly follow the path traveled by its government. U.S. citizens may not be particularly well-informed on the specifics of international affairs, but they do know what they want in a Soviet policy: a combination of firmness founded on reasonable strength and genuine efforts at cooperation.

The public's resistance to militarism is also reflected in its uneasiness with the idea of armed intervention in the Third World, even where a Soviet challenge to U.S. interests is said to exist. For example, President John F. Kennedy viewed Fidel Castro's Cuba, with its rabid anti-Americanism and close links to Moscow, as a thorn in America's side, and most of the public agreed with him. Yet, when asked whether U.S. troops should be sent into Cuba to get rid of Castro, only 20 percent agreed.[18] A more recent example of the distaste for unnecessary force was provided during President Jimmy Carter's term in office. Throughout the crisis of 1979-1980, when American diplomats were being held hostage in the embassy in Teheran and humiliated by Iranian students acting in connivance with their government, there was never a majority favoring the use of armed force to free them.[19]

Again, during the Reagan administration, when the U.S. government made known its strong opposition to the Sandinista government in Nicaragua and the leftist revolutionaries in El Salvador—Jeane Kirkpatrick, the U.S. ambassador to the United Nations, declared in 1981 that "Central America is the most important place in the world for the United States today" [20]—the public nevertheless did not want U.S. troops to intervene in the region. Whatever the public may have thought or known about the situation—and it did not seem to know much about the specifics—74 percent opposed a U.S. invasion of Nicaragua to dislodge its government,[21] and 72 percent feared that U.S. involvement in Central America could lead to another Vietnam.[22]

In sum, it is hard to recognize Kennan's prehistoric monster wildly lashing out when shaken from its complacency. Even in a situation that would seem so certain to provoke a nation's wrath as the spectacle of the hostages in Iran, the public reaction was mature and restrained. The Soviet invasion of Afghanistan was certainly disquieting, and Americans responded with anger and a substantially revised view of the Soviet Union—but they recognized the need for continued arms control negotiations and for cooperation in areas of mutual interest. The image of an unmanageably volatile public may have been accurate at one time, but it clearly no longer is. Perhaps the most plausible explanation for this change is that Rosenau's attentive public has been growing at the expense of the mass public. Rosenau himself predicted in 1961 that the ranks of the attentive public would grow because of better education, improved quality of the media, and the activity of civic groups that were stimulating people's interest in foreign affairs.[23]

This does not mean that the public is always opposed to any use of military force, for it is not. When crucial interests are believed to be at stake, it does not flinch from the prospect of military action. A majority, for example, supports the use of force to defend West European nations if attacked by the Soviet Union, and a majority is willing to have troops dispatched to the Persian Gulf if the Soviet Union were to invade that oil-rich region.[24] Also, the public will usually rally round the government when the latter has already resorted to military force. Such support, as we shall see, rarely survives a protracted involvement; but initially at least, the government can count on public support. Americans are thus not systematically opposed to the use of troops abroad, but the need must be very clear and the action must produce rapid success at a moderate price. Still, the bias is definitely against military solutions to foreign policy problems.

Friends and Allies

There is nothing surprising about the distrust that people in the United States feel toward the Soviet Union. History and the differences of national political cultures make it the expected, though not necessarily the most desirable, attitude. By the same token, we should not be surprised at the warmth that they feel for their industrialized allies in the West. These are countries whose commitment to electoral representation, civil rights and liberties, and other important democratic principles places them in the same ideological camp as the United States, and their foreign policies appear unthreatening. For the most part, they have stood at the side of the United States at crucial junctures in the twentieth century; Germany and Japan are obvious exceptions, but even they are now authentic democracies, vital U.S. economic partners, and indispensable parts of Western security alliances. Americans relate to these nations in personal terms as well. Many have traveled to Europe, Canada, or Japan, know the countries and have personal friends there, consume the goods they produce, watch the films they make, and so forth. All of these bonds—historical, political, and personal—are reflected in public opinion.

In contrast to their feelings about the Soviet Union, most people in the United States express regard and affection for the Western allies. While the Soviet Union was registering 26 degrees on the public's "feeling thermometer" in 1982 and 31 percent in 1986, every Western industrialized nation registered at least 55 degrees.[25] As against the 20 to 40 percent of the public that typically expresses some degree of favorable attitude toward the Soviet Union, most of the allies of the United States enjoy the approval of 70 to 90 percent of U.S. citizens (see Table 3-2).

Predictably, too, most Americans believe that their national security is closely linked to that of the other industrialized democracies. In 1986, for example, 77 percent of the public thought that the United States had vital interests in West Germany, 83 percent thought that this was the case for Great Britain, and 78 percent for Canada and Japan.[26] The great majority of U.S. citizens strongly support NATO and their country's military commitment to its chief allies. Because they are convinced that the fortunes of the West are indivisible, U.S. citizens are far less reticent about using force in its defense than in pursuing the East-West rivalry in developing regions. This further strengthens the conclusion that Americans do not shy away from the use of military instruments of foreign policy when the national interest compellingly suggests that force is called for (although, even then, the public would probably urge caution and would almost certainly wish to limit the escalation of hostilities).

In other ways, however, public pressure could undermine Western unity. As pointed out earlier in this chapter, the U.S. public is usually concerned with its economic welfare above all else. Since the effects of economic problems are easily recognized, and since governments are being increasingly held responsible for such problems, political authorities may be urged to take measures to protect national economic well-being, even at the expense of other nations. Because many allies of the United States have become its economic competi-

Table 3-2 Thermometer Ratings of Twenty-three Countries by U.S. Public, 1982 and 1986

Country	1982	1986
Canada	74	77
Great Britain	68	73
West Germany	59	62
Japan	53	61
Mexico	60	59
Israel	55	59
Philippines	—	59
France	60	58
Italy	55	58
Brazil	54	54
Poland	52	53
China	47	53
Taiwan	49	52
South Korea	44	50
Saudi Arabia	52	50
Egypt	52	49
India	48	48
South Africa	45	47
Nigeria	44	46
Nicaragua	—	46
Syria	42	34
Soviet Union	26	31
Iran	28	22

Sources: John E. Reilly, "America's State of Mind," *Foreign Policy* (Spring 1987), 47, and John E. Reilly, ed., *American Public Opinion and U.S. Foreign Policy* (Chicago: Chicago Council on Foreign Relations, 1983), 19.

tors, they may well be the victims of those measures. When U.S. producers appear particularly vulnerable, pressures develop to keep foreign goods out, wherever they are coming from.

Most Americans perceive the world as economically interdependent and understand that the U.S. economy is strongly affected by foreign policy. Typically, more than 70 percent of those asked say that foreign policy has a major impact on the nation's economy generally, and approximately 60 percent think it affects unemployment at home.[27] Concern over these effects has led many Americans to support economic nationalism in the form of protectionism. For example, when asked whether they preferred higher tariff barriers or freer trade as strategies to preserve jobs, more than twice as many respondents chose the former as chose the latter. Political leaders were far more inclined toward freer trade,[28] but they may nevertheless succumb to popular pressure when their political interests demand it.

The Third World

It was noted in Chapter 2 that there are two dimensions of U.S. relations with the Third World: an East-West or political dimension, associated with attempts by the superpowers to carry their rivalry into the developing regions, and a North-South or economic dimension, which springs from the economic disparities between the developed and the less-developed nations. Because of the nature of the government's concerns and priorities, the first of these dimensions comes to the public's attention much more frequently. The media contributes to this focus as well: it is more likely to report on struggles between right-wing and left-wing regimes or on Cuban or Libyan adventurism than on meetings devoted to the North-South economic problems.

Nevertheless, the U.S. public seems unconvinced that essential national interests are at stake in the Third World. In 1986, while 83 percent of the public thought that the United States had vital interests in Great Britain, only 36 percent said this was true of India and 31 percent that it was true of Nigeria.[29] And, as was pointed out earlier in this chapter, most Americans are quite unenthusiastic about military intervention in developing regions. More than two-thirds of those interviewed in 1986 said they would be willing to defend major European allies against the Soviet Union, but only 24 percent would defend South Korea from North Korea (even though the United States had already done so in a war from 1950 to 1953), or Honduras (another U.S. friend) if it were attacked by Nicaragua.[30]

This does not imply a complete absence of any desire to promote national objectives within the Third World, even by subversive activity, which—despite some public uneasiness—is not opposed as strongly as is military intervention. Support for covert action depends in part on its form. Although the vast majority of the public agrees that "every country should have the right to determine its own government by itself without outside interference from other countries," a plurality (43 percent) maintains that it is all right for the CIA to work "inside other countries to try to strengthen those elements friendly to the U.S. and to weaken anti-U.S. forces."[31] But the public does not seem to endorse the more extreme kinds of subversion. When Salvador Allende, Chile's elected president, was overthrown by the military in 1973, it was widely believed that the CIA had a hand in the affair; in a poll taken not long afterward, 60 percent of the respondents said that it was wrong for the United States to intervene in Chile's internal affairs, while only 18 percent claimed that it was right.[32] Likewise, when it was reported that the CIA had contemplated making a deal with members of the Mafia to assassinate Fidel Castro, 74 percent of U.S. citizens said that they thought that was improper.[33] Public support of such activities also fluctuates with the state of East-West relations. In 1982, when relations were at an especially low point, a slight majority agreed with the statement that it was acceptable for the CIA "to work secretly inside other countries to try to weaken or overthrow governments unfriendly to the U.S."[34]

As for the use of foreign aid as an instrument of foreign policy in the Third World, fewer people support it when it is given for the sake of economic development than do so when it is associated with a political quid pro quo (that is, when it amounts to bribery). While Americans are often very generous when there is a natural disaster or a famine in the Third World, not many seem to be concerned about persistent poverty abroad. Since the 1960s, there has rarely been a majority in favor of foreign aid. In 1986, only 37 percent of the public felt that improving the standard of living in the less-developed countries (LDCs) was a very important goal.[35] In fact, the U.S. public generally does not approve of foreign aid unless there is some clear political advantage in giving it. In one survey, a majority of the public opposed giving help to other countries "if they don't stand for the same things we do."[36] In another survey, 75 percent of the respondents said they would reduce aid, or cut it off completely, if the recipient country failed to support the United States in a "major foreign policy decision."[37] These are not attitudes of disinterested beneficence; rather, they indicate a willingness to use bribery as a tool of foreign policy.

Since the U.S. public is unwilling to endorse foreign assistance merely to promote development, it is also unlikely to accept a relaxation of protectionism in order to help the Third World. In several fields of production—such as textiles, for example—the major competitive challenge to the United States comes not from the other industrialized nations but from developing countries. Yet if the LDCs are to expand their economies or even pay their debts, they must be able to export much of what they produce. Consequently, a major thrust of the Third World's demands is for access to the markets of countries such as the United States. This, in turn, seems threatening to many producers in the United States, and resistance to that access can be expected. In short, not too much can be expected by the Third World from the American public when economic issues are at stake.

The Public's Impact on Foreign Policy

We do know, then, what the public's views are—to the extent that it has views—on some of the most important issues of U.S. national objectives and the appropriate means of pursuing them. But there remains the question of whether public opinion makes any difference. Is it a major influence on foreign policy? The answer seems to be that for most foreign policy decisions, it has very little influence, but on a few issues it does matter.

As pointed out at the beginning of this chapter, the public's views on international affairs rest on shallow understanding and skimpy information. Though this exacerbates the dilemma of aggregation, it does not disqualify these views for consideration by the nation's political authorities. After all, as has also been pointed out, the data show that the public generally does know what it wants—at least with regard to such major matters as war or peace, or free trade versus protectionism. But its low level of information limits the public's ability to play a vital and continuous role in foreign policy.

For most U.S. citizens, voting is their only significant form of political participation, but it can be an effective form. If the public knows what it wants (and does not seek inconsistent goals), it can use the vote to reward or punish elected officials for the foreign policy decisions they make. However, voters must know how their elected officials acted on the issues if they are to wield the electoral sanction in accordance with their preferences. But, while the president's policies may be known to much of the electorate, the votes cast by senators and representatives escape the attention of most people. If only about half the voters can correctly identify their representative, many fewer are likely to know how their representative voted on foreign aid or the military budget. As one would expect, then, research indicates that there is but a weak correlation between representatives' foreign policy votes and the opinions of their constituents.[38]

It is true that, at the presidential level, things are different. The chief executive's actions are covered daily in both the national and the local media, and the intense publicity that surrounds presidential campaigns means that the candidates' records are exposed to close popular scrutiny. Nonetheless, foreign policy probably does not have a major impact even on presidential elections. Elections involve a great many issues, and domestic problems are the ones that loom largest in the minds of voters. As one political scientist has observed, "It has been a tenet of presidential campaigns that barring exceptional foreign policy problems of the incumbent party (such as the Vietnam War posed for Democrats in 1968), the major issues will be the economic ones."[39] This is consistent with the observation already made that, at least in the United States, economic issues are generally given greater importance than foreign policy matters. In fact, there has probably not been any recent presidential election which was determined primarily by external affairs. Despite the public's disapproval of the Vietnam War, few voters found major differences on this issue between Hubert Humphrey, the Democratic candidate for president in 1968, and Richard Nixon, his Republican rival. Thus, although the disastrous course of that war had made President Lyndon B. Johnson abandon the idea of seeking a second term, it probably did not account for Nixon's triumph. Indeed, it has been estimated by statistical procedures that views on Vietnam accounted for only between 1 and 2 percent of the variance in voting behavior in 1968.[40] In 1980, even though President Carter's foreign policy was not very popular, his defeat probably had more to do with inflation and unemployment. Conversely, President Reagan's popularity and reelection in 1984 rested more on his economic successes (and sunny disposition) than on widespread admiration for his foreign policy record.[41] It is not that foreign policy makes no difference in presidential elections, but that, in most cases, it has a marginal rather than a decisive influence. A president who reduces unemployment and controls inflation can probably afford a few foreign policy failures; only if the president's domestic record is less bright will his foreign policy play a role in his reelection campaign.

On the other hand, some foreign policy issues may weigh heavily at election time, whatever domestic successes a president or party might claim. At the height of the Cold War, for instance, U.S. politicians were haunted by the fear that their electoral fortunes might fall victim to accusations of "appeasement," or of "losing" a nation to communism. The anticommunist hysteria of the early 1950s, the witch hunts associated with the name of Senator Joseph R. McCarthy, and the general paranoia which gripped the nation and twisted its sense of perspective made for extreme caution on the part of elected leaders. No greater onus could befall a president at the time, no greater anathema could be hurled at him, than the charge of being "soft on communism." It is likely that the 1952 election, won by the Republican candidate, Dwight D. Eisenhower, was influenced by these themes. The victorious party focused much of its campaign on denouncing the "failure" of Democrats to stand up to "international communism." Presidents Franklin D. Roosevelt and Harry S Truman were upbraided for their "tragic blunders" at Yalta and Potsdam, blunders which, the Republicans said, paved the way for subsequent Soviet expansionism and accorded Moscow an unduly important role in the postwar international order. Moreover, Truman's policy of "containment" of Soviet power was held to be weaker than the Republican goal of forcing a "rollback" of Soviet dominance in Eastern Europe. The Democrats were accused not only of "selling out" the Eastern European nations but also of allowing Chiang Kai-shek's regime in China to be overthrown, thus permitting the world's most populous nation to "go Communist" and to become a major new asset in the Kremlin's international position. Many voters were apparently convinced. Eisenhower, the affable hero of World War II, was swept into office over Adlai Stevenson, the man the Democrats had nominated to succeed President Truman.

Since that time, accusations of "appeasement" or of insufficient assertiveness toward the Communists have been less lethal electoral weapons. Cold War themes have continued to simmer below the surface of many presidential actions. For example, President Johnson's initial decisions to involve the United States in Vietnam were probably dictated as much by internal political calculations as by perceived international necessity. "If I don't go in now," he is said to have reasoned, "and they show later I should have gone, then they'll be all over me in Congress. They won't be talking about my civil rights bill, or education, or beautification. No sir, they'll push Vietnam up my ass every time. Vietnam, Vietnam, Vietnam." [42] Yet, although Reagan, during his 1980 election campaign, brandished charges reminiscent of 1952, he ultimately marched to victory on a path littered with the economic failures of the previous administration. The atmosphere of détente and the increased maturity of the public have made Manichaean views of the world somewhat less credible. In any case, anticommunism loses some of its edge as a political issue in a world where purportedly communist nations are at odds with each other, as China and the Soviet Union are.[43] The cordial relations of the United States with Communist Yugoslavia and more recently with Communist China and leftist Zimbabwe, and U.S. support in the late 1970s of avowedly Marxist Somalia against professedly Marxist Ethiopia, have further blurred the issue.

With the disappearance of anticommunism as a salient electoral issue, there remain two other foreign policy issues that are politically important. One of these is the broad area of foreign economic policy.

We have seen that economic issues matter a great deal to the public, and we know that the ups and downs in U.S. economic conditions are partly influenced by what happens abroad. Americans therefore do worry about the impact upon themselves of foreign economic policy, and so it is to be expected that if, for example, an increase in unemployment was to be attributed to foreign competition, the administration that had failed to turn the competition aside would lose votes. Political leaders recognize that, and they are attentive to their electoral needs when making foreign economic policy. Politicians' needs might, then, drive them to support a greater measure of economic nationalism and protectionism than might otherwise be the case. In short, the influence of public opinion may make itself more strongly felt in external economic policy than in many other areas of foreign policy. The public need not even grasp exactly how these policies affect its economic well-being. All that is required is that elected authorities understand that economic conditions and foreign policy are often linked and that they should act according to their own electoral interests.

The second foreign-policy issue with important potential electoral consequences is that of armed intervention abroad. As was pointed out above, the U.S. public tends to be wary of foreign military involvement. Especially since the Vietnam misadventure forced Lyndon Johnson not to run for president in 1968, one might assume that national leaders would be reluctant to arouse the public's antagonism by sending troops into combat overseas. But the matter isn't quite so straightforward, since the public has a tendency to oppose military intervention *before* it occurs but then to turn around and endorse it *after* it has occurred. Before U.S. combat troops were dispatched to Vietnam as a result of the Gulf of Tonkin incident in 1964, only 42 percent of the public supported involvement in Southeast Asia; afterward, however, 72 percent approved. Again, only 7 percent of Americans endorsed the idea of invading Cambodia, yet after President Nixon did just that in April 1970, 50 percent favored it.[44] When U.S. troops landed in Grenada in 1983 to oust that country's Marxist government, 59 percent of the public thought it was the right decision,[45] yet it is more than likely that, had they been asked before the invasion, most respondents would have opposed the intervention.

This is not to say that, no matter how the public feels before the fact, U.S. presidents can invade any country they choose, secure in the knowledge that, once troops begin wading onto foreign shores or parachuting onto foreign soil, most Americans will enthusiastically rally around their leader. One cannot be certain of rapid victory at acceptable costs (unless the territory is small and militarily insignificant, as in the case of Grenada), and the U.S. public has shown that, except for crucial conflicts such as World War II, it is unwilling to support anything other than quick, low-cost success. Support erodes with protracted ensnarement in the conflict, growing casualties, and a rising tax bill. Few people initially expected the engagements in Korea and Vietnam to last as long as they did or to produce the number of casualties they did. The first ended inconclusively, and the second, by any criterion, ended in defeat. The Democratic party, which controlled the presidency at the time of both involvements, failed to maintain its hold on power through the duration of either war. In sum, when a president contemplates sending troops to fight on foreign shores, the danger of being repudiated by public opinion is apt to outweigh the promise of popular approval. A president will decide to intervene only if he feels confident that quick and easy victory is within reach, as Truman felt in Korea and Johnson in Vietnam.

Today, then, it appears that the only two foreign policy issues that might be subject to electoral control are foreign economic policy and foreign military intervention. These are important issues, but they represent only a small part of U.S. foreign policy. For the most part, the conduct of external affairs escapes electoral accountability because of the apathy and ignorance of the mass public. But there is a further problem, one that compounds the dilemma of aggregation. Even if every presidential decision were taken with a view to popular preferences, it still is not certain that U.S. foreign relations would reflect the national mood.

The president is head of the executive branch of government, but he himself can make only a fraction of the decisions that have to be made, and monitor the implementation of only a fraction of his administration's policies once they are formed. Below the president, decisions are made by the cabinet officers, agency heads, undersecretaries, and assistant secretaries whom he appoints. These officials are supposed to carry out presidential policies, but things are not quite that simple. The heads of government agencies and departments develop loyalties to the institutions they administer, and each institution has its own organizational interests. Typically, each seeks to expand its power, personnel, and budgetary resources. To do so, it strives to take on new and bigger functions and missions, and it will promote policies that entail a need for its services and expertise. For example, the Department of Defense is unlikely to welcome arms-control agreements that deprive it of the hardware, manpower, and tax dollars upon which its organizational influence and status depend. The secretary of defense may consequently be torn between his organization's demands and his chief executive's arms-control efforts. In addition, bureaucracies have their established ways of performing their functions and are resistant to change, even when it is initiated at the top. As Franklin D. Roosevelt, an accomplished political manipulator, explained:

The Treasury is so large and far-flung and ingrained in its practices that I find it almost impossible to get the action and results I want.... But I find the Treasury is not to be compared with the State Department. You should go through the experience of trying to get any changes in the thinking, policy and action of career diplomats and you'd know what a real problem was. But the Treasury and the State Department put together are nothing compared to the Na-a-vy.... To change anything in the Na-a-vy is like punching a feather bed. You punch it with your right and you punch it with your left until you are finally exhausted and you find the damn bed just as it was before you started punching it.[46]

Thus, presidential power is limited by the nature of the bureaucracies, and bureaucracies are not directly subject to electoral control and public accountability. The problem is evident and will be examined in more detail in Chapter 5.

Not everyone laments the fact that foreign policy is not as closely controlled by the electorate as is domestic policy. A number of informed observers do not think that the public has a useful role to play in setting the nation's course in international affairs. Apart from concerns that "public ignorance and apathy remain appalling"[47] and that the public can rarely provide sensible guidelines for specific decisions, there are sometimes thought to be intrinsic grounds for discouraging public involvement in foreign affairs. One view is that the public is driven by personal interests and myopic vision, while foreign policy should be guided by the long-term interests of the nation as a whole. Political leaders, by this reasoning, are more likely to take the national interest as a whole into account if they are not subjected to the pressures of a narrow-minded public. It has also been argued that the public is emotional, perhaps to the point of irrationality, while the leadership is sensible and cool, better able to make thoughtful decisions in times of crisis. This is certainly a debatable generalization, but some people do feel that the requirements of foreign policy are simply at odds with the emotions by which the masses are moved.[48]

Still others, finally, are of the opinion that the need to defer to public opinion limits the nation's freedom of action in a dangerous world. Nondemocratic governments, with their concentration of political power and unconcern for public opinion, are said to enjoy a more coherent and directed foreign policy than do democracies, which are thus placed at a disadvantage in world affairs. For example, when the Kremlin decided to wage a military struggle against nationalist forces in Afghanistan, it did not have to worry about how this would sit with Soviet citizens. Why then should the United States be hobbled in pursuit of its geopolitical and strategic interests by allowing the public to be a back-seat driver? The answer may simply be that the United States ought not to seek to resemble the Soviet Union. But one could still ask at what point a nation's freedom of international maneuver should be constrained by domestic politics, particularly if one feels that popular pressure does not always run parallel to the national interest.

Such views also imply that the government's duty is to shape, rather than to follow, public thinking, and that democratic controls should be relaxed on crucial foreign policy matters. Taken to its extreme, this perspective could justify manipulating and misleading the public when the government decides that the national interest so requires. During the height of the Cuban missile crisis, when it became known that the government had initially misrepresented the gravity of the situation, one of President Kennedy's aides maintained that the nation's leaders had a "right, indeed the duty, to lie." [49] In this instance, deception may have been justified. Public emotions at the peak of the crisis could, if unleashed, have pushed Kennedy and his advisers into precipitate action during one of the most delicate and dangerous situations that the United States (and the world) has ever faced.

But where should the line be drawn? Recent history presents other cases of governmental deception and manipulation that are more difficult to justify. Two examples are the Gulf of Tonkin incident and the bombing of Cambodia. In 1964, President Johnson announced that two U.S. destroyers, which he maintained were on routine patrol in international waters in the Gulf of Tonkin, had been fired upon by the North Vietnamese. In response to this, a congressional resolution was passed, apparently with public support, endorsing retaliation against North Vietnam, thus opening the door to the lengthy and costly U.S. military engagement in Southeast Asia. Johnson had hidden from the nation the fact that the incident was provoked by the destroyers' participation in secret harassment activities against North Vietnam, within that country's territorial waters.[50] The impression of an unprovoked attack was intentionally conveyed to secure domestic support for the president's war plans. In a similar lack of candor, President Nixon in 1969 secretly authorized the bombing of areas in Cambodia (now Kampuchea) that were thought to be used as sanctuaries by the guerrillas the United States was battling in South Vietnam. This widening of the war was concealed from public knowledge by an elaborate system of falsified military reports.[51] A more recent example is the Reagan administration's secret sale of weapons to Iran in an effort to get Iran's help in releasing U.S. hostages being held by terrorists in Lebanon, an action that was especially egregious in view of the administration's simultaneous campaign to persuade other nations not to supply arms to nations supporting terrorism.

It seems that once any violation of a principle is accepted, it becomes very difficult to limit the scope of subsequent deviations. Certain instances of willful deception of the public by the government may be so patently justifiable (as during the Cuban missile crisis) as to arouse no serious opposition. But such instances are very exceptional. In a democratic society, any doubt about whether the public can be trusted to respond in the national interest must be resolved in the public's favor. Otherwise, an unrestrained defense of the national interest could undermine the very ideals that are being defended.

Notes

1. Senate Committee on Governmental Affairs, *Confidence and Concern: Citizens View American Government. A Survey of Public Attitudes by the Subcommittee on Inter-Governmental Relations*, 93d Cong., 1973, 73.
2. Robert Weissberg, *Public Opinion and Popular Government* (Englewood Cliffs, N.J.: Prentice-Hall, 1976), 33.
3. *Harris Survey*, November 26, 1984, 3.
4. Lloyd A. Free and Hedley Cawtril, *The Political Beliefs of Americans* (New York: Simon and Schuster, 1968), 60.
5. Reported in David W. Moore, "The Public Is Uncertain," *Foreign Policy* (Summer 1979): 70-71.
6. Alexis de Tocqueville, *Democracy in America* (New York: Alfred A. Knopf, 1945), 2:136.
7. *Gallup Poll: Public Opinion 1980* (Wilmington, Del.: Scholarly Resources, 1981), 47.
8. James N. Rosenau, *Public Opinion and Foreign Policy* (New York: Random House, 1961), 4.
9. George F. Kennan, *American Diplomacy, 1900-1950* (New York: New American World, 1959), 59.
10. Norman Podhoretz, *The Present Danger* (New York: Simon and Schuster, 1980), 85.
11. "Factors in America's Greatness," *Current Opinion* (January 1976): 2.
12. John E. Reilly, ed., *American Public Opinion and U.S. Foreign Policy* (Chicago: Chicago Council on Foreign Relations, 1983), 19, and John E. Reilly, "America's State of Mind," *Foreign Policy* (Spring 1987): 47.
13. For details, see Charles Mathias, Jr., "Habitual Hatred, Unsound Policy," *Foreign Affairs* 61 (Summer 1981): 1019-1020.
14. Reilly, ed., *American Public Opinion*, 15.
15. *Harris Survey*, July 23, 1984, 7.
16. Ibid., May 28, 1984, 3.
17. Both the October and the January polls are reported in Hedrick Smith, "Poll Shows Skepticism on Arms Pact," *New York Times*, January 8, 1984, 1.
18. *Gallup Poll: Public Opinion 1935-1971* (New York: Random House, 1972), 1807.
19. *Gallup Opinion Index*, January 1980, 3.
20. Quoted in Walter Lefeber, *Inevitable Revolution: The United States in Central America* (New York: W. W. Norton, 1983), 5.
21. *Harris Survey*, November 26, 1984.
22. *Gallup Report*, July 1984, 26.
23. Rosenau, *Public Opinion*, 40.
24. Bruce M. Russett and Donald R. DeLuca, "Don't Tread on Me: Public Opinion and Foreign Policy," *Political Science Quarterly* 96 (Fall 1981): 389.
25. Reilly, ed., *American Public Opinion*, 19.
26. Reilly, "America's State of Mind," 47.
27. Reilly, ed., *American Public Opinion*, 23.
28. Reilly, "America's State of Mind," 47.
29. Ibid.
30. Ibid., 48.
31. "Most Feel U.S. Intervention in Chile Was Wrong," *Current Opinion* 3 (January 1975): 1.
32. Ibid.
33. *Harris Survey*, December 1975, 1.

34. Reilly, ed., *American Public Opinion*, 21.
35. Reilly, "America's State of Mind," 52.
36. Barry B. Hughes, *The Domestic Context of American Foreign Policy* (San Francisco: W. H. Freeman, 1978), 32.
37. *Gallup Poll: Public Opinion 1935-1971* (New York: Random House, 1972), 1995.
38. A major study on this issue is Warren E. Miller and Donald E. Stokes, "Constituency Influence in Congress," in Angus Campbell, Philip E. Converse, Warren E. Miller, and Donald Stokes, *Elections and the Political Order* (New York: John Wiley and Sons, 1966).
39. Hughes, *Domestic Context*, 92.
40. Benjamin I. Page and Richard A. Brody, "Policy Voting and the Electoral Process: The Vietnam War Issue," *American Political Science Review* 66 (September 1972): 979-995.
41. Shortly after the 1984 election, 57 percent of the public approved of President Reagan's performance with respect to inflation and the cost of living, and 42 percent approved of his performance in the area of taxes, but only 37 percent approved of his policy in Central America and 33 percent his policy in Lebanon and the Middle East (though 43 percent said they approved of the way he had been handling relations with the Soviet Union). *Harris Survey*, January 21, 1985, 2-3.
42. Quoted in David Halberstam, *The Best and the Brightest* (Greenwich, Conn.: Fawcett, 1972), 643.
43. The decline of monolithic communism has in fact, left some conservatives at a loss. As Norman Podhoretz complained, it "increases the difficulty of explaining to ourselves and our friends what we are fighting for and what we are fighting against. It may therefore make it harder to mobilize the political support without which a steady and consistent strategy of containment is impossible." Podhoretz, *The Present Danger*, 98.
44. Weissberg, *Public Opinion*, 235.
45. *Gallup Report*, December 1983, 29.
46. Quoted in Marriner S. Eccles, *Beckoning Frontiers* (New York: Alfred A. Knopf, 1951), 336.
47. I. M. Destler, Leslie Gelb, and Anthony Lake, *Our Own Worst Enemy: The Unmaking of American Foreign Policy* (New York: Simon and Schuster, 1984).
48. See, for example, Louis Halle, *Dream and Reality: Aspects of American Foreign Policy* (New York: Harper, 1959), 155.
49. Paul N. McCloskey, Jr., *Truth and Untruth: Political Deceit in America* (New York: Simon and Schuster, 1972), 47.
50. Anthony Austin, *The President's War* (Philadelphia: J. B. Lippincott, 1971), 182-183.
51. See William Shawcross, *Sideshow: Kissinger, Nixon, and the Destruction of Cambodia* (New York: Pocket Books, 1979).

The Role of Congress

IF THE PUBLIC cannot play a direct and continuous role in foreign affairs, its representatives in Congress, who are closer to the levers of power yet answerable to those who elected them, might be able to do so on the public's behalf, so that, at least indirectly, the people would rule in foreign as well as domestic policy. It is true, as already discussed, that voters are not likely to monitor their representatives' and senators' foreign policy records and vote accordingly on election day. But if members of Congress cannot really be considered the citizens' proxies, they are at least their "trustees." Representatives and senators are not usually elected with the idea that they will solicit and weigh their constituents' views each time they vote (and in most cases, the constituents simply will not have any explicit views). Rather, they are elected because voters generally trust them to make the right decisions and to correctly interpret their preferences. Moreover, it is not Congress's only function to ensure that foreign policy making is democratic; its job is also to promote U.S. foreign policy objectives—and the two tasks are not always fully compatible. Thus in addition to having both a dilemma of aggregation and a dilemma of effective choice, it is also possible that solutions to the two dilemmas place different demands on foreign policy.

Foreign policy authority is constitutionally divided between Congress and the president, and, as usually happens when power is jointly exercised, there is much contention over each side's appropriate share. In the case of foreign policy, this division has been said to amount to "an invitation to struggle" between Congress and the president[1]—certainly a good description of the situation since the late 1960s. Before examining this tug-of-war between the two branches of government, let us see just what the Constitution does say on the matter of foreign policy authority.

Constitutional Provisions

Before the U.S. Constitution was drafted by the Constitutional Convention in 1787, the conduct of the new nation's external affairs was entrusted, by the Continental Congress, to a five-member Committee for Foreign Affairs. Its performance was apparently not illustrious, and the framers of the Constitution thought it advisable to place foreign policy making in a firmer institutional context, one in which both the executive branch and Congress would have an important role. The powers accorded to Congress can be viewed in two ways: first, from the point of view of the specific areas of international affairs that are placed under congressional authority; and secondly, in terms of the instruments of control that Congress is given over the foreign policy activities of the executive.

Areas of Explicit Authority

It can be argued that the Founding Fathers intended to give Congress a controlling role in foreign policy, since the responsibilities they assign to it cover some of the most crucial facets of international affairs: war, treaties, and economic relations.

A nation can engage in no more dramatic and costly act than the act of war, and the Constitution grants Congress the exclusive power to "declare war" (Article I, Section 8). However, the actual conduct of hostilities is plainly not something that can be managed by a deliberative body of that size. The Constitution therefore states that the president shall be "commander in chief" of the armed forces (Article II, section 2), which implies that he has ultimate responsibility for the way the war is fought. An early draft of the Constitution had given Congress the power to "make" war, but this was changed to "declare" so that the president, without waiting for congressional approval, could take immediate measures to repel a sudden attack. Thus, the president can in fact order troops into combat even without a formal declaration of war by Congress—a principle that has been confirmed by the Supreme Court.[2] In addition to its authority to declare war, Congress must authorize and appropriate money for the armed forces. This means that, even in the conduct of war, the president does not have unlimited authority, since Congress can deny funds for military operations of which it disapproves.

While the implications of a congressional declaration of war are a bit fuzzy, the Founding Fathers' apparent intention was that a president's decision to commit the country to war would have to be ratified by Congress as soon as possible. Still, the vagueness surrounding this principle, as well as changing historical circumstances, have made for considerable disagreement between the two branches of government on its proper interpretation.

The second major area of congressional responsibility concerns treaties. Since the Constitution stipulates that a treaty "shall be the supreme law of the land" (Article VI), and at the same time Congress is responsible for making laws, it follows that it should have a voice in the nation's treaty commitments. The Constitution empowers the president to make treaties "by and with the advice and consent of the Senate" (Article II, section 2). Although there is no set manner in which the Senate's advice must be sought, various mechanisms (such as having senators participate in treaty negotiations and informal consultations with key members of the Senate at some point during the negotiations) have been employed. Consent, on the other hand, requires a two-thirds majority vote—more than the simple majority required for domestic legislation.

While most often the Senate votes either in favor of treaties or against them, it can also try to alter particular treaty provisions or to make explicit interpretations of their meaning. This is usually done by means of amendments, changes in one or several treaty provisions. Because amendments alter the treaty, they must be accepted by both nations, which means that the agreement may have to be renegotiated, and that cannot always be done. (When negotiations for the SALT II treaty were completed, the Soviet Union informed the United States that no amendments would be accepted.) Occasionally, however, the other nation may go along with the changes. The Panama Canal Treaty of 1977, by which the United States returned to Panama sovereignty and control over the canal (which the United States had owned and operated since 1903), was bitterly opposed by a number of senators; they considered it a "sellout" or "giveaway" of U.S. property. As a result, a number of amendments further protecting U.S. interests in the canal were adopted by the Senate. In this case, Panama's government agreed to accept the changes without renegotiating the entire treaty.

The Constitution also empowers Congress to make rules governing foreign trade, a prerogative that is important not only in its own right but also because of its political implications. For example, Congress can affect the tone of the nation's relations with its allies by loosening or tightening restrictions on their exports to the United States. Conversely, the Soviet Union has been denied a variety of trade preferences because of the state of relations between the two countries; and when relations between Beijing and Washington improved, China was granted many of the concessions denied to the Soviets. Thus, by regulating access to American markets, Congress can wield both a carrot and a stick over foreign countries—either in a policy pursued jointly with the executive branch or despite its wishes. Indeed, it has been said that "few of the economic powers of Congress have more significant implications for foreign policy than its power to regulate commerce." [3]

Instruments of Congressional Control

In addition to the specific areas placed under its jurisdiction, Congress also has several instruments of control that apply to many facets of foreign policy. It can influence the choice of the people selected to manage the nation's international affairs, and it appropriates the money for foreign policy programs. Such powers give it, in theory, considerable control over the direction of foreign affairs. The question is how closely practice corresponds to theory.

The Constitution grants Congress the power to confirm major appointments. The heads of executive departments—such as the secretary of state, the secretary of defense, the director of the Arms Control and Disarmament Agency—and their principal deputies, U.S. ambassadors, and many other officials are appointed by the president but must be confirmed by the Senate. Since the substance of foreign policy is very much shaped by the beliefs of key people, this would appear to give Congress an important if indirect means of influencing the course of foreign affairs. However, as we shall see, the Senate rarely rejects a candidate put forth by the president.

As far as the purse strings are concerned, the president proposes a budget, but both houses of Congress must approve the funds for any foreign policy (or other) programs, first in an authorization bill and then in an appropriation bill. Thus, there are two stages of the funding process at which Congress can block foreign policy programs of which it disapproves, and this makes the "power of the purse" a theoretically potent instrument of congressional control. This is true not only of diplomatic activities and economic assistance to foreign countries. Because military means of pursuing national objectives play a large role in U.S. foreign policy (whether for compellence or deterrence), and because military programs are costly, control over the Pentagon's budget is another potential instrument of congressional influence.

Considering the powers granted it by the Constitution, it is hard to believe that Congress does not have a major function in external affairs. Nonetheless, its influence has been surprisingly modest throughout most of U.S. history. Although things have changed somewhat since the mid-1970s, the matter of its proper role has not yet been resolved.

The Era of Acquiescence

Until recently, Congress has willingly refrained from taking an active role in foreign policy: in fact, it played less of a part than what the Constitution seems to have intended for it. Acquiescence to presidential decisions has generally been the rule, and representatives and senators, like the public that elects them, have shown greater interest in domestic than in foreign affairs. They have displayed interest in matters of international trade, but this is a pocketbook issue, often with a direct effect on their constituents. Beyond this, members of Congress have traditionally been content to simply follow the presidential lead.

This passivity is reflected in the fact that, of twenty-one important foreign policy decisions between the 1930s and 1961, Congress initiated a mere three, and congressional influence was ultimately dominant in only six cases.[4] Perhaps this is not really surprising. After all, congressional power in foreign policy mostly involves telling the president what he cannot do rather than what he shall do. But even within that limitation, Congress has been remarkably unassertive in foreign affairs.

The Senate's power to confirm or reject the president's appointments to key policy-making jobs has been used very sparingly, and even when the Senate has challenged a presidential choice, this has rarely altered the government's actual policies. All in all, Congress has not acted as a very forceful gatekeeper of leadership positions in the foreign affairs bureaucracy.

Congress does exercise more control over foreign policy budgets, but, although it has occasionally been willing to pare down the president's requests for foreign aid, it has customarily accepted his defense budgets. At times, it has even given the president more than he has asked for.[5] But even if Congress had been more willing to wield the budgetary ax, the effect might have been more modest than is sometimes expected, since certain policies cannot be effectively influenced merely by withholding money. For example, President Ronald Reagan's verbal taunting of Moscow in the early 1980s, or President Jimmy Carter's attacks on several nations' human rights policies in the late 1970s, had major foreign policy implications but required no funding. Moreover, some actions actually make expenditures unnecessary and thus again escape congressional budgetary control. When the Reagan administration decided to withdraw the United States from UNESCO (the United Nations Educational, Scientific, and Cultural Organization), which it felt had become too politicized and anti-American, the immediate budgetary consequence was to obviate future U.S. contributions to the organization. *Programs* must almost always be funded, but not necessarily *policies*.

Congressional influence has not been very notable with respect to treaties, either. Although the Senate did reject U.S. adherence to the Treaty of Versailles (which sought to give international relations a new foundation after World War I), more often it has simply accepted the international agreements negotiated by the president. In the two centuries of its existence, the Senate has failed to provide the needed two-thirds majority on only eleven occasions, and it has rejected a treaty only twice since World War II.[6]

What is more important, the Senate has not even had an opportunity to vote on the great majority of U.S. foreign policy commitments, since so many of them have taken the form of *executive agreements* rather than treaties. The difference between treaties and executive agreements has never been satisfactorily defined. The legal fiction is that the former are agreements between nations, while the latter are agreements between governments. Nevertheless, executive agreements are just as binding as treaties; once they are signed, they are the law of the land, and they must be respected by subsequent governments as well. However, from the president's point of view, there is an important difference: because executive agreements are not agreements "between nations," they do not have to be ratified by the Senate. As has been said, "The executive agreement is an undeclared treaty which, like an undeclared war, seeks to avoid paying its Constitutional dues by changing its name." [7] All presidents, from George Washington to Ronald Reagan, have relied on these agreements, and it is easy to see why. Senate approval involves a fairly lengthy process and consumes the energies of senators, the president, and other government officials. The United States currently enters into several hundred agreements with other nations each year, and it would be impractical to submit each one to the Senate for its endorsement. Moreover, the necessity for secrecy sometimes makes formal submission undesirable on national security grounds.

The need for executive agreements is thus evident, but some find the extent of their use disturbing. Although the Senate has ratified over one thousand treaties since 1789, some seven thousand external commitments have been made by executive agreement. Since World War II, approximately 95 percent of U.S. agreements with foreign nations have been of this type.[8] Most of them have been concerned with routine and noncontroversial activities, but some have dealt with momentous matters. Both the Yalta and Potsdam agreements with the nation's World War II allies were executive agreements, as were a number of U.S. commitments to Vietnam at the time of America's involvement in that country. Most arrangements for U.S. military bases abroad are also made by executive agreement. Congress is not always left in the dark about these agreements; occasionally, the president may find it useful, for diplomatic and other reasons, to seek support for an agreement in the form of a joint congressional resolution, but that is the exception rather than the rule. Whatever the virtue of executive agreements, the more that is done by executive agreement, the less is Congress's influence over foreign policy.

Two Examples of Congressional Passivity

It has been noted that, although Congress is solely empowered to declare war, the president as commander in chief can take emergency military measures to deal with foreign threats without waiting for congressional authorization. This raises a fundamental question: At what point *is* it necessary for Congress to endorse the commitment of U.S. troops abroad? For a long time, presidents seemed to feel that they could dispense with formal congressional approval altogether, as long as they believed that a national consensus supported the military involvement that they wanted to undertake. Indeed, on more than 125 occasions, presidents have asserted their prerogative to send troops abroad on their own authority. Only five of the eleven major wars fought by the United States were accompanied by a congressional declaration of war.[9] In most cases, the military imperative has been accepted by both Congress and the public, and strict adherence to constitutional provisions has usually been subordinated to the desire to avoid unnecessary political debate during a state of national emergency.

The failure of Congress to insist upon its constitutional prerogatives has been particularly apparent in the years since World War II. Neither the 1958 intervention in Lebanon, nor the invasion of the Dominican Republic in 1965, were given explicit authorization by Congress. But congressional acquiescence was especially remarkable with regard to America's two major military commitments after World War II: in Korea and in Vietnam.

KOREA. Under the terms of a postwar settlement, Korea was divided at the thirty-eighth parallel. North Korea soon came to be ruled by a Communist government closely linked to the Soviet Union, while in South Korea a right-wing and pro-American regime was established. In January 1950, Secretary of State Dean Acheson, when defining the area of U.S. security interests in the Pacific, excluded Korea from the scope of immediate concern. Possibly encouraged by this, on June 24, 1950, North Korea launched ninety thousand troops against its southern neighbor, but the North Koreans miscalculated what Washington's response would be. President Harry S Truman was convinced (perhaps wrongly, in retrospect) that the Soviet Union was behind the invasion, and he declared that "if South Korea was allowed to fall Communist leaders would be emboldened to override nations closer to our own shores." [10] Truman ordered Gen. Douglas MacArthur to prepare to defend South Korea. The United States obtained a resolution from the United Nations Security Council (the Soviet Union was absent from the meeting at which the resolution was adopted) recommending "such assistance to the Republic of [South] Korea as may be necessary to repel the armed attack and to restore international peace and security in the area." U.S. air and naval forces were ordered into action.

On the day this decision was taken (and for the first time since the North Korean invasion), Truman met with fourteen members of Congress from both parties and summarized the situation as he saw it. When he requested the opinion of those present, he was told that it was enough to know that "we were in there with force and that the President thought the force adequate." [11] Three days later, U.S. naval and air involvement was extended to include targets in North Korea itself, and on the day after that, MacArthur was authorized to commit American ground troops as well. A meeting with a larger group of members of Congress was held at the White House. The president's actions reportedly met a "chorus of approval," [12] and, although Sen. Alexander Smith (R-N.J.) suggested that a congressional resolution approving the action might be useful, Secretary Acheson did not like the idea, and no resolution was introduced.

General MacArthur's military action at first succeeded, and by September, North Korean troops were retreating back across the thirty-eighth parallel. By most standards, the goal of defending South Korea against external aggression had been achieved. But MacArthur was not satisfied; he wanted to take the military action into North Korea itself, to do away with the Communist regime and to reunify Korea outside of the Soviet orbit. But there was a risk: North Korea bordered on China, and MacArthur's plan could lead U.S. troops up to its frontiers. Beijing gave notice that this would bring China into the fray. However, MacArthur did not take these warnings seriously, and in early October, U.S. troops were sent across the thirty-eighth parallel. This was a substantial expansion of the war and a major extension of initial U.S. objectives, but Congress requested no say in the matter.

Ten days later, true to their warnings, Chinese armed forces moved into North Korea, and the tide of combat began to turn against the United States. The stage was now set for a major international confrontation, one which could draw the Soviet Union (then allied with China) into the war. MacArthur, undaunted, responded by seeking to escalate the war even further, with air attacks against China itself. But the Truman administration was concerned about the possible consequences of further escalation, and the president refused MacArthur permission to carry the war to Chinese territory. Even the Joint Chiefs of Staff were adamantly opposed to the idea. Despite his enormous popularity with the U.S. public, MacArthur was recalled, and in July 1953 an armistice was signed with North Korea, ending the Korean War exactly where it had started—at the thirty-eighth parallel. A congressional burst of sympathy for the ousted general notwithstanding, neither the Senate nor the House of Representatives had played a significant role in initiating, or authorizing the extension of, U.S. involvement in a war that lasted three years, claimed thousands of American lives, and threatened to lead to a conflict of even greater proportions.

VIETNAM. The Vietnam War was an even more jarring chapter in U.S. history. It led to the engagement at times of over half a million U.S. troops and it ultimately cost some fifty thousand American lives. It alienated the United States from many of its allies and from a large portion of international public opinion. It also proved to be the most divisive event in the country's history since the Civil War. Yet it was largely the consequence of presidential actions, with very little input from Congress. It was only several years after U.S. troops had been committed to Vietnam—indeed, after they had reached peak numerical strength and after public opinion began turning against the war—that Congress felt emboldened to question the president's policies and to assert its own powers.

Vietnam had been a French colony. After a protracted war of liberation, conducted by an organization called the Viet Minh and led by the Marxist revolutionary leader Ho Chi Minh, the French were thrown out in 1954. Vietnam was then (like Korea, but along the seventeenth parallel) "provisionally" divided into two parts: Communist North Vietnam, under Ho Chi Minh and with its capital in Hanoi; and non-Communist South Vietnam, under the Catholic and pro-American Ngo Dinh Diem and with its capital in Saigon. From the very outset, the United States had staked an interest in Vietnam. It had supported France in its unsuccessful struggle against the Viet Minh, and it had given South Vietnam substantial economic and military assistance. However, Diem's rule became increasingly repressive, and South Vietnam was turned into a quasi-police state, which, in turn, bred an insurgency led by the remnants of the Viet Minh in the south, known as the Viet Cong. The prospect of Diem's collapse was real and very dismaying to Washington. In President Dwight D. Eisenhower's words:

The loss of all Vietnam, together with Laos in the west and Cambodia in the southwest, would have meant the surrender to Communist enslavement of millions. On the material side, it would have spelled the loss of valuable deposits of tin and prodigious supplies of rubber and rice. It would have meant Thailand, enjoying buffer territory between itself and Red China, would be exposed on its entire Eastern border to infiltration and attack. . . . And if Indochina fell, not only Thailand but Burma and Malaya would be threatened, with added risks to East Pakistan and South Asia as well as to all Indonesia.[13]

In retrospect, this "domino theory" appears to be a rather overheated assessment of the threat. But it appeared perfectly reasonable to many U.S. leaders at the time, and concerns such as it expressed provided the stimulus for further U.S. involvement. Around 1960, the Viet Cong began receiving active support from North Vietnam, and in 1961 President John F. Kennedy expanded aid to the Saigon regime, including an additional one hundred military advisers and some four hundred troops especially trained for antiguerrilla warfare. Over the next year and a half, U.S. troop strength in Vietnam rose above ten thousand. No congressional declaration of war, no resolutions by the House or Senate, indeed very little consultation with Congress at all, preceded or accompanied the growing military commitment to this remote country.

In 1963, U.S. troop strength reached fifteen thousand (still with no mandate from Congress), but the Viet Cong's operations continued unabated, and North Vietnamese assistance, in the form of regular troops, showed no sign of decreasing. In January 1964, the administration of Lyndon B. Johnson decided to begin an intense bombing campaign against North Vietnam, which (like MacArthur's incursion into North Korea) would amount to a major widening of the war. Thus far, Congress had had little to say about the growing U.S. combat role; indeed, its passive concurrence may have sprung from relief that the involvement was not even deeper. But by 1964, some form of congressional sanction was deemed necessary by the administration.

The events leading up to the Gulf of Tonkin resolution were alluded to in Chapter 3. What was then portrayed as an unprovoked attack against two U.S. destroyers engaged in a routine patrol in international waters was later discovered to be a response to secret harassment operations against North Vietnam.[14] On the same day that the ships were attacked, President Johnson ordered bombing raids against North Vietnamese naval bases and an oil depot. He then requested a congressional resolution authorizing him to take similar measures in the future. With very little objection, Congress, by overwhelming majorities in both houses, passed the Gulf of Tonkin resolution, declaring that it "approves and supports the determination of the President . . . to take all necessary measures to repel any further armed attack against the forces of the United States and to prevent further aggression." The administration considered this the "functional equivalent" of a declaration of war.

One White House official in a "position to know" later confided to a *New York Times* columnist that "the President had been carrying around the text of the resolution 'in his pocket' long before the Tonkin episode gave him the right opportunity to lay it before Congress." [15] Yet there was little congressional inquiry into the incident and no serious debate on the implications of what was a virtually open-ended resolution. Some members later charged that Congress had been duped by the administration, but it could not claim to have done much to reach an informed decision itself.

In April 1965, an increase of nearly 20,000 in the U.S. troop presence was authorized. In July, Gen. William Westmoreland, who was commanding the U.S. troops in Vietnam, requested an additional 100,000 men; in November, 154,000 more; in December, Westmoreland asked for a total of 443,000 troops by the end of 1966; a month later, this figure was augmented by an additional 16,000; in August 1966, he requested a total of 542,588 men by the end of 1967. The bombing campaign had expanded to include massive bombing of Hanoi. U.S. casualties were mounting. The first tremors of public disaffection rippled through the country. Congress, too, began to have second thoughts about the country's ensnarement in the conflict. We shall see shortly what action it took.

Reasons for Congressional Acquiescence

Why was Congress so often content to support presidential decisions, even in areas of major national importance, including executive appointments, treaty approval, and war involvement? Why did it, by passive acquiescence, in effect sanction the curtailment of its own foreign policy role?

Partly, it may be that Congress has never felt that it should, by its very nature, be called upon to play a major or continuous foreign policy role. Senators and representatives naturally tend to think of themselves, first and foremost, as the trustees of their constituents—the people who elected them and to whom they are accountable at the polls—and as we have seen, domestic issues matter most to voters. It is, therefore, understandable that foreign policy issues should not loom particularly large in the concerns of most members of Congress; they are absorbed with problems closer to home, and they do not have the time to deal with everything. As a leading political scientist described the situation:

> The Congressman is a rather ordinary person in some respects, not much wiser than the average small town lawyer, banker, doctor, or bartender, frequently confused, almost always harassed, excessively overworked, busy with an enormous variety of problems presented by his constituents, and sometimes called upon to make decisions on foreign policy that will affect man and his institutions over a large part of the earth's surface for generations to come. [16]

This parochialism is not shared by the executive branch, which is, in principle, trustee of the whole nation rather than of a local constituency. It is therefore more likely to act out of national rather than local considerations, which is what foreign policy requires. The difference should not be exaggerated—for example, a decision by President Reagan to lift the grain embargo against the Soviet Union was largely the result of pressure from the farm states. Still, there is a difference of degree, and it is a difference that argues against excessive congressional interference in international affairs.

A second reason—though things have changed somewhat in this respect more recently—is that Congress does not have the resources or foreign policy expertise available to the president and the executive agencies. Thus, even if it were able to rise above parochial interests, Congress might not be in as good a position to deal effectively with foreign challenges. The Department of State, which is the principal agency responsible for the daily conduct of foreign policy, has a staff of some twenty-three thousand. Among them are highly trained specialists in various functional aspects of international affairs (political-military affairs, economic and business affairs, and so forth) and in various regions of the world. Many of them are located in diplomatic and consular posts abroad, and the department can thus call upon first-hand knowledge of the domestic conditions and foreign policies of just about every country. Three specialized agencies—the Arms Control and Disarmament Agency, the Agency for International Development (AID), and the United States Information Agency—are also attached to the Department of State. The Defense Department is an even larger bureaucracy, with over ninety thousand civilian employees, including experts in virtually every aspect of military affairs and national security. The Office of International Security Affairs (ISA) within the Defense Department is organized along lines similar to the Department of State, and it manages the spectrum of foreign policy interests connected to military affairs. The Central Intelligence Agency is the largest and best-equipped intelligence organization in the world; it acquires and interprets vast amounts of information, some obtained openly and some through covert efforts, about political conditions and military capabilities of countries throughout the world. In addition, many other executive departments have responsibilities that spill over into international affairs (the Department of Commerce, the Department of Labor, the Department of the Treasury, and so on).

Compared to these enormous resources, those available to Congress are paltry. Members of Congress may well believe, therefore, that they should not try to second-guess those who are presumably in a much better position to understand what is going on and how best to deal with events.

But in the final analysis, perhaps the main reason that Congress has rarely challenged the president on foreign affairs is that it has usually agreed with his policies. Episodes of disagreement between the executive and legislative branches have occasionally occurred (one dramatic example, the Senate's refusal to ratify the Treaty of Versailles, has already been mentioned), but only occasionally. Consensus was particularly evident in the decades following World War II, and it was founded on three beliefs that were shared by the two branches. The first of these was the conviction that the United States was called upon to play a major role in international affairs. Isolationism had once been the dominant sentiment in the country, but it was weakened by World War I and completely dispelled by World War II. Secondly, virtually all U.S. political leaders believed in the benefits of free trade and of an open international economy. There was wide agreement that protectionism in the interwar period was responsible for the depth of the Great Depression, and since the United States had no real competitors in the international economy at the time, free trade would benefit the nation at least as much as it would the rest of the world. Thirdly, and most fundamentally, long-standing anticommunism was now merged with the specter of the Soviet menace to peace and democracy. So serious was the threat believed to be that it was thought not only irresponsible, but downright unpatriotic, to display anything less than national unity or to undermine the president's leadership.

This harmony of views produced a foreign policy rooted in firm bipartisan consensus. Occasionally, especially around election time, each party did try to score some points with the voters by criticizing the other's actions, but between elections, almost everyone professed adherence to the basic beliefs. The legislation for the Marshall Plan was approved by a vote of 318 to 75 in the House; in the Senate, it was passed by a nearly unanimous voice vote. The Senate ratified the NATO treaty by a vote of 82 to 13; the Gulf of Tonkin resolution sailed through by a vote of 88 to 2.

But this consensus seems to have ended, and during the 1970s a number of steps were taken to reassert congressional prerogatives in foreign affairs. Although there was no single event that changed Congress's perception of its proper role in foreign policy, a major catalyst was surely the Vietnam War. Along with changes in the country and in Congress itself, the disastrous embroilment in Southeast Asia modified the terms of executive-legislative relations and, in several important respects, recharted the course of U.S. foreign policy.

Congressional Resurgence

The Vietnam War marked the first time that many, perhaps most, Americans doubted the wisdom and morality of a cause for which they had previously been willing to fight and which their government depicted as a crusade in defense of national ideals. It brought into question the country's righteousness and the values it claimed to be defending. It produced mass demonstrations and, during its darkest moments, the death, by gunshot from the Ohio National Guard, of student protesters at Kent State University. It brought to light examples of presidential misconduct, including efforts to mislead the public and Congress. It generated economic inflation, the effects of which were felt long after the last U.S. soldier had returned home. And it fired Congress with a resolve never to permit the nation to slide into such a calamitous misadventure again.

It had not been easy to muster enthusiasm for the Vietnam War. North Vietnam and the Viet Cong did espouse communism, but South Vietnam's regime inspired no admiration, either. Even after Ngo Dinh Diem was gone, his successors were no less repressive. Nguyen Cao Ky, who became prime minister in 1965, had declared a year earlier: "I have only one other hero—Hitler. . . . We need four or five Hitlers in Vietnam." [17] As reports of governmental corruption and repression in South Vietnam reached the United States, and as the ineptitude of Saigon's armed forces became increasingly evident, the justification for the U.S. commitment became increasingly nebulous. Meanwhile, U.S. troops were being called upon to play a greater and greater combat role in the defense of the regime. By the end of 1967, more bombs had been dropped on Vietnam than on the whole of Europe during World War II. Still, after several years of escalating involvement, accompanied by wartime brutalities, victory was nowhere in sight.

Public outrage finally boiled over in 1968. That year, despite the administration's claims that good military progress was being made, the Viet Cong struck hard. During the lunar new year holiday known as Tet, large-scale attacks were launched throughout the country, and Viet Cong forces penetrated every major city, including Saigon, where part of the compound housing the U.S. embassy was temporarily seized. Although the attacks were ultimately repelled, the Tet offensive belied the administration's claims that the war was being won. Three years of military involvement showed no signs of accomplishing any of its supposed aims.

But the United States had never lost a war, and neither the Nixon nor the Johnson administration was eager to lead the nation to its first military defeat—particularly not at the hands of a nation once described by Johnson as "that raggedy-ass little fourth-rate country." [18] As the quagmire engulfed the United States, the country's image became more and more tarnished in the eyes of its own people. Not only were ultimate objectives questioned, but people were viewing the spectacle of carnage—not all of it at enemy hands—with increasing disquiet. A U.S. colonel, after ordering a village reduced to rubble to rid it of Viet Cong, was widely quoted as saying, "We had to destroy it in order to save it." [19] In March 1968, a U.S. infantry company shot more than a hundred civilians, women and children included, in the village of My Lai. Pictures of the massacre were published by a major magazine, shattering beliefs about the country's purity. Scenes of the war shown on television deepened the national revulsion.

As public indignation spread, opinion swung against both the war and President Johnson. Dissatisfaction was also brewing in Congress. Sen. J. William Fulbright (D-Ark.), chairman of the Foreign Relations Committee, held hearings that challenged the country's role in Vietnam. Sen. Eugene McCarthy (D-Minn.) campaigned in the 1968 presidential primaries on a peace platform and won more than 40 percent of New Hampshire's Democratic vote. Sen. Robert F. Kennedy (D-N.Y.) entered the race as another antiwar candidate.

The domestic signals were clear, and negotiations with North Vietnam and the Viet Cong were initiated in Paris. But they remained deadlocked for several years as the nation's most unpopular war dragged on.

In 1969, without informing the public or Congress, President Richard Nixon launched an air war against alleged North Vietnamese supply areas in neutral Cambodia, and this was expanded into an actual invasion in 1970.[20] The war seemed to be on the brink of spreading, and Congress reacted. In 1970, it formally repealed the Gulf of Tonkin resolution. The Senate even passed an amendment (which was defeated in the House) cutting off further funds for operations in Cambodia. This was the beginning of a congressional resurgence that challenged the foreign policy dominance that presidents had enjoyed. Congress acquired a greater degree of self-confidence than it had had before and the consensus of the post-World War II years was weakened. Congress's challenge embraced several areas of foreign policy, but, in light of Vietnam, it was focused on military and security commitments abroad.

Military Commitments

Vietnam galvanized Congress into a determination to reassert its foreign policy prerogatives. Some feel that it ultimately went too far, excessively weakening the president's ability to conduct an effective and coherent policy. But at the time, presidential misuse of foreign policy power appeared to be the more pressing problem.

In 1969, Congress passed the National Commitments resolution, which declared that henceforth all U.S. commitments abroad should be based on an agreement between the executive and legislative branches of government. A much stronger move was the War Powers Act of 1973, a measure that was passed over President Nixon's veto and that imposed significant restraints on the chief executive's ability to deploy U.S. troops abroad. Although Congress has not been especially firm about enforcing its provisions, the War Powers Act was certainly a major step away from passive acquiescence. It required the president to consult with Congress in any situation where hostilities threatened to erupt. Furthermore, if U.S. forces were sent into combat or into a situation where combat appeared "imminent," the president was obligated to report to Congress within forty-eight hours on the likely duration and scope of hostilities. Most importantly, the forces were to be withdrawn within sixty days (ninety days in certain circumstances) unless Congress authorized an extension. The act also allowed Congress, by a concurrent resolution (one passed by both houses), to order the president to remove the forces even before the end of the sixty-day period, but this provision was struck down in 1983 by a Supreme Court decision ending the practice of legislative veto (whereby Congress permits the executive to do something unless and until it revokes this authority). President Nixon attacked the act as "unconstitutional and dangerous to the best interests of our Nation." [21] Nevertheless, it remains the law of the land, although, as mentioned, it has not been rigorously applied.

Congress has sought to limit military commitments abroad in other ways as well. The case of Angola was a good illustration of this new congressional activism. In 1974, after fourteen years of guerrilla warfare, Angola, a Portuguese colony, was poised on the verge of independence. Several factions had been competing in the struggle against the Portuguese, including the Marxist and Soviet-backed MPLA (see Chapter 3). The United States found itself backing the MPLA's rivals, the FNLA and UNITA (which also enjoyed some support from South Africa). Eventually, eleven thousand Cubans were sent to help the MPLA, and the Ford administration began channeling military assistance to its opponents. But Congress, fearing another imbroglio in a distant country, included a provision in a 1976 appropriations bill that prohibited the use of any funds for "activities involving Angola directly or indirectly." By then, Angola was firmly under the MPLA's control, and the administration could do no more than express its ire toward the Soviet Union for supporting the Cuban intervention. (The prohibition was repealed in 1985.)

Congress also took action to exercise control over the supply of weaponry to other countries. Arms sales (which may be regarded as a subcategory of bribery) have often been used to induce foreign countries to support U.S. positions or to bolster friendly governments by strengthening their military capacity (either with respect to other nations or with respect to domestic opposition). Such sales have become an important facet of international security policy, as well as a source of export earnings. They had been mainly directed to U.S. friends and allies among the developed nations, but during the 1970s they began to focus on Third World countries—mainly those of the Middle East, but also some in Latin America, Asia, and Africa.[22] Thus, some poor nations, in some of the more volatile areas of the world, became major buyers of sophisticated and expensive U.S. weaponry. Unlike his predecessors, President Carter was uncomfortable with the idea of providing arms to countries that could ill afford them and that were all too likely to use them. The United States, he remarked, could not "be both the world's leading champion of peace and the world's leading supplier of the weapons of war." [23] Some members of Congress shared his view. The fact that sophisticated armaments were shipped to war-prone parts of the world could, they believed, exacerbate regional tensions, fuel local arms races, and make military conflicts both more likely and more destructive. Moreover, if relatively destitute countries squandered scarce resources for weapons purchases, their prospects for development could be jeopardized even further. The role of international arms merchant was, in any case, not one which many people in the United States relished nor one which fitted their self-image. In 1976, Congress passed the Arms Export Control Act, by which major arms sales to foreign countries could be prohibited by a resolution passed by both the House and Senate within thirty days of receiving a presidential notification of the proposed sale. Thus, in this area, too, Congress began to exert some control over foreign policy.

An example of this legislation in action was provided by the proposed sale of AWAC (Advanced Warning and Control) airplanes to Saudi Arabia. In October 1981, President Reagan notified Congress that he intended to sell five AWACs to Saudi Arabia, which was one of the Persian Gulf's major oil producers, a regional power, and a country with considerable antipathy toward the Soviet Union. With the fall of the Shah of Iran in 1979 and his replacement by an anti-American Muslim regime, Saudi friendship had become particularly important to U.S. interests in the Middle East. But Congress now had thirty days within which to disapprove of the sale, and it had other factors to consider. Probably the most important of these was the possible effect of the AWACs on the security of Israel—an important concern for many voters. Pro-Israeli organizations lobbied strenuously against the sale of the AWACs, and, perhaps for the first time, an Arab lobby also emerged to work in favor of the sale. The president maintained that the aircraft, which were primarily designed to give early warning of enemy attack, were defensive and thus represented no threat to Israel, but opponents of the sale were not convinced. The House passed a resolution disapproving the sale, and the Senate Foreign Relations Committee recommended that the Senate do the same. The president promised to provide Israel with radar-jamming equipment to counter the AWACs, and he wrote to Senate majority leader Baker offering assurances that the Saudis would not use the planes against Israel and would not compromise secrets by letting them fall into hostile hands. Finally, by a slight majority (52-48), the full Senate declined to join the House in rejecting the sale. The president had won, but only by dint of great effort and by mollifying senators with various compromises and assurances that, ten years earlier, would probably not have been needed.

Another example of increased congressional assertiveness concerns Central America. As part of the Reagan administration's commitment to combat left-wing influence in that part of the world, the CIA, in 1982, planned a major program to train and support a force of anti-Sandinista Nicaraguans, known as contras, based in Honduras, whose purpose was to launch military operations against Nicaragua. There were many signs of congressional concern, and Representative Edward P. Boland (D-Mass.), chairman of the House Intelligence Committee, introduced an amendment to the fiscal 1983 intelligence authorization bill prohibiting support for military activities designed to overthrow the government of Nicaragua. It was adopted by a unanimous vote.

Executive Agreements

In 1954, Sen. John Bricker (R-Ohio), a conservative and an isolationist, fearing that U.S. membership in the United Nations could lead to agreements with leftist regimes, had introduced a bill aimed at requiring that all executive agreements be reported to Congress. The bill was defeated, but, with the Vietnam experience and the decreased tolerance for executive secrecy, the issue of executive agreements was raised again. Following passage of the

National Commitments resolution, Sen. Stuart Symington (D-Mo.) launched an investigation of existing commitments. He found that their number and import was far greater than had initially been supposed and that several involved security guarantees of which Congress was quite unaware. As a result, Congress in 1972 passed the Case Act (named for Sen. Clifford Case, R-N.J.), requiring that it be informed of all executive agreements (some four thousand of which were in force at the time) within sixty days. Disclosure could be limited to the Senate Foreign Relations and House Foreign Affairs committees, under an injunction of secrecy, should the president determine that national security so required.

The Case Act does strengthen the hand of Congress in foreign policy by reducing the range of activities that the executive can keep secret from it. Its impact should not, however, be overestimated. In the case of a treaty, the president is under pressure to seek congressional advice even while it is being negotiated, to increase the chance that the Senate will ratify it, while for executive agreements the only need is to inform Congress about the finished product. Moreover, there are ways around this as well. For example, the president can convey personal assurances to another nation, binding the United States to a certain extent without any written agreement. In order to secure South Vietnam's acceptance of his plans for a settlement of the Vietnam War, President Nixon offered Prime Minister Nguyen Van Thieu secret assurances of continued support in the postsettlement period. Nevertheless, congressional power regarding commitments to other countries has been strengthened, and this represents another (if only partially successful) measure of its determination to alter the domestic balance of power in foreign policy.

Human Rights

Although it has long been a stated objective of U.S. foreign policy to promote, even outside of its own borders, the basic political values which the United States itself espouses, the country's record of support for human rights has been quite spotty. For a long time, almost any ruler, however repressive, who supported U.S. security objectives and proclaimed his anticommunism loudly enough was able to obtain American backing and praise. But during the late 1960s and especially in the 1970s, many people began to feel uncomfortable about the nation's ties to oppressive and unpopular regimes. This was particularly true with regard to several Latin American countries.

Latin America was not a region with a history of stable democracy. Unrest born of poverty and inequality spawned dictatorships, with which the United States usually came easily to terms. In Brazil, for example, a democratic, mildly leftist, generally ineffective government was overthrown by the armed forces in 1964 and replaced by a brutally repressive (though at first economically successful) military dictatorship. Washington welcomed the new regime, but soon news of arbitrary imprisonments, torture, and other violations of human rights began to reach the U.S. public and Congress. Unease was intensified by allegations (never confirmed) that a program sponsored by AID had provided training for the Brazilian police and that torture equipment might have been furnished as well. Senate hearings were held on the matter amid a groundswell of concern about the neglect of human rights in foreign policy. In Chile, a popularly elected Marxist president, Salvador Allende, was overthrown in 1973 and was succeeded by a particularly vicious military dictatorship. Torture, imprisonment, and "internal exile" were the regime's manner of dealing with opposition. It was even implicated in the assassination, in Washington, of Chile's former ambassador to the United States, who had publicly criticized the military rule. The Nixon and Ford administrations welcomed Allende's overthrow but had little to say about the new regime's flagrant brutality. Other instances of dictatorships in the region included Nicaragua under Anastasio Somoza, which was supported by every U.S. administration until that of President Carter.

Outside Latin America, there was the case of the Philippines under President Marcos (see Chapter 1). South Africa practices institutionalized racial segregation and ruthlessly crushes any hint of opposition, yet it has been an important U.S. trade partner as well as a tacit ally in the struggle against Soviet influence in Africa. Many other unsavory regimes were recipients of American foreign aid. It became painfully obvious to a growing number of U.S. political leaders, and to the U.S. public, that many of the governments to which the country was linked consistently trampled upon the very principles the United States was pledged to uphold. Prior to that, criticism of other nations' human rights practices was reserved for the Soviet Union and its allies, but by the early 1970s it was impossible to ignore the abuses of friends and allies in the Third World. The country could not escape consciousness of the dilemma of political principle.

In 1974, Congress issued a report entitled "Human Rights in the World Community: A Call for Leadership," which reaffirmed the nation's obligation to promote human rights abroad, and it proposed a number of ways of doing this, such as the suspension of U.S. assistance to countries guilty of gross violations. In the same year, a provision was written into the Foreign Assistance Act stating that,

> except in extraordinary circumstances, the President shall substantially reduce or terminate security assistance to any government which engages in a consistent pattern of gross violations of internationally recognized human rights, including torture or cruel, inhuman or degrading treatment or punishment; prolonged detention without charges; or other flagrant denials of the right to life, liberty, and the security of the person.[24]

If "extraordinary circumstances" were invoked to justify disregard of the provision, the president would have to explain them to Congress. The act also required that the State Department annually report the status of human rights in all countries receiving U.S. aid. This was later expanded to include all countries, whether or not they were recipients of aid. The Foreign Assistance

Act of 1975 continued the prohibition of economic aid to any country that violated human rights, unless "foreign assistance will directly benefit the needy people in such country."

The executive branch was not at all enthusiastic about these congressional initiatives. Secretary of State Henry Kissinger complained that the government's ability to maneuver in dealing with foreign countries was being limited too much, particularly when it came to dealing with those nations which, their domestic political practices notwithstanding, were useful to U.S. foreign policy objectives. His preference was for "quiet diplomacy" rather than public criticism—which he said might be counterproductive—but many members of Congress suspected that quiet diplomacy would be an excuse for doing nothing. These views fit in well with those of President Carter, who frequently criticized not only the Soviet Union but also several friendly nations for human rights violations.

In sharp contrast, President Reagan deemphasized human rights as a foreign policy goal, and that often placed him at loggerheads with Congress. In El Salvador, for example, so-called death squads (apparently with support from portions of the Salvadoran armed forces) regularly and with impunity murdered advocates of social reform and democracy. In 1981, Congress had passed a law making continued U.S. aid to El Salvador contingent on presidential certification that meaningful progress toward remedying human rights abuses was being made. President Reagan was opposed to the certification requirement, and in late 1983 he vetoed a bill to extend it, and Congress failed to override the veto. Congress subsequently passed legislation retaining the requirement, and it did become law.

Congress's determination to persist in its concern for human rights was reflected in one of its rare rejections of a presidential nominee for executive position. In 1975, the State Department, bowing to the newly emerging concern, had established the position of coordinator for humanitarian affairs (with a staff of two). Two years later, Congress upgraded this position to that of assistant secretary of state for human rights and humanitarian affairs. In 1981, President Reagan submitted to the Senate the name of Ernest Lefevre as his nominee for the post, a man whom many senators considered thoroughly unsuitable for the job. Indeed, Lefevre had once argued that the United States had "no responsibility . . . to promote human rights in other sovereign states." [25] He had also publicly opposed the use of foreign assistance and public criticism to exert pressure on regimes that, though repressive internally, sided with the United States on East-West issues. When questioned on his views on human rights by the Senate Foreign Relations Committee, he seemed evasive and inconsistent.[26] The committee voted 13 to 4 to reject the nomination, and Lefevre's name was withdrawn from further consideration.

While the Reagan administration believed that the active promotion of human rights was often incompatible with national security objectives, Congress appeared more drawn to the view enunciated in 1948 by Secretary of

State Marshall that "governments which systematically disregard the rights of their own people are not likely to respect the rights of other nations and other people and are likely to seek their objectives by coercion and force in the international field." [27] Congress has thus considered it a matter of principle to make the promotion of human rights a major objective of U.S. foreign policy. By supporting the ethical as well as the more pragmatic elements of national objectives, Congress rounded out the scope of its foreign policy concerns.

Future Directions

One might conclude that recent congressional activism in foreign policy is the outgrowth of a specific chapter in U.S. history, when the ideological pendulum had swung toward the liberal end of the political spectrum and the need for firm foreign policy leadership was subordinated to the goal of promoting democracy abroad. But this would be mistaken, for conservatives have also used the new balance of governmental power for their own purposes. For example, President Nixon and Soviet leader Brezhnev signed, in 1972, an economic agreement that would have bestowed certain commercial advantages on the Soviet Union that it had not previously enjoyed. But congressional opponents, led by Senator Henry Jackson (D-Wash.), made these concessions conditional on Moscow's agreement to allow more Jews to emigrate from the U.S.S.R.—a condition that the Soviet Union refused to accept. Similarly, Senate hawks had effectively ensured that the SALT II treaty, signed by Carter and Brezhnev in 1979, would not receive the two-thirds majority needed for ratification (although the treaty was not submitted for ratification anyway, because of the Soviet invasion of Afghanistan).

Thus, politicians of different political stripe have used the strengthened congressional authority to promote their policy preferences, and perhaps their electoral interests, and this has subjected foreign policy to ideological and political pressures from which it had previously been largely exempt. This creates problems of its own and highlights the pervasive dilemma of aggregation. It may be that broader democratic participation in the making of foreign policy is achieved only at the cost of increased difficulty in fashioning a unified, coherent, and credible external posture. Presidential military commitments may or may not be supported by Congress, arms control agreements may or may not be ratified, and foreign aid may or may not be approved. Foreign policy may swing together with lurches in domestic politics, or each branch of government may speak for itself amid rancorous debate and struggles over power. Such a situation could confuse both friend and foe and greatly complicate the management of the nation's international affairs.

The dangers of a foreign policy that reflects the variety of domestic political interests have been recognized. Henry Kissinger, for one, has lamented "the growing tendency of Congress to legislate in detail the day-to-day or week-to-week conduct of our foreign affairs." [28] Of course, congressional assertiveness directly impinged on his authority, so his complaint is scarcely surprising. But criticism of the new balance has been voiced from within Congress as well. For example, Senator Fulbright, who, as we have seen, was a critic of presidential foreign policy behavior during the Vietnam War, nevertheless confessed in 1979 that he had "increasingly serious misgivings about the ability of the Congress to play a constructive role in our foreign relations . . . those of us who prodded what seemed to be a hopelessly immobile herd of cattle [Congress] a decade ago, now stand back in awe in the face of a stampede." [29]

The problems that come from making Congress a full-fledged participant in foreign policy must be taken seriously, but so also must the dangers of an imperious presidency on the Johnson and Nixon models. There is as yet no clear solution to the problem posed by the dual requirement of democracy and firm leadership in a complex and sometimes threatening world. It is very unlikely that either the House or the Senate will revert to the previous degree of acquiescence; the memories of the misuse of presidential power will never entirely fade, and in any case the legislative foundation for increased House and Senate participation in major decisions has been laid. Congress is unlikely to tear down the structure that it has itself created, and most of the institutional controls over foreign policy will probably stay in force. The questions that remain are: How rigidly should Congress try to exercise its newly acquired powers? How willing is the executive branch going to be to tolerate congressionally imposed limitations?

Congressional Flexibility

The limits on the ability of the legislative branch to play a useful foreign policy role have not changed much since the Vietnam War. Congress has taken steps to improve the resources and expertise at its disposal in the area of foreign policy. The 1970s witnessed the expansion of congressional staff and the creation of a variety of institutions, such as the Congressional Budget Office and Office of Technology Assessment, which strengthen the legislature's ability to analyze the policies of the president. Nevertheless, this has only narrowed the knowledge gap between the two branches, not eliminated it. In any case, Congress is a large deliberative body, with a decentralized structure and time-consuming modes of operation, while foreign policy often requires quick decisions and prompt policy adjustments.

The legislative branch seems to recognize the constraints on its role in foreign affairs. It has sought to establish its foreign policy prerogatives but has not felt systematically impelled to exercise them, and it will often give the executive more leeway than law requires it to grant. Indeed, once Congress establishes its ability to influence external policy, it often shies away from the burden of actually doing so. An illustration came in the first real test of the War Powers Act during the U.S. participation in the Lebanese civil war between late 1982 and early 1984. Initially, eight hundred American marines had been dispatched to Beirut as part of a multinational force designed to monitor the fragile peace between Lebanese Muslim and Christian forces; subsequently, this was expanded to twelve hundred troops. Progressively (as is almost always the case), the U.S. role in Lebanon departed from what it started out to be. A politically neutral participation in a multinational peacekeeping force designed to assist national reconciliation evolved into military support of Lebanon's Christian Phalangist and pro-American President Amin Gemayel against Syrian-supported Muslim insurgents. Eventually, this led to the death of more than two hundred U.S. Marines, to an involvement of naval forces, and to direct participation in Lebanon's internal conflict on the government's side. This gave rise to the risk that U.S. forces would collide with the Soviet-backed Syrians, thus creating the specter of a major conflict.

Congress was understandably perturbed. U.S. troops had not been sent to Lebanon under congressional authorization, and they had greatly exceeded the sixty-day stay allowed under the War Powers Act. Congress could therefore have ordered an end to the military presence or cut off the funds that it required. But it did not do so. The Reagan administration vehemently opposed what it deemed congressional meddling in foreign policy, and Secretary of State Shultz even suggested that the War Powers Act was unconstitutional. President Reagan declared that the U.S. military role was "central to our credibility on a global scale," implying that Congress was not capable of placing foreign policy issues in proper perspective. Despite its qualms, Congress did not press the point; it simply authorized an eighteen-month extension of the military presence, thus avoiding a showdown over its prerogatives. The U.S. naval activities that were undertaken in the Persian Gulf in 1987 might also have come under the War Powers Act, but President Reagan thought otherwise and once again Congress refrained from challenging him.

Oversight of the CIA furnishes another example of insistence on establishing a principle coupled with a reticence to fully implement it. The CIA was created by the National Security Act of 1947, and for the first twenty-five years of its existence it was not subject to meaningful congressional oversight; even its budget was secret. But in 1974, revelations of clandestine activities of dubious merit and legality led Congress to include a provision in the foreign aid bill requiring that covert CIA activities be reported to the appropriate congressional committees. This was followed by the creation of a Senate Select Committee on Intelligence in 1976 and a parallel committee in the House a year later. Both committees were given jurisdiction over appropriations for the intelligence community and, hence, the power to check on clandestine activities. But despite these actions, congressional oversight of the CIA seems rather lax. For example, it was reported in 1983 that only two members of the House had bothered to visit the committee's offices in order to examine classified documents regarding intelligence activities and operations that Congress was about to authorize.[30] These apparent congressional inconsistencies may simply be examples of a pragmatic compromise between democratic control and an effective foreign policy.

Executive Recalcitrance

Congress has perhaps shown more adaptive flexibility than has the executive branch. Edwin Meese III, at the time Reagan's chief political adviser, truculently announced in 1985 that "it is the responsibility of the President to conduct foreign policy; limitations on that by Congress are improper as far as I'm concerned." [31] Subsequent events revealed that the administration was indeed willing to flout congressional restrictions on its freedom of action. The most evident example of its attitude was provided by the Iran-contra scandal, which first surfaced in the fall of 1986. The affair contained two major strands. Several Americans had been taken hostage in Lebanon by Muslim extremist groups with connections to Iran. As part of the Reagan administration's efforts to secure their release, an attempt was made to bribe the Iranians to intercede with the hostages' captors. This was done by secretly selling sophisticated weapons to Iran that it could use in the war it was fighting with Iraq. This seemed inconsistent with the public U.S. stance of neutrality in the Iran-Iraq war; it was expressly contrary to the administration's own policy of refusing to bargain with terrorists or to supply weapons to nations that support terrorism; and it was apparently a violation of the Arms Export Control Act.

In addition, a small group of people in the CIA and the National Security Council secretly decided to use the proceeds from the sale of weapons to Iran to finance military support for the Nicaraguan contras. This clearly violated the requirement that covert activities be reported to the congressional intelligence committees, and it appeared to be a violation of the Boland amendment as well. Plainly, the executive branch was showing no inclination to let congressional restrictions stand in the way of pursuing its foreign policies. Outright illegalities, however, may have been the exception, and it is possible that, as a result of the congressional hearings and prosecutions growing out of the Iran-contra affair, subsequent administrations may refrain from breaking the law, even if they continue testing the limits of congressional forbearance. (The affair and its implications will be discussed further in Chapter 5.)

The search for an equilibrium between the legislative and executive branches will undoubtedly continue. Wherever it may lie, it must contain certain elements. Democratic theory requires that Congress participate in charting the nation's course in international relations. Congress must keep policy within bounds that reflect an informed national consensus, and to do so, it must be prepared to challenge the executive when it deems that policy has departed from the guidelines it has laid down. But Congress cannot exercise detailed supervision of foreign affairs, for that demands a flexibility, a promptness, and a submerging of domestic political differences for which it is institutionally ill-suited. As long as Congress sketches the contours of national goals and sets overall limits on what the president can and cannot do, the actual implementation and day-to-day management of foreign relations must remain the responsibility of the executive if the United States is to behave in a consistent and purposive fashion in international affairs. This assumes that the executive branch itself is capable of acting in a consistent and purposive manner, and this is a question that the next chapter will examine.

Appendix: Milestones in
Congressional Foreign Policy Activism

1969   National commitments resolution: Requires that foreign commitments be based on "affirmative action" taken by both the executive and the legislative branches

1971   Repeal of Gulf of Tonkin resolution: Rescinded the authority given to President Johnson to pursue the war in Vietnam

1972   Case Act: Requires that the executive branch inform Congress, within sixty days, of executive agreements reached with other nations

1973   War Powers Act: Obligates the president to consult with Congress if military forces have been sent to region where hostilities appear imminent; unless Congress authorizes otherwise, troops are to be brought home within sixty (in special cases, ninety) days

1974   Foreign Assistance Act: Requires that the president "substantially reduce or terminate" aid to governments that systematically violate human rights

   Hughes-Ryan amendment to Foreign Assistance Act: Requires that covert operations abroad be reported to the "appropriate committees of the Congress"

1976   Foreign Assistance Act: Strengthens the human rights provisions of the 1974 Foreign Assistance Act

   Clark amendment: Bars use of funds for direct or indirect military participation in the Angolan conflict

   Arms Export Control Act: Gives Congress thirty days within which it may disallow major foreign military sales

   Creation of Senate Select Committee on Intelligence: Conducts Senate oversight of U.S. covert activities abroad

1977   Creation of House Permanent Select Committee on Intelligence: Conducts House oversight of U.S. covert activities abroad

   Human rights provision of Agricultural Trade Development Assistance Act: Denies assistance to countries that engage in human rights abuses and requires the executive branch to report on the status of human rights in countries receiving U.S. aid (in 1979 the reporting requirement was extended to all nations)

1982   Boland amendment to the 1983 intelligence authorization bill: Prohibits support for military activities designed to overthrow the government of Nicaragua

Notes

1. The expression was first used in Edwin S. Corwin, *The President: Office and Powers* (New York: New York University Press, 1940), 200. It is also the title of a current book on Congress and foreign policy: Cecil V. Crabb, Jr., and Pat M. Holt, *Invitation to Struggle: Congress, the President and Foreign Policy*, 2d ed. (Washington, D.C.: CQ Press, 1984).
2. See the *Prize* cases, 67 U.S. (2 Black) 635 (1863).
3. Crabb and Holt, *Invitation to Struggle*, 55.
4. James A. Robinson, *Congress and Foreign Policy*, rev. ed. (Homewood, Ill.: Dorsey, 1967), chap. 2.
5. See James L. Sundquist, *The Decline and Resurgence of Congress* (Washington, D.C.: Brookings Institution, 1981).
6. Congressional Research Service, *Treaties and Other International Agreements: The Role of the United States Senate* (Washington, D.C.: Congressional Research Service, 1984), 117.
7. Thomas M. Franck and Edward Weisband, *Foreign Policy by Congress* (New York: Oxford University Press, 1979), 141.
8. Crabb and Holt, *Invitation to Struggle*, 17.
9. The precise numbers vary from author to author. See Louis Henkin, *Foreign Affairs and the Constitution* (New York: W. W. Norton, 1972), 53, 306 n. 43.
10. Harry S Truman, *Memoirs: Years of Trial and Hope* (Garden City, N.Y.: Doubleday, 1956), 333.
11. Dean Acheson, *Present at the Creation: My Years in the State Department* (New York: W. W. Norton, 1969), 409.
12. Ibid., 413.
13. Dwight D. Eisenhower, *Mandate for Change* (Garden City, N.Y.: Doubleday, 1963), 333.
14. Anthony Austin, *The President's War* (Philadelphia: J. B. Lippincott, 1971), 182-183.
15. Tom Wicker, *J. F. K. and L. B. J.: The Influence of Personality upon Politics* (Baltimore: Penguin, 1972), 224-225.
16. Robert A. Dahl, *Congress and Foreign Policy* (New Haven: Yale University Press, 1950), 10.
17. Bernard A. Weisberger, *Cold War, Cold Peace: The United States and Russia since 1945* (New York: Houghton Mifflin, 1984), 233.
18. Quoted in Walter LaFeber, *America, Russia, and the Cold War: 1945-1984*, 5th ed. (New York: Alfred A. Knopf, 1985), 264.
19. Weisberger, *Cold War, Cold Peace*, 246.
20. See William Shawcross, *Sideshow: Kissinger, Nixon, and the Destruction of Cambodia* (New York: Pocket Books, 1979).
21. House of Representatives, 93d Cong., 1st sess., 1973, H. Doc. 93-171.

22. See Andrew J. Pierre, *The Global Politics of Arms Sales* (Princeton, N.J.: Princeton University Press, 1982).

23. Speech before the Foreign Policy Association, August 1976.

24. P.L. 93-559, sec. 46.

25. Quoted in Russell Watson, "How America Can Help," *Newsweek*, February 14, 1983, 55.

26. The Lefevre controversy is described in House Committee on Foreign Affairs, *Congress and Foreign Policy*, Committee Print, 1982.

27. Quoted in Walter Lacqueur, "The Issue of Human Rights," in Barry Rubin and Elizabeth P. Spiro, eds., *Human Rights and U.S. Foreign Policy* (Boulder, Colo.: Westview, 1979), 51.

28. Quoted in I. M. Destler, Leslie H. Gelb, and Anthony Lake, *Our Own Worst Enemy: The Unmaking of American Foreign Policy* (New York: Simon and Schuster, 1984), 156.

29. J. William Fulbright, "The Legislator as Educator," *Foreign Affairs* 57 (Spring 1979): 723-727.

30. *New York Times*, October 19, 1983.

31. Ibid., January 25, 1985.

c h a p t e r   f i v e

The Presidency
and the Bureaucracy

IT IS PROBABLY clear by now that most of the power to shape and manage U.S. external affairs is vested in the executive branch of government, headed by the president. Public opinion has proven to be a secondary force; the average citizen has neither the inclination nor the information needed to mold most foreign policy decisions, and, though public tolerance does define the limits of what the government can do, these boundaries are usually fairly broad and fluid. Congress is in a better position to influence the direction of foreign policy, but its role is limited by its own nature and by the character of international affairs; despite recent changes, it is incapable of doing more than patrolling the outer frontiers of foreign policy. Thus, most foreign policy problems are left to the judgment and responsibility of the president and his administration.

The executive branch is itself not a uniform organism. In particular, it is important to distinguish between the *presidency* and the *federal bureaucracy*. There are similarities and overlap between the two, but the dissimilarities are significant as well. The presidency is composed of, in addition to the president himself, the people and institutions that immediately surround him, communicate with him, and bear directly on the performance of his duties. The bureaucracy is that complex structure of departments and agencies that administer specific categories of policy and are, partially at least, independent of the president. Both segments of the executive branch influence foreign policy, and both will be discussed in this chapter, but it is important to understand the differences in their nature and structure.

Presidential style and policy are very much shaped by the pressures of electoral politics. The president has won his position in an electoral struggle and may, if in his first term, face another such struggle. His claim to office is rooted in a set of policy goals and personal skills by which he has distinguished himself from other aspirants to the nation's highest political office. As Lincoln Bloomfield observes, "One tries out for the part by showing or demonstrating, not that one can administer a huge government, but that one can win an election (plus dozens of state primaries beforehand)." [1] Few presidents have had much experience in foreign affairs, yet since a president's tenure is constitutionally limited to eight years, he must put his imprint on policy rather quickly in order to ensure a meaningful place in history. The presidency is of necessity a combination of ideology and pragmatism, of commitment and personal ambition, of rush and reflection.

By contrast, the federal bureaucracy is an established, routinized, highly structured, and rather plodding set of institutions, decision-making mechanisms, and people. It is conscious of its relative permanence and of the fact that most of its components will be around long after the current president has left office. It is not buffeted by political winds as much as is the presidency, if only because most of those who occupy bureaucratic positions enjoy civil service status and therefore retain their positions when the administration changes. Few major initiatives originate from within the bureaucracy, but it is charged with implementing and managing the policies that are formulated by the presidency and Congress—which places it in a good position to block activities of which it disapproves.

The major interface between the presidency and the bureaucracy is provided by the political appointees who head the various governmental departments and agencies and by their principal deputies. They are chosen by the president and thus reflect his philosophies and policy preferences. But at the same time, they are part of the bureaucratic organizations that they head, and they come to identify with the interests and ways of doing things that characterize their organizations. Occasionally, the head of an executive department will be subject to conflicting influences because of this dual position. For example, if the president wishes to decrease defense spending or abandon a major weapons system that had previously been contemplated, his secretary of defense might be torn between loyalty to the president and the interests of the Department of Defense in opposing the reduction.

The Chief Executive

The French king, Louis XIV, once proclaimed, "I am the State!" *(l'état, c'est moi)*. A U.S. president could not go that far, but he could at least justifiably declare, "I am its symbol!" No person as powerfully connotes the United States as does the president. [2] This is true both at home and abroad. When Iranian demonstrators wished to flaunt their scorn for the United States while hostages were being held in the U.S. embassy in Teheran in 1979 and 1980, they brandished posters ridiculing President Jimmy Carter. When demonstrators in many foreign countries attacked U.S. involvement in Vietnam during the 1960s, their denunciations were as often directed against President Lyndon B. Johnson as against the United States. Americans, too, tend to identify the president with the nation and, separation of powers notwithstanding, see him at its political pinnacle. Children, subject to political socialization yet with less capacity for coyness than adults, provide a simplified yet distilled representation of the general public and its perceptions. Their image of the president is that of a benevolent and important leader, whereas members of Congress are viewed as merely "the President's helpers" who are appointed by him.[3] For most adults, whether they agree with the president or not, he *is*, in many important ways, the United States.

But the president is far more than a symbol. He is the nation's chief executive, and so he commands enormous formal and informal resources for the conduct of policy. Often, he wields these resources more effectively in external than in internal affairs.[4] Since the emergence of the United States from isolationism after World War II, its presidents have usually relished playing a major role on the international stage. The drama and impact of the issues they confront abroad is often more heady than the matters they must deal with at home—fighting "for freedom and against oppression" or establishing a "generation of peace" versus, say, arguing for agricultural price supports. Moreover, particularly before Vietnam, they could usually be assured of domestic support for foreign policy and could seek a place in history unfettered by the squabbles that so often accompany domestic politics.

As we saw in Chapter 4, the Constitution confers on the president the authority to make treaties with foreign nations (though these must be ratified by the Senate) and names him as commander in chief of the armed forces (which has sometimes been interpreted as giving him the power to commit the country to war without the approval of the legislative branch). It also authorizes him to appoint (again subject to the Senate's approval) the heads of the executive departments and agencies within the foreign policy establishment, as well as their principal deputies. But the constitutional provision that does the most to give him the ability to shape foreign policy is the one that vests in him "the executive power" of the national government (Article II, section 1). This power, as chief executive, has been further enhanced by the nature of international affairs in the nuclear age.[5] From one perspective, the president's role in foreign affairs can be viewed negatively: his power comes to him by default, because of the unwillingness or inability of the public and Congress to seriously challenge it. But it can also be explained in positive terms: by the resources at his disposal by virtue of his position as chief executive.

To begin with, the wide variety of powers and prerogatives of his office give the president many carrots to wave and many sticks to wield when seeking endorsement for the foreign policies he wishes to pursue. He can provide payoffs to political allies and, in various ways, punish opponents. When Sen. Frank Church (D-Idaho) argued with President Johnson in favor of a negotiated settlement rather than a military solution to the war in Vietnam, and cited the political columnist Walter Lippmann as being on his side, Johnson glared at him and said, "The next time you want a dam in Idaho, you just go to Walter Lippmann for it." [6]

The president is also well placed to persuade the nation of the desirability of his policies.[7] He enjoys the constant attention of the media and can use it, as well as the respect which his office attracts, to appeal directly to the public for support when his policies are opposed by others in the government. Often, his visibility and popularity enable him to bend Congress to his will by arousing public support for his views. Given President Ronald Reagan's talent as a "great communicator," he has been particularly prone to go over Congress's head by appealing directly to the public when his programs seem threatened by legislative resistance. There are, however, limits to the effectiveness of this tactic. Even President Reagan had difficulty convincing Congress to appropriate aid for the Nicaraguan contras, despite appeals to the public in which the contras were hailed as "our brothers," comparable in their qualities to the Founding Fathers, and despite pleas not to "walk away from one of the greatest moral challenges in postwar history" and not to sink to the depths of a "shameful surrender." Nevertheless, a president does have great resources close at hand, and quite frequently they do work.

Finally, the fact that the president is chief executive means not only that he appoints the heads of all executive departments and agencies, but also that they report to him. Since, as we have seen, so much information, expertise, and other resources are concentrated in these organizations, the president is plainly in an excellent position to make and implement foreign policy decisions. Again, however, matters are not that simple and it often turns out that the components of the executive branch are not as responsive to the presidential will as one might think.

The Major Institutions

There are many institutions within the executive branch whose functions in some way touch on foreign affairs. In fact, one could reasonably claim that most executive agencies, directly or indirectly, have responsibilities that are affected by the behavior of foreign nations or whose own decisions have ramifications abroad. The Treasury Department and the Commerce Department are obviously concerned with matters of international trade. The Postal Service is involved in the international flow of mail, and the Environmental Protection Agency has to recognize that pollution is not always confined within national borders. Even the American Battle Monuments Commission has an overseas staff, since it maintains monuments and cemeteries where U.S. citizens are buried. However, most of these agencies engage in routine operations that rarely produce visible ripples in international politics, while our interest is in those institutions that participate in shaping the major elements of U.S. foreign policy, and these are not very numerous. Some are properly considered part of the presidency, others part of the federal bureaucracy. Most specialize in wielding one of the foreign policy instruments identified in Chapter 1.

The Department of State

The executive department with primary formal responsibility for the nation's foreign affairs is the Department of State. Its major function is diplomacy. One of the first acts of Congress following ratification of the Constitution in 1788 was to create the State Department (originally called the Department of Foreign Affairs), and its first head was Thomas Jefferson. It was not a very impressive organization at the outset: Jefferson started with only four clerks, one part-time translator, and one messenger, and there were just two permanent U.S. missions abroad. Today, the Department of State has some twenty-three thousand employees and operates diplomatic missions in over one hundred thirty countries. It is headed by the secretary of state, who is regarded as the senior cabinet member. He is assisted by a deputy secretary, four undersecretaries (for political affairs; economic affairs; security assistance, science, and technology; and management), and several assistant secretaries.

A particular feature of the Department of State's organization is that responsibility is structured along both *geographic* and *functional* lines (see Figure 5-1). For example, there is an assistant secretary for each major region of the world (Europe, Africa, and so on) and one for each special area of policy (human rights and humanitarian affairs, economic and business affairs, and so on). This means that each issue comes, in principle, within the purview of two parts of the department and is seen from two perspectives. Another important unit in the department is the Bureau of Politico-Military Affairs, which was established to provide it with its own analyses of military issues—a crucial need, since military policy and diplomacy are often closely related, and State would not want to be entirely dependent on the Pentagon's assessments.

As noted in Chapter 4, three specialized agencies are also attached to the Department of State. The Agency for International Development (AID) was established in 1961; it dispenses foreign economic assistance, and in some cases "security support assistance" (designed to strengthen internal security forces), to certain developing nations. (AID is nominally an arm of the International Development Cooperation Agency, but this parent body has few other significant functions.) The Arms Control and Disarmament Agency (ACDA), which was also created in 1961, studies matters concerning arms control policy and assists in arms control negotiations. The United States Information Agency (USIA—known overseas as the U.S. Information Service) is essentially the nation's propaganda unit; it administers the Voice of America radio stations, which broadcast primarily to the Soviet bloc, and it arranges cultural exchange programs, exhibits in foreign countries, and lectures abroad by prominent Americans.

Figure 5-1 Organization of the Department of State

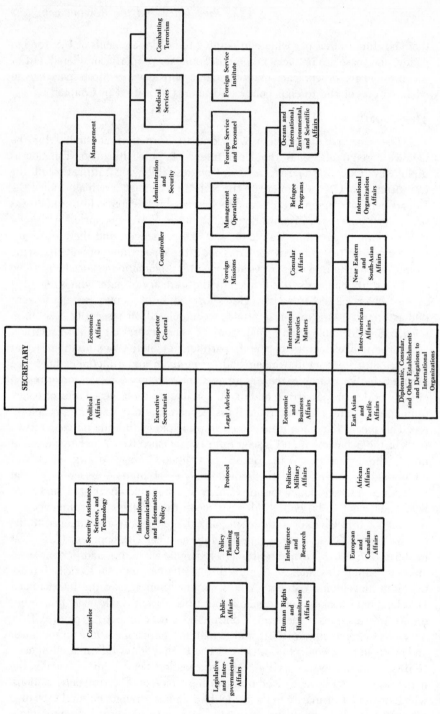

Source: *Washington Information Directory, 1987-1988* (Washington, D.C.: Congressional Quarterly, 1987), 366.

The highest officials in the department are political appointees, but most of the important career positions are filled by Foreign Service Officers (FSOs), an elite corps of professional diplomats. The FSOs are divided into three categories of functional specialization: political affairs, economic affairs, and consular affairs. They constitute the greatest repository of expertise on foreign nations and international affairs in the U.S. government. Former secretary of state Henry Kissinger has said that the Department of State is "staffed by probably the ablest and most professional group of men and women in public service. They are intelligent, competent, loyal, and hardworking." [8]

Nevertheless, the personnel of the department have on occasion been subject to severe criticism. The most damaging of these episodes came in the late 1940s and early 1950s, when the loyalty of State Department officials was impugned by Sen. Joseph McCarthy. FSOs who had warned of corruption in the government of China and the domestic unpopularity of its leader, Chiang Kai-shek, and who predicted the victory of Mao Zedong revolutionary forces, were forced out of government service. In 1948, Whittaker Chambers, a self-confessed former Communist, testified before the House Un-American Activities Committee that Communists had infiltrated the State Department. In 1950, McCarthy made the absurd claim that "I have here in my hand a list of two hundred and five that were known to the Secretary of State as being members of the Communist Party and who, nevertheless, are still working and shaping policy in the State Department." [9] Although McCarthy never produced this alleged list, right-wing politicians sought to capitalize on the climate of distrust that was thereby created. Sen. Robert Taft (R-Ohio), campaigning for the Republican presidential nomination in 1952, castigated "the pro-communist group in the State Department who surrendered to every demand of Russia at Yalta and Potsdam, and promoted at every opportunity the communist cause in China." [10] Although such charges were later determined to be unfounded by a Senate committee, and the Senate ultimately censured Senator McCarthy, the accusations and witch hunts undermined the Department of State's morale and probably did much to inhibit boldness in policy recommendations and analysis. As a group of former U.S. diplomats put it, "A premium has been put upon reporting and upon recommendations which are ambiguously stated or so cautiously stated as to be deceiving." [11]

The character of international relations has served to downgrade the State Department's importance in the postwar period. Before the United States entered the international arena as a power with global interests, confronted by a powerful rival who some thought was bent on its destruction, diplomacy was generally considered a sufficient instrument of foreign policy. But as the Cold War developed, the role of military and subversive instruments rose in importance, and as diplomacy lost the dominant position it had once occupied, the influence of the State Department declined.

Finally, State has often lacked support from presidents who felt that its bureaucratic slowness and deliberate caution made it too sluggish an instrument for dealing with pressing issues. President Franklin Roosevelt, it is reported, complained that "dealing with the State Department is like watching an elephant become pregnant; everything's done on a very high level, there's a lot of commotion, and it takes twenty-two months for anything to happen." [12] For its part, State Department officials have sometimes felt that presidents are unreasonable in supposing that international problems are amenable to quick and simple solutions—that, indeed, presidential attitudes and lack of understanding make their task all the more difficult and thankless. For example, President Kennedy, who often sought to bypass the Department of State— because, he said, according to the department "the risks have always outweighed the opportunities" [13]—once asked Charles E. Bohlen, a veteran U.S. diplomat, "What is wrong with that God-damned department of yours?" Bohlen replied very frankly: "Mr. President . . . one one of the reasons, of course, is that foreign affairs is an extremely complex question. I do not have to tell you this, but you cannot give answers off the top of your head and quick ready-made solutions. . . . In regard to the department as a whole, the fault is yours." [14]

Of course, prudence and reflection may often be precisely what foreign policy most requires, but, as already pointed out, the nature of presidential politics is such that quickness and boldness are often thought preferable to sober caution. The State Department may represent an anchor to international reality, but domestic politics often dictates its moorings.

The Department of Defense

While the major function of State is diplomacy, that of the Department of Defense (DoD) is coercion. It is entrusted with the task of organizing the nation's capabilities for defense, deterrence, and compellence. DoD is a relatively new department. Until 1947, the army and the navy were separate cabinet departments and had independent command structures and programs of weapon procurement, leading to much duplication of effort and making it difficult to integrate defense planning. As the gravity of the U.S.-Soviet rivalry became evident, a reform of the military services was deemed necessary. Under the National Security Act of 1947, a single Department of Defense was established, which went part way toward unifying the services under a single cabinet secretary and the Joint Chiefs of Staff.

The secretary of defense—who, like other cabinet officers, is appointed by the president and confirmed by the Senate—is one of the president's main advisers on military and defense matters and administers one of the largest bureaucracies in the world, employing nearly 90,000 people, exclusive of members of the armed forces (see Figure 5-2). Because of the fear that a completely unified military organization could threaten the primacy of civilian authority, the three armed services were retained as separate departments within the DoD—the Department of the Army, the Department of the Navy (which includes the Marine Corps), and the Department of the Air Force—

Figure 5-2 Organization of the Department of Defense

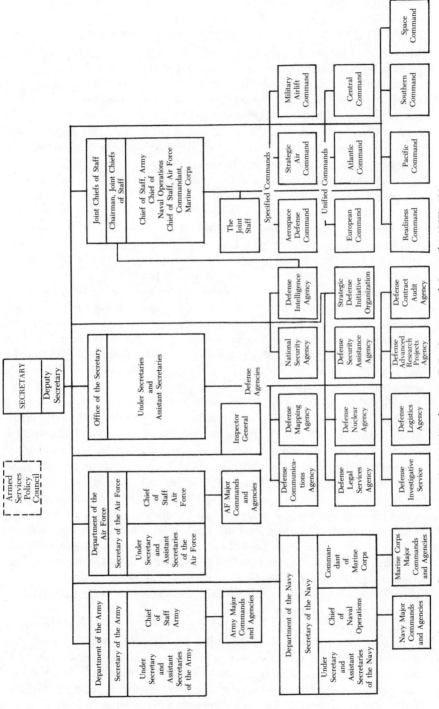

Source: *Washington Information Directory, 1987-1988* (Washington, D.C.: Congressional Quarterly, 1987), 436.

each headed by a secretary (though these heads are not cabinet members). Each service has its chief of staff, a military officer who is responsible for providing operational direction to his service and who is the military adviser to the service's civilian secretary. The chiefs of staff meet collectively as the Joint Chiefs of Staff (JCS), which is headed by a chairman, a high-ranking officer of one of the services who is appointed by the president and confirmed by the Senate. The JCS functions as the nation's principal military planning body and provides strategic and operational advice to the president, the National Security Council (NSC), and the secretary of defense.

DoD thus has a civilian side and a military side, which have, on the whole, coexisted fairly well. The major task of the civilian side is to plan for and administer the financial resources needed to ensure the military's ability to accomplish its functions. The major task of the military side is to develop operational plans for the use of armed force. The principle of ultimate civilian authority over the military has always been accepted, and largely for this reason the law requires that the secretary of defense be a civilian.[15]

One unit in the Pentagon that is especially relevant to foreign policy is the Office of International Security Affairs (ISA), which is headed by an assistant secretary of defense. As already mentioned, its main task is to analyze the foreign policy matters that are related to DoD's functions. Like the State Department, it is organized along both geographical and functional lines, and it has at times been a significant source of foreign policy initiatives. It has been described as "a lean and adaptable body that can be galvanized into bureaucratic shock troops by a Defense Secretary who wants to play a major role in formulating American foreign policy."[16] ISA is the DoD's counterpart to the Bureau of Politico-Military Affairs in the State Department, and like that bureau, it reflects the interdependence of foreign policy and military policy, neither of which can be effectively dealt with by entirely separate institutions.

The scope of military activity and the size and reach of the Pentagon in relation to foreign policy are occasionally a source of controversy. It is sometimes argued that the military's role in foreign policy is not compatible with the principle of civilian control—that the military tail comes to wag the civilian dog by virtue of its control over the instruments of coercion. On the other hand, it cannot be expected that the nature of these instruments will be irrelevant to the determination of the ends to which the instruments will be applied.[17] A related concern is that too strong a military influence in external affairs might lead to a distorted and even dangerous foreign policy. Because the military establishment is often thought to be best equipped to gauge the gravity of foreign threats to the United States, it is usually called upon to provide such assessments. Yet the military's own organizational interests lead it to try to maximize its missions, its hardware, and its budgetary resources—which in turn may predispose it to provide the most menacing assessments of the capabilities and intentions of potential rivals, leading to an overly paranoid and militaristic foreign policy.

Moreover, if military solutions come to dominate foreign policy, the result may be that policy will become both less effective and more dangerous. Its effectiveness may be reduced by neglect of the social, political, and economic roots of turmoil in many parts of the world, which cannot be dealt with by military force. Its perilous side may be increased because even modest military involvements abroad often carry substantial costs in lives and because there is never a guarantee against further escalation once hostilities are initiated.

Other criticisms of the military establishment spring from apprehension about its role within American society. For example, because of the enormous expenditures and procurement programs administered by the Pentagon, the military has become a major force in the U.S. economy. Consequently, a major reduction in military activity might be very hard to achieve, even if it were compatible with national security, because of the immediate economic consequences that could follow, in the form of unemployment or even recession. It is also feared that the foundations of a free-market economy may be weakened when so much production is oriented toward the needs of the military establishment, and is therefore governmentally administered and relatively noncompetitive.[18]

The Intelligence Community

Virtually every nation, and certainly every major power, has one or more intelligence organizations within its governmental structure. The need to acquire information about other nations' intentions and capabilities and the fact that some of those nations are rivals or adversaries means that the information must sometimes be gathered by clandestine methods. Both the United States and the Soviet Union have invested considerable resources in creating a powerful national intelligence capacity. The major Soviet intelligence organization is the KGB, which combines the functions of domestic secret police and counterintelligence with foreign espionage and subversive operations. The intelligence community in the United States is said to employ at least 150,000 people and to involve the expenditure of billions of dollars. Its foremost and by far most notorious member is the Central Intelligence Agency (CIA).

The CIA is the successor to the Office of Strategic Services (OSS), which was created during World War II to collect military and political intelligence in support of the war effort and to undertake covert political operations and sabotage activities behind enemy lines. With the end of the war, the OSS was disbanded, but its core became the Central Intelligence Agency, which, like the DOD and NSC, was established by the 1947 National Security Act. Officially, its principal functions are to collect, correlate, and evaluate intelligence data and to advise the NSC on intelligence matters concerning national security. It is also mandated to coordinate the collection and evaluation of intelligence by other departments and agencies and to perform vaguely defined "other" functions requested of it by the NSC. This last duty has been interpreted to mean covert subversive operations against foreign governments. The agency was barely six years old when it organized the overthrow of Prime Minister Mohammed Mossadegh in Iran, and at age seven it did the same to the Arbenz government in Guatemala. Between 1962 and 1970, more than half of its budget and personnel were devoted to covert operations;[19] in the 1970s, such activities accounted for nearly 40 percent of its budget.[20]

Still, the principal function of the agency remains the collection and evaluation of information about the capacities, intentions, and political conditions of foreign countries, particularly those that are considered hostile. This does not necessarily involve spying or sophisticated electronic eavesdropping. Perhaps the bulk of foreign intelligence information is acquired through public sources (for example, foreign newspapers); but the most sensitive information usually does require clandestine collection. Some of this bears on a country's military capacity, but much of it concerns its political and economic conditions—how stable the government is, whether there are major disaffected groups, how its foreign policy is evolving, and so forth. The CIA has had its successes in this mission, but it has also had some embarrassing failures. It did not foresee the downfall of the Shah of Iran—a major U.S. ally in a volatile and geostrategically important part of the world—and it wrongly assured President Kennedy in 1961 that the invasion of Cuba by CIA-organized Cuban emigres was militarily feasible and would meet with widespread popular support with Cuba. In fact, no Cubans flocked to the invaders' side, Castro's forces handily fought off the invaders, and the enterprise ended in fiasco.

Unlike the KGB, the CIA officially does not engage in domestic counterintelligence activity, the task of combatting foreign espionage in its own country. By law, this is the responsibility of the Federal Bureau of Investigation (FBI). In fact, the CIA is barred by its charter from engaging in domestic surveillance. Consequently, it came as a shock to many people to learn that the agency had been doing just that in the 1960s and 1970s—for example, in Operation Chaos, directed against domestic opponents of the Vietnam War and other political dissidents. Several organizational changes and new regulations were instituted to ensure against future abuses. As mentioned in Chapter 4, some congressional oversight of CIA activities has also been introduced, and new executive controls have been established as well. In 1976, President Gerald R. Ford issued an executive order limiting CIA intrusions into the lives of American citizens, and in 1978 President Jimmy Carter reinforced NSC control over sensitive intelligence collection procedures. A three-person Intelligence Oversight Board has also been established to verify the legality of intelligence activities. Although President Reagan has sought to loosen some of the constraints on CIA operations, it no longer has the freedom of action it enjoyed earlier.

The CIA is not the only member of the intelligence community. In fact, DoD has more people working in this area than does the CIA. The largest intelligence organization in the country is the ultrasecret National Security Agency

(NSA), which is located within DoD and seems to have resources that exceed those of the CIA.[21] Housed in Fort Meade, Maryland, the NSA (not to be confused with the NSC) apparently has two primary functions. The first involves cryptology, the making and breaking of secret communications codes. National security often requires that communications be concealed from foreign knowledge and, conversely, that efforts by other countries to do the same be outwitted. Presumably, every nation has an organization for this purpose, but probably none has resources comparable to those of the United States; for example, the NSA is said to have the most elaborate system of computers in the world. Its second function is that of electronic surveillance—that is, eavesdropping on the overt electronic communications (such as telephone and telegraph) of other nations.

Each of the military services has its own intelligence unit, which gathers information pertaining to the needs of that particular service, and the Pentagon's Defense Intelligence Agency (DIA) was created in 1961 to integrate their work. The DIA does not do much intelligence gathering itself; rather, it evaluates the data provided by the separate services in order to obtain intelligence estimates of value to DoD as a whole. The State Department also has an intelligence unit, the Bureau of Intelligence and Research (which is generally known by the initials INR). Like the DIA, INR does not itself gather raw intelligence data but analyzes and evaluates the stream of information from U.S. embassies and other diplomatic missions abroad.

Thus, the intelligence community is large and far-flung, and some coordination of its numerous activities is necessary. One way this is achieved is by having the head of the CIA, acting in the capacity of director of central intelligence (DCI), coordinate the foreign intelligence activities of all the agencies that engage in such work. The DCI also chairs a National Foreign Intelligence Board, a management group that formulates the official position of the U.S. intelligence community on the capacities and vulnerabilities of foreign countries.

Obviously, the existence of a vast and powerful network of organizations engaged in covert operations and using clandestine methods is potentially incompatible with democratic principles. Much of their work is done in secret, whereas democracy demands public accountability of government and hence public disclosure of information. As two former high officials of the CIA have themselves pointed out, "The secret work of intelligence agencies inherently conflicts with the idea of openness; such secrecy can easily undermine individual rights in the name of protecting them." [22] Thus, there may be an inevitable tension between national security and democracy. While each president has sought to achieve the proper balance between these values, they have been differently weighted by different administrations: from Carter's determination to avoid improper CIA intrusions into American life to Reagan's readiness to unshackle its domestic operations in order to pursue the U.S.-Soviet rivalry more effectively. There always remains the possibility, however, that the very ideals that the intelligence community is supposed to protect can be eroded by their efforts and activities, and this is another instance of the overall dilemma of aggregation.

The Executive Office of the President

The State Department and the Department of Defense are parts of the federal bureaucracy, and they are large institutions, with their own history, institutional routines, and established perspectives. While they are responsive to presidential policy, they also have their own organizational interests, and when these interests collide with official policy, it is not always the policy that prevails. Often, in fact, presidents have bemoaned their inability to prod the bureaucracy into doing what they want it to do. As President Richard Nixon once exploded, when one of his instructions was ignored, "Well God damn it, I'd told them two weeks ago not to put this out. See, [White House Chief of Staff Alexander] Haig didn't follow up on it. Nobody follows up on a God damn thing." [23] Similar outbursts by other presidents have probably gone unrecorded. Because the bureaucracy is not always as tractable as they want it to be, presidents have tended to surround themselves with institutions within the presidency itself, to which a number of functions have progressively been transferred. The organizational framework for the president's own bureaucracy is the Executive Office of the President (EOP), which employs some sixteen thousand people.

The EOP includes a number of agencies that perform general management and coordinating functions for the executive branch (see Figure 5-3). The unit with the most direct contact with the president is the White House Office, composed of his immediate advisers and staff: various special assistants, political counselors, the press secretary, the chief of staff, and others who, for the most part, have offices in the west wing of the White House, which is also where the president's office (the Oval Office) is located. By virtue of their proximity, many of these people have the president's ear and some of them play a role in shaping foreign policy. For example, Hamilton Jordan, President Carter's chief of staff, was involved in behind-the-scenes negotiations concerning the Panama Canal treaty and the U.S. hostages held in Iran.

No unit within the EOP has a more continuous foreign policy role than the National Security Council (NSC). Like the DoD, the NSC was created by the National Security Act of 1947,[24] and it has four statutory members: the president, the vice president, the secretary of state, and the secretary of defense. The director of central intelligence and the chairman of the Joint Chiefs of Staff are not statutory members but regularly participate in its meetings, as does the president's special assistant for national security affairs. In addition, the president can invite other cabinet members and national leaders to attend NSC meetings.

The purpose of the NSC is to "advise the President with respect to the integration of domestic, foreign, and military policies relating to national

Figure 5-3 Organization of the Executive Office of the President

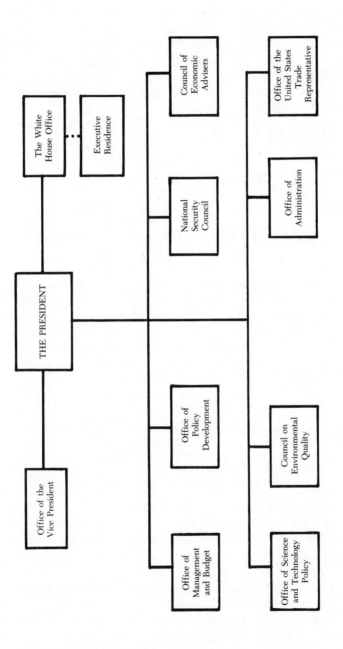

Source: The United States Government Manual, 1984-1985 (Washington, D.C.: U.S. Government Printing Office, 1987), 822.

security." In other words, its primary function is to coordinate the various strands of national policy which bear on national security and the use of military power. It thus hovers over and cuts across several bureaucratic organizations, but it is an advisory body, and the president is free to decide how much or how little he wishes to use it. Presidents Eisenhower and Nixon made ample use of the NSC; Presidents Johnson and Reagan relied on it considerably less. On balance, the NSC has not been a major force in the making of foreign policy, even though certain of its members have individually been very influential.

The NSC has a staff, which is headed by the special assistant for national security affairs, usually known as the national security adviser. Its members are specialists in various geographical regions and in functional areas such as arms control and international economic affairs. While the State Department is principally staffed by career civil servants, the NSC staff's composition is more varied. Besides civil servants, it includes military officers, academic experts on foreign policy issues, and others whom the president and his national security adviser trust and respect. It is a much leaner institution than either DoD or the State Department: during the Kennedy presidency, the staff had as few as ten or fifteen members; under President Nixon, it expanded to about fifty and under President Carter to about seventy, but it has been reduced in the Reagan administration. The NSC staff serves as a clearinghouse for information and policy proposals emanating from various federal agencies, but it is also a source of foreign policy expertise which, unlike the federal bureaucracy, is immediately responsive to the president. It is thus far more powerful than its size would suggest, and it has acquired an institutional personality of its own, acting, as two observers have put it, "as a minidepartment."

> In theory, the assistant to the President for national security affairs and his staff are only a neutral link between the departments and agencies involved in the national security process and the President, transmitting their recommendations, summarizing their disagreements, and, where appropriate, transmitting back the President's instructions. On actual practice, the staff often acts as a minidepartment of its own, participating actively in interdepartmental working groups, and pressing its own views on foreign policy.[25]

Unlike civil servants, national security advisers have a personal and exclusive loyalty to the president, and unique among high-ranking officials, they are not subject to confirmation by the Senate. For this reason, and also because they meet with the president on a regular basis and have access to a wide range of intelligence information, they often exert a major influence on foreign policy. President Kennedy seems to have relied more on the advice of McGeorge Bundy, his national security adviser, than on that of Dean Rusk, his secretary of state, in his conduct of foreign policy. Similarly, in the Carter administration, National Security Adviser Zbigniew Brzezinski soon displaced Cyrus Vance, the self-effacing secretary of state, from his initially preeminent position in formulating foreign policy. Perhaps the single most powerful figure in the postwar diplomacy of the United States was Henry Kissinger, a former professor of government at Harvard University who served as national security adviser to Presidents Nixon and Ford. He was instrumental in initiating diplomatic relations with the People's Republic of China, promoting détente with the Soviet Union, negotiating a cease-fire with North Vietnam (for which he received the Nobel Peace Prize), and achieving a temporary settlement of the Arab-Israeli war of 1973. His strong personality, diplomatic skills, and scholar's understanding of the complexities of international politics gave him exceptional stature. For a time, he was both national security adviser and secretary of state, the only person ever to occupy both those posts simultaneously.

At no time was concern over the foreign policy role of the national security adviser and the NSC staff as acute as it was upon the revelations of the Iran-contra affair during President Reagan's second term in office. With or without the president's knowledge, the national security adviser, John Poindexter, and several members of the NSC staff undertook a plan to sell arms to Iran and to use the proceeds from the sale to provide military equipment to the Nicaraguan contras—clandestine activities that were apparently in violation of the Boland amendment and probably of the Arms Export Control Act as well. Here, the NSC was not merely displacing the State Department; it was virtually conducting its own foreign policy, and an illegal one at that.

Ultimately, however, the power of the national security adviser and the NSC staff is whatever the president decides it will be, and there have been several administrations in which the secretary of state has played the dominant foreign policy role. John Foster Dulles, for example, probably influenced diplomacy during the Eisenhower administration more than did the president himself. More recently, and despite the Iran-contra scandal, George Shultz proved to be a more visible foreign policy presence than President Reagan's several national security advisers. Thus, the president remains the final arbiter of foreign policy power among his chief associates, and the structure of foreign policy decision making is largely of his own making.

Still, it cannot be overlooked that, because the federal bureaucracy is not as pliable as presidents usually wish, institutions have emerged within the presidency itself that rival the traditional organizations of the foreign policy establishment. The relative freedom of one of these institutions, the NSC, from congressional scrutiny has had the effect of reducing executive accountability for external affairs. Although the president is certainly not omnipotent, the process by which foreign policy is made has become more complex, and presidential power has benefited from that fact.

Foreign Policy Making in the Executive Branch

There is no doubt that the president is the most powerful political leader in the United States and one of the strongest heads of government in the West.

Still, his position is not equivalent to that of a traditional monarch or of a modern military dictator. His power is limited by constitutional provisions and by decisions of Congress, the Supreme Court, and the electorate, however modest these limitations sometimes are in practice. What is frequently not realized, however, is the extent to which limits on presidential power come from within the executive branch itself. Presidents may seek ways to circumvent an occasionally intractable bureaucracy, and some do so more successfully than others, but foreign policy making is rarely a matter of the chief executive issuing directives which are then implemented at lower levels of government. As President Harry S Truman observed regarding his successor: "He'll sit there and he'll say, 'Do this! Do that!' and nothing will happen. Poor Ike—it won't be a bit like the Army. He'll find it very frustrating." [26] The president's orders may be executed most of the time, if he makes a point of insisting on it and following up on his subordinates' actions, but this certainly cannot be taken for granted.

Consider the case of President Kennedy during the Cuban missile crisis, which was probably the most perilous moment in the nation's history.[27] Approximately a year and a half before the crisis, Kennedy had ordered that U.S. Jupiter missiles, which were not regarded as useful strategic weapons, be taken out of Turkey, and he instructed the State Department to negotiate their removal. But the Turkish government disliked the idea and State, not wishing to ruffle an ally's feathers, let the matter drop. At the height of the missile crisis, the Soviet Union pointed out that the United States should not complain too strenuously over the Cuban missiles, because the United States itself had missiles near Soviet territory—in Turkey. Upon inquiring, Kennedy discovered that his instructions had been ignored, and his bargaining position in the crisis was, as a consequence, weakened. During the crisis itself, the president ordered a naval blockade of Cuba to prevent the Soviet Union from completing its planned missile deployments. However, he soon realized that the blockade line was so distant from Cuba that it did not give the Soviet Union time to reconsider before its ships would be challenged. Kennedy therefore ordered that the blockade line be drawn closer to Cuba. But the Navy strenuously objected to this change and attempted to ignore the presidential directions. Also, to lessen the likelihood of exacerbating tensions, the president directed that no provocative intelligence operations be undertaken at that time. His orders notwithstanding, a U-2 spy plane penetrated Soviet airspace at a particularly tense moment during the crisis.

These examples are unusual only in that they involve a particularly dramatic moment in the nation's history and are, as a result, more frequently cited than others. But the general inference is clear: although nominally the head of the executive branch, the president only imperfectly controls the individuals and agencies that comprise it. Some presidents regard their situation philosophically; others are more bitterly resentful of bureaucratic recalcitrance. President Nixon, who felt that the civil service was packed with

Democrats appointed by Kennedy and Johnson and fundamentally hostile to his policies, was willing to take strong measures. As he told George Shultz, then director of the Office of Management and Budget:

> You've got to get us some discipline, George. You've got to get it, and the only way to get it, is when a bureaucrat thumbs his nose, we're going to get him. . . . There are many unpleasant places where Civil Service people can be sent. We just don't have any discipline in government. That's our trouble. . . . So whatever you do—well, maybe he is in the regional office. Fine. Demote him or send him to the Guam regional office. There's a way. Get him the hell out.[28]

The limits of presidential power do not stem solely from bureaucratic refusal to obey the chief executive's orders. A great many matters simply do not cross the president's desk at all but are resolved at lower levels of government. The most crucial decisions—military intervention, economic sanctions, and the like—do require an explicit presidential directive, but there are far more issues to be dealt with than a president can handle personally, and decision-making power must be delegated to subordinate levels of authority. In principle, all policy within the executive branch is supposed to follow the general course set by the president, but there is almost always room for interpretation of what that course requires, and even mutually incompatible policies are sometimes claimed to lie within presidential guidelines. Thus, decisions that are not made by the president are made by others who have—or believe they have—considerable latitude. At times, lower-level decision makers actually feel that their chances of success are better if the president is deliberately excluded from the decision. In the Iran-contra affair, National Security Adviser Poindexter and NSC staff member Oliver North, who together apparently initiated and managed it, appear to have made diligent efforts to avoid presidential involvement in the operational decisions related to the enterprise. The point has been stated in the following general terms:

> Participants have a tendency to compromise an issue among themselves rather than submit it to the president. They do so in the belief that they can better protect their own organizational interest by getting a compromise which leaves other participants and themselves free to pursue their respective goals than by submitting the issue to unpredictable presidential arbitration.[29]

All of this sharpens the dilemma of aggregation.

Bureaucratic Bargaining

Thus, whether because they disagree with the president or simply because they must make many decisions without his participation, officials of executive departments bring their own perspectives to bear on foreign policy. They will have a conception of the president's foreign policy imperatives, but, while the president is the elected leader of the nation, they are members of organizations with specific functions and outlooks, and they usually see problems from a narrower point of view, partly because of the restricted perspective that their jobs offer, and out of concern for their institution's corporate interests.[30]

Whatever preferences, perceptions, and political predilections government officials bring with them to their job, the position they occupy will largely determine their behavior in their official capacity. It has been said that "where an official stands will depend on where that official sits." Each position requires the incumbent to play a defined role, such as ambassador to France or trade negotiator, and the incumbent will be expected to promote certain objectives and points of view and to act in a way that conforms to this job-defined role. Though there may be exceptions, the director of the Arms Control and Disarmament Agency is not likely to be as enthusiastic about a new missile as a general in the Strategic Air Command. From the former's perspective, the new weapon could undermine hopes for arms control, which he is expected to encourage, while for the latter it may improve U.S. military strength vis-à-vis the Soviet Union, which is his primary concern.

Besides being influenced by the perceptual constraints that bureaucratic roles impose on their occupants, foreign policy is also shaped by a variety of specific institutional objectives. Institutions, like individuals, acquire their own interests, and these may be only partially consistent with those of the nation as a whole. Each organization seeks to increase the resources it is allocated and the range of issues within its jurisdiction (often referred to as "expanding its turf"). The NSC and the State Department may both feel that they should have a larger share in the making of foreign policy; so will the Pentagon and the CIA. Their definitions of external problems, as well as the proposed solutions, will be formed so as to buttress each organization's claim to expanded authority. What State might see as an issue calling for a diplomatic foray, the CIA might consider best suited for a clandestine venture.

The evidence of bureaucratic rivalry in foreign policy is abundant. Two of the major antagonists in this struggle during the past few decades have been the State Department and the NSC. When Kissinger was national security adviser, he apparently did his best to shunt Secretary of State William Rogers to the sidelines, and he was largely successful. Ironically, however, when Kissinger took over Rogers's job, he managed to shift power back to the Department of State—while Brent Scowcroft, who succeeded him as national security adviser, found himself in a much less powerful position. Again, during the Carter administration, Secretary of State Vance and National Security Adviser Brzezinski engaged in skirmishes over both jurisdiction and policy substance. Brzezinski proved to be the more skillful infighter and emerged as chief spokesman for U.S. foreign policy and as the major influence on President Carter's positions. When President Reagan came into office, the traditional NSC-State rivalry surfaced once more, pitting Richard Allen, the administration's first national security adviser, against Alexander Haig, its first secretary of state. Both men soon left office under inglorious conditions and Haig's successor, George Shultz, seemed to reclaim his office's grip on the reins of foreign policy. Yet, as we have seen, the Iran-contra affair demonstrated that significant and delicate areas of foreign policy remained within the NSC's purview, if only because of its willingness and ability to undertake clandestine operations—and despite the dismay and vigorous objections of both the State and the Defense departments.

The Pentagon's Office of International Security Affairs also tends to act like a little State Department, which, naturally enough, places it at loggerheads with the real department. During the Reagan administration, the two have vied over various policy issues. The headline on a *New York Times* article once asked, in this connection, "Is Washington Big Enough for Two State Departments?" [31] The NSC staff and the Pentagon have also been known to distrust each other. When Kissinger excluded the Joint Chiefs of Staff from information to which they felt entitled, they reportedly infiltrated a spy as a clerk at the NSC, in order to obtain the information that had been denied them. [32]

Thus, the various agencies of government pursue their organizational objectives and struggle with each other when their interests collide. Foreign policy is often the resultant of these competing organizational drives, and many presidential decisions embody the outcome of such struggles. This may or may not be compatible with the national interest, or with presidential preferences, but it is undeniably the stuff of which foreign policy decisions are often made.

Conceptual Models

Graham Allison, a Harvard political scientist, has tried to capture the various types of decision making in a set of three conceptual models. [33] In the first of these, the *rational actor* model, decisions are made by a leader, or by a group acting as a unitary body, which considers all courses of action, defines preferred outcomes, and then chooses the actions that are most likely to produce the preferred outcomes. In some ways, this is a highly idealized version of decision making; it neglects not only the facts that people often do not know what they really want and that they usually operate with imperfect knowledge of the consequences of various activities, but also the fact that the participants in decision making have different outlooks and preferences. In the second model, the *organizational process* model, decisions are the outcome of institutions acting simply on the basis of their routinized modes of operation. Governmental behavior is less a rational response to existing conditions than the implementation of standard operating procedures by various bureaucracies, and the consequence is a very predictable and conservative style of behavior.

In the third model, *governmental bargaining*, policy is a weighted resultant of the interests and preferences of the various individuals and institutions that, in one way or another, participate in the process of government. Each may be following a rational or an organizational mode of decision making, but the ultimate policy is the net outcome of their strivings. It is this third model that most closely approximates the reality of foreign policy decision making, although the other two also have some explanatory value (and it must be borne in mind that the influences on policy do not originate exclusively from within the governmental structure).

Two important conclusions can be drawn at this point. First, power in government, despite its apparently hierarchical structure, does not always flow smoothly from the top down. Second, policy is often as much shaped by a process of interorganizational struggle as by a rational and comprehensive assessment of national interests. To some extent, therefore, the executive branch lacks the qualities that seemed at first to make it superior to Congress as a source of foreign policy.

Politics and the Presidency

It must also be observed that the executive branch, or at least the presidency, is no less "politicized" than is Congress. The president, like a representative or senator, cannot help but have elections on his mind. If he is in his first term, an election will determine whether he, and the people he appointed, will enjoy another four years in office. If he is in his second term, he will want to ensure that his party retains control of the White House. Moreover, the president will want to improve his party's prospects in congressional elections, if only to strengthen likely legislative support for his policies. Thus, the sort of short-term electoral concerns that weigh on every elected official affect the president as well (and those who owe their jobs to his continued incumbency). For example, the reluctance of most presidential administrations to wholly embrace free trade is rooted in the anticipated wrath of labor and other interests if jobs are lost to foreign imports. Whether or not free trade is good for the nation as a whole, it does arouse opposition from those who may suffer from international competition, and this is often translated into political costs for the president and his party. Thus, even so nominally vocal a free-trader as President Reagan has trod very gingerly on this issue, and, when political expedience has so demanded, he has adopted protectionist policies.

Foreign policy and domestic politics therefore merge even in the executive branch, a merger that is especially conspicuous at election time. During the 1952 presidential campaign, Dwight Eisenhower made the clearly far-fetched, but electorally promising, claim that he would not only contain the Soviet Union but that he would actually "roll back" communism, and with reduced military expenditures to boot. After his election, he dropped these themes. Vice President Nixon enthusiastically endorsed support of anti-Castro Cuban exiles as a member of the Eisenhower administration, but during his own first campaign for the presidency in 1960, he berated John Kennedy for proposing to help these very same Cubans. Kennedy, for his part, hammered at the existence of a "missile gap" between the two superpowers, which the Republican administration allegedly had allowed to develop; after he was elected, it turned out that no such gap had ever existed.[34] U.S. involvement in Vietnam began while Kennedy was in office, but he apparently soon concluded that it was a mistake, and in 1962 he told Senator Mike Mansfield (D-Mont.)

that he wanted to withdraw U.S. forces—not before 1965, however, for he feared that if he announced a withdrawal of U.S. military personnel from Vietnam before the 1964 election, there would be a conservative outcry against returning him to the presidency for a second term.[35] Thus, even the military presence in Vietnam, with all of its implications and consequences, was partly a product of perceived electoral necessity.

President Johnson's years in office were marked by the escalating involvement in Southeast Asia, but that was not what Johnson had promised during his campaign against the Republican candidate, Barry Goldwater, in 1964. He had strongly criticized Goldwater for supporting the bombing of North Vietnam, a move that Johnson said would risk widening the war. He also promised that "we are not going to send American boys nine or ten thousand miles away from home to do what Asian boys ought to be doing for themselves." [36] Yet after he was elected, Johnson ordered a massive bombing campaign against North Vietnam and increased U.S. forces in South Vietnam to over 500,000 troops. Domestic politics led him to make promises he did not keep. Richard Nixon ran his second presidential campaign, in 1968, largely on a promise to end the war in Vietnam, but neither peace nor withdrawal from Vietnam occurred during his years in office.

East-West relations have not escaped the effects of electoral politics, either. When President Ford was campaigning for the Republican nomination in 1976, he came under attack from Ronald Reagan and the Republican right wing, and in order to deflect it, he announced that he didn't "use the word 'détente' any more," [37] and he suspended movement toward a SALT II treaty. Conversely, Jimmy Carter made grandiose promises in 1976 about reducing military spending, nuclear proliferation, and the arms trade, but he did little to carry out his pledges after he was elected. In 1980, Ronald Reagan promised a tough policy toward the Soviet Union, but—despite occasionally virulent anti-Soviet rhetoric—he actually followed a rather prudent course in East-West relations. In fact, under pressure from agricultural interests during the congressional elections of 1982, he suspended the grain embargo against the Soviet Union that President Carter had imposed after the Soviet invasion of Afghanistan. The relationship between electoral politics and foreign (as well as domestic) policy has been summarized in these words:

> Too often the motivating force for our Presidents in making key decisions during the past two decades has been either gaining short-term political advantage—keeping political adversaries at bay, diverting attention from domestic problems, and scoring political points—or satisfying some set of values that bore little relation to reality but pleased political ideologues.[38]

Although it is sometimes argued that "politics should stop at the water's edge," it does not.[39] Within both the legislative and the executive branches, foreign policy tends to be subordinated to domestic politics rather than to hover loftily above it. If it is charged that Congress cannot deal effectively with external affairs because it is too concerned with short-term political goals, then a similar charge can be made about the president.

Two more conclusions can now be drawn: (1) the president's control of foreign policy is far from perfect, and (2) a president's foreign policy is very much influenced by domestic politics. Congress is often driven by short-term political interests, but so is the presidency. The federal bureaucracy is less subject to electoral pressures, but it is only one part of the executive branch. Many observers consider Congress incapable of formulating a coherent foreign policy, but so frequently is the myriad of feuding executive organizations. Congress may not be well structured for rapid and decisive action, but even the president cannot count on having his directives implemented. Arthur Schlesinger, Jr., writing in the aftermath of the Vietnam War, expressed these doubts about the executive's superiority in the making of foreign policy:

> Unity? This had been a strong argument in the 1790s when the State Department consisted of Thomas Jefferson and half a dozen clerks. But unity was an illusion in the vast and refractory executive branch of the 1970s, where a cluster of quarreling departments and bureaus and hundreds of people contended (generally in vain) for a share in the making of foreign policy. . . . Expertise? The test of expertise was the judgments it produced; and no episode in American history had been more accompanied by misjudgment, misconception and miscalculation than the war in Vietnam. Information? The newspapers provided far more accurate information about the progress of the war in Indochina than Top Secret cables from Saigon.[40]

However, the case should not be overstated. The executive branch does indeed share many of Congress's problems, but it is nevertheless probably more suited to deal with dilemmas of effective choice in the nation's foreign affairs. Differences of degree are still differences, and the executive branch has somewhat more unity of purpose, superior resources, and a marginally better capacity for quick decisions than does Congress. Occasionally, too, it exercises more tact and discretion than can be expected of a legislative body. On the other hand, even if Congress is not in a position to become engaged with the details of foreign policy, the executive branch has no claim, based on its allegedly superior position, to operate free of congressional oversight. Similarly, while Congress cannot be charged with the day-to-day conduct of foreign affairs, there is no compelling reason not to have it participate in charting the overall course of the nation's foreign policy.

Notes

1. Lincoln P. Bloomfield, *The Foreign Policy Process: A Modern Primer* (Englewood Cliffs, N.J.: Prentice-Hall, 1982), 78.
2. Good treatments of the presidency are James D. Barber, *The Presidential Character* (Englewood Cliffs, N.J.: Prentice-Hall, 1977); Louis W. Koenig, *The Chief Executive*, 4th ed. (New York: Harcourt, Brace, 1981); and Arthur M. Schlesinger, Jr., *The Imperial Presidency* (New York: Popular Library, 1973).

3. Fred I. Greenstein, "What the President Means to Americans: Presidential 'Choice' between Elections," in James D. Barber, ed., *Choosing the President* (Englewood Cliffs, N.J.: Prentice-Hall, 1974), 121-147.

4. See Aaron Wildavsky, "The Two Presidencies," in Aaron Wildavsky, ed., *The Presidency* (Boston: Little, Brown, 1969), 230-243.

5. See, on this issue, Michael Mandelbaum, *The Nuclear Revolution* (Cambridge: Cambridge University Press, 1981), chap. 7, "The Nuclear Presidency."

6. Quoted in Ronald Steel, *Walter Lippmann and the American Century* (Boston: Little, Brown, 1970), 49.

7. This theme is developed in Richard E. Neustadt, *Presidential Power: The Politics of Leadership*, rev. ed. (New York: John Wiley and Sons, 1976).

8. Henry Kissinger, *White House Years* (Boston: Little, Brown, 1979), 27.

9. James A. Nathan and James K. Oliver, *United States Foreign Policy and World Order*, 2d ed. (Boston: Little, Brown, 1981), 128.

10. Quoted in Richard P. Stebbins, *The United States in World Affairs, 1950* (New York: Harper and Row, 1951), 57.

11. Quoted in Eric F. Goldman, *The Crucial Decade—And After: America, 1945-1960* (New York: Vintage, 1960), 142.

12. Quoted in Bloomfield, *Foreign Policy Process*, 41.

13. Arthur M. Schlesinger, Jr., *A Thousand Days: John F. Kennedy in the White House* (Boston: Houghton Mifflin, 1965), 414.

14. Charles E. Bohlen, *Witness to History* (New York: W. W. Norton, 1973), 490.

15. Congress made an exception for Gen. George C. Marshall, who was secretary of defense for a brief period in 1950-1951.

16. Leslie Gelb, "Is Washington Big Enough for Two State Departments?" *New York Times*, February 21, 1982, 1.

17. See Adam Yarmolinsky and Gregory D. Foster, *Paradoxes of Power* (Bloomington: Indiana University Press, 1983).

18. See, for example, Seymour Melman, *The Permanent War Economy* (New York: Simon and Schuster, 1974).

19. Senate Select Committee to Study Governmental Operations with Respect to Intelligence Activities, *Final Report*, 94th Cong., 2d sess., 1976.

20. James Dull, *The Politics of American Foreign Policy* (Englewood Cliffs, N.J.: Prentice-Hall, 1985), 79.

21. The most comprehensive book on the National Security Agency is James Bamford, *Puzzle Palace: A Report on America's Most Secret Agency* (Boston: Houghton Mifflin, 1982).

22. Stansfield Turner and George Thibault, "Intelligence: The Right Rules," *Foreign Policy* (Fall 1982): 122-138.

23. Quoted in Bloomfield, *Foreign Policy Process*, 76.

24. The historical context in which the NSC was created is well described in Bernard A. Weisberger, *Cold War, Cold Peace: The United States and Russia since 1945* (Boston: Houghton Mifflin, 1984), chap. 3.

25. Yarmolinsky and Foster, *Paradoxes of Power*, 35.

26. Cited in Neustadt, *Presidential Power*, 22.

27. A good account of American decision making during the Cuban missile crisis is Elie Abel, *The Missile Crisis* (New York: Bantam, 1966).

28. *New York Times*, July 20, 1974, 14.

29. Morton H. Halperin and Arnold Kanter, "Leaders versus Bureaucrats," in Robert J. Art and Robert Jervis, eds., *International Politics: Anarchy, Force, Political Economy, and Decision Making*, 2d ed. (Boston: Little, Brown, 1985), 453.

30. See Morton H. Halperin, *Bureaucratic Politics and Foreign Policy* (Washington, D.C.: Brookings Institution, 1974).

31. Gelb, "Is Washington Big Enough for Two State Departments?"
32. Yarmolinsky and Foster, *Paradoxes of Power*, 38.
33. Graham T. Allison, *Essence of Decision: Explaining the Cuban Missile Crisis* (Boston: Little, Brown, 1971).
34. See Tom Gervasi, *The Myth of Soviet Military Supremacy* (New York: Harper and Row, 1986), chaps. 1 and 2.
35. Kenneth O'Donnell, "LBJ and the Kennedys," *Life*, August 7, 1970.
36. Nathan and Oliver, *United States Foreign Policy*, 328.
37. I. M. Destler, Lesie H. Gelb, and Anthony Lake, *Our Own Worst Enemy: The Unmaking of American Foreign Policy* (New York: Simon and Schuster, 1984), 69.
38. Ibid., 23.
39. See Paula Stern, *Water's Edge* (Westport, Conn.: Greenwood, 1979).
40. Schlesinger, *The Imperial Presidency*, 283.

Interest Groups

Organized private interest groups are extremely influential in the making of U.S. foreign policy. They are neither constitutionally mandated to play this role nor popularly elected to do so, yet they are a major source of political power. Many citizens in democracies, especially in the United States, are members of several special interest groups and thus do not limit their political activity to the act of casting a ballot every few years. Rather, they attempt to influence public policy, particularly as it affects the specific interests or beliefs of the groups to which they belong.[1] Farmers are most likely to get involved in politics when questions of agricultural price supports are at issue. Religious fundamentalists climb into the political arena when the matter of school prayer is raised. Labor unions become most aware of the value of political action when jobs are threatened by foreign competition. As previously noted, the United States is not a nation of political animals where the overall national interest is concerned, but its citizens are like lions defending their young when their group interests are involved. Indeed, it is likely that the most vigorous form of political action in which Americans participate is their activity as members of interest groups.

An *interest group* is an association of people who, through their collective action, seek to influence domestic or foreign policy so as to promote their common interest. They are very much a part of political life in the United States. As Alexis de Tocqueville observed more than 150 years ago: "In no country in the world has the principle of association been more successfully used or applied to a greater multitude of objects than in America."[2] Many of our most important interests are those we derive from membership in professional, economic, or other groups, and we often seek to further those interests through the political system. Policy is then not merely a matter of citizens making decisions through their representatives, but also of groups struggling to promote their corporate welfare through competitive political pressure. It is the activities of interest groups, above all, that generate the dilemma of aggregation.

One political scientist has observed that interest groups exist "for everything from abrasives and absorbent paper to Zionism and zirconium" and that "a substantial part of government in the United States has come under the influence or control of narrowly based and largely autonomous elites." [3] Republicans frequently accuse Democrats of being the captives of "special interests" (by which they generally mean labor unions), and liberals criticize conservatives for being subservient to the interests of "big business." In fact, it may be that the "most important difference between liberals and conservatives, Republicans and Democrats, is to be found in the interest groups they identify with." [4]

It is not a fundamental defect in a political system if private associations play an active role in it. On the contrary: freedom of association and of private organization is one of the basic principles of democracy. Conversely, the right to associate freely and to pursue group interests is antithetical to the idea of an all-powerful state; neither Stalin's Soviet Union nor Hitler's Nazi Germany had the slightest tolerance for independently organized interest groups. On the other hand, it does not follow that, where freedom of association is allowed, democracy will necessarily follow. A society in which a few powerful interest groups dominate political life, while others are too weak to make much of a difference, would be a society ruled by a privileged minority. A country in which the military or the wealthy have imposed a stranglehold on political life, designed to perpetuate their privileged position to the detriment of the rest of society, would scarcely qualify as a model democracy, even if freedom of organization had not been formally abolished. Democracy assumes not just that interest groups have a right to exist, but also that they will balance each other and check any tendency toward a monopoly of power.

There is a sense, however, in which the existence of interest groups presents a problem in a democratic society. Democracy requires the accountability of those whose decisions and actions affect other members of the society. Congress is accountable to the electorate, the executive branch answers to both Congress and the electorate, but interest groups are responsible only to their own membership. The American Tobacco Institute, for example, may influence the level of cigarette smoking in the country by belittling the dangers of smoking, but it does not have to answer to those whose health is thereby endangered. Democracy and accountability are supposed to go together, but there is no mechanism for rendering interest groups accountable. Thus, the status of interest groups in the sort of political system that most people in the United States seem to desire is problematic.

Interest groups can be highly organized (the American Petroleum Institute, the AFL-CIO) or amorphous and informal (the defense industry, automobile producers). Their concern may be with broad interests (the U.S. Chamber of Commerce speaks for the business community on a wide range of issues), or it may be highly focused (the National Rifle Association simply wants to minimize control of firearms). They may grow out of the common economic concerns of their members, or they may be based on an ideology or on a common identity. Ideological groups seek to promote specific beliefs; examples are the American Civil Liberties Union, the National Right to Life Committee (which attempts to have abortion outlawed), and the Committee on the Present Danger (which advocated militantly anti-Soviet policies). Occasionally, such groups manage to exert considerable influence on public policy, as did the Committee on the Present Danger, which in the late 1970s contributed to mobilizing public opposition to détente and to the SALT II arms control agreement. Members of identity groups share a common identity from which a presumption of common interests arises, usually going beyond economic gain or the promotion of a specific ideological goal; examples are the National Organization for Women (NOW), which seeks to promote the socioeconomic and political well-being of women, and the American-Israel Public Affairs Committee (AIPAC), which lobbies on behalf of the interests of Israel.

How Interest Groups Operate

The main instrument of interest-group influence is the lobby—an organization with a staff (the lobbyists), a budget, and, usually, an office in Washington.[5] A lobby may work by either *direct* or *indirect* means. In direct lobbying, personal contact is established with policy makers in order to influence their decisions through persuasion. The lobbyists communicate with members of Congress, other policy makers, or their staff in order to present the best case for the policies believed to be most favorable to the interests and beliefs of the group's membership. For example, representatives of an arms-control lobby may visit key senators to persuade them to vote in favor of an arms-limitation treaty or against certain items in the defense budget. Representatives of the United Auto Workers (UAW) might seek to convince members of Congress to vote in favor of legislation limiting the sale of Japanese automobiles to the United States. Lobbies may also communicate with a number of policy makers simultaneously, as when they offer testimony before relevant congressional committees.

In indirect lobbying, third parties, or voters and the general public, are mobilized and urged to put pressure on policy makers. One way of doing this is to organize mail campaigns; the White House and Congress receive millions of letters each day. Often the lobby will send out huge numbers of preprinted letters addressed to the president or a member of Congress advocating the lobby's position; the recipients of these letters—a selected segment of the public—are asked to sign the letter and mail it to the policy maker. During the debate in 1978 over ratification of the Panama Canal Treaty, Richard Viguerie, head of the National Conservative Political Action Committee and a specialist in these direct-mail campaigns, claimed credit for having 2.5 million letters sent to Congress in opposition to the treaty (which, as we have seen, was nevertheless ratified, although by a very slim majority). The interest group might also sponsor a number of "advocacy ads" in the newspapers or on TV or radio, promoting the lobby's position on an issue, or op-ed articles and letters to the editors of major newspapers might be written by representatives of the lobby in their own name.

Lobbies also sometimes engage in what is called *dollar lobbying*, a practice that is of uncertain ethical status. It consists of making campaign contributions to incumbents or to candidates for elective office whose support the lobby would like to acquire. These financial contributions may be quite well intentioned, but they may also have unsavory consequences. During the 1968 presidential election campaign, the ITT Corporation contributed $400,000 to the Republican National Committee. Following the victory of Richard Nixon, Attorney General John Mitchell, who had been Nixon's campaign manager, ordered the Justice Department to drop its effort to force ITT, on antitrust grounds, to give up ownership of the Hartford Insurance Company. A confidential memo from an ITT lobbyist seemed to suggest that the Nixon administration explicitly and purposely decided to do the company this favor in return for its contributions.[6] There are other examples of shady practices, but outright bribery does not seem to be a major objective of the campaign contributions of interest groups. More often, the purpose is to make sure that the lobby will have access to the policy maker when it wishes to argue its position. In other words, dollar lobbying is usually engaged in to gain entree for direct lobbying. However, political campaigns can be tremendously costly; in 1982, the average winning congressional candidate spent $265,000 on his election,[7] and the costs have increased significantly since then, giving rise to a pressing need for financial support and making elected officials susceptible to requests for special treatment from campaign contributors.

In order to prevent bribery and other malodorous practices, while still preserving the freedom to support political candidates, Congress has sought to regulate campaign financing. Unions and corporations have long been forbidden to make campaign contributions out of their own funds, but the Federal Election Campaign Act of 1971 did allow them to solicit funds from their members for the specific purpose of campaign contributions. This was further institutionalized by an amendment to the act in 1976, in effect permitting most corporations and labor groups to establish *political action committees* (PACs). These are theoretically independent organizations that are permitted to collect money from members and pass it on to their preferred candidates. Thus, via PACs, interest groups can play a substantial role in political campaigns. In 1982, PACs contributed $87.3 million to congressional campaigns.[8] Typically, corporate PACs favor Republicans while labor-union PACs favor Democrats, and there are ideological PACs on both ends of the political spectrum.

Since the international system impinges in so many ways on the interests of U.S. citizens, it can be expected that many interest groups will direct some of their efforts to lobbying on matters of foreign policy. This causes some concern for, while domestic politics are widely accepted as an arena for competition among interest groups, many people feel that foreign policy ought to represent the general interests of all citizens rather than the special interests of those who are best able to influence foreign affairs. Whatever position one may take on this issue, the present reality is that special interests do play an active part in foreign policy formation, and we must therefore become acquainted with the major ones.

Business Groups

A public-opinion survey conducted in 1979 found that business was ranked second among twenty-nine major institutions in perceived degree of influence on national policy in the United States.[9] Its power derives from several sources, especially from interests that are usually clearly identified, narrowly focused, and that are supported by substantial financial resources. It engages in political activity in three principal fashions: (a) through business and trade organizations, (b) through informally concerted efforts, and (c) through individual companies. Obviously, the bigger and more powerful a company is, the more able it is to act independently to influence the conduct of foreign affairs.

Of the several major business organizations, the three largest are the National Association of Manufacturers (NAM), the United States Chamber of Commerce, and the Business Roundtable. The NAM, which was founded in 1895, has a membership of some fifteen thousand corporations. The Chamber of Commerce, formed in 1912, is a federation of some 2,500 local and state branches, trade and professional associations, and corporations. The Business Roundtable, the most recently established of the three (1974), consists of the chief executive officers of the 180 largest corporations in the United States. These three groups act both jointly and separately to promote the interests of their members. While each includes organizations from various sectors of economic life, a second kind of business group, the trade association, is comprised of firms that produce similar goods or services. For example, the American Petroleum Institute represents the producers, refiners, and distributors of petroleum and petroleum products. Questions concerning relations with oil-producing nations would obviously be of special interest to its members. In a slightly different vein, the National Council for United States-China Trade is composed of several hundred corporate members who engage in trade with China.

Occasionally, industries that are not formally bound together in a trade association find that they have sufficiently similar interests to act together to promote some particular foreign policy objective. For example, U.S. automobile makers and their many suppliers have a common interest in limiting imports of Japanese cars, and they have coordinated efforts to raise trade barriers accordingly. Finally, individual businesses are likely to act on their own if their foreign interests are substantial enough and if they have sufficient resources and political clout. The major defense producers are in that category, as are a number of multinational corporations, whose activities span several countries and which are among the wealthiest economic entities in the world.

The interests represented within the three major business organizations are quite diverse, and often there will not be sufficient commonality of interest among their members to provide them with an unambiguous set of policies for which to lobby. The NAM's members, for example, include some manufacturers who rely on foreign markets for a significant part of their sales; as exporters, they would suffer from other nations' trade barriers, and since one nation frequently imposes such barriers in retaliation for restrictions imposed on its own goods, these manufacturers usually oppose U.S. restrictions on imports. On the other hand, NAM members such as textile, steel, and automobile producers are subject to intense competition from foreign-made goods, and so they are likely to lobby for higher trade barriers. Thus, an association encompassing a wide variety of interests may simply have no clear preference when it comes to international policy. On the whole, therefore, the more focused lobbies, such as those representing individual corporations or trade associations, are more active in foreign affairs. The best way to get an idea of the sorts of policies they pursue and of how they pursue them is to examine a few instances of their activities.

The Copper Producers in Chile

Until the early 1970s, Chile had been closer to the ideal of a political democracy than most Latin American countries. Political life was open, the press was free and vigorous, and political power was acquired though competitive elections. It was also a country which, because of its size, resources, and relative prosperity, had attracted large investments by several U.S. multinational corporations, including ITT and the Anaconda and Kennecott copper-mining companies. Toward the end of the conservative Alessandri presidency (1958-1964), these and other corporations, and the U.S. government, were concerned that the political left might emerge victorious in the next election. It is reported that the CIA undertook a variety of actions to assist the center-right Christian Democratic party, led by Eduardo Frei, against its major opposition, a left-wing coalition led by Salvador Allende. The Christian Democrats won, but the Chilean left maintained considerable strength, and in 1970 Allende was elected president on a platform strongly colored by economic nationalism.

At this point, ITT, fearing for the future of its assets in Chile, apparently entered into a joint effort with the U.S. government to prevent Allende from assuming office and to reinstate a less threatening government.[10] It seems that, immediately after the election, a senior ITT official contacted the NSC staff specialist on Latin America and offered his company's financial assistance for such an effort. Shortly afterward, an ITT vice president, Edward Gerrity, met with William Broe, a CIA official. According to revelations that were later made at hearings, the two men discussed ways of promoting economic instability in Chile, including such measures as inducing U.S. banks not to renew credits to the country and withdrawing U.S. technical help. According to an ITT memorandum, the hope was that "a swiftly deteriorating economy (bank runs, plant bankruptcies, etc.) will touch off a wave of violence resulting in a military coup." [11]

The inauguration did take place, but U.S. economic pressure, including a credit blockade, against Chile was maintained with the support of other U.S.-based multinationals that were interested in Allende's downfall. Chile's economy was heavily dependent on copper exports, and most of the copper mining was in the hands of Anaconda and Kennecott. The Allende government believed that a greater measure of domestic control over copper production was essential for improved economic growth, and one of its first acts was to nationalize the assets of these two companies. Nationalization and expropriation of foreign-owned assets occur quite often in the developing world and are generally permitted by international law as long as appropriate compensation is provided. The Chilean government offered compensation, but it declared that it would deduct from it what it considered to be the "excess profits" that the copper producers had realized in Chile. The companies as well as the U.S. government rejected the Chilean contention of excess profits and demanded full compensation. The record indicates that the companies, Kennecott in particular, acted in concert with the NSC and the State and Treasury departments to exert pressure on Allende.[12] Kennecott sought, through the courts, to have Chilean copper destined for export to European buyers seized pending settlement of the compensation issue. This made importers apprehensive about purchasing Chilean copper. At the same time, Washington imposed a credit squeeze by inducing the World Bank and the Inter-American Development Bank to suspend loans to Chile. As mentioned earlier, the CIA was apparently also trying to foment dissatisfaction with the Allende government among Chileans.

These efforts eventually produced the desired results. The joint activities of the companies and the U.S. government almost certainly contributed to the military coup that overthrew Allende in 1973 (although policy mistakes by the Allende government were also partly responsible). Allende himself was killed, and the successor government, under Augusto Pinochet, proved to be a spectacularly repressive military dictatorship.

This was an instance of corporate pressure on a U.S. administration (which was in any case hostile to leftist governments in the Third World) and of their joint success in achieving a political goal. It may not represent what has been typical in recent U.S. history, but it does illustrate what is, under certain circumstances, possible. It also suggests that major U.S. corporations with global interests are likely to go to great lengths to influence U.S. foreign policy in defense of these interests.

The Steel Industry and Import Restraints

Steel was one of the bases for the industrial ascent of the United States and for its emergence as the world's leading economic power. Steel production, concentrated in the northeast and midwest, became one of the nation's most important "smokestack" industries, but it went into a major decline in the 1980s. In late 1982, it was operating at only 40 percent of capacity, lower than at any time since the Great Depression, and more than 40 percent of steelworkers had lost their jobs. Industry executives blamed European and Japanese steel producers for their fading fortunes. They charged that these producers were being subsidized by their governments and that their exports to the United States therefore amounted to unfair competition. During 1982, imports constituted more than 22 percent of the U.S. steel market. The industry lobbied hard for protection, and Washington responded by persuading Japan and the European Economic Community to restrict their exports of steel to the United States. During the first nine months of 1983, Japanese shipments were reduced by 35 percent relative to the same period in 1982, and the European Community trimmed its exports by 36 percent.[13]

But the steel industry did not recover, and this was now blamed on competition from another set of countries. Producers from Mexico, Brazil, South Korea, South Africa, and other nations seemed to be making up for the reduction of imports from Japan and Europe, so that imports still accounted for approximately 20 percent of the sales of steel in the United States. The industry pressed for additional protection. U.S. Steel, charging that these imports amounted to "dumping" (the practice of selling exported goods below their cost of production, which is generally considered unfair competition), filed complaints with the Commerce Department against several Latin American nations, asking that special tariffs be imposed on their shipments to the United States. The industry also demanded restrictive quotas on foreign steel. But the Third World producers had amassed large foreign debts, and their sales of steel were seen as necessary to earn the foreign exchange with which to pay the interest on these debts. Measures against their exports would surely have been considered an unfriendly gesture, and the Reagan administration's relations with the developing world were already frayed. Moreover, the president had repeatedly voiced his commitment to free trade. Nevertheless, the steel producers prevailed. At the administration's prodding, Mexico and South Africa agreed to cutbacks in their shipments to the United States. In 1984, with an election approaching, the president announced "voluntary" quotas that would further reduce the foreign steel producers' share of the U.S. market.

The Farm Lobbies

Farmers have always had a marked influence on U.S. politics, both because farming regions possess, in the aggregate, considerable voting power, and because farmers are very vocal when they feel that their interests are threatened. Indeed, the farm vote has been crucial in several presidential elections, including Harry S Truman's unanticipated triumph over Republican candidate Thomas E. Dewey in 1948 and John F. Kennedy's narrow victory over Nixon in 1960.

Like business, agriculture is organized into several broad groups. The oldest is the National Grange, founded in 1867; the largest is the American Farm Bureau Federation (AFBF). Another organization, the National Farmers Union (NFU), draws most of its membership from the Great Plains. Other groups, such as the National Turkey Federation and the Southwestern Peanut Growers Association, are established on narrower geographical or commodity lines. The farm lobbies specialize in direct persuasion, particularly with reference to members of the agricultural committees of the House and Senate, but they also engage in indirect lobbying and in campaign contributions through their PACs (of which the dairy lobby has been the most notable).

Agricultural lobbying has focused mainly on matters of domestic farm policy, and its major accomplishment has been a system of support prices and supply controls. However, farmers' lobbies have occasionally been active in foreign policy as well. For example, Public Law 480 (Food for Peace) authorized the federal government to purchase a certain amount of surplus agricultural production, which is then to be allocated to needy countries as food aid. This program, which farm interests have energetically supported, is primarily intended to take surplus production off the market, preventing it from lowering domestic agricultural prices. It is thus at least as much an agricultural price-maintenance program as it is a foreign assistance program.

Because the Soviet Union has become a major buyer of their output, U.S. grain producers have been major beneficiaries of détente. While farm lobbies have not, for the most part, been prominent advocates of détente for its own sake, concerned producers, particularly through the National Association of Wheat Growers, have consistently sought expanded grain sales to the Soviet Union. Just as President Jimmy Carter had embargoed grain shipments to the Soviet Union after the invasion of Afghanistan, President Reagan suspended negotiations with the Soviet Union on grain sales when the Polish government, possibly at Moscow's behest, clamped down on political dissent in 1981 to cope with the challenge of the Solidarity movement. But as the 1982 congressional elections approached, the president reversed course and tried to coax the

Russians to buy large quantities of U.S. grain.[14] Thus, farming interests benefited from the fact that, when elections are imminent, foreign policy is often subordinated to the needs of domestic politics.

Organized Labor

While it does not occupy quite the powerful political position enjoyed by unions in many other industrial democracies, organized labor in the United States does influence policy on a variety of domestic and international issues. Even though less than one-quarter of the U.S. work force is unionized, labor unions represent a sizable number of voters, and they are very well organized, capable of effective lobbying, and able to make substantial financial contributions to political candidates. The largest union in the United States is the American Federation of Labor and Congress of Industrial Organizations (AFL-CIO), which is comprised of some 130 craft or industrial unions. Its PAC is the Committee on Political Education (COPE). The UAW, the International Brotherhood of Teamsters, and the United Mine Workers have also been influential unions. In addition to COPE, there are nearly two hundred labor PACs.

Most of organized labor's lobbying efforts are directed toward domestic issues such as labor legislation and economic policy. But labor unions are also occasionally active in foreign affairs, and this is particularly true of the AFL-CIO. Its views are characterized by an intensely anticommunist orientation, and it is especially aroused to activism when it believes that workers' jobs and incomes are being affected by events abroad. For example, the union has lobbied hard for restrictive immigration legislation, especially for provisions requiring the government to certify that an applicant for immigration to the United States is not, by dint of his profession, likely to take a job that might otherwise be filled by a U.S. worker. As illegal immigration from Mexico and other Latin American countries has increased, the AFL-CIO has vigorously supported measures to end it. Such measures have broader foreign policy implications than might appear on the surface. Since unemployment is an enormous problem in these countries, efforts to halt illegal immigration increase the social problems with which they are burdened and tend to harm their relations with the United States.

U.S. workers' jobs are threatened not only by the influx of foreign labor, but also because goods previously made in the United States come to be imported from abroad. This can occur in two ways. First, foreign manufacturers may effectively compete against U.S. manufacturers, as the familiar examples of Volkswagen and Toyota show. Secondly, U.S. producers may decide to shift some of their own manufacturing operations abroad, in order to take advantage of cheaper labor or proximity to needed raw materials. Thus, goods that had been made by U.S. workers will then be made by foreign workers, employed by the foreign subsidiaries of U.S.-based corporations. Labor unions have been active both in erecting barriers against imports and in discouraging the transfer of production activities to other countries.

If a nation exports more than it imports, more jobs will be gained than lost from international trade, and it can be expected that labor unions will then endorse free trade. However, if imports outstrip exports, they can be expected to support protectionism. After World War II, the United States emerged as the world's dominant economic power, while European and Japanese manufacturers usually could not compete with U.S. producers in external markets or even in their own domestic markets. The U.S. balance of trade had a large surplus of exports, and so the major U.S. labor unions enthusiastically supported free trade. But the European and Japanese economies eventually recovered from the destruction of the war, and later, inflation, generated largely by the Vietnam War, made U.S. products more expensive than they had once been. By the late 1960s and early 1970s, U.S. industry was besieged by foreign competition, and the AFL-CIO, along with several other unions, took an entirely different attitude toward international trade. In 1971, the AFL-CIO declared that "regulation of trade, designed to soften the impact of concentrated imports from other nations with lower wage standards, has become an absolute necessity if we are to avoid growing disruption, loss of job opportunities, and sharp rises in our costs of job training and public assistance." [15] Organized labor in the beleaguered sectors of production has since become a most energetic opponent of free trade.

Unions have become similarly aroused by the transfer of production abroad. George Meany, head of the AFL-CIO from 1955 to 1979, maintained that, by the 1970s, 20 percent of U.S.-made cars, 60 percent of sewing machines and calculators, 100 percent of cassettes and radios, and "large proportions of U.S. production of shirts, work clothes, shoes and knitgoods" had been displaced by imports, many of which came from the foreign subsidiaries of U.S.-based multinationals.[16] Consequently, the AFL-CIO has tried very hard to have restrictions placed on the transfer of U.S. technology and capital abroad. In the early 1970s, it lobbied for the proposed Foreign Trade and Investment Act of 1973 (the Burke-Hartke bill). Had it become law, it would have placed serious obstacles in the path of U.S. companies that wanted to operate outside the country. It would have repealed most of the credits they had been receiving for taxes paid abroad, limited capital and technology outflows from the United States, and imposed tight quotas on imports, whether produced by U.S. multinationals or by foreign producers. Business groups opposed it, and the Nixon administration sided with them and against the unions, assuring that the proposed legislation did not come to a vote in Congress (where it might well have passed). Thus, organized labor does not always get its way, particularly when it is opposed by business or other powerful interests. Nevertheless, because of the political pressure unions can bring to bear on policy makers, they have frequently shaped decisions to conform with the interests of their members.

Ethnic Lobbies

Because the United States is a nation of people with different national and ethnic backgrounds, and since immigration into the country still occurs at a substantial rate, many Americans take an interest in events in the countries to which they trace their roots and to which they continue to feel emotional ties. Many Chinese Americans worry that, in its increasingly cordial relations with Beijing, Washington might neglect the interests of Taiwan. Jewish citizens generally sympathize with Israel, and they occasionally fear that the United States might tilt too far away from that country and toward the Arab nations of the Middle East. Greek Americans side with Greece in its quarrels with Turkey, while their fellow citizens of Turkish origin have the opposite set of loyalties. Frequently, such sentiments give rise to well-organized and effective political lobbies.

A particularly powerful lobby is that of U.S. Jews, who seek to encourage a foreign policy that is supportive of Israel. Although the nation's Jewish population amounts to only about 2 percent of the total, its political strength is magnified by the intensity of its commitments, its generally high level of education and political activism, its substantial campaign contributions, and its concentration in states that account for a large number of electoral votes. There are a number of organizations that lobby on behalf of Israel, including B'nai B'rith, the American Jewish Committee, and the American Zionist Council, but by far the most active and powerful on foreign policy issues is the American-Israel Public Affairs Committee (AIPAC).

AIPAC employs all three forms of lobbying: direct, indirect, and dollar. It has enjoyed close connections with many important legislators and their staffs, especially in the Senate. For example, it has been very close to the offices of former senators Henry Jackson (D-Wash.), Abraham Ribicoff (D-Conn.), and Jacob Javits (D-N.Y.). Its indirect lobbying has benefited from effective media contacts and an ability to mount grass-roots campaigns to gain public endorsement of pro-Israel policies. While it does not disburse campaign contributions itself, AIPAC maintains lists of many important individual contributors. Thus, it has been extremely well equipped for lobbying, and its successes have been noteworthy.

At the height of the period of détente, President Nixon signed an important commercial agreement with the Soviet Union. Moscow had been seeking closer economic cooperation with the United States for some time, and the agreement was viewed as a reward for Soviet cooperation on arms control and an inducement to continued good behavior. AIPAC saw the agreement as a lever with which to move the Soviet Union toward more liberal policies regarding the emigration of Soviet Jews. It was able to persuade the Senate to adopt a provision in the Trade Reform Act of 1974, the Jackson-Vanick amendment, which severely limited the benefits the Soviet Union could obtain from the agreement unless it substantially increased the number of Jews allowed to leave. Soviet leaders viewed this as interference in the internal affairs of their country, and they refused to comply. Consequently, the commercial agreement was nullified. Ironically, Moscow then retaliated by further restricting the right of Soviet Jews to emigrate.

AIPAC's influence was felt in other areas as well. In the spring of 1975, the Ford administration was trying in vain to bring about negotiations between Israel and Egypt. Secretary of State Henry Kissinger, in particular, felt that the stumbling block was Israeli intransigence, and at his suggestion, the president suspended arms deliveries to Israel and ordered a "reassessment" of U.S. Mideast policy. AIPAC, alarmed, mobilized its forces. A letter urging vigorous support of Israel, which had apparently been drafted by AIPAC's director, Morris Amitay, was circulated as a "Dear Colleague" letter from Senators Javits and Birch Bayh (D-Ind.) for signature by other members of the Senate. AIPAC lobbied the senators strenuously, and even some who were at first opposed to the letter eventually added their names to the list of signatories. In all, seventy-six senators signed. AIPAC's efforts were successful: on May 27, the *New York Times* reported that, "buoyed by recent demonstrations of congressional support, Israel has decided to ignore repeated United States requests that it produce new negotiating proposals before the American-Egyptian meeting in Salzburg next Sunday, according to senior Israeli officials." [17]

Although AIPAC may be one of the most powerful lobbies in Washington, it has experienced defeats as well. One of them concerned the sale of AWAC aircraft to Saudi Arabia (see Chapter 4). The lobby had undertaken a major campaign to rouse public opposition to the sale, and it argued directly with members of Congress against its endorsement. The sale was nevertheless approved, though the vote was close and President Reagan provided assurances that the planes would not endanger Israel's security.

Among other effective ethnic lobbies was that representing the Chinese Nationalists on Taiwan, the so-called "China lobby," which for a long time managed to block U.S. diplomatic recognition of the People's Republic of China. More recently, the Greek lobby, spearheaded by the American-Hellenic Institute (AHI), has worked against U.S. and NATO concessions to Turkey, a country with which Greece has competed both for influence in Cyprus and for naval control of the Aegean Sea. One of its major successes came after the Turkish invasion of Cyprus in 1974, when the AHI managed to bring about an embargo on U.S. arms shipments to Turkey (in response to which the Turkish government closed U.S. military bases on its territory). Arab Americans have tried to offset the influence of pro-Israel lobbies with organizations of their own; they did succeed in countering the pressure from AIPAC during the controversy over the sale of AWAC airplanes to Saudi Arabia. East European refugees and their descendants also have modest lobbying organizations, usually with a strongly anticommunist orientation.

Ethnic lobbies represent legitimate interest groups with a strong emotional commitment to their cause. There is a question, however, as to how far loyalties to more than one country are compatible, since the foreign cause and the U.S. national interest do not always overlap—as, for example, when U.S. bases in Turkey were closed in response to the arms embargo on that country that had been demanded by the Greek lobby. Thus, the ethical and political issues involved in the operation of ethnic lobbies are more complex than for other lobbies.

Lobbies for Foreign Governments

While most lobbies act on behalf of interests in the United States, a considerable number act on behalf of foreign governments. Normally, relations between sovereign states are conducted by direct interaction between their executive branches, but it is also possible to influence another country's foreign policy by acting on its legislators, at least insofar as the legislative branch has power in that area. Since Congress does play a role in U.S. foreign affairs, other countries occasionally seek to establish useful contacts with its members.

Lobbyists acting on behalf of foreign governments in the United States are required by law to register as "foreign agents." The term "foreign agents" carries cloak-and-dagger connotations, but there is rarely anything insidious about these people. Their activities are generally carried out in an above-board manner, and the "foreign agents" themselves are usually U.S. citizens— frequently lawyers or public-relations specialists.

Most foreign lobbying revolves around economic issues. One lobby of long standing represents Latin American sugar exporters. Some sugar is produced in the United States, but so much sugar is consumed in the country that a portion of it has always been imported. Ever since the rupture of relations with Cuba, which had been the major source of imported sugar for the United States, a number of Latin American countries have been competing to fill the void. But domestic sugar producers are unhappy about imports, since they tend to lower the prices they themselves can charge, and so they try to have Congress enact restrictions. Accordingly, the foreign exporters have hired lobbyists, including some prestigous Washington law firms, to defend their interests. Similarly, the United States-Japan Trade Council, which is predominantly financed by the Japanese government, has lobbied (not always successfully) against the import restrictions that U.S. producers of cars, electronic apparatus, textiles, and steel have sought.

While foreign lobbying is not necessarily improper, it sometimes bears on major issues of foreign policy and consequently raises troubling questions. For example, when foreign governments, perhaps acting in association with ethnic lobbies, attempt to guide U.S. foreign policy in the direction of their own international objectives, they are manipulating internal U.S. politics for their own purposes, and the resulting policies may be at variance with the interests of the United States. There is no doubt that a number of ethnic lobbies are aided and influenced by foreign governments: the China lobby was created with the skillful help of Taiwanese diplomats, and AIPAC's staff is regularly briefed by people from Israel's embassy in Washington. While one may agree or disagree with the political goals these organizations promote, it is at least debatable whether their activities have always been consistent with the international needs and objectives of the United States.

Occasionally, foreign lobbies, like domestic ones, go over the borderline into improper and even illegal activities. One of the best-publicized instances involved the South Korean government. A wealthy South Korean, Tongsun Park, posing as a rice broker, secretly attempted—together with a former member of Congress and several members of the South Korean Central Intelligence Agency—to bribe senators and representatives to vote in ways that were favorable to the South Korean government and to deliver speeches supportive of it. These activities were uncovered by reporters for the *Washington Post* and by congressional investigators, and Park was indicted by a federal grand jury. He fled the country before his case came to trial.

It should be emphasized, though, that such operations are the exception rather than the rule. Foreign lobbying is legal, and foreign lobbies—again, like domestic ones—operate, for the most part, in legitimate ways. In many cases, they actually serve as a useful complement to official diplomacy.

"Public Interest" Groups

An interesting development of recent decades has been the emergence of "public interest" groups, established to promote not the parochial interests of their members but rather some more general notion of the public good. Because of this, they stretch the definition of an "interest group," although they are lobbies in all other respects. Sometimes, their beliefs are sufficiently explicit and coherent to represent identifiable ideologies. Examples are the Moral Majority and Americans for Constitutional Action, which are conservative groups, and the World Federalists, the United Nations Association, and Americans for Democratic Action, which are liberal groups. Most such organizations, especially the liberal ones, address themselves chiefly to the college-educated and middle-class strata of the public.

A number of these groups came into existence to lobby for or against arms-control negotiations. The most influential of the opposition groups has been the Committee on the Present Danger, which was mentioned earlier in this chapter. Its founders were Paul Nitze and Eugene V. Rostow. Nitze had occupied a variety of high-level positions, including secretary of the navy and deputy secretary of defense, in Republican administrations. In 1950, he was one of the authors of National Security Memorandum 68, which called for increased vigilance against the U.S.S.R. and for a major U.S. rearmament effort. In 1974, Nitze resigned from the U.S. SALT delegation, accusing it of being too weak in its dealings with Moscow. He later became an adviser on arms control to President Reagan. Rostow, a former high-ranking State Department official, was one of the architects of the U.S. involvement in Vietnam and a man of strongly anti-Soviet views. Among the principal objectives of the Committee on the Present Danger have been to dispel what Nitze called "the myth of détente" and to lobby against the SALT II negotiations, which its members believed were making too many concessions to the Soviet Union.

One of the group's first goals was to defeat the confirmation of Paul Warnke, President Carter's nominee to be director of the Arms Control and Disarmament Agency. Warnke, who had previously worked with Nitze at the Department of Defense, had been unenthusiastic about the Vietnam War and was a vigorous proponent of arms control. In testimony before the Senate Foreign Relations Committee, Nitze characterized Warnke's views as "absolutely asinine, screwball, arbitrary, and fictitious." [18] In the Senate vote, Warnke was approved by a vote of 58 to 40—sufficient for confirmation but less than the two-thirds margin that would be required for ratification of any arms-control treaties. The Committee on the Present Danger continued to campaign against arms control, and its efforts were supported by other right-wing groups. One of these, the American Security Council, included in its leadership a large number of retired defense and intelligence officials. It called for a "national strategy based on overall military and technological superiority over the Soviet Union," [19] and it produced a series of widely circulated films dramatizing the Soviet military threat and portraying the U.S. strategic position as one of vast inferiority.

Among the groups supportive of arms-control negotiations and of better relations with the Soviet Union in general is one that called itself SANE and has conducted a public-education campaign on the benefits of arms limitation and détente. The membership of the American Committee on East-West Accord has included such luminaries as the late senior statesman Averell Harriman, the diplomat and historian George Kennan, and Donald Kendal, a former president of the U.S. Chamber of Commerce. The Arms Control Association, the Center for Defense Information, and the Union of Concerned Scientists are other groups that have attempted to explain the benefits of arms control. On the whole, the relative resources of the two kinds of groups and the political climate of the late 1970s favored those that were hostile to arms control, and, as we have already seen, the negotiating process collapsed in late 1979—though the efforts of these organizations were far from being the only reason.

Other public interest groups are concerned with a broader range of issues. Common Cause, founded in 1970 by John Gardner, a former secretary of

health, education, and welfare, is one of these. Its main goals are "to change political structures so they will be more responsive to social needs and to produce
a major reordering of national priorities." [20] Although the organization is
bipartisan, its orientation is generally considered liberal, and its membership of
some 350,000 is essentially upper-middle class and well-educated. While it has
mostly addressed itself to domestic issues (the congressional seniority system,
the vote for eighteen-year-olds, financing of election campaigns), it has also
taken positions on several important issues of foreign policy. It was, for
example, an opponent of military involvement in Vietnam and lobbied
energetically for its termination. In the wake of disclosures about covert CIA
activities abroad, it worked for stricter controls on subversive operations.
Common Cause has also taken a strong stand in support of nuclear arms
limitation, and it has tried, through its Citizens Campaign on War and Peace,
to bring pressure on Congress to curb the arms race. However, while Common
Cause has placed its imprint on some areas of domestic politics, it has not as yet
made much of an impact on foreign policy.

Conclusions

Freely organized associations are an essential part of democracy, but they
can also usurp a disproportionate share of political power. Wealthy landholders
and the armed forces in several Central American nations are examples of
interest groups that have made it difficult or impossible for groups that oppose
them to pursue their own interests and that have, therefore, undermined
democracy. Such extreme cases are not found in the United States, but here,
too, one may ask whether organized special interests have more political power
than they ought to have.

A principle of successful democracy is that power should be broadly
distributed throughout society, in a manner roughly proportionate to the
fraction of the societal interest represented by power holders. Since Congress
represents the entire electorate, it should therefore have more power than, say,
the AFL-CIO or the American Tobacco Institute. The question regarding
interest groups and their lobbies, then, can be more precisely stated as whether
they exercise more power over national policy—in the present case, foreign
policy—than is warranted by the fraction of the societal interest which they
represent. The issue is particularly important when a group's interests seem to
be at variance with those of the nation as a whole.

There are many observers who are disturbed by the amount of political
power exercised by special interests. Most conservatives, for example, are
convinced that organized labor is too powerful, while radicals, and at times
liberals, believe that big business is too powerful. Distrust of interest groups has
been a perennial theme in U.S. history. It was one of the stimuli for populism,
and, in the early twentieth century, for a political movement known as

Progressivism, whose goal was to purge the influence of interest groups, especially that of big business, from the political system. The sociologist and social critic C. Wright Mills has argued that political power in the United States has been lodged in the hands of an "interlocking directorate" or *power elite* of business executives and military leaders who, acting in collusion with government officials, shaped the nation's domestic and foreign policies in accordance with the interests of the military-industrial complex.[21] Even such a defender of the political role of private associations as Robert Dahl has expressed some misgivings about their possible influence. While he acknowledges that private associations "are necessary to the functioning of the democratic process itself, to minimizing government coercion, to political liberty, and to human well-being," he also fears that "organizations may use the opportunity to increase or perpetuate injustice rather than to reduce it, to foster the narrow egoism of their members at the expense of concerns for a broader public good, and even to weaken or destroy democracy itself." [22]

On the other hand, there are those who, while admitting that the goals of special interests are selfish, feel that, because of the nature of the U.S. political system, their power is not excessive. This *pluralist* view has been stated in the following way:

> Power is widely dispersed among various groups which represent diverse interests. Those interests that are unrepresented in groups are represented by the state, which ordinarily is an umpire, one of whose functions is to oversee the struggle between groups and set the rules for conflict among them. Finally, the groups tend to be in equilibrium in the sense that none continually dominate governmental decision-making and all are subject to veto by other groups.[23]

Thus, there is considerable disagreement about the impact of interest groups on policy, and no final judgment can yet be made. But perhaps some tentative conclusions can be suggested, at least with respect to foreign policy.

There is very little doubt that some interest groups have more of an effect on foreign policy than appears justified by the scope of the interests they represent. The success of certain business groups in lobbying for protection against imports is a case in point. The influence wielded by a number of ethnic lobbies over U.S. policy in particular regions of the world is another. Both these types of groups act on behalf of a rather narrow segment of society, yet both have displayed an ability to shape foreign policy in the areas of their concern. Whatever may be true of domestic policy, it is not always true of foreign policy that the power of interest groups is moderated by the mediating role of government and by an equilibrium among competing groups.

In the first place, it is difficult for the government to act as umpire when strong interests within the government itself are tied to those of private groups. According to Mills's conception of a power elite, it is precisely because industrial groups and the military are closely connected that they can shape national security policy in their own interests. The steel lobby and the powerful ethnic lobbies exert their influence via the electoral interests of members of Congress, rather than through relationships with government bureaucrats. In either case, the lobbies have powerful allies within the political system, and government is unlikely to act as an impartial umpire under such circumstances.

Secondly, the equilibrium argument assumes that groups have more or less equal resources at their disposal, and that is not always the case. Some groups have more prestige, credibility, and, in particular, money than others do. Business groups, for example, are usually in the strongest position, and when their interests clash with those of other groups (as in the case of the Burke-Hartke bill), they will usually prevail. It is true that the interests of some business groups may collide with those of others, but again, they do not necessarily balance each other. For example, while companies producing steel have lobbied for import quotas, those that buy steel (and who have to pay more when foreign competition is reduced) opposed protection, through the efforts of the American Institute for Imported Steel. While the opponents may have helped thwart the most drastic forms of protection, its advocates, whose political and financial resources are considerably greater, have evidently had the upper hand.

Clearly, it cannot be assumed that the interests of powerful groups are identical with those of the nation as a whole, or even that they overlap. Given U.S. dependence on foreign oil, it could be argued that something like impartiality in the Middle East conflicts would be, objectively speaking, in the national interest, but AIPAC certainly does not want the United States to be impartial. Because protectionism drives up the prices that domestic consumers must pay and reduces pressure for improved efficiency, it is presumably detrimental to the national economy as a whole. If so, then the interests of the industries seeking tariffs, quotas, and other kinds of restrictions on imports are at variance with those of the larger society.

Often, of course, it is difficult to determine just where the national interest really lies. Foreign policy conservatives, for example, may feel that ITT's and Kennecott's participation in Allende's downfall was consistent with the interests of the United States, since it led to the removal of a left-wing government. Others may feel that the ensuing right-wing dictatorship was less in accord with U.S. values than the freely elected Allende government was. Differing values and ideologies can thus cloud the issue, but there is no denying the principle that interest groups often pursue goals that are at variance with the national interest.

Finally, it should be emphasized that lobbies do not dictate national policy. Foreign policy results from the interplay of all the forces that have been considered in this and the three preceding chapters: public opinion, Congress, the executive branch, and private groups. Their influence is not generally equal, but none regularly and unambiguously dominates the others.

Notes

1. The tendency of U.S. citizens to act through private organizations has been well documented in Gabriel A. Almond and Sidney Verba, *The Civic Culture: Political Attitudes and Democracy in Five Nations* (Princeton, N.J.: Princeton University Press, 1963).

2. Alexis de Tocqueville, *Democracy in America* (New York: Alfred A. Knopf, 1945), 1:45.

3. Grant McConnell, *Private Power and American Democracy* (New York: Alfred A. Knopf, 1966), 131, 339.

4. Theodore J. Lowi, *The End of Liberalism* (New York: W. W. Norton, 1979), 53.

5. Lobbyists must register with the clerk of the House of Representatives and the secretary of the Senate.

6. Peter Navarro, *The Policy Game: How Special Interests and Ideologues Are Stealing America* (New York: John Wiley and Sons, 1984), 97.

7. "Cost to Get Elected Jumped in 1982 Campaign," *Wall Street Journal*, May 3, 1983.

8. *Wall Street Journal*, April 29, 1983.

9. William Eberstein et al., *American Democracy in World Perspective*, 5th ed. (New York: Harper and Row, 1980), 110.

10. For detailed studies of the U.S. role in Allende's downfall, see James Petras, *The United States and Chile* (New York: Monthly Review Press, 1975), and Elizabeth Farnsworth, "More Than Admitted," *Foreign Policy* (Fall 1974): 127-141.

11. Cited in Petras, *The United States and Chile*, 33.

12. Kennecott's activities are described in ibid., chap. 4.

13. *Time*, December 19, 1983, 50.

14. Compare these two headlines in the *Wall Street Journal*: "Farmers Losing Hope of New Grain Accord With Soviets as U.S. Widens Sanctions," June 28, 1982; "Reagan Fails to Coax Soviets into Raising Grain Purchases; Stepped Up Bid Is Urged," December 1, 1982.

15. Barry Hughes, *The Domestic Context of American Foreign Policy* (San Francisco: W. H. Freeman, 1978), 166.

16. Quoted in Richard J. Barnet and Ronald E. Muller, *Global Reach: The Power of the Multinational Corporations* (New York: Simon and Schuster, 1974), 304.

17. Quoted in Russell W. Howe and Sarah H. Trott, *The Power Peddlers: How Lobbyists Mold America's Foreign Policy* (Garden City, N.Y.: Doubleday, 1977), 273.

18. Quoted in Arthur Macy Cox, *Russian Roulette: The Superpower Game* (New York: Times Books, 1982), 78.

19. Ibid., 85.

20. See Andrew S. MacFarland, *Common Cause: Lobbying in the Public Interest* (Chatham, N.J.: Chatham House, 1985).

21. C. Wright Mills, *The Power Elite* (New York: Oxford University Press, 1982).

22. Robert A. Dahl, *Dilemmas of Pluralist Democracy* (New Haven: Yale University Press, 1982), 1.

23. Kenneth Prewitt and Alan Stone, *The Ruling Elites: Elite Theory, Power, and American Democracy* (New York: Harper and Row, 1973), 119.

Friends and Adversaries

Sources of Conflict
and Cooperation

IN MOVING FROM process to substance, from questions of how foreign policy is made to a discussion of the external challenges facing the United States, it is useful to begin with the simplest, and probably the most fundamental, distinction in international politics: that between conflict and cooperation. Of course, an image of the international system in which all other countries are either friends or foes would be a gross distortion. Although this is how the world is sometimes viewed, even by otherwise sophisticated political leaders, the conception is too stark and simplistic to do justice to the complexity of international relations. There is no country with which the United States maintains exclusively cooperative or conflictual relations: there are problems between even the best of friends, and there are bonds among even the most bitter rivals (not the least of which is common survival). Nevertheless, the mix of enmity and amity is different in, say, U.S.-Soviet than in U.S.-Canadian relations, and because the nature of the mix has a major influence on foreign policy, we should understand how both of its elements are produced. This will help us understand why we get along better with some countries than with others, and it should also provide clues as to how friction can be lessened and cooperation strengthened.

We are not treading on virgin territory here, since a large proportion of the scholarship on international relations deals with questions of conflict and cooperation. Although a fully articulated and convincing theory of how and why relations between countries become hostile or friendly is not yet available, certain propositions can nonetheless be stated. We will begin by reviewing those that seem most apparent, illustrating them in terms of U.S. diplomatic history and international relations. The discussion will reflect some of the issues raised in previous chapters concerning national objectives and the impact of various segments of society on the course of foreign policy.

The causes of political behavior are often most usefully examined by distinguishing two separate levels: the level of *initiating* causes and the level of *reinforcing* causes. An initiating cause can produce the attitude or event in question whether or not other causes are also present. A reinforcing cause, on the other hand, may amplify the effect of an initiating cause, or sustain the behavior once it is produced, but it will not, in and of itself, give rise to the behavior. To take a simple example outside of political life: the reasons why I choose to drive at a certain speed on a specific occasion (perhaps because there is little traffic) are quite different from the reason I decided to drive somewhere in the first place (say, to get to the beach). Although these categories sometimes break down (what is ordinarily a reinforcing cause sometimes itself yields an event or attitude and an initiating cause may also amplify the impact of a different cause), the distinction is usually helpful, especially in the case of relations between hostile nations.

Initiating causes of hostility can, in turn, be divided into two types: (a) *objective conflicts of interest* between two nations, and (b) *domestic needs* that are satisfied by bellicose external postures. Both may, independently of other circumstances, lead nations toward hostility. Reinforcing causes of hostility are also of two sorts: (a) *dissimilarities* between nations, in particular between their fundamental belief systems, and (b) *perceptions* of other nations, which sometimes maintain hostility even after the initiating causes have ceased to operate. Following a discussion of each of these categories, we will consider the ways in which friendly relations are established.

Hostility: Initiating Causes

Objective Conflicts of Interest

It may appear, at first blush, that there is little mystery about why nations sometimes do not get along: each wants something that can be acquired only at the other's expense or at least is thought to be obtainable only at the other's expense. When this is the case, the two countries experience an objective conflict of interest: a situation in which one side's gain is the other side's loss, and vice versa. In terms of individual persons, for instance, the existence of two qualified candidates for one available job places them in a conflict of interest, since if one is hired the other will not be.

Objective conflicts of interest involve the sorts of things that are desired in their own right, not those that are incidental to a conflict that already exists. If two hostile nations want the same country as a military ally, then it can be assumed that they are seeking the means to pursue a rivalry in which they are already engaged; competition over the ally is part of the conflict but not its original cause. Objective conflicts, on the other hand, are primary causes of international contention. Broadly speaking, there are three sources of such conflicts: territory, economic advantage, and competitive belief systems. The specific character of these bases of conflict, as well as the rank order of their importance, will be determined by how interests are aggregated in a given society and by its historically specific circumstances.

TERRITORY.   There is probably nothing over which nations have more frequently quarreled than territory. The existence of a state is defined in terms of the territory over which it exercises sovereignty, and, as a rule, larger territories are preferred to smaller ones. A larger territory is associated with greater prestige, wealth, and military power. It often implies a larger population as well, and the two together mean that the nation is more difficult to invade and to occupy. A larger population also means that the pool from which armed forces can be drawn is greater, making the nation a more formidable military entity. A larger territory usually confers access to more and varied natural resources and thus is conducive to national prosperity. Moreover, wealth comes not only from access to natural resources but also from having a large market—which again may be associated with the size of the country. Finally, a richer country is also likely to be a militarily more powerful country (and, under certain conditions, the obverse is true as well).

It is not surprising, then, that nations have historically sought territorial aggrandizement. It is also obvious that, since the amount of available territory is finite, territorial expansion can be achieved only at another nation's expense. Consequently, the competitive quest for territory has, throughout history, been a major cause of international confrontation. The wars of expansion conducted by Europe's classical empires are good examples, but there are more recent instances as well. The Balkan Wars of the early twentieth century were largely fought over rival territorial claims, and Hitler's drive toward Poland and Russia was intended to provide a larger territory (*Lebensraum*) for the German people. In the 1970s, Ethiopia and Somalia fought over the Ogaden region, which both claimed as their own, and the war between Iran and Iraq that began in 1980 and still continues was also rooted in a territorial dispute.

The United States enjoys a large and bountiful territory, and its quasi-insular character has meant that, compared to many other countries, it has had neither the urge nor the opportunity to expand its boundaries in recent time. Because of this geographical position, it has also been spared the threats of foreign invasion that so many other of the world's nations have had to face. Nevertheless, even U.S. history has witnessed territorial conflict: the war with Mexico over Texas in 1835 is one example, and the struggles with the American Indians were rooted in conflicts over land.

Territorial contention has also generated hostility without erupting into warfare. Current relations between Spain and Great Britain are marred by rival claims to Gibraltar, Yugoslavia and Bulgaria have unsettled disputes over parts of Macedonia, and Greece and Turkey continue to quarrel over control of Cyprus as well as the Aegean Sea.

ECONOMIC GAIN.   The pursuit of wealth at the expense of other countries has also driven many nations into confrontation. Of course, that pursuit often overlaps with a drive for territory. Primitive societies seeking to acquire new territory for their tribal domain have usually done so because their ability to adequately feed themselves depended on it. Colonial expansion, especially in the late nineteenth century, was closely linked to economic objectives. But economic gains can be made independently of territorial control—preferential access to the markets or raw materials of a nation can be obtained as a side effect of a political alliance—though even then, one country's gains may be perceived to be another's loss.

Very few economies can prosper entirely without exports. By selling abroad, a nation achieves two objectives. First, it acquires the foreign currencies with which to buy from abroad those goods it cannot itself produce. Japan, for example, buys most of its minerals from other countries, financing these purchases from the proceeds of its exports of manufactured goods. The Soviet Union, on the other hand, exports natural resources for the most part and applies its modest earnings to buying technology and manufactured goods from the West. Second, exports allow longer production runs on goods that are also being produced for domestic consumption, and the longer a production run is, the more overhead costs can be spread and the cheaper the products will be when sold on the domestic market. Thus, in at least these two ways, a nation's prosperity is enhanced by access to foreign markets. But foreign markets, at any specific time, are limited. It is interesting to recall that economic competition brought the United States and Russia into hostility even before 1917. In the latter part of the nineteenth century, as the U.S. economy began expanding, businesses felt a need to gain access to Asian markets, to which Russia was intent on having preferential access. Relations between the two nations suffered from the effects of this rivalry.

The search for sources of raw materials has also been a frequent cause of international conflict. In fact, many of the colonial wars of the late nineteenth century may be seen as struggles for industrial minerals. However, the pursuit of secure access to natural resources has not been a historically important cause of U.S. confrontation with other countries, because, as already noted, the United States has enjoyed an abundance of the raw materials its economy has required. Only recently has this country become significantly dependent on foreign supplies.

BELIEF SYSTEMS.   A nation often defines itself in terms of the major values it claims to stand for. In earlier periods, religion provided the principal set of beliefs and symbols around which many national identities were forged. More recently, political ideology has replaced religion as a major source of the values by which nations distinguish themselves from each other. In both cases, international antagonisms have often sprung from differences in belief systems.

It is important to understand that these antagonisms do not arise merely from one nation's dislike of the values another espouses. The fact that one nation stands for values that another disapproves of does not necessarily make it a threat to that other nation. For example, Albania's regime has embodied a

Stalinist form of Communism, while Chile's is rooted in extreme right-wing values, but neither feels jeopardized by the other. If a difference in belief systems is to produce an objective conflict of interest, one or both of two conditions must be met. First, at least one of the two nations would have to be convinced that its values require it to *actively combat* the other's value system. In this case, of course, one side's success would be defined as the other's failure, and there is a genuine clash of interests between the two. Second, at least one of the two nations would have to be seeking converts to its own belief system at the expense of the other. Though it is sometimes difficult to decide whether antagonism is caused by simple intolerance for another belief system or by an actual conflict of ideological interest as here defined, examples of the latter are not hard to find. The struggles between Napoleon and much of monarchical Europe stemmed largely from the feeling by each side that the other's form of political organization threatened its own fundamental political beliefs, and the coalition that eventually developed against Hitler was born of the feeling that Nazism objectively threatened the survival of political democracy.

Domestic Needs

INTERNAL TENSIONS. At least as much has been written about the domestic drives behind aggressive foreign policies as about the role of international conflicts of interest. One hypothesis is that external hostility is intended to allay internal tensions. Social psychologists have pointed out that, for many people, aggressive behavior serves a cathartic function by relieving internal frustrations.[1] The person who is the target of the aggression need not be the cause of the frustration; sometimes, all that is needed is that this person be conveniently available. A number of scholars have reasoned, by analogy, that tension and instability within a nation might lead it to engage in hostile international behavior. Quincy Wright, one of this century's best-known analysts of international conflict, has argued that many wars have been rooted in domestic causes and that confrontational foreign policies are often associated with internal disunity and civil strife.[2] The government of a strife-torn nation may hope that internal differences will be submerged in the face of a foreign threat and that this threat will mold a sense of national identity and draw domestic factions closer together. The creation of international tension would therefore be a mechanism for resolving intranational tension.

A variant of this theory maintains that hostility flows from the self-serving calculations of a beleaguered government. If its policies have failed, and if domestic conditions have deteriorated as a result, the government's hold on power may become tenuous. Political opposition might become particularly vocal, stirrings of popular unrest might be felt, and so forth. The government might then decide that the way to stay in power is to provoke some external hostility or to exaggerate a foreign threat. If the people believe that the nation is imperiled, they will rally behind the government, despite its failures, on the ground that the time is not appropriate for a challenge to established authority.

At the extreme, the existence of a real, inflated, or fabricated danger from abroad might provide a regime with an excuse to tighten the reins of domestic control—perhaps declaring a state of emergency, curbing the rights of political opponents, outlawing criticism of the regime, all purportedly because of the urgent need to deal with a foreign peril. Anthropologist Margaret Mead has suggested that one purpose of all foreign conflicts is to provide external targets when the maintenance of power is threatened from within.[3] Many political scientists would probably agree.

Some proponents of this view have maintained that nondemocratic governments are particularly likely to behave in this way. The argument is that a dictatorial regime does not enjoy much spontaneous public support and that it will therefore require international tension to quell or deflect public dissatisfaction. Quincy Wright has gone so far as to express doubt that a totalitarian regime could hope to remain in power without taunting or attacking a foreign scapegoat.[4]

Despite the widespread acceptance of such theories, their validity is not unqualified. It cannot be taken for granted that a government faced by domestic unrest can effectively deal with the problem by fomenting external trouble, at least not to the extent of starting a war. Conflict with another nation is, at best, a risky proposition for any regime. While a "rally-round-the-flag" effect may be produced in the short term, the scheme could eventually backfire; populations do become war-weary, and the original dissatisfaction with a government may actually be amplified as the distress of warfare makes itself felt. The enormous suffering imposed on the Russian people by the nation's involvement in World War I was one of the factors leading to the overthrow of the tsarist regime. In 1871, the people of Paris, sick of the privations caused by the Franco-Prussian War, rose up against the French government and created the Paris Commune, which embodied a number of revolutionary principles. Closer to home, popular support for the U.S. government may never have been quite as shaken as during the height of the country's involvement in Vietnam.

On the other hand, governments beset by internal problems have found that conflict short of actual warfare can shore up their position. Perhaps nothing has helped cement the Castro government's grip on power as much as the hostility directed at it by the United States, which probably caused many Cubans to rally around a leader about whom they may otherwise have had grave misgivings. Similarly, the governments of both North and South Korea (neither of which is particularly popular) have probably benefited from the threat that they experience from each other. To a certain degree, therefore, the internal-tension hypothesis is a useful explanation of international hostility. But other domestic conditions may be just as important.

THE ROLE OF NATIONAL-SECURITY BUREAUCRACIES.   Although a government's policies are strongly influenced by the structure of political interests and power in the nation at large, it is also true that all modern states rely on the expertise of specialized organizations and groups to analyze their needs and propose and implement solutions to their problems, and policy will depend to some extent on the views and power of these organizations and groups. Different organizations have different kinds of expertise and different sorts of responsibility, but none are likely to behave in a manner that would reduce their own role or influence. On the contrary: They are usually inclined to interpret the common weal in terms of their own interests.[5] To put it bluntly, governmental organizations' policy preferences are apt to be self-serving (adding to the dilemma of aggregation).

Even aside from self-interest, conceptions of reality are very much colored by professional concerns. One is most likely to see and to recognize that which one is trained to deal with. These biases are not peculiar to governmental organizations; they are displayed by most people. As Lord Salisbury once said, "If you believe the doctors, nothing is wholesome; if you believe the theologians, nothing is innocent; if you believe the soldiers, nothing is safe."[6] The views of Joseph Kennedy, a former banker and head of the Securities and Exchange Commission, on Hitler's Germany at the time when Kennedy was ambassador to Great Britain, have been described as follows:

> His primary interest lay in economic matters. . . . The revolutionary character of the Nazi regime was not a phenomenon that he could grasp. . . . It was far simpler, and more in accord with his own premises, to explain German aggressiveness in economic terms. The Third Reich was dissatisfied, authoritarian, and expansive largely because her economy was unsound.[7]

It follows that external hostility may flow partly from the bureaucratic and professional interests of the governmental organizations that are in a position to shape foreign policy (see also Chapter 5). Since national-security bureaucracies are professionally disposed to interpret the world in a threatening light, and since their own resources and influence depend on such interpretations, as well as on an emphasis on external toughness, the extent to which nations act in a hostile fashion may be a function of the position that national-security bureaucracies occupy within the governmental structure. In other words, governments in which military establishments and intelligence and counterintelligence organizations are high on the bureaucratic totem pole are most likely to place a threatening interpretation on foreign events and to propose bellicose responses to those events.

ECONOMIC PRESSURES. Some analysts of international relations believe that certain domestic economic needs are best satisfied by belligerent external behavior. This perspective on international hostility and conflict has been most notably embodied in two types of theories: those of imperialism and those of militarism.

Imperialism refers to a tendency by a state to expand its sovereignty, or at least its informal control, over other countries and territories. Its classic expression was colonialism, but more modern forms, involving looser and less overt forms of control, have been identified as well. Obviously, imperialism is incompatible with most concepts of international cooperation; it has usually implied the coercive subjugation of other peoples and has frequently involved conflicts over rival spheres of influence. Various theories have sought to account for the imperialist drive,[8] but the most influential ones have been built on economic foundations. Although doing justice to the range and complexity of economic theories of imperialism would require far more space than is available here, their common denominator is a conviction that imperialism is designed to forestall domestic economic decline. J. A. Hobson, a liberal British economist and journalist writing at the end of the nineteenth century, linked imperialism to an unequal distribution of wealth within capitalist societies. According to Hobson, when a large portion of society was poor, domestic markets were not adequate to sustain high profits. This led to a search for external markets, often in the less-developed part of the world, and to an associated need for political control over those markets. Imperialism was the result. The logical remedy, according to Hobson, was to promote more equality within capitalist societies, which would expand domestic markets and decrease the need for imperial expansion.[9] V. I. Lenin, the chief architect of the Bolshevik Revolution, also linked capitalism and imperialism, but proposed a quite different solution. According to Lenin, capitalist economies inevitably experienced declining rates of profit, due largely to an inability to continue to extract "surplus value" from exploited labor. External economic expansion was once again the outcome, but Lenin saw it as a necessary consequence of capitalism per se. Doing away with imperialism meant, therefore, doing away with capitalism.[10]

There are more recent theories of imperialism as well, and while they differ in many respects from those of Hobson and Lenin, they, too, link territorial expansion and international conflict to the economic needs of capitalist societies.[11] Scholars are very much divided on the merits of these theories, but at least two conclusions are apparent: (a) because of their influence and the diversity of thinkers who have advocated them, they must be treated with respect, but (b) such theories account for only a limited aspect of international conflict.

Militarism is a somewhat broader concept than imperialism. It refers to the whole gamut of domestic interests that somehow benefit from military growth. Bureaucratic drives of the sort examined in the preceding section can certainly be one facet of militarism, but it has more commonly been attributed to economic forces. The principal impetus behind economic theories of militarism has come from radical authors, particularly prominent among whom are Paul Baran and Paul Sweezy. Their research led them to conclude that, in advanced capitalism, there is a tendency for profits to accumulate in the hands of monopolies and oligopolies and thence to lack sufficient investment outlets. Large corporations tend to "suffocate" in their own profits. Since it would be politically unacceptable to tax away these surplus profits to support extensive welfare spending, the solution is to resort to either artificially generated, and socially useless, consumption, or to the creation of a huge military machine.[12]

While one need not accept this explanation in its entirety, it cannot be denied that military spending has occasionally been an economic boon to societies experiencing recession. Hitler's preparations for war pulled the German economy out of the Great Depression, and it is often suggested that the U.S. economy of the same era was rescued not by the New Deal but by vastly expanded military production to meet the Nazi threat in Europe.[13] However, at least in the United States, military spending has not grown only during periods of recession but under a variety of economic conditions. Thus, at best, economic explanations of militarism shed but a partial light on military growth. Moreover, they are of little use when dealing with nonmarket economies, such as that of the Soviet Union. Nevertheless, as later chapters will suggest, there may indeed be a link between arms races and economic needs, and more nuanced theories of the link may be quite useful.

Hostility: Reinforcing Causes

Neither the three sources of objective conflicts of interest nor the three types of internal needs that produce hostility in foreign affairs by themselves account for the intensity or duration of international antagonisms. For an understanding of those phenomena, we must consider the reinforcing causes.

Dissimilarities

Relations between two countries can sometimes be strained, even if objective interests do not collide, simply because the two countries are, in some fundamental respect, different. Differences in everything from skin color to religious beliefs have been the basis of intolerance and hatred, and differences in cultures, systems of social organization, and political ideologies have also been known to amplify (and sometimes even to cause) tension between nations.[14] Aversion born of difference is certainly present at the level of individuals. A poor man might dislike a rich man even though the latter's wealth may have no identifiable bearing on the former's condition, and racial and ethnic hostilities have been all-too-common components of social existence. Still, nations are not individuals. To dislike or distrust those who are different may be a common human tendency, but so complex an organization as a nation state need not mirror the psychological makeup of individuals. Be that as it may, history suggests that dissimilarity does contribute to international contention. It may not, in and of itself, suffice to ignite a quarrel, but it can amplify antagonism arising from other sources, and it may make the resolution of objective conflicts of interest more difficult than would otherwise be the case.

Of all the national attributes that have generated intolerance between states none has probably created such bitter animosity as discordant belief systems. As already mentioned, core national belief systems used to derive from religion. The sixteenth and seventeenth centuries witnessed a number of religious wars, pitting monarchs who had chosen Protestantism against those who remained faithful to Catholicism. The longest and most costly of these wars was the Thirty Years War (1618-1648), involving France, Germany, Spain, and other countries. But by the late eighteenth century, political ideology overtook spiritual convictions as the basis of the beliefs by which nations primarily identified themselves. In this respect, the French Revolution was a turning point. The attempted overthrow of monarchy, feudalism, and aristocracy by a quasi-popular and republican form of political organization in 1789 aroused profound fears in the established European monarchies. In 1791, Austria and Prussia sought to crush the Revolution, and soon after, the Napoleonic Wars ushered in a new phase of the confrontation. The content of the major ideologies has since changed, but their capacity to generate distrust and intolerance is as much a part of international life in the late twentieth century as it was in the early nineteenth.

The chasm dividing communism and capitalism, the one rooted in an ideal of economic equality but uncommitted to political freedom, the other wedded to political liberty and an ideal of economic opportunity, has recently replaced the gulf between Catholicism and Protestantism, or between monarchy and republicanism, as the principal focus of international ideological intolerance. While it could be argued that these two belief systems do objectively threaten each other, it nevertheless appears to be the case that the differences between the two often reinforce hostility in and of themselves (an argument that will be discussed in greater detail in Chapter 8).

Bearing in mind that nations do not have the psychological attributes of individual humans, why might ideological differences exacerbate hostility even in the absence of objective conflicts of interest? To begin with, one nation may fear that the basis for its own regime's legitimacy is weakened when an incompatible set of beliefs is adopted elsewhere. Whatever set of legitimizing principles a political system is built upon, these principles are virtually always taken to be the only correct ones. Though some latitude for interpretation may be permitted, and though the punishment for apostasy might be mild or harsh, few political systems fail to claim that only the principles they themselves espouse are right and just. Thus, no political system feels entirely comfortable with the challenge represented by rival belief systems. An absolute monarchy would not be comfortable with a republican and democratic neighbor, no matter how little interest that neighbor shows in undermining the monarchy. Secondly, it is easy to magnify the extent of those interests which do objectively clash when ideological intolerance clouds one's perceptual lenses. There is a tendency for people to think that bad things go together: countries with bad ideologies must have aggressive foreign policies. Finally, hostility generated by domestic forces is more easily directed at nations with values that are disapproved of than at nations with values similar to those of one's own country.[15]

Faulty Perceptions

In the discussion so far, it has been assumed that political leaders act in response to objective conflicts of interest or to objective domestic forces. Strictly speaking, however, no one acts on anything but a perception of reality, a set of images which may constitute an entirely accurate, a somewhat distorted, or an altogether misleading picture of the world. As an influential student of the issue has reminded us, "It is what we think the world is like, not what it is really like, that determines our behavior." [16]

This raises the possibility that international hostility may sometimes be based on false perceptions. Not only does it suggest that many instances of international confrontation may be "unnecessary," but it also indicates that one way to improve relations may be to correct perceptual distortions. History is indeed replete with instances of international tension which, in retrospect, was based on misperceptions which one or both parties had of the other. Moreover, few nations perceive their own attributes and actions in exactly the same way other nations do. The United States has always presented itself as a virtuous nation, one that is highly principled yet, for any nation exhibiting a modicum of good will, reasonable and easy to get along with. Still, this has not been every other country's perception. More than a century ago, for example, Prime Minister Palmerston of Great Britain made this assertion, in the course of a minor dispute with the United States:

> In dealing with Vulgar minded bullies, and such unfortunately the people of the United States are, nothing is gained by submission to Insult & wrong; on the contrary the submission to an Outrage only encourages the commission of another and a greater one—such People are always trying how far they can venture to go; and they generally pull up when they find they can go no further without encountering resistance of a formidable Character.[17]

Such a statement might almost be mistaken for one made about the Soviet Union by a hawkish politician in the United States today! Robert Jervis, a political scientist who has brought many psychological insights to bear on foreign policy analysis, has pointed out that "there is an overall tendency for decision-makers to see other states as more hostile than they are." [18]

How do distorted perceptions of foreign hostility originate? Usually, they have, or at least they had at one time, an objective basis. One important clue to the process by which they are created or reinforced is given by the psychological principle of *cognitive consistency*.[19] According to this principle, people tend to seek a balance or a structured consistency among the various beliefs they have. They do not easily tolerate *cognitive dissonance*—that is, clashes between elements of their belief systems—and the need for consistency is so strong that inconsistent perceptions are usually modified to bring them into balance. For example, we typically expect a person whom we like and admire to have ideas that we agree with. If someone toward whom we felt affection were to espouse beliefs we found repulsive, we would have a sense of cognitive dissonance, which would be resolved by deciding either that we didn't much like the person after all or that the belief is really not so bad as we initially thought it to be.

Similarly, we dislike dissonance in our perceptions of other nations. We expect a country whose human rights practices we abhor to have objectionable foreign policies as well; it is hard to accept the idea that a regime that condemned its political opponents to hard labor in concentration camps would be committed to international peace or to generous assistance to the development of poor countries. As Jervis has put it, "We tend to believe that countries we like do things we like, support goals we favor, and oppose countries we oppose. We tend to think that countries that are our enemies make proposals that would harm us, work against the interests of our friends, and aid our opponents." [20] If, therefore, a country has domestic policies that we disapprove of but a foreign policy that is to our advantage, cognitive dissonance may lead us to find that its domestic policies are not so bad after all. Some right-wing Third World dictatorships are considered supportive of U.S. positions in the East-West rivalry, and so there is a tendency to minimize their internal repressiveness. Similarly, the Reagan administration, which considers South Africa a bulwark against Soviet influence on the African continent, has praised the modest steps Pretoria has taken to mitigate the most objectionable manifestations of racial discrimination, describing them as major steps akin to those taken earlier in the United States itself to end segregation.

But the process may operate in the other direction as well. The absence in Soviet-bloc countries of the democratic principles considered so fundamental in the United States impedes the establishment of friendly relations with them. In the eyes of many people, regimes that pursue such distasteful internal policies could not help but be hostile to a nation that, like ours, stands for quite different values. But this is a psychological rather than a logical inference; there is no convincing reason why a nation with a different political philosophy should inevitably wish the United States ill. Different political philosophies do not necessarily imply clashing interests, for indifference to the other is perfectly compatible with discordant beliefs. Nevertheless, marked dissimilarities easily lead to perceptions of objective conflicts of interest or of the other side's inherent bellicosity. Consequently, a world of very diverse nations, in which the attributes of some are abhorred by others, is less likely to be a cooperative world than one in which countries are broadly similar. Particular attention must then be paid to the effects of cognitive dissonance if one is to avoid misperceptions of other nations' foreign policy intentions.

Psychologists also tell us that our perceptions depend to a large extent on our expectations. In other words, we usually see what we expect to see, and we interpret incoming information to make it consistent with our expectations. For example, when experimental subjects are presented with ambiguous images and are given different indications of what they should expect to see, in most cases the subjects interpret the unclear images as the sort of objects they had been told to expect. [21] In one experiment, for example, people viewing a skit were given different bits of information about what the skit would deal with; predictably, they saw different things in the identical skit. Along similar lines, reports of unidentified flying objects (UFOs) appear in most cultures, but the way in which they are described reflects objects that are familiar in the describer's culture; in the United States they are described as the high-technology interplanetary vehicles of science fiction stories, whereas in the stories of Tibetan travelers, the UFOs are reported to resemble the pictures of devils found in Tibetan books.[22]

The implication for present purposes is that if objective circumstances have led to a state of antagonism between two countries, then each may expect the other to exhibit hostility even when the original circumstances no longer exist. Evidence that squares with this expectation will be noted, while evidence that does not will be ignored, and ambiguous evidence is apt to be interpreted as signifying unfriendliness. The acquisition of a weapon by the other country will be taken as a sign of aggressive intentions even if the weapon was intended to be defensive. A diplomatic overture made by the other side to a third party may well be interpreted as an attempt to build a hostile coalition. Not only what the rival does but how he does it will be viewed with suspicion.

Perceptions of hostility, whether justified or not, produce specific perceptual distortions as well. To begin with, the rival's behavior will usually be seen as guided by centralized decisions. In previous chapters, we saw that, in the United States, foreign policy decisions were more often the result of a process of internal political bargaining than of a unified foreign policy plan. To some extent, this is true of most nations; even authoritarian countries have competing bureaucratic factions and divergent views and interests among their leaders. Yet the policies of a nation that is distrusted or is considered unfriendly will usually be seen as the product of a deliberately formulated policy implemented by a homogeneous leadership, and this will make the other nation appear more threatening than if its actions were understood to come from political and bureaucratic jockeying. Furthermore, we rarely believe that the policies of a distrusted nation do not follow some "master plan." Although we may regard our own policies as a matter of "muddling through," of dealing piecemeal with a fluid and unpredictable environment, the policies of nations perceived as hostile will be viewed as the product of deliberate machinations, a "master plan" aimed at some nefarious ultimate goal. Such nations are likely to be considered more dangerous than if they, too, were thought to be merely coping, on a day-to-day basis, with a difficult world.

Finally, if another nation is always expected to behave in an unfriendly manner, and if most of its acts are interpreted accordingly, we are ourselves likely to act in unfriendly fashion toward it. The *other* country's expectation of hostility will then be confirmed, and the process will assume a life of its own, quite independently of whatever objective circumstances may have brought about the antagonism. At that point, the best explanation of what the antagonism is all about might simply be that it is about itself.

Thus, the drives behind hostility are numerous and powerful: objective conflicts of interest and perceptions, domestic needs and ideological dissimilarities. However, there are forces operating in the other direction as well.

The Bases of Friendship

Friendship in international relations implies cooperation between two countries, mutual benefits in the maintenance of good relations, and predominantly positive feelings on the part of the people and government of each toward the people and government of the other. International friendship is not easy to achieve but it is more attainable than many cynics imagine. Friendly relations generally characterize relations between Western European nations, U.S. relations with both of its next-door neighbors, and relations between most South American countries and between most African nations as well. Even countries linked by bitter hostility at one time can, under the right circumstances, become friends at another time. France and Germany, which had fought against each other in the Franco-Prussian War and in both world wars, came to be considered traditional, almost instinctive enemies—yet their friendship is today one of the main pillars of European cooperation. Relations between China and the United States had been extremely bitter in the 1950s and 1960s, but currently the two countries are virtual allies. Thus, there is nothing inevitable about hostility nor chimerical about friendship; both simply require certain conditions.

Nonconflicting Interests

First of all, nations are likely to enjoy good relations when the sources of hostility are absent. This implies that there should be no major objective conflicts of interest and that there should have been no such conflcts in recent history (so that the self-perpetuating perceptual mechanisms can be avoided). Territorial contention should be absent, neither nation should seek to undermine the fundamental principles of the other's belief system, and their prosperity should not be considered mutually incompatible. Each of these conditions applies to relations between the United States and Canada, the Soviet Union and Bulgaria, Sweden and Norway, Venezuela and Peru. Indeed, these are fairly common conditions—but a mere absence of conflicts of interest at any historical point does not guarantee that they will not arise later. Hitler's territorial drives against the nations of Eastern Europe had no precedent in German policy prior to the triumph of Nazism; the United States and Russia were not previously divided by the ideological rift that has marked their relations since 1917. Thus, the foundations of cooperation and amity must involve more than just the current absence of objective conflicts of interest.

Absence of Major Dissimilarities

It seems obvious that the more nearly parallel are the belief systems of two countries, the less likely it is that conflicts of interest will emerge between them. Not only is it tautologically true that they will not regard each other as ideological threats, but they are also less likely to wrangle over territory or economic actions if they are bound by common normative principles. Moreover, as has already been suggested, if another nation espouses values very similar to one's own, it is unlikely to become a target of internally generated hostility. For example, the nations of the Organization for Economic Cooperation and Development (OECD), which includes the capitalist democracies of Europe, Yugoslavia, the United States, Canada, Australia, New Zealand, and Japan, is in many ways a "club" of industrialized nations which (except for Yugoslavia) have similar political systems. It is the largest such grouping of nations in the world, and it is also the most peaceful and cooperative one: no violent conflict has occurred among its members since its founding in 1960 (or indeed, since the founding of its predecessor organization, the OEEC, in 1948). Whatever the drawbacks of too much international homogeneity might be, a world of relative uniformity might well be less bruised by conflict. But the point must not be overstated. China and the Soviet Union, both communist nations, have been antagonists for a quarter of a century, while the United States and China, on the other hand, have been getting along quite well recently despite their obvious ideological differences. Similarity helps cement cordial relations but is not a sufficient condition for their emergence.

The conclusion so far is that friendship between nations must rest on more than either similarity or the absence of conflicts of interest. It requires positive as well as negative foundations—the presence of certain conditions and not just the absence of others, if it is to be truly stable.

Positive Interdependence

If nations quarrel when their interests are objectively incompatible, then it is logical that they should cooperate with each other when their interests are positively linked—that is, when they are, in some meaningful fashion, interdependent. Instead of a situation in which one side can achieve what it wants only at the other's expense, friendship arises out of a situation in which one side can get what it wants only if the other side does so as well, so that a cooperative effort is needed if either is to satisfy its wishes. To some degree, even the most bitter adversaries feel some interdependence and engage in a certain amount of cooperation; for example, they may both realize that they can escape substantial destruction only if each allows the other to do the same, by avoiding armed conflict between them or by controlling the level of violence should fighting break out. Centuries ago, when wars were fought by mercenary armies, armed conflict was quite expensive for monarchs; consequently, they tended, by tacit mutual consent, to keep battles as short and as bloodless as possible. More recently, the threat of mutual nuclear annihilation has demanded explicit cooperation between the two superpowers, even when their relations were at their worst. This cooperation has involved an implicit agreement not to let relations degenerate into violence, measures to prevent the accidental initiation of conflict, and some mutual tolerance for intelligence activities (so that neither side will have to make worst-case estimates of the other's intentions and capabilities). Still, this can hardly be called friendship; international cooperation is usually thought of in positive terms—the mutual attainment of something desirable, rather than merely the avoidance of something undesirable.

Perhaps the most significant form of positive international interdependence is that which comes from economic and commercial exchanges. Indeed, the idea that free trade is conducive to peace has a long tradition. By the nineteenth century, most notably in England, it was generally believed that commercial progress had eliminated many of the frictions that had previously afflicted international relations. Adam Smith was thought to have conclusively demonstrated in *The Wealth of Nations* that all countries gained from mutually advantageous economic relations and that free trade rather than aggressive mercantilism was the path to economic well-being. Indeed, trade did expand considerably in the nineteenth century, and this was also one of the most peaceful periods in Europe's history. As one author has put it, "Paradise is an International Bazaar." [23]

Advocates of this theory can also point to evidence that a contraction in international trade leads to a breakdown of cooperation. It is, for instance, noteworthy that the years preceding the rise of Hitler and the collapse of international order that set the stage for World War II were marked by a large reduction in world trade (see Table 7-1 and Figure 7-1). As one scholar pointed out, "When foreign trade is scanty, unemployment is rife [and] governments may think the time suitable for setting more men to work on preparations for war. Hitler did that on a vast scale when he first came to power." [24] A return to free trade was also one of the foundations of America's postwar foreign policy, largely out of the belief that peace could not be dissociated from vigorous international commerce.

It is true that trade allows countries to increase their separate and joint prosperity by concentrating on producing that for which each has the greatest comparative advantage and importing the rest from others. It can also create powerful domestic interests committed to maintaining good relations with the country's trading partners. At times, the power of such interests outweighs the influence of those groups, such as national security bureaucracies, whose interests call for a modicum of international tension.

According to some authors, economic cooperation can also provide the building blocks for actual political integration between nations. These authors, frequently referred to as *neofunctionalists*, maintain that political cooperation and integration cannot always proceed by explicit political decisions, for the sources of resistance are too numerous and the obstacles too great. They argue for beginning with economic cooperation in various specialized areas instead,

Table 7-1 Total Imports of Seventy-five Countries, January 1929 to March 1933 (monthly values in terms of U.S. gold dollars in millions)

	1929	1930	1931	1932	1933
January	2,997.7	2,738.9	1,838.9	1,206.0	992.4
February	2,630.3	1,454.6	1,700.5	1,186.7	944.0
March	2,814.8	2,563.9	1,889.1	1,230.4	1,056.9
April	3,039.1	2,449.9	1,796.4	1,212.8	
May	2,967.6	2,447.0	1,764.3	1,150.5	
June	2,791.0	2,325.7	1,732.3	1,144.7	
July	2,813.9	2,189.5	1,679.6	993.7	
August	2,818.5	2,137.7	1,585.9	1,004.6	
September	2,773.9	2,164.8	1,572.1	1,029.6	
October	2,966.8	2,300.8	1,556.3	1,090.4	
November	2,888.8	2,051.3	1,470.0	1,093.3	
December	2,793.9	2,095.9	1,426.9	1,121.2	
Average	2,858.0	2,326.7	1,667.7	1,122.0	

Source: Charles P. Kindleberger, *The World in Depression, 1929-1939* (Berkeley: University of California Press, 1973), 170.

without making a major political issue of it. Eventually, one form of economic cooperation will lead to another, and the process will gain momentum. For example, two nations that expand trade between themselves may discover that they must cooperate to improve the necessary transportation networks. Two nations might decide to jointly produce a good in order to benefit from economies of scale which neither could attain separately; if this works, they might decide to produce another good in the same way. One form of economic cooperation leads to another, and eventually this produces spillover effects in noneconomic areas. The cooperating countries might find that, in order to realize the full benefits from their cooperation in production, they must coordinate their fiscal systems as well. As these successive steps are taken, the web of interdependence becomes so dense that hostility becomes unthinkable, for too much is at stake, and even political integration begins to appear useful and feasible.[25]

The European Economic Community (EEC) was established on largely neofunctionalist assumptions. The organization started out in 1952 as the six-member European Coal and Steel Community (ECSC), whose task was to integrate the heavy-industry sectors of the members' economies and, more than incidentally, to thus limit their separate war-making capacity. By 1957, it evolved into the EEC, commonly known as the Common Market, with wide powers to regulate trade and working conditions, eliminate tariffs, and provide for the free movement of people. The hope is to eventually create the conditions for political integration of the nations of Western Europe. This was long one of

Figure 7-1   The Contracting Spiral of World Trade, January 1929 to March 1933: Total Imports of Seventy-five Countries (monthly values in terms of U.S. gold dollars in millions)

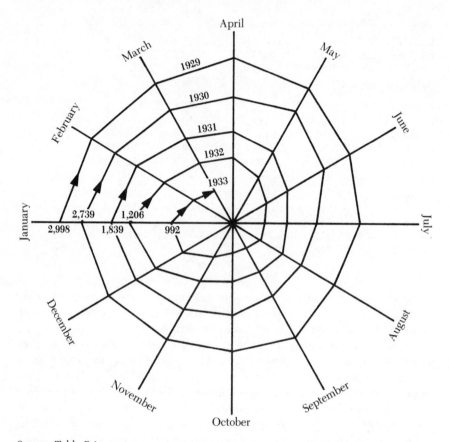

Source: Table 7-1.

the most war-prone regions of the world, but economic integration has perhaps made violence there, and even milder forms of hostility, a thing of the past.

Self-Reinforcing Perceptions

We have seen that negative perceptions of other countries may be reinforced by dissimilarities. Conversely, we find it hard to believe that a country that resembles our own in fundamental respects could wish to injure us. While similarity by itself does not produce friendship, it does make it somewhat harder to view another country in a threatening light. Germany's transition from Nazi dictatorship to political democracy following its defeat in World War II made it much easier to believe that its interests were consistent with those of the United States. Nonetheless, not much practical advice can be drawn from this kind of observation, since ideologies and political systems may never be much more uniform than they are today and since, in any case, they can rarely be changed from the outside. Thus, the main hope is that the tensions that political differences generate can be overcome rather than that the differences themselves will be eliminated.

It is also true, though, that expectations created by past experience can reinforce positive as well as negative perceptions. If we see more or less what we expect to see, and if what we expect to see is friendly, cooperative behavior, then that is probably just what we will see. If the Soviet Union were to propose negotiations with the United States on the future status of Antarctica, the reaction might be to wonder what Moscow had up its sleeve. If Britain were to make the same proposal, it would probably be seen as a useful and cooperative gesture. If we believe that the other side is acting in good faith, our own behavior is more likely to be helpful, the other side will probably continue to be friendly and cooperative, and so on. That is, expectations of friendship are just as likely to create the reality of friendship as expectations of hostility are to produce the reality of hostility. But again, it is not easy to draw useful policy implications from this conclusion. Expectations are derived from past experiences, and these cannot be erased from memory except perhaps in the very long term.

Interaction and Reciprocity

From what has been said so far, it might appear that once negative perceptions congeal there is very little that can be done to decrease tension— that once relations start to deteriorate, they are irrevocably launched on a downward spiral. But this is not necessarily the case. Several suggestions have been made for ways of producing patterns of interaction that can reverse hostility and set relations on a stable and cooperative track.

One such proposal has been put forward by the social psychologist Charles Osgood. He argued that, if two nations were engaged in a series of reciprocally hostile actions, the process could be reversed if one of the two undertook unilateral initiatives leading to what he called Graduated Reciprocation in Tension-Reduction, or GRIT.[26] The premise is that rewards for acts that dampen hostility are more effective than punishments for those that increase it; that is, positive reinforcements can do more to modify an adversary's behavior in a favorable direction than can further hostile actions.

Accordingly, the country initiating GRIT should make conciliatory moves toward its adversary. These moves should not jeopardize national security, but they should be more than mere cosmetic gestures. They should be unambiguously friendly and appear entirely voluntary, so that they will not be attributed to external or internal pressure. Examples of such moves in the U.S.-Soviet case might be deactivating nonessential overseas military bases or sharing technology for early warning of nuclear attacks. The moves should be made without regard to reciprocity by the adversary; the object is not to elicit immediate reciprocal moves but rather to make an unmistakable demonstration of good will. When a favorable response does occur, another step should promptly be taken, and the expectation is that a progressive process of tension reduction would be set in motion. Each side would gradually revise its opinion of the other, threat perceptions would be attenuated, and appraisals of the other's actions would become more rational.

This line of reasoning has an appealing logic: If the process can operate in one direction, why not simply turn things around and make it operate in reverse? Perhaps the main objection, though, is that it demands far more unilateralism than domestic politics (on either side) would permit. There is a likelihood that the nation making the first moves would have a much more re-stricted idea of what it takes to establish its good will than would its rival. While the initiator might feel that it had done more than enough for that purpose, the rival might regard the steps as tricks designed to lull it into an un-warranted feeling of complacency and might take much longer to be convinced than the initiator's patience and sense of security could bear. An even more ominous situation would arise if the second party interpreted the conciliatory moves as a sign of weakness and proceeded to adopt an even harder line of its own. Even if this problem does not occur, it may nevertheless be true that, when conciliatory moves are made by national leaders, "the probabilities are all too high that the competence, courage or patriotism of one or both sets of elites will be challenged by a 'hard-line' domestic opposition, be it a legitimate political party in a democratic system or a less institutionalized faction in a more autocratic system." [27] GRIT therefore requires true courage on the part of governments, and failure can carry significant penalties.

Not everyone agrees that unilateralism is the best way to encourage cooperation between nations. Another method has been suggested by Robert Axelrod, a political scientist at the University of Michigan. Axelrod defines cooperation in a modest, not to say minimal, way, as meaning the avoidance by two parties of behavior that will be mutually harmful. Assuming that the two sides' interests are largely in conflict, and that all they have in common is an in-terest in avoiding the long-term effects of continuous confrontation, they can still engage in cooperative behavior if they follow three basic rules: (1) Never initiate confrontation. (2) If the other side does act in a confrontational manner, make sure that you reciprocate, but if it behaves cooperatively, reciprocate that as well. (3) After you have responded appropriately to a confrontational move, start acting cooperatively again. [28]

Research indicates that patterns of interaction that have been established in this way remain quite stable, and they appear to have characterized cooperation between a wide variety of actors whose interests are to some extent conflicting yet who can benefit from a mutual avoidance of confrontational behavior. It has been found among competing business firms, soldiers engaged in trench warfare during World War I, and a variety of living organisms from bacteria to primates. It has the advantage over GRIT of being politically less demanding, for here one is not required to make a whole series of concessions. All that is required is that a nation should reciprocate when a normally hostile nation behaves cooperatively, that it should not engage in punishing behavior beyond the initial retaliation, and that it should not be the first to embark on confrontation. However, this procedure has its difficulties as well. Behavior considered cooperative by one side may not be so defined by the other, and the same is true of confrontational and retaliatory behavior. If basics of this sort are not agreed upon, the rules of behavior cannot be meaningfully followed. Also, it is still conceivable that *domestic* forces may lead one side or another to initiate confrontation, to punish the other side more severely than is needed, or to fail to reciprocate when the other side behaves cooperatively. There have been many such instances in the case of U.S.-Soviet relations. Nevertheless, in terms of domestic politics, the rules are not as difficult to apply as are those required by GRIT.

It is still somewhat unsatisfying that Axelrod's proposal assumes a world in which many of the conditions of hostility are present. His only claim is that the parties would do even worse if some level of cooperation were not established. Yet one should not forget that when the conditions of friendship are firmly established, the very structure of the situation changes: the parties cooperate not simply to avoid the costs of noncooperation, but because they want to cooperate and will benefit from doing so. In other words, establishing stable rules of cooperation under conditions of antagonism is not the same as creating the bases for international friendship.

To sum up, hostility can be the product of objective conflicts of interest or of domestic needs, and it is often amplified by the effects of political dissimilarities and perceptual distortions. Hostility can be directed toward another nation for reasons which have little to do with that nation's behavior, as when the belligerence produced by domestic forces seeks a dissimilar nation to serve as its target, or when perceptual mechanisms continue to brand another country as a dangerous rival although the objective bases for that assessment have been altered.

The forces behind hostility are often powerful: The internal interests that seek gratification through external hostility may be embedded in the political system, or objective conflicts of interest may be considered intractable. Nevertheless, even the bitterest of enemies occasionally become friends and there is nothing necessary or predetermined about international rivalries. Even if some objective conflicts of interest cannot be resolved, they can often be offset by bonds of positive interdependence—and an economic basis for cooperation can be very firm indeed. There are also some ways of mitigating the problem of self-reinforcing perceptions. Although asymmetric concessions require more political will than can usually be expected, some of the psychological pitfalls in international relationships can be guarded against. It is, for example, important to be as clear as possible about the assumptions underlying one's perceptions of an adversary in order to identify any weak links in one's chain of reasoning. Similarly, it is useful to be aware of widely held misperceptions. Open discussion is to be encouraged even within the innermost councils of government.[29] Where there is too much uniformity of views, clichés replace analysis and suppress both objective understanding and creative solutions.[30] Finally, even if antagonism is not removed, it may be possible, by following Axelrod's rules, to establish a stable basis of minimal cooperation, although even this could be precluded by domestic political resistance.

Notes

1. See, for example, Leonard Berkowitz, "The Expression and Reduction of Hostility," *Psychological Bulletin* 55 (1958): 257-283; idem., *Aggression: A Social-Psychological Analysis* (New York: McGraw-Hill, 1962); idem., "Experimental Investigations of Hostility Catharsis," *Journal of Consulting and Clinical Psychology* 35 (1970): 10-17; and James C. Davies, *Human Nature in Politics* (New York: John Wiley and Sons, 1963).
2. Quincy Wright, *A Study of War* (Chicago: University of Chicago Press, 1942), vol. 2, Chapters 28 and 32.
3. See her comments in the symposium volume edited by Morton Fried, Marvin Harris, and Robert Murphey, *War: The Anthropology of Armed Conflict and Aggression* (Garden City, N.Y.: Natural History Press, 1968), 221-222.
4. "War," *Encyclopedia Britannica* (1962), 23:325.
5. See especially Anatol Rapoport, *Conflict in Man-Made Environment* (Baltimore: Penguin, 1974), Chapter 18, and Richard J. Barnet, *Roots of War* (New York: Atheneum, 1972).
6. Quoted in Samuel Huntington, *The Soldier and the State* (Cambridge: Harvard University Press, 1967), 66.
7. William Kaufmann, "Two American Ambassadors: Bullitt and Kennedy," in Gordon Craig and Felix Gilbert, eds., *The Diplomats* (Princeton: Princeton University Press, 1955), 658-659.
8. See Benjamin J. Cohen, *The Question of Imperialism* (New York: Basic Books, 1973).
9. John A. Hobson, *Imperialism, A Study* (Ann Arbor: University of Michigan Press, 1965) (originally published in 1902).
10. V. I. Lenin, *Imperialism, the Highest Stage of Capitalism* (New York: International Publishers, 1939) (originally published in 1917).
11. See Michael Barrat Brown, *After Imperialism*, rev. ed. (New York: Humanities Press, 1970).
12. Paul A. Baran and Paul M. Sweezy, *Monopoly Capital* (New York: Monthly Review Press, 1966).
13. See, for example, Oscar Handlin and Mary F. Handlin, *The Wealth of the American People: A History of American Affluence* (New York: Basic Books, 1975), Chapter 12.
14. Similar phenomena have been known in the animal world, where, for example, a bird painted a different color by a human hand may be pecked to death when it re-

joins a flock of its own species. This metaphor is the theme of Jerzy Kosinski's autobiographical work, *The Painted Bird* (Boston: Houghton Mifflin, 1965).

15. Miroslav Nincic, "Understanding International Conflict: Some Theoretical Gaps," *Journal of Peace Research* 20 (1982): 49-59.

16. Kenneth E. Boulding, "National Images and International Systems," in James N. Rosenau, ed., *International Politics and Foreign Policy* (New York: Free Press, 1969), 182.

17. Quoted in Kenneth Bourne, *Britain and the Balance of Power in North America* (Berkeley and Los Angeles: University of California Press, 1967).

18. Robert Jervis, "Hypotheses on Misperception," in Rosenau, ed., *International Politics*, 251.

19. See Leon A. Festinger, *A Theory of Cognitive Dissonance* (Stanford: Stanford University Press, 1957), and Robert Zajonc, "Cognitive Theories in Social Psychology," in Gardner Lindzey and Elliot Aronson, eds., *Handbook of Social Psychology*, 2d ed. (Reading, Mass.: Addison-Wesley, 1968), 2:345-353.

20. Robert Jervis, *Perception and Misperception in International Politics* (Princeton: Princeton University Press, 1976), 118.

21. Jerzy Zadny and Harold Gerard, "Attributed Intentions and Informational Selectivity," *Journal of Experimental Social Psychology* 10 (1974): 34-52.

22. Carlos Garcia-Mata, "UFO Iconography," *Science* 159 (March 15, 1968): 1187.

23. Geoffrey Blainey, *The Causes of War* (New York: Free Press, 1973), 18.

24. Francis A. Beer, *Peace against War* (San Francisco: W. H. Freeman, 1981), 131.

25. Representative of the neofunctionalist literature are Ernst B. Haas, *Beyond the Nation State* (Stanford: Stanford University Press, 1964); Leon Lindberg and Stuart Scheingold, eds., *Regional Integration* (Cambridge: Harvard University Press, 1971); Phillipe Schmitter, "Three Neofunctionalist Hypotheses about International Integration," *International Organization* 24 (1969): 161-167.

26. Charles Osgood, *An Alternative to War and Surrender* (Urbana: University of Illinois Press, 1962).

27. David Singer, "Disarmament: The Domestic and Global Context," in John H. Gilbert, ed., *The New Era in American Foreign Policy* (New York: St. Martin's, 1973), 179-180.

28. Robert Axelrod, *The Evolution of Cooperation* (New York: Basic Books, 1984).

29. On this issue, see Alexander George, "The Case for Multiple Advocacy in Making Foreign Policy," *American Political Science Review* 66 (1972): 751-785.

30. Irving Janis, *Victims of Groupthink* (Boston: Houghton Mifflin, 1972).

The Causes of
U.S.-Soviet Rivalry

MOST OF THE animosities and antagonisms in U.S. relations with other countries seem to flow, in one way or another, from its rivalry with the Soviet Union. Leftist movements and governments in developing countries, even those that have grown out of conditions of extreme social inequity, are opposed for fear that they could become extensions of Soviet power. The East European countries are disliked, if not actually feared, because of their dependence on Moscow and their tendency to be servile toward its policies. Even when relations with friends become frayed, it is sometimes because these countries are thought to be excessively accommodating to the Soviet Union.

Because this rivalry so pervades U.S. foreign relations, because it is so fraught with consequences for humanity, and because it poses some of the most crucial instances of the dilemma of effective choice, it deserves extended discussion. Surprisingly, the causes of Soviet-American antagonism are not often subjected to rational analysis. Instead, facile assumptions, reflex reasoning, and unexamined misconceptions provide the prism through which many people view the Soviet Union and U.S. relations with it. The ease with which totally different conceptions of these relations take root reflects the superficiality of thinking on the subject.

According to one perspective, usually associated with the conservative end of the U.S. political spectrum, there is little good to be said about the Soviet Union and little to be gained by seeking to cooperate with it. The Soviet system is inherently evil and its foreign policy is consistently aggressive. The Kremlin's overriding goal, which, despite tactical retreats, it has never abandoned, is to ensure the global spread of communism and the destruction of democracy and free enterprise. A world thus reshaped would be subservient to Moscow's dictates. Accordingly, the highest priority of Soviet leaders is to acquire military supremacy and to undermine the international position of the United States. This has meant, among other things, an ever-expanding nuclear arsenal, far in excess of legitimate defensive needs. Occasionally, the Kremlin may make gestures of good will and even negotiate arms control treaties and other agreements designed to reduce tension, but they are likely to be part of an attempt to lull the United States into complacency, for Moscow must always be assumed to be acting in bad faith. Soviet designs can be thwarted only by U.S. strength and determination; any sign of weakness or of flaccidity will lead Soviet leaders to bolder encroachments on the interests of the United States and other democracies. Soviet expansionism can be contained only through superior military might and constant vigilance. Toughness and distrust are the appropriate attitudes; anything less would amount to an abdication of U.S. responsibility in world affairs.

A second perspective, which is usually found at the liberal end of the political spectrum, makes less absolute statements and is willing to grant that, in some important ways, the two superpowers can have satisfactory relations. While the Soviet Union would certainly like to encourage the international spread of communism, its overriding concern has always been national security, and what it is most concerned about is external aggression. Because the Soviet Union has suffered so much from foreign invasion, its frequently paranoid behavior toward other nations is understandable. This experience has also led to the belief that the nation will be secure in the future only if it is stronger than it has been in the past. To be sure, the Soviet Union is engaged in competition with the United States, and interprets U.S. foreign policy defeats as actual or potential Soviet gains, but in this respect it is merely behaving as any major power does when dealing with a rival. In any case, the Kremlin has repeatedly demonstrated that it is unwilling to take major risks to pursue its international goals, especially when these goals involve remote regions. Under the circumstances, the United States is justified in increasing the costs and risks to the U.S.S.R. for its objectionable activities, but it is very important to understand the historical foundations of Soviet anxieties and to try to reduce, not exacerbate, the Soviet sense of insecurity. Military superiority is an evanescent goal, and its pursuit merely fuels the arms race and heightens tensions. Thus, vigorous efforts should be made to negotiate verifiable arms-control treaties and to eliminate sources of friction.

These two conceptions of Soviet behavior cannot both be right, and the policies they lead to are incompatible. Such differences suggest that we must probe more deeply into the nature of superpower relations. It is usually because our thinking is superficial and dominated by ideological preconceptions that apparently intelligent people can disagree so totally. There will be no sound basis for formulating policies toward the Soviet Union until we achieve better understanding of the forces that shape relations between the two countries.

In the preceding chapter, the distinction was made between the initiating and reinforcing causes of conduct in foreign affairs. This distinction will be applied here in the attempt to understand what propels the United States and the Soviet Union into rivalry and mutual intolerance.

Initiating Causes

Objective Conflicts of Interest

If two nations regard each other as adversaries, it is easy for people on both sides to fall into the trap of assuming that everything gained by the other must be a loss to themselves. "If they really want something badly enough, they probably should not be allowed to get it!" is an attitude often implicit in the behavior of leaders and advisers in superpower relations. But such thinking assumes that an adversary relationship already exists. The arms race, for example, indicates that each side perceives an increase in the other's military strength as a threat to its own security, but this presupposes that some other conflict has preceded the military rivalry. The arms race is not an initiating cause of the antagonism; rather, it is both a symptom and a reinforcing cause. The three sources of objective conflicts of interest that operate as initiating causes were identified in the preceding chapter as territory, economic gain, and belief systems.

TERRITORY. It is axiomatic to many Americans that the Soviet Union is an aggressive nation bent on aggrandizement. Former President Richard M. Nixon has said, "Most of the obstacles to peace today result from the Soviet Union's expansionist policies." [1] Richard Pipes, a historian at Harvard University and a frequent consultant to conservative foreign policy groups, has written that, "in the history of Russia, expansion is not a phase but a constant . . . the Russian state has been expanding since the early fourteenth century with extraordinary vigor." [2] Although it is not always clear in such statements whether "expansion" refers to territory or merely to political influence, the image of seizure of territory is often implicit, and if that is really what is involved, the ingredients of an objective conflict of interest could be present. Is the Soviet Union, then, a ruthlessly expansionist nation?

Many countries have had a history of imperial growth. While people in the United States do not usually think of their country as expansionist, the historical record says otherwise. After all, the descendants of the Mayflower, starting from Plymouth Rock, ended up conquering a large part of North America, taking it not only from the American Indians but from a number of foreign nations as well. Still, it is probably true that Soviet expansionism has lasted longer than is the case with most other countries and that it has been exceptionally successful.

The origins of the Russian empire lay in the principality of Muscovy (now known as the city of Moscow) in the thirteenth century. Muscovite history was steeped in warfare, as its princes fought foreign assailants, mainly the Mongols, and sought territorial acquisitions. Muscovy eventually became Russia, which, under such rulers as Ivan the Terrible, Peter the Great, and Catherine the Great, spread its sovereignty through both Europe and Asia. When Alexander II, who is best known for his emancipation of the Russian serfs, died in 1881, Russia controlled a territory of nearly eight million square miles—about thirteen thousand times as much as the six hundred square miles occupied by Muscovy in the fourteenth century. Thus, territorial growth was an integral part of Russian history.

Economic necessity was a major reason for this expansion. Unlike the more arable land of Western nations, Russian soil is capable of supporting only a fraction of its population, and the country's population was growing. But security concerns also played a part. The experience of Mongol and other foreign forays into Russian land, including Napoleon's devastating invasion in 1812, encouraged expansion into adjacent areas, to push the frontiers as far out as possible in order to keep potential aggressors distant from the centers of population. According to some scholars, this history has repeated itself in the twentieth century. For example, no other nation (with the possible exception of Poland) suffered such enormous losses from Nazi aggression, and the Soviet Union was one of the few countries to emerge from World War II with more territory than it had before. It acquired Latvia, Estonia, Lithuania, and parts of Germany, Czechoslovakia, Finland, Poland, Romania, China and Japan.

It must be reiterated, however, that expansionism of this sort has not been unique to Russia. Several nations that today are thought to exemplify peaceful international conduct have had histories marked by periods of aggressive expansion: Sweden in the seventeenth century, France under Napoleon, Germany under the Nazis. Why should it be assumed, then, that expansionism is a "constant" of Russian behavior and that the Soviet Union is therefore a permanent threat to its neighbors and to the United States? Besides the existence of natural barriers to growth and the difficulties in absorbing new ethnicities, the Soviet Union may well have reached the outer limit of the territory it can hope to control politically and to manage administratively.

Moreover, it is far from clear that there are territorial conflicts of interest between the Soviet Union and the United States specifically. The land acquired by Russia has never been territory to which the United States aspired (with the possible exception of Alaska, which was, in any case, sold to the United States). One can argue that the Soviet military presence in Afghanistan or Vietnam threatens U.S. security in some way, but that is only because an adversary relation between the two superpowers already exists and the Soviet presence in those two countries is viewed as conferring a military advantage on the U.S.S.R., not because there are rival claims to the territories. Again, one may object to the Soviet annexation of the Baltic states on political or ethical grounds, but this is as irrelevant from the point of view of competing territorial interests as were the Louisiana purchase or the U.S. acquisition of Texas from Mexico. In short, whatever the threat that Soviet military activities in other countries represent to the United States, it has little to do with land.

ECONOMIC COMPETITION. Much of the ill feeling between the United States and prerevolutionary Russia stemmed from economic rivalry. In the 1890s, the United States came to believe that its continued prosperity required an "open door" to trade in China's wealthy province of Manchuria, while the Russians wished to colonize parts of Manchuria and close its markets to outside competition. Because of this, the United States tried to contain Russian expansion into the area by supporting Japan, which also had its eye on Manchuria. But this was nearly a century ago, and we must ask whether conflicts of economic interests exist today.

One possible basis for such conflicts would be competition for export markets. However, differences between the economic systems of the two superpowers and between the nature of the goods they produce make this unlikely. The U.S. economy, like all market economies, is largely driven by aggregate demand. Consumers, investors, and the government all seek to purchase various goods and services, and, generally, the greater their demand, the more robust the economy will be as it mobilizes to supply what is needed. However, domestic demand usually does not suffice to ensure economic vigor; it must be supplemented by demand from foreign buyers. Consequently, securing access to external markets is an important U.S. foreign policy goal. In the Soviet Union, however, supply and demand are supposed to be matched through central planning. The Soviet economy is driven not by demand but rather by supply: it grows in accordance with how much it produces, and all that is produced will normally be absorbed. By implication, exports are not needed in quite the same way as in the United States. For the Soviet Union, the main purpose of exports is to earn the foreign currency needed to buy sophisticated technology from the West.

The Soviet economy grew quite rapidly in the early postwar decades, but growth rates have been less impressive since the 1970s. Soviet economic strategy was initially based on *extensive* growth—that is, on the use of large quantities of labor and capital to expand production. But this strategy could not be sustained, for several reasons. First, as any factor of production is used in increasing amounts it becomes subject to the law of diminishing returns: each additional unit of capital or labor produces a smaller output. Second, there are simply limits to the availability of capital and labor. Because of demographic factors, the Soviet labor force is no longer expanding, and the female population is already largely absorbed into the labor force. As for capital, some 30 percent of national income is already devoted to capital formation (more than twice the U.S. figure), and it is not feasible to allocate much more for this purpose.

Faced with these conditions, the Soviet leadership has moved to a strategy of *intensive* growth. Instead of using more and more labor and capital, it seeks to make them more productive, especially by the application of modern technology. Yet, outside the military and space sectors, the Soviet Union has not been a very technologically innovative society. The technological gap that separates it not only from the United States but also from other industrialized countries as well is quite wide, perhaps because an economy based on bureaucratic planning is not well suited to the tasks of rapid technological growth. Under the circumstances, the Soviet Union finds itself compelled to acquire technology from abroad—primarily from the West.

But it confronts several obstacles to that course of action. There are political impediments to technological exports in the Western countries, particularly if the desired technology seems likely to have military applications. There are economic problems as well, among them the need to pay for purchases from the West with convertible currencies, which the Soviet Union does not have in great quantities. The ruble itself is not convertible, which means that hard currencies must be earned by exporting to the West. Thus, by providing the means to purchase foreign technology, exports could serve a vital function for the Soviet economy.

However, the Soviet Union is not in a good position to compete with the United States for export markets. The major U.S. exports are manufactured goods and grain and other agricultural products. Since the Soviet Union, far from being an exporter of grain, actually imports it—indeed, its major supplier is the United States—there is obviously no rivalry in that area. On the other hand, the major Soviet exports are not manufactured goods but raw materials, and, to the extent that it does attempt to sell finished goods abroad, they do not seriously compete with those exported by U.S. producers. The quality of Soviet goods is so inferior to that of U.S. products that they represent virtually no competitive threat. Consequently, competition over export markets cannot reasonably be considered a cause of the U.S.-Soviet rivalry.

Another common basis for economic conflict has been rivalry for access to raw materials. In 1980, Secretary of State Alexander Haig declared that, "as one assesses the recent stepup of Soviet proxy activity in the Third World . . . one can only conclude that the 'era' of the resource war has arrived." [3] Yet closer scrutiny reveals that this concern, too, rests on fragile foundations.

Oil has been at the focus of U.S. concerns. Ever since the Arab members of the Organization of Petroleum Exporting Countries (OPEC) suspended shipments of oil to the United States in late 1973 in retaliation for U.S. support of Israel, the danger of heavy reliance on imported oil has loomed large. A few years after that event, the Central Intelligence Agency issued a report predicting a sharp decline in the Soviet Union's oil production and suggesting that it would soon have to rely on external sources of oil as well—presumably the Middle East. [4] Thus was raised the threat of U.S.-Soviet competition for access to Middle Eastern oil fields—a rivalry that might be pursued by regional proxies for a while but that might eventually come to involve the superpowers directly.

In retrospect, this threat seems to have been considerably overdrawn. To begin with, the United States has taken significant steps toward lessening its dependence on OPEC oil; by 1983, no more than 10 percent of domestic oil consumption came from OPEC sources. Also, the CIA has altered its own forecasts and now believes that the Soviet Union has a reasonably reliable supply of oil from domestic sources. In any case, the Soviet economy is not as dependent on oil as other economies are, and an expanded reliance on natural gas (which the Soviet Union has in ample amounts) or on nuclear power (which in the Soviet Union does not have to face the opposition of environmental groups) could further reduce that dependence. Finally, even if some of the bleaker predictions on future Soviet oil production should be borne out, the petroleum which Russia now exports to its friends and allies could provide a comfortable cushion for domestic needs. The East European countries might have to turn elsewhere for much of their petroleum supply, but the U.S.S.R. it-self could remain relatively self-sufficient for quite some time.

Much the same conclusion can be drawn for other minerals. Although the United States is a mineral-rich country, it is dependent on external sources for a number of strategic raw materials used for military and aerospace purposes. Such minerals as chromium, cobalt, platinum-group metals, manganese, and vanadium are obtained largely from politically unstable parts of the world, such as Zimbabwe and especially South Africa. However, the Soviet Union is nearly entirely self-sufficient in minerals (see Table 8-1); in fact, it is one of the world's biggest producers and exporters of chromium and manganese, and it is also an exporter of platinum-group metals and vanadium. It does import

Table 8-1 Percentage of Domestic Consumption of Minerals Obtained from Imports, United States and Soviet Union, 1984

Mineral	United States	Soviet Union
Titanium (rutile)	100	0
Columbium	100	0
Mica (sheet)	100	0
Manganese	98	0
Bauxite	94	39
Cobalt	91	42
Tantalum	91	0
Chromium	90	0
Platinum-group metals	85	0
Tin	80	24
Asbestos	80	0
Nickel	72	0
Zinc	67	0
Cadmium	63	0
Tungsten	52	14
Selenium	49	0

Source: U.S. Department of Defense, *Report of the Secretary of Defense Caspar W. Weinberger to the Congress, Fiscal Year 1985* (Washington, D.C.: Government Printing Office, 1984), 96.

substantial amounts of cobalt, mainly from Cuba, Zaire, and Zambia, and the latter two nations are suppliers to the United States as well, but that alone can hardly be considered to make conflicts over minerals an important source of rivalry.

Of course, it might be argued that Moscow could seek to deny the United States access to needed minerals whether or not the Soviet economy itself required them. But even if that were so, it would imply that the conflict was the effect of an already existing adversarial relationship, and perhaps a reinforcing cause, but not its initiating cause. Indeed, the whole issue of competition over resources between the United States and the Soviet Union is relatively recent; it surfaced long after the two nations had come to regard each other as rivals. No matter how we look at it, it does not appear that the economic interests of the superpowers are inherently in conflict.

IDEOLOGICAL CLASHES.   Probably the most common belief about the U.S.-Soviet conflict is that it springs from clashing ideologies. The struggle between the two is viewed as a duel between democracy and communism, the state-run economy and free enterprise, religion and atheism, pluralism and totalitarianism—in short, between fundamentally incompatible principles. While there is no space here for a thorough appraisal of what the Soviet Union stands for ideologically, and though Soviet behavior is often at variance with its professed ideology, the major components of the official belief system of the U.S.S.R. can be briefly outlined.

The foundation of Soviet ideology is provided by the writings of Karl Marx and Friedrich Engels, especially the *Communist Manifesto* and the much longer and turgid analysis of capitalism entitled *Das Kapital*. The work of Lenin, particularly his action-oriented treatise *What Is To Be Done?* is another pillar of Soviet ideology. From this body of work, and its interpretation by Soviet leaders and commentators, several themes emerge.

The most fundamental of these concerns the existence of an inevitable *class struggle* within capitalist societies. History is the record of a continuous conflict between the interests of those who possess the means of production (anything from a plow to a factory) and those who have only their labor to sell, but the conflict reaches its culmination under capitalism. Property owners (capitalists) exploit workers (the proletariat) by extracting a *surplus value* from their labor, representing the difference between what the workers are paid and the contribution their labor makes to the end-value of the product. As a result, the working class becomes increasingly impoverished, and its standard of living becomes merely the minimum required to physically sustain it as a work force.

A second theme is that capitalism is not an economically viable system. Competition among firms leads to monopolies, as weaker capitalists are squeezed out and are relegated to the proletariat. The production of these monopolies cannot be absorbed, because so large a portion of society has become impoverished; hence, profits can be maintained only by extracting an ever larger surplus value from the already severely oppressed labor force. Ultimately, the contradictions of the system will become so obvious, and the plight of the proletariat so extreme, that the foundations of the system will crumble and the workers will rise up to destroy it.

A third element of Soviet ideology, and the one that owes most to Lenin, is the belief that, inevitable though all of this may be, the demise of capitalism will be expedited if organized communist parties assert leadership of the proletariat and guide it toward its historical destiny—replacing capitalism with a workers' state. Even after a successful communist revolution, however, the state cannot be expected to wither away overnight; because the revolution will continue to face the opposition of unrepentant "class enemies," a strong, even coercive, state will be required to ensure the security of the new system. This principle has also been inferred to mean that the Soviet Union, as the first nation to experience a revolution of this sort, is obliged to don the mantle of leadership in the international struggle against capitalism, and that other communist movements owe it loyalty and obedience.

This sketchy outline of what the U.S.S.R. officially stands for highlights a set of beliefs that are incompatible with the principles on which the U.S. political and economic system is based. But are these differences at the root of the U.S.-Soviet rivalry?

Though this may appear very likely, there are reasons for caution. We have already seen that the rivalry between the two nations preceded the Bolshevik Revolution of 1917, that relations deteriorated in the late nineteenth century, well before the Communists came to power. Still, it might be contended that political ideology has always been part of the problem. As pointed out in Chapter 2, Americans fell out of sympathy with Russia at a time when tsarist rule was imposing repressive political conditions. Prison camps, arbitrary arrests, and censorship of the press existed long before the Communist state. Thus, the basic quarrel may be not between capitalism and communism, but between democracy and *non-democracy*, whether of the left or of the right. It may simply be that the United States cannot get along with countries that violate the political principles it holds sacred, no matter where on the political spectrum they happen to be situated.

But this contention also fails to carry conviction for, as we have seen in previous chapters, the United States has had friendly relations with many repressive dictatorships of the right, nations whose records on human rights are not obviously better than the Soviet Union's. Surely, the Philippines under Marcos, Chile under Pinochet, Nicaragua under Somoza, or Indonesia under Suharto could not, by any stretch of the imagination, be considered democracies. Perhaps, then, the only nations that the United States cannot get along with are those that do not respect private property, implying that it is the *economic* characteristics of communism rather than its political practices that Washington most objects to. However, the evidence does not support this hypothesis either, for there are a number of avowedly Marxist regimes with which the United States manages to get along quite well; the People's Republic of China and Yugoslavia are the most obvious examples.

Of course, Americans' dislike of communism, and the Soviet leaders' disapproval of capitalism, may have much to do with the two nations' rivalry, but that is not the same as saying that these differences are the *cause* of the rivalry. For there to be an objective conflict of interest in the ideological sphere, as was pointed out in Chapter 7, one or both of two conditions must be met: the proponents of one ideology must try to subvert the other side's values and institutions within the latter's own society, or one side must attempt to make ideological converts among the rival's allies or among previously neutral countries.

The first of these conditions was met, to some extent, by both sides in the years immediately following the Bolshevik Revolution. As mentioned in Chapter 2, more than ten thousand U.S. troops were dispatched to combat the Bolsheviks after their seizure of power, and they did not leave Soviet territory until 1920. Most people in the United States today are probably unaware of this intervention, but it was certainly the most direct step either side has ever taken to rub out the other's political system. Meanwhile, during the same period and continuing through the 1920s and 1930s, the Soviet regime was making efforts to export its revolution. The major vehicle for these efforts was the Communist International, or Comintern, a Soviet-led organization of Communist parties, which many people believed was engaged in subversive activity in the United States and several other countries. Something of the kind probably was going on, but it was on a very limited scale and had no effect at all on U.S. political values or institutions (other than to stimulate anti-Communist witch hunts). But many decades have elapsed since those times, the stability of both political systems is firmly established, and it is extremely unlikely that either superpower believes that its rival's values and institutions can be subverted by outside efforts. Conversely, although the Soviet regime may continue to justify internal repression by the need to struggle against foreign "class enemies," and McCarthyist paranoia may occasionally erupt in the United States, it strains credulity to believe that either superpower actually fears that its political system will be undermined by the other's efforts.

The second condition for an ideological conflict of interest is a more credible source of superpower antagonism. Many people in the United States are convinced that it is a matter of high Soviet priority to promote, through conversion or coercion, the international spread of communism. Still, the importance of this kind of behavior on the part of the Soviet Union should not be exaggerated.

It is unlikely that Soviet leaders have ideological pretensions with regard to the Western democracies. It must be amply apparent to the Kremlin by now that these nations are genuinely inhospitable to the values and practices of communism and that neither proselytizing nor active subversion is likely to alter the forms of government they have chosen for themselves. The Bolshevik revolutionaries may have been convinced in the post-1917 years that capitalism was on the verge of collapse, but responsible Soviet officials today must be impressed by the vitality of the industrialized capitalist societies and firm popular support their political systems enjoy. Despite the slogans referring to the "inevitable" triumph of the "proletarian" states and the half-hearted attempts to explain away the popularity of capitalist democracy with comments about "false consciousness," it is hard to believe that the Soviet rulers are not fundamentally realists, with a fairly accurate understanding of political trends in the contemporary world. Accordingly, they would not be inclined to make large investments in the conversion of, say, Denmark or France to Soviet-style communism. Consequently, ideological competition within the industrialized democracies is scarcely an issue in U.S.-Soviet relations.

The situation is somewhat different in the developing world, where political preferences are less clearly defined and political systems are generally less stable. There, the existence of ideological competition between the superpowers is more credible. Richard Pipes, the conservative historian who has been mentioned before, has asserted that the ultimate objective of Soviet strategy is "the elimination, worldwide, of private ownership of the means of production and the 'bourgeois' order which rests upon it, and its replacement with what Lenin called a 'worldwide republic of Soviets,'" and that the main target of this strategy is now the Third World.[5] Another interpretation of Soviet behavior in the developing regions, however, is that it is guided more by pragmatic security and diplomatic interests than by the desire to advance international communism. Indeed, when the Soviet leaders have had to choose between support for a local Communist movement and the promotion of other foreign policy objectives, they have almost invariably abandoned their ideological comrades. For example, Moscow's support for Mao Tse-tung's forces in China when they were fighting for survival against the armies of Chiang Kai-shek in the 1940s was, at best, tepid. Stalin was not convinced that the Chinese Communists would emerge victorious and considered it prudent to avoid alienating Britain and the United States. Similarly, when Greek Communists were fighting a civil war with right-wing monarchists in the late 1940s, they received no support from the Soviet Union; Moscow's diplomatic interests at the time led to a hands-off policy.

Such ideologically neutral pragmatism has been evident more recently as well. When Moscow established cordial diplomatic relations with newly independent India, it turned its back on the Indian Communist Party, and later it went so far as to inform the party that, if forced to choose between it and "progressive bourgeois nationalism," it would choose the latter.[6] In spite of the persecution of Communists in Egypt, Moscow furnished arms to the Cairo government and provided assistance for its Aswan Dam project. Egypt's president, Gamal Abdel Nasser, was even awarded the decoration of "Hero of the Soviet Union," an honor rarely bestowed on foreigners. Despite repression of Communists in Iran, Iraq, and Uganda during the Brezhnev era, Moscow supplied arms to all three countries. As one observer notes:

> Despite the rhetorical support for revolution, Moscow did little to promote social upheavals in the Third World. All the revolutionary changes of the last two decades took place without Soviet involvement in the overthrow of the old regime—Cuba, Nicaragua, Iran, Afghanistan, Ethiopia, and the collapse of the Portuguese empire. Only in the case of Afghanistan, Angola, and Guinea-Bissau had Moscow ever had any previous contact with some of the new leaders.[7]

In short, while Soviet activity in the Third World is prompted by a desire to weaken the international position of the United States (and vice versa), it is not primarily motivated by ideological goals. This is not to say that Soviet leaders are indifferent to their proclaimed beliefs, but rather that the security of the Soviet state, its power and its international position, rank higher than the spread of Marxist-Leninist precepts in the hierarchy of national goals. Furthermore, even in the Third World, the payoffs of ideological activism cannot be considered very attractive. Although Third World countries are generally not as committed to traditional democratic principles as are the West European nations, few are enamored of the Soviet political model and of the beliefs from which it springs. In any case, these countries generally eschew too close an identification with either superpower, preferring to think of themselves as "nonaligned."

Plainly, Moscow would prefer a world of like-minded countries. Some level of ideological commitment must be assumed, and, in any case, countries shaped in the Soviet mold would presumably be more responsive to the interests of the Soviet state. These propositions, too, must be qualified. Even a professedly Marxist nation may not be a servile ally, as the cases of Yugoslavia, Zimbabwe, Romania, and especially China demonstrate. Moreover, in economic as well as political respects, the Soviet model has aroused little enthusiasm in the Third World. Although a number of socialist or Marxist concepts may be appealing because of their egalitarian implications and suggestions of a break with a history of exploitation, the well-known Soviet lethargy and bureaucratic ossification, and the unimpressive rate of Soviet economic growth in recent years, do not offer much promise to societies whose dominant goal is rapid economic development. Thus, the Kremlin must realize that ideological bedfellows are unlikely to be found in the developing world and that, even if they could be created, their responsiveness to Soviet state interests could not be assumed.

The discussion so far can be summarized in the statement that ideological differences between the superpowers are relevant to their relationships but do not constitute objective conflicts of interest. But perhaps the discussion has been too restricted. Could we not simply assume that both countries seek *power* and that, since power is relative—the more that one side has, the less powerful is the other—there is an inevitable conflict of interest between the United States and the Soviet Union? This is not an indefensible position, but it does raise a further issue—namely, why do the two sides want power? Unless one is willing to believe that power is an "elemental bio-social drive," [8] one has to assume that nations want it because it allows them to pursue their rivalry more effectively. But then the quest for power would be a manifestation of the rivalry, not its cause. At most, the competition for power could be regarded as producing a derivative conflict of interest, not as being its initiating cause. We must turn, therefore, to the other category of initiating causes of hostility: domestic forces within one or both countries.

Domestic Forces

In the previous chapter, we distinguished three possible domestic causes of external hostility: (a) internal tension and instability, (b) the pressure of national-security bureaucracies, and (c) economic drives. Each of these forces might operate within both superpowers.

ON THE SOVIET SIDE. It could be argued that, since there is little room for opposition to the Soviet regime and no significant signs of domestic instability, the Kremlin has no internal reason to pick foreign quarrels. Another view, however, is that the Soviet government, and tsarist governments before it, have never managed to establish a sense of citizen identification with the political process and have rarely managed to improve the people's material lot sufficiently to ensure legitimacy on the basis of popular loyalty or economic performance. Consequently, these regimes have tried to compensate for domestic failures by impressing their citizenry with external achievements. Pipes, for example, has argued that

> Russian governments have always felt the need to solidify their internal position by impressing on the population the awe which they inspire in other nations. . . . Psychologically speaking, the greater the awe in which a Russian government is held by foreigners, the stronger is its claim to rule and the more satisfying the compensation that it offers to its people.[9]

According to this line of thought, even without overt manifestations of domestic instability, Russian governments have usually had a *latent* concern with their fragile legitimacy and hence have felt a need to shore it up by success abroad. Pipes does not back his hypothesis with much explicit evidence, though. A somewhat different twist to the argument is that the Russian people have historically experienced a sense of inferiority toward the West and that their leaders have felt called upon to offset this feeling with foreign successes and international strength. Again, the government's legitimacy is thought to be strengthened by acts that bolster the nation's sense of self-assurance. As one scholar put it:

> The dominant trait of the Russian national character has been a lack of political, economic, military, or psychological security. . . . It is because the Russians have failed throughout their history to establish self-assured and prosperous conditions at home that they are driven to equate stability and security with political domination abroad rather than with the attainment of social justice or economic well-being.[10]

There is not enough persuasive evidence for this version either, and yet the idea that the Soviet regime feels that its legitimacy depends on external toughness, either to compensate for its failures or to offset a historically conditioned sense of inferiority, cannot be lightly discarded.

Beyond questions of regime legitimacy-building, we must ask whether there are forces within the governmental structure, and especially the national security bureaucracy, that benefit from external hostility and might wish to promote it. The notion that entities within the governmental structure may be shaping national policies to suit their own needs and interests may seem less applicable to the Soviet Union than to the Western democracies. In the Soviet case, it is generally assumed that the bureaucracies simply do as they are told, whereas in the West, political discipline is much less tight and a diversity of views and preferences is regarded as the desirable state of affairs. Consequently, bureaucracies are more likely to make themselves felt. Nevertheless, there is evidence that policy preferences are less uniform in the U.S.S.R. than the nature of the regime might lead us to believe. As George Kennan observes,

> Many of the more alarmist visions of Soviet behavior . . . seem to reflect a view of the top Soviet leadership as a group of men who, having all internal problems effectively solved and nothing to do but plot our destruction, sit at the pinnacle of a structure of power whose blind and unquestioning obedience resembles that of a tremendously disciplined military force, poised for attack and only awaiting superior orders. This is unrealistic even from the standpoint of the actual relations between the leadership and its own bureaucracy.[11]

Interorganizational rivalry for resources, missions, and status is characteristic of every policy-making machine, no matter how well-oiled it might appear from the outside. Furthermore, in the state-run economy of the Soviet Union, economic pressures are exerted not through the market and through political lobbies, as in the West, but primarily through the bureaucracies. Thus, although it is plainly impossible to learn as much about the operations of the Soviet regime as about democratic governments, it is almost certain—and indeed it is a matter of general agreement among observers—that different bureaucracies have discrepant interests when it comes to relations with the United States. In a country where economic resources are tight, devoting more resources to one kind of policy objective means that noticeably fewer will be available for others; even more than elsewhere, policy becomes, in the words of one expert on the Soviet Union, a matter of "robbing Pyotr to pay Pavel." [12] Specifically, the pursuit of ambitious military policies deflects resources from investment, the production of consumer goods, and agriculture. Long-suffering Soviet consumers have received very little from the regime and are probably quite aware of how much lower their standard of living is than that of the West. Moreover, the Ministry of Agriculture and the agriculture department of the Central Committee of the Communist party are presumably concerned about low levels of agricultural productivity and the country's embarrassing dependence on the United States for grain, and it can be assumed that the Ministry of Light Industry and the Ministry of the Meat and Dairy Industry are more concerned with the lot of the consumer than are the military organizations. These bureaucratic agencies might be inclined to prefer a placid international situation, one that did not require major investments in defense. Those sectors of the civilian economy that are especially dependent on advanced technology, which is obtainable mainly from the West, might also prefer a state of superpower relations that would enable them to acquire this technology with fewer political obstacles.

On the other hand, many powerful Soviet interests are better served by confrontational policies. The military could not justify the share of national income it claims, nor the KGB the power it wields, in the absence of international tension. Similarly, the Ministry of General Machine Building (which is responsible for the development and production of strategic missiles) and the Ministry of Medium Machine Building (which produces the nuclear warheads) would not prosper in a world of détente and arms control. Consequently, heavy industry probably supports more defense production and the foreign policies that require it, while agricultural groups and those associated with light industry presumably prefers policies that allow the allocation of more resources to their own sectors of the economy.[13]

In the past, bureaucracies that benefited from some measure of hostility have had the upper hand, but this may be less true in the future. While it is hard to predict just how the balance of power between these discrepant interests will evolve, there are reasons to think that it will tilt toward those who favor the objectives of consumer goods production and détente. In the first place, the generational turnover implies that fewer Soviet leaders will have experienced World War II at first hand, and they may consequently be less obsessed with the need for military strength and ceaseless vigilance. The more open and cooperative outlook on world affairs shown by Mikhail Gorbachev and his associates confirms this belief. Moreover, as the rate of economic growth slows down, satisfaction of consumer demands will become increasingly important to the regime's legitimacy. The Gorbachev regime, in particular, seems determined to remove the many obstacles to successful economic growth. This requires significant reforms, including a relaxation of economic planning; it also requires improved relations with the West, to lighten the economic burden of the arms race and to increase Soviet access to Western technology. Still, the international climate will ultimately determine whether the strength of the Soviet national-security interests will be allowed to wane in favor of other national needs.

One important conclusion to be drawn is that, in the U.S.S.R. as in other countries, a true understanding of policy requires a constant attentiveness to the structure of internal interests behind the policy, especially the interests of relevant governmental bureaucracies. How the Soviet Union behaves toward the United States will be at least partly determined by the nature of these interests and the relative power of the organizations that represent them.

ON THE U.S. SIDE. The U.S. political system is, if anything, more stable than that of the Soviet Union, and, in contrast to the U.S.S.R., the legitimacy of U.S. political institutions and practices rests on their performance and on the public's identification with and involvement in the system. U.S. governments would therefore seem not to require a belligerent foreign policy. Nevertheless, various political actors often do derive some benefit from a tough stance toward the Soviet Union. In Chapter 3, it was pointed out that the U.S. public distrusts Moscow and believes in a strong military posture. Under those circumstances, it is sometimes possible to gain political advantage by accusing opponents of being "soft on communism" and neglecting the needs of national defense. As a result, incumbent administrations are anxious not to appear weak on East-West issues. Thus, even if U.S. governments need not pick quarrels with the Soviet Union to deflect attention from unsolved domestic problems or to create an excuse for tightening their grip on power, political leaders and candidates could well believe that a position of "firmness" toward the Soviets will at least deprive the opposition of a potentially damaging issue.

On another level, a large portion of the national-security bureaucracy is, through a combination of habit and organizational interest, inclined to interpret most Soviet activities in a predatory light and to advocate militaristic methods of dealing with the Kremlin. People in the Department of Defense and the intelligence community are trained to perceive threats rather than opportunities for cooperation; moreover, like their Soviet counterparts, they would have difficulty promoting their interests in a world where international hostility had been eliminated. This is not to suggest that they consciously subordinate the national interest to their own, or that they are mindlessly committed to confrontation. Rather, their experiences, interactions, and ambitions bring them to identify the nation's interests with those of their organization. In the same way, the State Department is more likely to view the world through the prism of diplomacy and to believe that most U.S. foreign policy objectives can be met through negotiation. Thus, it is not surprising that such a champion of toughness in foreign affairs as Henry Kissinger found that, as secretary of state, he was usually more "dovish" than Secretary of Defense James Schlesinger, just as Secretary of State George Shultz, a man with a strong distrust of Moscow, frequently argued for more moderate policies than did Secretary of Defense Caspar Weinberger.

Along similar lines, cabinet departments such as Commerce and Agriculture tend to place more emphasis on the benefits of closer economic relations with the Soviet Union than does Defense; indeed, they have occasionally sought State's support in trying to overcome Defense's objections to improved commercial ties between the two countries.[14] However, in the pecking order of bureaucracies, those that deal with commerce and agriculture stand far below those dealing with national security, and the competition between them is necessarily uneven when East-West relations are at issue.

The impact of bureaucratic interests and perceptions on U.S. policy toward the Soviet Union should not be overstated or understated. On the one hand, short-term fluctuations in policy are probably not determined by bureaucratic jockeying. The balance of influence among various parts of the federal bureaucracy does not change enough to account for most of the zigzags in U.S.-Soviet relations. On the other hand, the existence of powerful governmental organizations that tend to see the other side in particularly threatening terms, and that have a vested interest in some level of confrontation, probably creates a floor below which, in the longer term, hostility is unlikely to fall. Thus, they ensure that superpower relations will be marked by a minimum degree of hostility.

Some critics of U.S. foreign policy, particularly those of a radical bent, claim that it is largely molded by the interests of domestic economic groups, often labeled the "military-industrial complex," rather than by overall national goals. Soviet commentators have made this argument, too, long attributing U.S. activities abroad to the machinations of weapons producers and the Pentagon, whose goals are to perpetuate the arms race and, as a means to that end, to promote a permanent Cold War. The economic basis of the arms race will be discussed in greater detail in Chapter 13, but it is appropriate to consider here the influence of the military-industrial complex in the United States.

It must be recognized that military activity accounts for a significant proportion of the country's overall economic activity. In 1985, it constituted approximately 7 percent of gross national product and nearly 30 percent of total federal spending.[15] Furthermore, many jobs are, directly or indirectly, linked to defense activity. Some four and a half million people are employed in federal defense-related agencies as civilian or uniformed personnel. In the private sector, more than seven hundred thousand people work in aircraft production, a major portion of which involves military aircraft; more than one hundred thousand are employed in producing guided missiles and space vehicles; several hundred thousand are engaged in producing military communication equipment, and so forth. In all, several million people are employed by civilian military producers.

But even this tells only part of the story, because for every job that is directly created by defense, a certain number of other jobs are indirectly created. For example, in addition to the people required to assemble an army truck, others are needed to produce the raw materials used in its production, to transport them to where they are processed, to deliver the processed materials to the truck factory, and so forth (to say nothing of those who maintain the roads along which this distribution takes place or who erect the buildings which house the offices of the military contractors). Thus, a substantial number of jobs are related to the defense effort, and one must assume that serious economic losses would be experienced, at least in the short term, if it were to be markedly reduced. It follows that the defense contractors, the unions representing the workers they employ, the officials of the towns where production takes place, and the senators and representatives from regions that have or want military contracts are likely to fight to avoid these losses. When the defense establishment is seeking expanded resources, these groups make powerful allies, and military growth—as well as the political climate needed to sustain it—may well be promoted by their joint efforts.

Nevertheless, it is easy to exaggerate the power and role of the military-industrial complex. Indeed, there are strong economic arguments against massive defense production as well. For example, the military dollar is probably more inflationary than alternate types of public expenditure, and it has been shown to produce fewer jobs than many other forms of economic activity.[16] Consequently, there are economic and bureaucratic interests pulling in the other direction as well, and policy is the product of a pluralistic tug of war rather than of a monolithic military-industrial complex. Nevertheless, this complex can wield considerable political power when its interests impel it to do so.

Reinforcing Causes

There is no doubt that both types of reinforcing causes, dissimilarities and faulty perceptions, have contributed to the antagonism between the Soviet Union and the United States.

Dissimilarities

Each of the superpowers holds a set of beliefs and a vision of the ideal society that it considers universally applicable: best not only for the superpower itself but for all nations. This vision is partly shaped by political assumptions, but there is more to it than that. The relative insularity of each country (geographical in the case of the United States, political on the Soviet side) has meant that their cultures have many autonomous elements, not directly traceable to external influence. In the United States these include egalitarian cultural symbols (the rich and the poor watch the same TV shows, enjoy many of the same sports, and do not talk or dress very differently), a strong work ethic, a belief that individual achievement is the ultimate good, a high regard for ephemeral cultural creations, and a belief that truth and other virtues are simple and straightforward. In the Soviet Union, they include a feeling of virtue acquired through historical suffering, a conviction of possessing more national "soul" than other nations, a belief in collective rather than individual destiny, and a respect for cultural creations that stand the test of time. Each views its cultural heritage and social practices as unique and, in many ways, superior to that of other nations.

The role of the state is also viewed very differently in the two societies, and this difference did not begin with the Bolshevik Revolution. It appears that most Russians believe that the purpose of the state is to guarantee national security and, if possible, minimal material security for the citizenry. Governmental coercion in pursuit of these goals may be condoned, since the ends are regarded as important enough to justify a degree of brutality in the means by which they are attained. For the average U.S. citizen, insecurity, either of a material sort or out of fear of external aggression, has never been an overriding problem, and the function of government is more narrowly defined. It is to provide the conditions for the full realization of each person's individual potential, and there must be severe limits on the state's ability to exercise coercion over its people.

These are substantial differences, and each nation is firmly convinced of the superiority of its own convictions. The intolerance that this self-righteousness breeds is expressed in many, sometimes subtle, ways. Each side, for example, tends to portray the other's history in the least flattering light; it has been noted, for example, that high-school textbooks in both countries make a point of minimizing the other nation's contributions to the victory of the Allies in World War II.[17]

Of course, the Soviet Union and the United States are not alone in believing that they stand for exceptional and lofty principles, but what sets these two countries apart from others is that their history of growth and their position as superpowers vindicate this belief in their own eyes. Each is therefore irritated that its rival, which embodies so many antithetical beliefs, has similar pretensions. Even if the rival does nothing specifically threatening, its mere profession of superiority linked to its international position undermines, to some extent, one's own claim to being the anointed nation.

What might otherwise be a vaguely expressed intolerance is crystallized by sharp political differences, and these differences are disturbing to each side even if they do not amount to objective conflicts of interest. The principles of Marxism-Leninism, particularly the concept of an inevitable class struggle, are directly opposed to the notions of essential social harmony characteristic of the United States. Moreover, the Soviet Union claims that it is the leader in this struggle, from which it is bound to emerge as victor over the political and economic system that the United States stands for. This seems to give the Soviet Union the status of a total enemy, simply on the basis of its own claims. Other enemies in U.S. history were defined by the stakes in a particular conflict (for example, the rival designs on Cuba during the Spanish-American War) or were limited to the duration of the confrontation (such as the four years of World War II). In the Soviet case, by contrast, the scope and duration of the conflict seem virtually unlimited. This is not to say that all Soviet leaders really believe in an inevitable class struggle with a preordained outcome; some may very well doubt this, and the United States perhaps should not take the notion too seriously. But it has certainly brought into focus differences that might otherwise have remained more amorphous, and it has provided a focus for resentment and hostility.

Perceptions

Although perceptions often acquire a life of their own, with but a tenuous connection to reality, they can usually be traced to some objective facts. In the U.S.-Soviet case, this factual origin has two facets. The first consists of the differences between the two countries that have just been discussed. The concepts of cognitive consistency and dissonance lead to the inference that unfriendly intentions are apt to be attributed to a nation that stands for vastly different things. People in the United States might well assume that a nation that stands for atheism, state control over the economy, and authoritarian rule backed by coercion must have hostile designs against a nation that represents piety, respect for private property, and democracy. Conversely, Soviet citizens could as easily believe that a nation that accepts social inequality, unemployment, racial tension, materialism, and so forth must harbor ill intentions toward one that stands for economic equality, full employment, and a collectivist ethic. Secondly, the effect of these differences is compounded by the fact that each nation has ample historical reasons for fearing the other.

U.S. PERCEPTIONS OF THE SOVIET UNION.   An important basis for U.S. perceptions of a Soviet threat was Soviet behavior after World War II. The United States understood the Yalta agreement (see Chapter 2) to mean that the East European nations would be allowed to determine their own political future, but instead Soviet troops in those nations were used to impose a Soviet-style system and Soviet control on those nations. The military invasions of Hungary in 1956 and Czechoslovakia in 1968 demonstrated that brute force would be used to prevent any significant deviation from the political line laid down by the Kremlin. The Soviet intervention in Afghanistan indicated that Eastern Europe was not the only part of the world in which Moscow felt it had proprietary rights. The Kremlin's military buildup during the 1970s, the frequently strident anti-American rhetoric in official Soviet proclamations and the mass media, and evidence of subversive activity in a number of countries, especially in the Third World, were also grounds for U.S. perception of a Soviet threat.

Soviet behavior has indeed appeared menacing at times, but perceptions often follow a logic of their own. A particularly revealing study of perception and misperception was made by the political scientist Ole Holsti. He had observed that Secretary of State Dulles seemed to maintain a uniformly negative image of the Soviet Union during his years in office, and he set out to discover the psychological mechanisms by which this was guided. He applied a technique called *content analysis* to Dulles's speeches and to his statements at press conferences and congressional hearings and on other occasions; from this analysis he derived measures of Dulles's overall evaluation of the Soviet Union as well as measures of his specific perceptions of Soviet hostility, the degree of Soviet success in foreign policy, and its general capability.

It appeared that Dulles's perceptions of Soviet hostility depended on his perceptions of Soviet success and capability. That is, when Soviet behavior was less threatening, he attributed it either to a lack of success in its recent activities (resulting in temporary discouragement) or to a reduced capability to do mischief (implying that the mischief would be resumed when the capability had been restored). However, changes in the perception of hostility did not bring changes in Dulles's overall evaluation of the Soviet Union; he continued to regard it as a nation inherently characterized by bad faith. If, for instance, men were released from the Soviet armed forces, Dulles would explain it as being due to economic problems: the men were being released so that they could be put to work building more weapons. As Holsti said, "So long as good behavior is attributed to necessity, there is no need to attribute it to virtue. . . . Dulles interpreted the very data that would lead one to change one's model in such a way as to preserve that model." [18]

Not every secretary of state has had such a rigid outlook. Another political scientist, Harvey Starr, applied Holsti's methods to the public statements of Henry Kissinger. He found that Kissinger was more willing than Dulles had been to alter his views of the Soviet Union as their behavior changed, and also that Kissinger had less of a tendency to attribute fluctuations in Soviet hostility to changes in degree of success or in capability.[19] That may help explain why U.S. relations with the Soviet Union were considerably better during Kissinger's tenure in office than they were during Dulles's.

SOVIET PERCEPTIONS OF THE UNITED STATES.   History has also provided the U.S.S.R. with indications of hostile U.S. designs. U.S. participation in the military intervention against the Bolshevik Revolution has never been forgotten. The conviction that the United States was bent on securing the demise of the Soviet system was reinforced by Washington's delay in opening a second front in Europe during World War II (which, as pointed out in Chapter 2, Soviet leaders interpreted to mean that the U.S. was willing to see their country mauled by Hitler's forces). Unease was compounded by U.S. acquisition of the atomic bomb in 1945. Periodic outbursts of anticommunist and anti-Soviet rhetoric have given additional grounds for Soviet beliefs about the unfriendly intentions of the United States, and U.S. interventions in Vietnam and Grenada have made American denunciations of Soviet military actions abroad seem highly hypocritical in Moscow's eyes.

But Soviet perceptions, too, often seem unresponsive to changed conditions, for they are affected by a need for ideological consistency. In the classical Soviet view, the objectives of U.S. foreign policy are class-based. According to Andrei Gromyko, who was minister of foreign affairs for the Soviet Union from 1957 to 1985 and is now its president, this policy reflects "the interests of the dominating class . . . the monopoly bourgeoisie. . . . Its main concern—to retain and strengthen American imperialism's position in the world—also predetermines its very long-term features and its continuity through different historical stages." [20]

Soviet ideologues hold that imperialism is inevitably associated with "barefaced anti-Sovietism" and relies upon subversion, psychological warfare, and especially on force—hence the important role that military-industrial interests are thought to play in the United States. This policy of force, in turn, leads to the "blatant flouting of international agreements and the sovereignty of other countries" and the "oppression of the weak by the strong." A major aim is to create foreign markets for the arms-manufacturing monopolies.[21] When Soviet analysts concede that the United States has departed from its aggressive policies, they argue that this is not because the nation or its class interests have changed, but because it has been forced to recognize that new realities, especially the U.S.S.R.'s ascending power, make aggression a difficult and often counterproductive tool of foreign policy. They refer to this as a change in the "correlation of forces," but one may recognize in it a mirror image of the Dulles mode of thinking.

The same psychological mechanisms are again seen at work in the ability of Soviet ideologues to interpret evidence that would logically refute a belief in such a way as to confirm it. For example, during the Vietnam War, Soviet observers were surprised to see that stock prices on Wall Street tended to rise with news of peace initiatives, whereas they had claimed that the war was being fought at the behest of capitalist interests. A major tenet of the Soviet belief system was thus threatened, but an authoritative Russian commentator explained that Wall Street's behavior was explained by its knowledge that, if the U.S. pulled out of Vietnam, the money saved on conventional forces would be put into the production of nuclear weapons.[22]

Nevertheless, there may be some basis for thinking that Soviet perceptions have become more flexible. A "realist" school of thought, with a slightly more differentiated view of the United States, has reportedly emerged alongside the more ideologically extreme "traditionalist" school that has long been dominant. Moreover, the generational turnover that has occurred in the Soviet Union since the mid-1980s may also portend more realistic images of the United States; the new leaders seem to have a more pragmatic bent than their predecessors.[23] Not having directly experienced the ravages of World War II, security anxieties may be less pronounced in their case, and since they are better educated and informed concerning the West, ideas about class struggles may loom less large in their minds than the desire to emulate some of the material achievements of the capitalist West.

Still, Soviet perceptions are not changing overnight, as is suggested by the views of the most prominent of the new leaders, the general secretary of the Soviet Communist party, Mikhail Gorbachev. According to U.S. diplomats who spoke with him in preparation for his November 1985 meeting with President Reagan, Gorbachev saw the United States as "a land controlled by wealthy capitalists and conservative business interests," where "right-wing forces dictate Government policy and would never permit a lasting improvement in relations with the Soviet Union.[24]

The Outlook

There is no single or simple explanation for U.S.-Soviet enmity. Objective conflicts of interest account for less than is usually assumed. Superpower goals in the Third World do clash at times, but this has little to do with territorial or economic ambitions, and even ideological goals may not be as important as is sometimes thought. Those limited areas where interests do objectively collide cannot, in and of themselves, explain the state of superpower relations. Although the two sides' security needs are usually considered incompatible, this is properly considered a consequence, not an initiating cause, of their rivalry.

Superpower hostility springs in part from domestic sources. The domestic legitimacy of the Soviet regime can apparently be enhanced by external toughness, and many politicians in the United States are unwilling to bear the costs of appearing "soft" toward the Soviet Union. Furthermore, the national-security bureaucracies on both sides of the Cold War make important contributions to the maintenance of tension and hostility. Nevertheless, there are also in both societies a variety of vested organizational interests that are better served through cooperative relations and détente, and their influence should not be dismissed.

Whatever its initiating causes, superpower hostility is greatly reinforced by crucial dissimilarities between the two countries. Both nations are firmly convinced, not only of their cultural and social exceptionalism, but also of the superiority of that which they stand for, and this conviction is reinforced, for each side, by the international stature and power it has achieved. Consequently, it is disconcerting for each to find that its rival has similar pretensions, particularly when its political beliefs appear so offensive. Because of the dissimilarities, and because each side has been an objective threat to the other at certain times in the past, perceptions of threat are to be expected. Yet there are psychological mechanisms that sustain these perceptions even after the objective threat has been weakened or eliminated. Thus, U.S.-Soviet relations bear many burdens, and friendly, cooperative relations should not be expected in the near future. Nevertheless, some of the more dangerous aspects of the antagonism can be controlled, as may be seen in the case of conflicts of interest in the Third World.

Although its extent is considerably overstated, there has been a certain amount of ideological competition between the Soviet Union and the United States in the Third World. It has not been a high-priority element in the foreign policy of either side, but it has been pursued when the costs and risks did not appear too great and when it did not clash with other national objectives. But even at that level, it has often damaged relations. The collapse of détente in the late 1970s was partly due to Soviet forays in the developing countries.

One problem is that the bounds of permissible superpower activity abroad have never been adequately defined, and the Soviet Union has thus sometimes underestimated the sharpness of U.S. reactions to its conduct. The disenchantment of the U.S. public with the Vietnam War and its rising opposition to any sort of external involvement was apparently seen by Moscow as an opportunity to expand its activities in Africa, which it did through Cuban proxies in Angola and Ethiopia. On the whole, the U.S. response to these incursions was moderate, and no firm steps were taken to counter them. This may have emboldened the Soviet Union to launch its military invasion of Afghanistan in December 1979—whereupon simmering resentment in the United States boiled over, and, in an eruption of anger that must have greatly exceeded Soviet expectations, whatever vestiges of détente remained were eradicated.

Perhaps, then, a joint attempt to define mutually tolerable behavior would reduce misunderstandings and ensure that no action in the Third World was taken whose costs might exceed the ideological and other benefits it was meant to produce. There was a tentative effort in this direction in 1972, when, as mentioned before, the United States and the Soviet Union signed a document known as the Basic Principles Agreement (BPA). It stated that ideological and social differences should be the object of peaceful negotiations and that "both sides recognize that efforts to obtain unilateral advantages at the expense of the other, directly or indirectly, are inconsistent with these objectives." However, these provisions were rather vague, and each side interpreted them to its own advantage.[25] A more explicit and detailed set of ground rules for permissible behavior in the Third World may be needed. It would not alter the fact of rival national objectives, but it could make it less likely that behavior considered acceptable by one side would be deemed provocative and aggressive by the other.

A proposal along these lines has been advanced by Arthur Macy Cox, a former U.S. official and now a writer on international affairs. Cox acknowledges that certain forms of superpower competition in the Third World are inevitable: whether in the form of economic aid, propaganda, or military assistance. He suggests that the United States and Soviet Union enter into a pact banning direct military intervention, indirect intervention by third-party proxy forces, and intervention with covert military or volunteer forces.[26] There would obviously be problems with such a pact—for example, neither side would be willing to call the forces it supports their "proxy," and proving the contention would be very difficult. Nevertheless, some such set of ground-rules might help avoid the most irritating and dangerous confrontations between the superpowers.

If the superpower rivalry arose out of objective conflicts of interest, the solution might be theoretically (if not practically) simple; disputed territory, for example, can be divided. But hostility that is embedded within the social, political, or economic structure is more intractable. The will to resolve the conflict would have to come from within the very society that has, in various ways, come to depend on the existence of the conflict—an especially disturbing aspect of the dilemma of aggregation. Indeed, one or both societies may judge that, even though the rivalry is undesirable, it is preferable to the dangers of upsetting accepted domestic arrangements.

While the United States and the Soviet Union may never actually be friends, the rivalry can be controlled and cooperation in limited areas of mutual interest can be achieved. The successful U.S.-Soviet summit meeting, held in Washington, D.C., in December 1987, testified to the possibilities for effective communication and limited agreement, even in the face of persistent differences.

Appendix: Milestones in U.S.-Soviet Relations

1917	Bolsheviks come to power in Russia.
1933	United States and Soviet Union establish diplomatic relations.
1941-1945	United States and Soviet Union collaborate in World War II.
1945	Yalta Conference sets guidelines for postwar reorganization and creates foundation for division of Europe into two blocs.
	U.S. explodes first atomic bomb.
1946	U.S.-Soviet friction arises over Turkey and Iran.
1947	Truman Doctrine announced: Commits United States to aid Greece and ushers in policy of containment.
1948	Communists come to power in Czechoslovakia.
	Berlin blockade: Soviet Union cuts ground traffic from West Germany to West Berlin; United States undertakes Berlin airlift.
	Marshall Plan is established for economic reconstruction of Europe.
1949	North Atlantic Treaty Organization, joint military organization of Western democracies, is established.
	Soviet Union detonates its first atomic bomb.
1950	Korean War begins; United States intervenes on South Korea's side.
1952	United States detonates first thermonuclear bomb.
1953	Stalin dies.
1955	Warsaw Pact signed, establishing joint military organization of Soviet and East European forces.
1956	Soviet Union invades Hungary.
1957	Soviet Union launches first artificial earth satellite.
1958	United States intervenes in Lebanon.

1959   Khrushchev and Eisenhower meet at Camp David.

1960   U-2 spy plane shot down over Soviet Union.
          Summit conference in Paris collapses over U-2 affair.

1961   United States involved in unsuccessful invasion of Cuba.
          Soviet Union builds Berlin Wall.
          Kennedy and Khrushchev meet in Vienna.

1962   United States and Soviet Union confront each other over issue of
          Soviet missiles in Cuba.

1963   Hot line established between Moscow and Washington for rapid
          crisis communications between heads of governments.

1965   Direct U.S. military involvement in Vietnam begins.
          United States intervenes in Dominican Republic.

1968   Soviet Union invades Czechoslovakia.

1969   SALT talks begin.

1970   Treaty signed between West Germany and Soviet Union acknowl-
          edging division between East and West Germany.

1972   Nixon visits Moscow (and the People's Republic of China), signs
          SALT I treaty limiting ABMs.

1974   Vladivostok agreement puts limits on strategic weapons.

1975   Jackson-Vanik amendment in effect ends U.S.-Soviet trade agree-
          ment.
          U.S. accuses Soviet Union of involvement, through Cuban forces,
          in Angolan war.

1977   Soviet Union supports Ethiopia (again through Cuban forces),
          United States backs Somalia, in conflict between the two African
          countries.

1979   SALT II treaty signed.
          Soviet Union invades Afghanistan.

1980   United States imposes economic sanctions on Soviet Union and
          withdraws SALT II treaty from consideration for Senate ratifica-
          tion.

1981   President Reagan describes Soviet Union as "evil force" bent on
          destroying the United States; undertakes major military buildup.

1982   Reagan announces end to negotiations on a comprehensive test
          ban for nuclear weapons.

1983   Reagan proposes "Star Wars" project for defense against nuclear
          missiles; describes Soviet Union as "evil empire."
          Soviets shoot down South Korean civilian airplane.

1985   Reagan and Gorbachev meet in Geneva; tone of relations improves.

1986   Reagan and Gorbachev meet in Reykjavik, Iceland.

1987   Gorbachev makes major proposals for nuclear arms control.

Reagan and Gorbachev meet in Washington; United States and Soviet Union sign treaty to destroy their intermediate- and short-range missiles.

Notes

1. Richard Nixon, *Real Peace* (Boston: Little, Brown, 1983), 5.
2. Richard Pipes, *Survival Is Not Enough* (New York: Simon and Schuster, 1984), 37.
3. Quoted in Michael Shafer, "Mineral Myths," *Foreign Policy* (Summer 1982): 154.
4. Central Intelligence Agency, *Prospects for Soviet Oil Production* (Washington, D.C.: Government Printing Office, 1977).
5. Pipes, *Survival Is Not Enough*, 51 and Chapter 2.
6. Jonathan Steele, *Soviet Power: The Kremlin's Foreign Policy—Brezhnev to Andropov* (New York: Simon and Schuster, 1983), 165.
7. Ibid., 167.
8. Hans J. Morgenthau, *Politics among Nations* (New York: Alfred A. Knopf, 1948), 146.
9. Pipes, *Survival Is Not Enough*, 40-41.
10. Michael Nacht, *The Age of Vulnerability: Threats to the Nuclear Stalemate* (Washington, D.C.: Brookings Institution, 1985), 15, 33.
11. George F. Kennan, *The Nuclear Delusion: Soviet-American Relations in the Atomic Age* (New York: Pantheon, 1983), 83.
12. Edwina Moreton, "Comrade Colossus: The Impact of Soviet Military Industry on the Soviet Economy," in Curtis Keeble, ed., *The Soviet State: The Domestic Roots of Soviet Foreign Policy* (Boulder, Colo.: Westview, 1985), 126.
13. Vernon V. Aspaturian, "The Soviet Military-Industrial Complex—Does it Exist?" *Journal of International Affairs* 26 (1977): 1-28.
14. See, for instance, Clyde H. Farnsworth, "The Doves Capture Control of Trade," *New York Times*, October 23, 1983.
15. These and the following data are from *Statistical Abstract of the United States, 1985* (Washington, D.C.: Department of Commerce, Bureau of the Census, 1985).
16. For some relevant data, see Miroslav Nincic and Thomas Cusack, "The Political Economy of U.S. Military Spending," *Journal of Peace Research* 2 (1979): 110-111. See also Robert W. DeGrasse, Jr., *Military Expansion, Economic Decline* (Armonk, N.Y.: M. E. Sharp, 1983).
17. David K. Shipler, "How We See Each Other: The View from America," *New York Times Magazine*, November 10, 1985, 48.
18. Ole R. Holsti, "The Belief System and National Images: John Foster Dulles and the Soviet Union" (Ph.D. diss., Stanford University, 1962), 140, 212. See also Ole R. Holsti, "The Belief System and National Images: A Case Study," *Journal of Conflict Resolution* 6 (1962): 244-252.
19. Harvey Starr, *Henry Kissinger: Perceptions of International Politics* (Lexington: University of Kentucky Press, 1983).
20. Andrei Gromyko, "Sovremennye tendentsii vneshnei politiki SShA" (Contemporary tendencies of U.S. foreign policy), *SShA* (April 1972): 40 (my translation).

21. John Lenczowski, *Soviet Perceptions of U.S. Foreign Policy* (Ithaca, N.Y.: Cornell University Press, 1982), 153.
22. Lenczowski, *Soviet Perceptions*, 63.
23. On this issue, see Jerry F. Hough, *Soviet Leadership in Transition* (Washington, D.C.: Brookings Institution, 1980), especially Chapters 6 and 8.
24. "How Gorbachev Sees America: A Gloomy Land," *New York Times*, November 15, 1985.
25. Alexander L. George, "The Basic Principles Agreement of 1972: Origins and Expectations," in Alexander L. George, ed., *Managing U.S.-Soviet Rivalry: Problems of Crisis Prevention* (Boulder, Colo.: Westview, 1983), 107-118.
26. Arthur Macy Cox, *Russian Roulette: The Superpower Game* (New York: Times Books, 1982), Chapter 6.

c h a p t e r   n i n e

Friendship and Friction
in the Western Alliance

F RIENDS ARE AS much a part of America's international environment as are rivals; therefore an understanding of U.S. foreign policy therefore requires an appreciation of the bonds that link the United States to its friends and of the occasional strains that these bonds endure.

The Foundations of Cooperation

International friendships have four primary sources: nonconflicting interests, positive interdependence, absence of fundamental dissimilarities, and favorable mutual perceptions. These are, of course, the opposites of the conditions that give rise to rivalry and enmity between nations. When we consider the principal friends of the United States, the other industrialized democracies—Canada, Great Britain, the nations of Western Europe and Scandinavia, Japan, Australia, and a few other countries—it is apparent that all four favorable conditions are met.

Nonconflicting Interests

Friends may squabble, but they are usually not separated by major incompatibilities of interest. None of the three major sources of clashing interests between countries seems to seriously mar relations between the United States and other industrialized democracies.

TERRITORY. The borders of the United States are geographically unambiguous and its territory is not coveted by any nation, certainly not by the democracies. Similarly, the United States has no territorial pretensions beyond its borders. In fact, problems of this sort are generally absent within the Western world. Europe, where much fighting over territory occurred in the past, now has settled borders, which as a rule encompass well-defined nation states. The general outline of European borders was set in the midseventeenth century, largely by the Treaty of Westphalia in 1648, which terminated the Thirty Years War. However, territorial changes were made after the Napoleonic Wars and the wars of German and Italian unification in the second half of the nineteenth century. The breakup of the Austro-Hungarian and Ottoman empires after World War I caused the map of southeastern Europe to be redrawn, and World War II brought some further, though not major, modifications to the boundaries of Central Europe. Today, the political map of Western Europe is generally unchallenged. The territorial boundaries of Japan and other developed democracies are also universally accepted. Rivalry over land is virtually absent in the Western world.

ECONOMIC RELATIONS.   The nations of the West do sometimes quarrel over economic matters, but these are the quarrels not of predators who wish each other ill, but of competitors whose economic relations are simultaneously competitive and cooperative. By the 1960s, Japan and the nations of Western Europe, which had previously been dependent on U.S. assistance for their postwar recovery, became both America's principal economic partners and its principal rivals. As we shall see later in this chapter, when the industrialized countries have competed for each other's markets, the United States has often been on the losing side, partly because of failures within the U.S. economy but also because of unfair trading practices on the part of the other industrialized democracies. Nevertheless, the economic clashes that occur are not significant enough to undermine the foundations of friendship and cooperation between the United States and its allies.

IDEOLOGY.   The Western democracies are a group of countries whose societies have willingly accepted a compatible set of political values and institutions. Moreover, they have often stood side by side in the face of common threats, most obviously against German autocracy in World War I and nazism and fascism in World War II. The formerly totalitarian nations of Germany and Italy have rejoined the fold, and ideological conflict is plainly not a problem within the West.

Positive Interdependence

In international politics, firm friendship requires more than just the absence of objective conflicts of interest. It requires mutual dependence in the pursuit of common goals—that is, positive interdependence. In the case of the United States and its friends, this has been built on two bases: security and prosperity.

SECURITY.   In 1949, the North Atlantic Treaty Organization was established in response to deteriorating East-West relations and the perception of a heightened Soviet threat. While NATO's mission includes various forms of political cooperation, the principal focus is on military matters.

It has been generally accepted for the past several decades that the European democracies could not repel a Soviet attack by relying exclusively on their own forces. The size of the military machine that the Soviet Union and its allies could mobilize is thought to exceed that which the Western European countries could themselves muster. Consequently, U.S. military participation is considered necessary. Upon the establishment of NATO, several hundred thousand U.S. troops were deployed to Europe, principally to West Germany, which would be geographically most exposed in the event of a Soviet invasion. The purpose was not so much to provide a defense capable of repelling a Soviet assault in and of itself, but rather to provide deterrence and to buy time. First, the presence of U.S. troops would serve as a "tripwire," in the sense that the casualties that the troops would suffer in the first stages of an attack would call forth a U.S. response with nuclear, possibly intercontinental, forces. Knowledge of the consequences was expected to be a strong deterrent to a Soviet invasion. Secondly, if deterrence failed and a Soviet attack did take place, U.S. forces would help slow down the advance of Soviet forces, even if intercontinental nuclear weapons were not used, while the United States mobilized to furnish reinforcements of troops and weapons to the European theater. In order to bolster NATO's capability to fend off an attack without resorting to intercontinental missiles, thousands of short-range or "tactical" nuclear weapons were deployed under U.S. control. In this way, the military security of Western Europe was entwined with that of the United States.

Europeans and Americans sometimes disagree on the proper use of nuclear weapons, the former preferring primary reliance on strategic missiles, whereby the superpowers would absorb most of the destruction, while the latter tends to place more emphasis on tactical missiles, which would cause Europe to bear the brunt of the destruction. However, under most assumptions some use of both sorts of weapons would be likely. Accordingly, the benefits and perils of the most destructive weapons available to mankind would be shared, cementing the links between the major Western industrialized democracies. These military bonds experience occasional strains but there is little doubt that the security of the Western nations has become indivisible.

ECONOMIC WELL-BEING. Trade between developed countries has expanded significantly during the past several decades, to the point where they have come to depend very much on each other for the goods they like to consume. French wines and kitchen appliances, Japanese cars and television sets, and Italian clothes are a major presence on the American market, and many U.S. goods, from personal computers to children's toys, are familiar abroad. Vigorous trade also affects employment, since many jobs in each industrialized economy grow out of production for export. Although the countries of Northeast Asia—Japan, Korea, and Taiwan—as well as a number of less prosperous Third World nations sell a great many products to the United States and buy a great deal from it, the Western industrialized democracies continue to account for the bulk of U.S. imports and exports. The nations of the

Organization for Economic Cooperation and Development have accounted for more than half of the total value of U.S. trade for at least two decades, and they currently account for about three-quarters.[1]

Interdependence is reflected not only in trade, but also in the industrialized nations' investments in each other's economies. The major vehicle of international investment today is the multinational corporation (MNC), and while U.S. MNCs are the most numerous and wealthy, those of other countries have been expanding their presence in the United States. This has consequences of various sorts. The presence of a foreign multinational on U.S. soil means that a good that the company might otherwise have produced in its own country and exported to the United States is instead produced here, creating domestic jobs and tax revenue. Although some of the profits might be transferred back to the home country, and although foreign ownership sometimes injures feelings of national pride, these investments complement domestic investments, which, in the U.S. case, are usually considered insufficient to ensure dynamic economic growth. Obviously, the operations of U.S. multinationals in France or Italy carry similar benefits for those countries. As Table 9-1 shows, the developed countries are the major direct investors in each other's economies, with the United States and the European Economic Community (EEC) nations being especially tied by this type of interdependence.

While this interdependence entails costs—and it is these that get most attention—its benefits almost certainly dominate. In any event, the developed countries simply cannot do without each other economically.

Absence of Basic Dissimilarities

There are many similarities between the United States and other industrialized democracies. To begin with, the great majority of U.S. citizens are of European descent; although the African, Latin American, and Asian components are significant as well, Europe remains the continent whence most people in the United States originally came. U.S. history has also been tightly bound up with that of Europe. U.S. participation in both world wars, the extensive cultural exchanges between the two continents, the dense network of commercial trade, and frequent travel in both directions have meant that much of Europe has rubbed off on Americans and vice versa.

These countries also share similar principles of social organization. All are open societies, committed to broadly based political participation, free elections, civil liberties, and vigorous political competition. Moreover, all have predominantly market economies, which have provided their citizens with standards of living that are the envy of the rest of the world.

European countries also have some traits that are not shared by the United States. For example, it is more widely believed in Europe than in the United States that society bears a responsibility for its least privileged citizens, a responsibility that is discharged through the state. Because of this, extreme poverty is less often encountered in Europe than in the United States, and

Table 9-1   Direct Investment by the United States and Other Developed Democracies in Each Other's Economies, 1984

	Percentage of U.S. Investments Abroad	*Percentage of Foreign Investments in the United States*
Canada	9	22
EEC	60	34
Other European nations	7	11
Japan	9	4
Total	85	71

Source: U.S. Department of Commerce, *Survey of Current Business* (Washington, D.C.: Government Printing Office, June 1985).

nonmilitary public spending is a larger part of national income in many European countries. Also, though all Western democracies have a plurality of political organizations, the U.S. political system operates with only two major parties, while many European countries have half a dozen or more significant parties. In part, this is a result of somewhat different electoral systems; for example, proportional representation is common in Europe but not in the United States. In part, it is rooted in a generally greater European tolerance for ideological diversity, as seen particularly in the prominent role of left-wing parties. For example, Socialist parties are frequently in power or are members of a governing coalition. By comparison, the political spectrum in the United States is not very broad; on most fundamental issues, the differences between Democrats and Republicans are relatively small.

But these dissimilarities are matters of degree rather than of kind. There is every reason to view the Western democracies as a category much more strongly distinguished from other countries than they are from each other.

Self-Reinforcing Perceptions

The peoples of the Western democracies view each other in a favorable light, and these feelings are shared by their governments. This is the joint result of the other determinants of friendship as well as an additional determinant in its own right. These favorable perceptions are strengthened by the psychological mechanism of cognitive consistency—the tendency, already discussed, to interpret a behavior in a more positive light if it comes from an already friendly country than if it comes from an adversary. The stability of friendship is further reinforced by the fact that, tending to perceive that which we anticipate, our expectations of friendly or praiseworthy behavior are usually confirmed.

The implication is that if the first three sources of friendship are substantially present in a relationship, then that relationship can withstand a fair amount of buffeting, since much that could threaten amity will be filtered out by psychological mechanisms. Hence, although the foundations of U.S. friendship with its Western allies have been shaken from time to time, they remain very firm. Nevertheless, problems have occasionally arisen, and will arise again, and foreign policy must deal with them.

The Sources of Tension

The most serious irritants among the Western allies have come from three sources: relations with the Soviet Union, burden-sharing within NATO, and economic competition. Let us look at each of these more closely.

Relations with the Soviet Union

Very few Europeans, in or out of government, sympathize with the Soviet Union's political practices or approve of its policies. The Soviet system has few advocates in Western Europe. Where there is disagreement with the United States, it is usually over the proper interpretation to be placed on the Soviet Union's *foreign* policies.

Moscow's intentions are not always seen in the same light on the two sides of the Atlantic. The tone of U.S. policy toward Moscow shifts with changes in the political climate, but it is almost always assumed that the Soviet Union is an expansionist nation, that it pursues its objectives through coercion or dissimulation, and that it is, in the final analysis, the source and focus of most of the world's problems. Europeans, on the other hand, are not quite as convinced of the Soviet Union's inherent aggressiveness or expansionism. They tend to view Soviet foreign policy and attitudes against a lengthy historical background. They are better acquainted with the numerous and devastating foreign onslaughts of which the country has been victim, and Moscow's security fears are consequently better understood. Thus, Soviet activities that might seem from the U.S. point of view to be unambiguously aggressive, a European might consider both offensive and defensive. In addition, Europe's long and rich diplomatic history has instilled in many of its leaders the realization that nothing lasts forever and no country is unalterably evil. Other European nations with inglorious chapters in their history have been admitted back into the fold and are now pillars of the Western community. Accordingly, not even the Soviet Union is considered implacably and immutably threatening. The relatively brief and simple international experience of the United States may not have allowed such convictions to take root to the same extent.

Western European nations have definite qualms about the U.S.S.R., but few of them place as extreme an interpretation on its menace or advocate quite as stern a response as that frequently adopted by the United States. The European allies of the United States do not like, and generally do not trust, Moscow and realize that, while current Soviet objectives may be defensive, a shift in the military balance to the disadvantage of the West could cause these objectives to become more threatening. Nonetheless, the majority of these countries probably do not believe that military expansion in Europe and the imposition of Soviet-style governments rank very high on the Kremlin's list of priorities. Most notably, European leaders are not as prone to stress a buildup of military forces and the use of tough rhetoric as methods of dealing with the Soviet Union. While the need for military deterrence is recognized, it is not viewed as the only effective instrument of the West's Soviet policy. Diplomacy and negotiated agreements are considered just as useful and just as important. Also, Europeans are somewhat less inclined than is the United States to put stock in economic leverage. Thus, different conceptions of the nature and immediacy of the Soviet threat have led to different notions of how best to confront it.

It is also significant that Europe's interests are not invariably identical to those of the United States. To begin with, most Europeans believe that their land would be the principal battlefield of a Soviet-U.S. confrontation, so that their people and cities, rather than those of either the United States or the Soviet Union, would bear the brunt of the devastation. Indeed, as we have mentioned, the history of U.S. and European efforts at nuclear deterrence has included policies on both sides that would transfer the likely nuclear costs to the other, with Europe favoring deterrence with strategic nuclear weapons based in the United States, while the United States has generally preferred to rely on shorter-range weapons based in Europe. At any rate, European memories of their suffering during both world wars has led them to be especially wary of the risks of armed conflict and to press for reduction of tensions.

In addition, there are peacetime benefits to be derived from interacting with the Eastern bloc, and these are more important to the West European nations than they are to the United States. To most Europeans, regardless of how they feel about Soviet-type political systems, détente is a desirable goal. It has meant, among other things, that West Germans can more easily visit, or be permanently reunited with, family members and friends in East Germany. Economic relations with the Eastern bloc are also important to some European countries (see Table 9-2). France and West Germany in particular are substantial exporters to the Soviet Union and its allies and are unwilling to sacrifice those markets on the altar of anticommunist purity.

These circumstances mean that there is more of an economic stake in improved East-West relations in Europe than there is in the United States. Many people in the United States, as a matter of principle, object to any show of warmth toward the Kremlin; at least, as one observer, Sovietologist Dimitri

Table 9-2   U.S. and EEC Trade with Soviet Bloc Members (percentage of total value of exports and imports)

	1965	1970	1975	1980	1984
U.S.	0.9	0.9	1.9	1.3	1.4
EEC	3.7	4.1	3.8	4.5	4.1

Source: OECD, *Historical Statistics of Foreign Trade, 1965-1980* (Paris: OECD, 1982), and OECD, *Monthly Statistics of Foreign Trade, Series A* (Paris: OECD, 1985).

Simes has put it, "There is no strong American constituency committed to improved relations with the Soviet Union." [2] But such constituencies do exist in Western Europe. Personal interest and fear of international conflict, as well as greater sympathy for Soviet historical experience, lead many Europeans to prefer a policy of cooperation with the Soviet Union.

It is therefore not surprising that the earliest postwar moves at establishing East-West relations on a more constructive footing came from within Europe. Some of the first such moves were made by the French president, Charles de Gaulle, in the 1960s. De Gaulle was convinced that it was not in the Soviet Union's interest to attack Europe and that it had no plans for doing so. In keeping with this conviction, he removed French forces from NATO and NATO headquarters from France. In July 1965, he became the first Western leader to visit Moscow since the beginning of the Cold War, a symbolic trip during which he called for a "Europe of the Europeans" stretching from the Atlantic to the Urals. De Gaulle did not view this initiative as a rebuff to the United States. As he pointed out to the West German chancellor, Willy Brandt:

> France is in no way opposed to America. On the contrary, she is America's friend. But nothing can be worse for the Europeans than an American hegemony which enfeebles Europe and prevents the Europeans from being themselves. Such hegemony also hinders agreement with the East—in fact, it hinders everything. The Americans are Americans, not Europeans. [3]

Brandt felt much the same way, and he decided to carry the cause of East-West détente further still, in an effort that was to win him the Nobel Peace Prize. In the context of a policy of reconciliation with the East, he signed treaties with Czechoslovakia, East Germany, Poland, and the Soviet Union, and he promoted a four-power treaty on the status of Berlin. Brandt's policies initially met with suspicion and disapproval from the administration of President Richard Nixon, but despite their misgivings, Nixon and Secretary of State Henry Kissinger eventually joined the moves toward reconciliation with Moscow. U.S.-Soviet détente proved to be short-lived—Moscow's adventurism in the Third World and a rightward drift in the U.S. political climate brought it to a halt in the late 1970s—but the European nations did not want to tear down the edifice of cooperation that had been built up. This led to strains within the Western alliance. The controversies over the natural-gas pipeline and U.S. actions in the Third World are good illustrations of the difficulties involved.

THE NATURAL-GAS PIPELINE. In 1948, at the height of the Cold War, Congress passed the Export Control Act, which restricted the types of goods that could be sold to Communist countries and set up a licensing system to enforce the restrictions. The United States hoped that its allies would emulate this initiative, and in 1949 a Coordinating Committee was established to discuss and coordinate the lists of "strategic goods" that would be subject to embargo. But, the United States argued for a broader definition of such goods than the European nations and Japan were willing to support. Although the disagreements moderated during the period of détente, they persisted and finally came to a head following a Soviet decision in 1978 to build a pipeline from western Siberia that would allow it to expand its sale of natural gas to Western European countries. The Soviet Union had begun selling gas to Western Europe in 1968, and its customers came to include France, West Germany, and Italy. The new pipeline would have allowed Western European nations to buy more of this relatively cheap gas and to reduce their reliance on energy supplies from the Middle East. It was to be largely financed by French and West German credits.

Following the imposition of martial law in Poland in 1981, the administration of President Ronald Reagan decided to tighten up its restrictions on trade with the Soviet Union. As part of this policy, it sought to halt construction of the Siberian pipeline. Besides wanting to express indignation at the repressive moves in Poland, which were presumably supported by the Soviet Union, the administration contended that the Soviet economy could be dealt a serious blow by depriving it of the hard currencies that would be earned by selling natural gas to the Europeans. Moreover, the Reagan administration warned, if Moscow became a major provider of gas to the Western European countries, its leverage over them would be significantly increased, because it could threaten to cut off supplies. In fact, the administration pointed out, Yugoslavia, China, and Israel had all had their energy supplies cut by the U.S.S.R. at one time or another.

The Europeans saw the issue in a very different light. Few leaders in Europe believed that the Soviet economy was in such desperate condition that it would be seriously affected by sanctions of this sort. They regarded this idea as a misconception dictated by wishful thinking rather than an accurate understanding of the facts. Moreover, the Europeans did not accept the notion that they would be placing themselves in a situation of dangerous dependence on the U.S.S.R. The fraction of total energy needs that would be met by Soviet gas was not very large, and they reasoned that the Soviet Union would be at least as dependent on the hard currency thus earned. Also, many Europeans surmised that their fuel supplies would be no better assured, probably less adequately so, if they relied on the turbulent Middle East for their natural gas, which would also have been more expensive. Another incentive to pursue the deal was that European firms would be the main suppliers of the steel pipes and compressor stations required for construction of the pipeline, making the project a source of employment for the European economies. In any case, the Europeans pointed out that the United States had little moral authority for asking them to abandon the pipeline arrangement since Washington was unwilling to accept the economic costs of giving up grain sales to the Soviet Union (which benefited the Soviet regime and pleased U.S. farmers). In other words, it did not appear that the administration was prepared to practice what it preached.

European qualms notwithstanding, in December 1981, the U.S. government suspended the General Electric Company's license to export turbine rotor sets for the pipeline's compressor stations, and it revoked the Caterpillar Tractor Company's license to sell pipe-laying vehicles to the Soviet Union (the latter contract was promptly snapped up by Komatsu of Japan). President Reagan went even further the following summer by extending the ban to West European firms manufacturing compressor stations under license from General Electric and using that company's parts.

Most allied governments were indignant at the U.S. measures and, in particular, at the attempt to impose Washington's jurisdiction on firms operating in Europe. The issue quickly went beyond questions of East-West policy and became a matter of principle, involving national sovereignty and pride. The French government was the first to defy the United States. It ordered all French firms to disregard the American decisions. Two days later, Italy followed suit, declaring that it would honor its contractual obligations to the U.S.S.R. Nine days later, British Prime Minister Margaret Thatcher, who had been a staunch supporter of President Reagan, vehemently denounced the sanction decisions and proclaimed that they would not bind her country. At the meeting of the leaders of the major Western nations held in Versailles in June 1982, the U.S. president found no support for the policy of economic warfare against the Soviet Union, and construction of the pipeline was continued.

However justified U.S. anger toward Moscow and the desire to inflict some economic punishment may have been, the decision to act in opposition to the common judgment of the European nations harmed the Western alliance more than the Soviet Union. This not only illustrates the differences of perspective on the two sides of the Atlantic, but it also shows how important it is for the United States to take into account the opinions of those allies who are most directly affected by its decisions. It also brings into view a recurring dilemma of effective choice: How far should confrontation with the Soviet Union be pursued at the expense of unity within the alliance that is the West's bulwark against the Soviet Union?

ACTIONS IN THE THIRD WORLD.   Although Washington's perceptions of conflicts and revolutionary violence in the less developed parts of the world have shifted somewhat from administration to administration, these are frequently viewed as the results of Soviet machinations. Instability in South Africa, conflict in the Horn of Africa, revolutionary violence in Central America, tension in the Middle East have all been interpreted as evidence of the Kremlin's willingness to challenge U.S. positions and to plant the seeds of Communist takeovers.

European governments with a strong Social Democratic or Socialist component, on the other hand, have not been inclined to view every instance of Third World turmoil as part of a Soviet grand design. Even governments ideologically further to the right do not always concur with the U.S. view. While most political leaders agree that instability in developing areas provides opportunities for an expansion of Soviet influence and that Moscow will usually try to take advantage of such opportunities, they see the causes of instability in more complex terms. Because many European societies have, in the past, suffered from great internal inequity, and because democracy and the first steps toward egalitarianism were often the product of political revolutions, they tend to perceive the domestic causes of instability in the Third World today in comparable terms. A feudal property system, the absence of representative government, and the arbitrary exercise of political power led to the French Revolution in 1789—a revolution that was to provide the model for social and political change in other parts of the Continent. In Britain, a major step away from monarchical despotism and toward representative government was taken with the Great Rebellion of 1642, and another step was made in the Glorious Revolution (1688-1689). True liberalism came to Great Britain in 1832 with the Reform Bill, leading to both an extension of suffrage and the first attempts at social legislation (for example, the regulation of child labor). Most European societies understand that revolutionary ideals may give way to new forms of injustice or oppression, but they are too well-versed in history to believe that all violent attempts at sociopolitical change must be the result of external subversion. Thus, the United States had little success in the early 1980s in its efforts to convince its allies that instability in Central America, for example, was principally engineered by the Kremlin.

Moreover, few of our allies have been willing to participate in or even to endorse U.S. military activity in the Third World. This was perhaps most apparent at the time of America's involvement in Vietnam. It is likely that President Lyndon B. Johnson initially expected some expression of allied support for his policy in Vietnam, and possibly even some token troop commitments, but he was disappointed. Except for mild expressions of sympathy from West Germany, the Europeans favored complete dissociation from the war. Prime Minister Harold Wilson of Great Britain, despite Johnson's urging, refused to support escalation in Vietnam. France's President de Gaulle vehemently denounced the U.S. military presence in Southeast Asia. Prime Minister Olof Palme of Sweden could be seen marching in demonstrations protesting the war. In 1967, a U.S. official admitted that 80 percent of the West

European public "is opposed to what the U.S. is doing in Vietnam." [4] There was distress in Japan as well, particularly since U.S. bombing raids against North Vietnam originated from Okinawa. The Japanese Diet passed a resolution declaring that "the attacks from Okinawa against Vietnam are bringing uneasiness and terror to the . . . inhabitants and are dragging Okinawa into the war. This has become a serious question threatening not only the safety of Okinawa but that of the Japanese homeland." [5] This lack of enthusiasm for what the administration and its supporters viewed as a crucial and selfless mission to halt the spread of communism and Soviet influence provoked bitterness. Some conservatives in the United States called for a punitive reduction of the U.S. troop presence in Europe. But the allies felt that the peril created by the U.S. response exceeded that caused by the Soviet challenge.

More modest examples of U.S. military involvement in the Third World have encountered an equally adamant allied opposition. The invasion of Grenada in 1983 was criticized by virtually every other industrialized democracy, including the Thatcher government in Great Britain. Similarly, when U.S. naval forces off the Lebanese coast bombarded the positions of radical and pro-Syrian Islamic groups in the autumn of 1983, both France and Britain objected. When the United States mined Nicaragua's harbors in 1984, France offered to help the Nicaraguans clear the mines away. Occasionally, the European nations have participated in peacekeeping activities, such as the multinational force in southern Lebanon, but they have eschewed participation in military confrontations with an East-West dimension.

Not only have many European governments taken a different view of the causes of Third World unrest, but, for reasons already discussed, they have also considered the preservation and promotion of détente in Europe more important than the pursuit of Cold War objectives in distant regions. For example, even after the U.S.S.R. invaded Afghanistan in 1979, U.S. allies in Western Europe were willing to condemn the Soviet action but not to join in the punitive sanctions desired by Washington. The difference was compounded by the view of many Europeans (which appears correct in retrospect) that the invasion was a serious strategic error, which would tie up Soviet resources and undermine its influence in the Third World, especially in Islamic societies.

Some people in the United States have expressed frustration at what they see as Europe's unwillingness to stand by the very country that is committed to Europe's defense in the event of Soviet aggression. But the Europeans' point of view is that East-West tension is usually a greater threat to their security than are Soviet forays in the Third World. This does not mean that Europeans are indifferent to Soviet footholds in other parts of the world, but they look at the problem somewhat differently. They believe that turmoil in the developing world has internal causes and does not usually threaten Western Europe directly. Besides, the costs of abandoning détente are, as we have seen, considerably greater for Western Europe than for the United States.

The Issue of Burden-Sharing

NATO was established in the aftermath of World War II, when the economic destruction of Western Europe, coupled with the postwar prosperity of the United States, made it clear that America would have to bear most of the costs of Western security. But as Europe recovered and actually became America's economic competitor, Washington began wondering whether the United States should continue to carry so large a share of NATO's military expenses. Sen. Mike Mansfield (D-Mont.) raised this question in the mid-1960s. In 1966, he offered a resolution in the Senate stating that Europe's ability to defend itself had improved, both economically and militarily, and calling for a smaller U.S. contribution to the common defense, to be achieved by reducing the number of U.S. troops stationed in Europe. The resolution was never passed, though it was introduced again several times in later years. Recently, several circumstances have made the issue reemerge.

When friends begin disagreeing on the substance of a common endeavor, it is not long before they start quarreling about who is bearing the greater burden in its pursuit. Accordingly, disagreements on the interpretation of the Soviet threat have led to discord on relative contributions to NATO's defense spending. The belief in the United States that it was carrying an unfairly large share of the costs has been compounded by displeasure with Europe's stance toward the U.S.S.R. The question of burden-sharing loomed especially large following the pipeline controversy and Europe's comparatively mild response to Soviet activity in Afghanistan and Poland.

An additional factor was the U.S. decision in 1979 to deploy theater nuclear weapons—the ground-launched cruise missile and the Pershing II—in West Germany, England, and several other countries. This generated fears that a nuclear war would be fought on European soil if deterrence failed and that the security of the continent might actually suffer as a result of the new deployments. As a result of these fears, the NATO partners decided to make a major effort to upgrade their conventional (that is, non-nuclear) military capacity, in order to improve their ability to fend off a Soviet attack without having to resort to nuclear weapons. However, this called for substantial expenses, and the United States did not want to bear the costs by itself. Consequently, with vigorous U.S. prodding, the European members of NATO pledged that each of them would increase its defense spending by an annual rate of 3 percent after inflation for each of five years. Their willingness to make good on this pledge was taken by many in Washington as a test of Europe's commitment to the Western alliance. If the European nations could not manage an increase of 3 percent a year at a time when the United States was increasing its defense spending at a much greater rate, then, it was felt, the advisability of continued U.S. exertions on Europe's behalf should be reexamined.

In fact, most of the countries failed to meet the 3 percent goal. In 1979, the second wave of oil price increases sent European economies into a recession, tax revenues dropped, and military spending grew by an average of barely 2 percent annually. Many Americans took this as evidence that their European allies would not make the necessary effort to deal with Soviet power and as grounds for reexamining the U.S. commitment to the defense of Europe. The United States pointed out that approximately 50 percent of its defense outlays were spent on NATO and that U.S. defense budgets had been growing rapidly since the late 1970s. Why should the United States pay so much to take care of countries that, in the eyes of some critics, would not help themselves?

In 1984, Sen. Sam Nunn (D-Ga.) proposed a reduction of U.S. troops in Europe by 90,000 (approximately one-third of their strength) by 1990, unless the Europeans increased defense spending by the 3 percent target or met other specified military goals. The proposal was opposed by the Reagan administration and was defeated in the Senate, but it was a sign of U.S. discontent with the European NATO members.

The issue is less clear-cut than it might seem. While U.S. military spending has been growing rapidly since the late 1970s, it had not been doing so in previous years. In fact, Europe did substantially better than the United States earlier in the decade: between 1969 and 1979, its share of NATO's total defense expenditures nearly doubled, rising from 22.7 percent to 41.6 percent. To many Europeans, the United States has overlooked that fact. Furthermore, they point out that the single-minded focus on military spending obscures the true magnitudes of the relative contributions to defense. A focus on actual military deployments would reveal that, of the ready forces in Europe, some 90 percent to the ground forces and 85 percent of the air forces come from Western European countries, and that includes 75 percent of NATO's tanks and 90 percent of its armored division.[6] The higher U.S. spending figure, European critics point out, comes largely from the fact that the United States has a volunteer army and thus must pay its soldiers nearly civilian salaries. Europe's armies are drawn from conscripts, who are much cheaper. Thus, military *spending* and military *contribution* are not synonymous.

If, nevertheless, the United States does bear a disproportionately large share of the defense burden, many social scientists would argue that this is exactly what should be expected. Western security, they point out, is a *collective good*, that is, a good that is jointly enjoyed, from which it is not possible to exclude those who do not contribute their fair share, and the consumption of which by some members does not really reduce the supply available for others. Fresh air, for example, is a collective good, because, though it involves certain costs, such as pollution control, those who do not contribute to the costs cannot be prevented from enjoying it, and one person's breathing of the air does not diminish the ability of others to do the same. Similarly, national defense is a collective good, because people in the United States who do not pay their taxes cannot very well be deprived of its benefits, and the enjoyment of national security by some people does not deprive other people of its benefits. With most collective goods, unless fair shares can be imposed coercively, the wealthiest members of the group get saddled with a large proportion of its costs while others enjoy more or less of a "free ride." [7] As an alliance provides something very much resembling a collective good, it should also be subject to this principle.[8] Certainly, the Soviet Union bears most of the costs of the Warsaw Pact just as the United States accounts for a large share of NATO's expenditures. In both cases, the leading nation in the alliance is in the best position to pay a large share. In addition, the military alliance may mean somewhat more to the leading nations than to the other members. While this is evidently the case for the Warsaw Pact (indeed, it is not obvious that most of its other members are really voluntary participants), in the case of NATO it may stem from a greater U.S. emphasis on military methods of dealing with the U.S.S.R. While all European nations recognize the need to be prepared to confront a Soviet military threat, they appear more eager than the United States to explore other ways of dealing with Moscow, including a stable détente. Under the circumstances, many social scientists consider the division of the financial burden to be quite logical, if not necessarily "fair."

Economic Competition

Almost everyone agrees that, in the long run, free trade benefits all trading partners. In principle, almost everyone is opposed to protectionism. Nevertheless, industrialized nations seem to be erecting an ever-expanding array of formal and informal trade barriers, and the gap between reality and declared preferences grows wider every year. Relations between the United States and other developed democracies have suffered in recent years because of an unwillingness to open national markets to each other's goods and services, and when economic relations turn sour, political relations usually deteriorate as well. At present, the damage to relations does not appear great enough to undermine the West's ability to meet its economic and security challenges, but observers have begun sounding warning bells.

Despite the benefits of free trade, some countries do suffer costs and dislocations from unimpeded foreign competition, especially in the short run, and a government that accepts these costs incurs political risks as a result. If certain sectors of the economy or parts of the country feel that they are bearing an unfairly large proportion of the costs, they will lobby for relief in the form of barriers against imports. If they do not get it, their ire will be directed against the incumbent government, and if they are sufficiently angry and well organized, the government might get thrown out of office. Consequently, pressures toward protectionism appear in most nations, though the demands are particularly vehement, and the political risks of rejecting them especially great, in countries whose competitive edge is slipping, for they have the largest number of losers.

The postwar recovery of Western Europe and Japan provided the United States with its first serious taste of economic competition. By the 1960s, its dominance in international markets was challenged. The inflation induced by the war in Vietnam accelerated the decline in the U.S. balance of trade, converting it from a surplus to a growing deficit. Beginning in the late 1970s, the situation deteriorated even further, for two reasons. In the first place, productivity in the United States did not grow as fast as that of most of its competitors, and U.S. goods therefore lost ground in quality and price to those made in Japan and Europe. Secondly, the value of the U.S. dollar increased relative to most other national currencies. This was an outgrowth of the high U.S. interest rates, generated by huge budgetary deficits. Such high interest rates led foreigners to place their money in the United States, and they had to buy dollars to do so, thus increasing the dollar's value relative to other currencies. A "strong" dollar may sound like something desirable, but it hurts the nation's balance of trade. Foreigners wishing to buy U.S. goods must pay more for the dollars they need; consequently, they buy less, and U.S. exports decline. Conversely, the "strong" dollar makes foreign goods cheaper in the United States; more are bought, and imports grow. The dollar began declining in value in 1986, but not enough to change the situation very much.

Expanding imports and shrinking exports mean a rising deficit in the balance of trade and less manufacturing activity, with an attendant loss of jobs and income. Between 1980 and 1984, the proportion of sales in the U.S. market accounted for by foreign products increased from 10 to 15 percent for manufactured goods, from 16 to 26 percent for capital equipment, from 3 to 10 percent for computers, and from 25 to 45 percent for semiconductors. Foreign producers' share of the textile market rose from 20 to 50 percent, while employment in the U.S. textile industry declined by 20 percent. In shoes, the import share rose from 50 to 71 percent; employment declined by 11 percent, and ninety-four shoe plants closed in 1984 alone.[9]

A frequent reaction in the United States has been to blame foreign competition—specifically, to declare that Japan and the European nations engage in unfair trade practices. Political action has usually focused on efforts to keep foreign competitors out of U.S. markets. This has not necessarily required quotas or tariffs; more often, protection has relied on barriers of a less formal, but equally effective, sort. For example, when the U.S. automobile industry experienced a near-depression in the late 1970s and early 1980s, the U.S. government imposed "voluntary" restraints on Japanese car exports, persuading Japan to reduce its sales 7 percent below those of the previous year. These restraints were maintained for four years. Japanese-made electronic goods have been under similar pressure. Steel production represents an endangered sector of American industry. Mainly because of lagging productivity, U.S. steelmakers have been unable to meet competition from other developed, and even some developing nations. Consequently, the industry has lobbied hard for protection. In 1982, the United States signed a "voluntary" quota agreement with the EEC, which put a limit on European steel exports, and at about the same time, similar limits were placed on exports of steel from Japan. In 1984, the United States began negotiating export restraints with other steel suppliers. Because of the high cost of U.S. labor compared to that of developing nations, the U.S. textile industry has also faced strong foreign competition, especially from Asian nations. Some protection was granted to the industry in 1974 by the Multi-Fiber Agreement, another case of "voluntary" export restraints. In 1983, textile quotas were substantially reduced, and they were extended to imports from the People's Republic of China, a nation of great diplomatic and geopolitical importance to the United States. In 1983, President Reagan increased tariffs on large motorcycles (which are mainly produced by Japan) from 4.4 percent to 49.4 percent. U.S. sugar producers are also protected by import quotas.

Such measures are typically explained not as an abandonment of the principle of free trade but as "temporary" provisions designed to give domestic producers an opportunity to recover their market positions. They are also said to be justified as retaliatory measures against the protectionism practiced by America's trading partners. The United States, it is argued, cannot be the only nation to play by the rules of free trade.

To a certain extent, the charges leveled against America's trading partners may be warranted. The EEC, for example, has long had its Common Agricultural Policy (CAP), which is designed to stimulate agricultural production within the community even at the expense of more efficient foreign producers, including farmers in the United States. The strategy has been to impose variable duties on all agricultural imports, ensuring that few foreign producers can undercut the prices charged by European agricultural producers. Since the United States is the country with the most productive agricultural sector, and since agricultural products account for a large fraction of total U.S. exports, the CAP has created resentment in the United States.

Protests against Japan have been even more vociferous, mainly because it has proven such a formidable competitor. "Japan-bashing" is a common reaction to the loss of jobs resulting from imports of Toyota automobiles or Hitachi television sets. The usual argument has been that Japan has engaged in "unfair" trading practices. The record, however, is not clear-cut on this score. Japan's tariffs are not especially high and, while it does not have fewer quotas than do other nations, neither does it have inordinately more. Rather, its barriers to imports tend to be of a bureaucratic and cultural character. Regulations, for example, are at times virtually impenetrable. In one frequently cited example, Japan had seventeen laws and safety standards that made it impossible for U.S. producers to sell aluminum baseball bats there. It took five years of pressure from the United States before Japan finally relented and modified these rules.

Neither the United States nor its trading partners are particularly pure when it comes to free trade, but the problem of the U.S. trade deficit has come at least as much from within its own economy: high costs, sluggish productivity growth, and goods of frequently inferior quality. While free trade cannot be dissociated from fair trade, long-term solutions to the problem will have to come from within. In particular, U.S. productivity must grow more vigorously. Yet, as MIT economist Lester Thurow points out, "Going back to Washington to extend protection is always easier than doing the research and development, building the new factories, acquiring the new skills, altering wages and work rules, and selling the new products that would be necessary to become competitive." [10]

There are reasons to decry protectionism on both economic and political grounds. While it may help economically inefficient producers in the short run, it helps virtually no one else. Freed of the pressure of foreign competition, domestic producers are no longer compelled to hold down their own prices, and consumers end up paying more for the goods they purchase (in addition to having a more restricted choice of goods). Other producers who must buy the higher-priced goods also suffer. For example, U.S. automobile makers who buy more expensive U.S.-made steel may find their own sales jeopardized. Eventually, consumption declines because of the higher prices, business activity goes down as sales volume shrinks, and jobs are lost in other sectors of the economy. Even protected producers feel the effects of the reduced activity. Finally, as nations begin retaliating against each other's protectionistic measures, the losses assume international proportions. It was just such successive rounds of protectionism that accelerated the demise of the developed economies in the 1930s and deepened the Great Depression.

Trade wars create noneconomic consequences as well, including a weakening of international solidarity. The situation has not reached a point in the Western alliance where commercial advantage is seen as outweighing the benefits of cooperation, but there are definite signs of friction. In 1985, the U.S. Senate passed a resolution accusing Japan of being an "unfair trader." Sen. Bob Packwood (R-Ore.), chairman of the Senate Finance Committee, declared that Congress had "run out of patience" with Japan, which had "dallied, stalled, and lied to us." After President Reagan tightened curbs on imports of European steel, former French finance minister Jacques Delors, who was about to take over as head of the EEC Commission (its executive body), described the state of trans-Atlantic relations as "abysmal" and said Europe was the victim of an "increasingly aggressive and ideological" U.S. administration that carries "a bible in one hand and a revolver in the other." [11] In March 1987, the Reagan administration imposed a 100 percent import duty on a number of Japanese electronic products, thus effectively doubling their price on U.S. markets. This is not the stuff of which friendship among allies is made.

The Alliance in Perspective

It has become fashionable to criticize America's Western friends and allies for insufficient toughness toward the Soviet Union, for unfair trading practices, for excessive welfare spending, and so on. Most of these criticisms originate at the conservative end of the U.S. political spectrum. Irving Kristol, a leading conservative commentator, has complained that, in Europe, the "social democratic temper, the inward-turning politics of compassionate reform has largely replaced the patriotic temper, the politics of national self assertion." [12] The impression conveyed is that Europe has become soft, "decadent," committed to pampering its people in an economically ruinous welfare state, while appeasing the Soviet Union rather than confronting it with proper firmness.

While these charges are principally directed against Western Europe, they could encompass other nations as well. Japan has never been willing to spend much for military purposes, and, though Japan's governmental expenditure is a relatively small fraction of national income, its outlays for social welfare exceed those of the United States. U.S. relations with New Zealand have also deteriorated. As a matter of policy, the New Zealand government has refused to permit U.S. ships carrying nuclear weapons to enter the country's harbors. In retaliation, the United States has reduced security cooperation between the two countries, and there has even been serious talk of scrapping the ANZUS treaty linking Australia, New Zealand, and the United States.

While the West does share an overriding commitment to preserving political democracy and resisting Soviet power, a commitment that nothing so far has undermined, perceptions and interests have evolved in somewhat different directions in Europe and the United States. As we have seen, commercial and other exchanges between the European nations and the Soviet Union are much greater than between the superpowers themselves. One consequence is that there is less to be lost in the United States from confrontation with the Soviet Union. Moreover, Europe fears that it would bear the brunt of the military destruction caused by an East-West conflict, and what might appear like appeasement to the United States seems more like prudence from Europe's perspective.

These are significant differences, but two other factors are no less crucial to the difficulties that afflict the Western alliance. The first of these is the difference of opinion as to the proper combination of military force and diplomacy in East-West relations. For many U.S. leaders, particularly in recent years, military force is the principal tool for dealing with Moscow; diplomacy is effective only to the extent that the Kremlin realizes that it is not dealing from a position of strength, and even then it is limited by the inherent bad faith of the Communists. For most European leaders, excessive reliance on military policies thwarts whatever chance diplomacy might have to bring about improvements in East-West relations, and these policies are often less effective and more dangerous than diplomacy. They agree that a strong deterrent posture is needed, but they do not want to reduce East-West relations to an arms race. Thus, while many U.S. leaders tend to view the Europeans as excessively soft, many Europeans worry that U.S. leaders seem to favor a gunslinging approach to the Soviet Union.

The second factor grows out of the very nature of relations within the Western alliance. The great disparity between U.S. and European power after World War II made Europe's dependence on, and deference to, the United States inevitable. As one scholar has observed, "Most of us grew up knowing a Europe that was indeed the perfect ally: too weak to disagree, yet not so weak as to be totally irrelevant for us." [13] But the disparity is no longer as great, and this has produced its own strains. When Europeans reject U.S. views and preferences, it evokes in the United States righteous indignation at the perceived ingratitude and a resolve to downgrade U.S. commitment to NATO. Most European leaders understand that, while the disparity in power and resources is not what it used to be, it remains too great for total equality in decision making—but they often resent the situation. The sense of humiliation at being dependent on the United States, compounded by the conviction that U.S. policies are not invariably right, makes them chafe at the terms of the relationship and attempt, whenever possible, to assert an independent view. The narrower the disparity becomes, the less acceptable is the asymmetry of decisional power. Frustration on the European side is the result.

Disagreements among allies are not unusual. On the contrary, they are inevitable in a democratic alliance, and they are healthy to the extent that they encourage adaptation to changing circumstances. Moreover, despite the disagreements, the basic foundations of the Western alliance have never been brought into question by responsible policy makers in any of its members. Although views differ on the proper mix of military and nonmilitary policy instruments, all parties share the opinion that the Soviet Union represents the most serious threat to the alliance and that deterrence must remain a cornerstone of their common policy toward the U.S.S.R. Although most European nations display a greater concern for social welfare and a greater readiness to consider it a governmental responsibility than does the United States, all Western industrialized nations are devoted to private enterprise as the basis of economic activity and to democracy as the foundation of political organization. In sharing these beliefs, they form a minority within the international community and are linked by an identifiable common destiny. The disagreements are thus much less significant than the bonds.

But, in people's minds, problems often loom larger than shared interests. They are irritating, they produce indignation, and they seem to call for immediate action. If the Europeans seem to be "exploiting" the United States by refusing to pay their share of the defense burden, if they persist in "unfair" trade practices, it is hard to concentrate on the overriding ties. Moreover, electoral rewards more frequently go to those who are prepared to indulge public moods than to those who are willing to go against them. Given the inevitable tension between allies, the principal challenge to responsible leadership will be to maintain a sense of proper perspective, refusing to act on short-term frustrations at the expense of long-term interests.

Notes

1. OECD, *Historical Statistics of Foreign Trade, 1965-1980* (Paris: OECD, 1982), and OECD, *Monthly Statistics of Foreign Trade, Series A* (Paris: OECD, 1985).
2. Dimitri K. Simes, "The Anti-Soviet Brigade," *Foreign Policy* (Winter 1979-1980): 8.
3. Quoted in Willy Brandt, *People and Politics* (Boston: Little, Brown, 1979), 132.
4. "Europe's Opposition to War in Asia Chills Its Relations with U.S.," *Wall Street Journal*, May 9, 1967.
5. Quoted in Richard J. Barnet, *The Alliance* (New York: Simon and Schuster, 1983), 268.
6. Earl C. Ravenal, "Europe Without America," *Foreign Affairs* (Summer 1985).
7. Mancur Olson, *The Logic of Collective Action* (New York: Schocken, 1968).
8. Mancur Olson and Richard Zeckhauser, "An Economic Theory of Alliances," *Review of Economics and Statistics* 46 (1966): 266-279.
9. John M. Culbertson, "Control Imports through Bilateral Pacts," *New York Times*, August 11, 1985.
10. Lester C. Thurow, *The Zero-Sum Solution: Building a World Class American Economy* (New York: Simon and Schuster, 1985), 104.
11. Quoted in Paul Lewis, "It's Far from Quiet on the European Front," *New York Times*, December 30, 1984.
12. Irving Kristol, *Reflections of a Neoconservative* (New York: Basic Books, 1983), 239.
13. James Oliver Goldsborough, *Rebel Europe: How America Can Live With a Changing Continent* (New York: Macmillan, 1982), 9.

c h a p t e r   t e n

Interventions
in the Third World

THOUGH THE UNITED STATES has been a participant in war less often than many other nations, military conflict has nevertheless been an integral part of its history. Settlement of the continent entailed warfare against the American Indians, independence was acquired by armed struggle against England, and territorial growth beyond the thirteen colonies was partially achieved through war (as with Mexico over Texas). Participation in World War I and World War II insured the victory of nations committed to democracy and created an international environment more hospitable to U.S. political values than might otherwise have been the case. In recent decades, however, the only form of U.S. involvement in conflict has been armed intervention in developing nations, and despite America's unrivaled military power these interventions have often ended badly. If we are to draw lessons from these experiences, we must understand why the interventions occurred, how they escalated, and what their consequences have been.

Recent Instances of Intervention

For a nation committed to peace, the United States has resorted to force surprisingly often. Between 1789 and 1940, by one count, it engaged in 116 acts of overt military intervention in the Third World (or what might then have been considered as such). Between 1946 and 1975, it employed its military power on 215 occasions.[1] Most of these incidents fell short of outright invasions of foreign countries, amounting usually to a mere show of force, but on several occasions since World War II the United States has actually intervened abroad with armed force (see the appendix to this chapter).

During the early part of the nineteenth century, U.S. military power was used mainly for such purposes as the control of piracy, the suppression of slave trading, and the protection of U.S. lives and economic interests in Latin America and the Far East. Some of these interventions seem mildly comical in retrospect; for example, Commodore Thomas Jones seized Monterey in Mexico in 1843 in the belief that a war with Mexico had begun, but upon learning that he was mistaken, he gave Monterey back.

In the twentieth century, U.S. military interventions abroad acquired a more pronounced political and ideological character. Participation in World War I and World War II was impelled by major political objectives, and the attempt to oust the Bolsheviks after they had seized power in Russia was dictated by ideological revulsion for Marxism. Several less well-known interventions during this period were also colored by political sentiments. For example, when a revolution seemed imminent in Nicaragua in 1926, U.S. Marines landed (for the ninth time since 1853) to avert it. Though the troops had not planned on a prolonged stay, circumstances caused them to extend their presence. Augusto Sandino (from whom today's Sandinistas draw their name) emerged as an opposition leader and began to attract leftist support from abroad. For the first time, the perception of a Communist threat in the Western Hemisphere prompted a lengthy U.S. military involvement; the troops remained in Nicaragua until 1933.

The largest and most costly U.S. interventions in the Third World occurred after World War II, in Korea and Vietnam. Approximately thirty thousand Americans lost their lives in the Korean action, some fifty thousand in Vietnam. The circumstances surrounding U.S. involvement in these two wars will be discussed in detail below, but it will be helpful to consider first the more modest interventions in Lebanon in 1958 and 1983, the Dominican Republic in 1965, and Grenada in 1983.

Lebanon, 1958 and 1983

In 1957, Lebanon was shaken by civil strife.[2] Groups opposing the government of President Camille Chamoun, a conservative Christian, took to the streets and engaged in sporadic acts of violence. The president's supporters launched a campaign of counterviolence, and the level of conflict escalated. Uprisings by various guerrilla groups brought resistance from paramilitary groups loyal to Chamoun. For the most part, the loyalists were Christians while the rebels were Moslems; moreover, many, though not all, in the opposition were considerably to the left of the president and his supporters, and many were fervent Arab nationalists as well. Rumors began circulating that Syria might seek to take advantage of the situation either by launching a direct invasion of Lebanon or by providing the guerrillas with necessary supplies.

This might appear to have been a local conflict of little direct concern to the United States, but the administration of President Dwight D. Eisenhower saw in it various threats to American interests. In particular, it feared that

Syria was on the verge of becoming a Communist state. In 1957, the State Department's Bureau of Intelligence and Research estimated that the Syrian and Lebanese Communist parties together had over twenty thousand members[3]— far more than other countries in the region—and the Syrian government was thought to be very unstable. Should Communists come to power in those two countries, Washington feared they might spread their influence throughout the region, a situation the Soviet Union might then exploit to establish its presence in the Middle East. At the very least, Egypt's president, Gamal Abdel Nasser, whom U.S. policy makers distrusted and also suspected of pro-Soviet leanings, might find his own regional influence increased if Arab nationalists came to power in Lebanon.

Chamoun asked for Western assistance, and President Eisenhower decided to provide it, even though there was little hard evidence of a threat to U.S. interests or of a Syrian invasion. On July 15, 1958, Eisenhower gave this explanation:

> What we see now in the Middle East is the same pattern of conquest with which we became familiar in the period 1945 to 1950. This involves taking over a nation by means of indirect aggression; that is, under the cover of a fomented civil strife the purpose is to put into domestic control those whose real loyalty is to the aggressor.[4]

On the same day, more than fourteen thousand U.S. Marines landed on the beaches of Beirut and stormed ashore amidst startled bathers and Coca-Cola vendors. Ironically, the United States later decided that political stability in Lebanon demanded the departure of Chamoun, the very man at whose request the invasion had been carried out, and a compromise government composed of both loyalist and opposition members was formed. A further irony was that this was the same solution that Egypt's Nasser had advocated all along but which, coming from him, had been considered unacceptable. Stability had returned to Lebanon temporarily but at the cost of increased anti-American Arab nationalism in the Middle East.

Although Lebanon subsequently enjoyed a period of internal peace and economic prosperity, relations among the country's religious and ethnic groups, especially Christians and Moslems, remained tense. By the early 1970s, there were new waves of civil strife in the country. Conflict intensified as the Arab-Israeli conflict resumed and began to intrude increasingly into Lebanese life. Christian forces had the backing of Israel, while Syria, whose military dependence on the U.S.S.R. had become considerable, supported the Moslems. To complicate matters, the Palestine Liberation Organization (PLO) had established a major presence in southern Lebanon.

In April 1982, fighting between Christians and Moslems reached its highest level since 1976, and Syria began moving surface-to-air missiles (SAMs) into position. Israel threatened military action against the Syrians if the SAMs were not removed, and it mounted air strikes against PLO positions in Beirut, resulting in large numbers of civilian deaths. On June 6, thirty thousand Israeli troops invaded southern Lebanon, moved to positions around Beirut, and inflicted substantial losses on Syrian forces, destroying in the process numerous Syrian fighter planes and SAM sites. The Soviet Union replaced Syria's lost equipment and began to take a larger role in training Syria's troops and even to man much of Syria's air defense system. The turmoil in Lebanon thus threatened to destabilize the whole region. After massive Israeli air and artillery strikes against Beirut, a U.S. proposal for a modest multilateral peace-keeping force (MLF) in Beirut was accepted. The main mission of the MLF, which included U.S., Italian, and French troops, was to supervise the with-drawal of Syrian and PLO forces from the area. It was thought that, if this were achieved, a major obstacle to regional peace would be removed and the task of rebuilding national unity in Lebanon facilitated.

The PLO and the Syrians did in fact pull out of Beirut, and the MLF be-gan withdrawing on September 10. Several days later, however, Christian Phalangist militiamen were allowed into two camps for Palestinian civilian refugees in Beirut and massacred the population of both camps, women and children included. Amidst the ensuing international outcry, the multinational force was rapidly reinserted and was reinforced by a contingent of British troops. In principle, its task was to secure peace in Beirut, but the position of the U.S. participants was somewhat ambiguous. Because Washington supported the Lebanese president, Amin Gemayel—a Christian Phalangist who was also supported by Israel—the United States was not perceived as neutral by Lebanon's Moslems. An additional problem was that the administration of President Ronald Reagan, more so even than previous U.S. governments, defined the Arab-Israeli conflict in East-West terms. It thus tended to ignore the issues behind the local antagonisms, focusing instead almost exclusively on the danger of Soviet influence in the area. Syria, which supported the Moslem forces (though not necessarily the PLO), was viewed by Washington as the Soviet advance force in the area.

When the Israelis withdrew from Beirut to more secure positions in southern Lebanon, fighting intensified between Syrian-supported militias and government forces seeking to occupy the positions vacated by Israel. In this context, the U.S. Marines in Beirut were attacked with increasing frequency and U.S. firepower was being used both to protect the Marines and to assist the Lebanese government's own military effort. A large U.S. naval force, including two aircraft carriers and the battleship *New Jersey*, was assembled off the Lebanese coast and began sporadic offshore bombardment of Moslem military positions in the hills surrounding Beirut. On October 23, a terrorist suicide mission blew up the Marine barracks in Beirut, killing 239 American soldiers.

The United States had now become a participant in the Lebanese civil war, and both Congress and the public were concerned that another major military involvement might be imminent for purposes that were, at best, of nebulous merit. Although President Reagan suggested that the Soviet Union was poised to move into the region in Syria's wake, such an eventuality appeared remote to many people. Furthermore, the military action seemed likely to further reduce Arab support for U.S. policies in the Middle East. As the violence intensified, other member nations of the MLF began reassessing the value of their presence. A small peacekeeping force was helpless in the face of intolerance and hatred among the country's ethnic and religious groups, and the foreign troops were a target for terrorist attacks. Accordingly, Italy and Great Britain announced that their contingents would be pulled out. Under a combination of domestic political pressure and, perhaps, a sense that the connection between military force and political goals was becoming obscure, in February 1984 Washington decided to withdraw the Marines and to cease naval action against Moslem forces. The second U.S. military intervention in Lebanon was terminated with a general recognition of its dubious utility.

The Dominican Republic, 1965

In many ways, U.S. intervention in the Dominican Republic in 1965 was rooted in Washington's obsession with the specter of "another Cuba." When Dominican dictator Rafael Trujillo was assassinated in 1961, Juan Bosch, a mildly leftist but non-Communist politician and writer, returned from a twenty-year exile to assume the nation's presidency. However, the Dominican military, with U.S. support, overthrew Bosch in 1963 and installed a three-member military junta at the country's head. Rifts soon appeared within the military, and an apparent coup attempt was discovered in late April 1965. Although the aim of the coup remains a mystery, some suspected its major purpose was to bring Bosch back to the presidency. A rebellion of a portion of the armed forces broke out shortly afterward; while many of the rebelling officers sought Bosch's return, others simply wanted elections, while still others wanted a purge of the military itself. The situation deteriorated, effective government disappeared, and the armed forces coalesced into two groups, Bosch supporters and Bosch opponents. Washington threw its support behind the latter, more conservative group, and U.S. intelligence services began reporting that Bosch's supporters seemed to include a number of local Communists. The evidence was far from clear-cut, but President Lyndon Johnson was convinced that the Dominican Republic was indeed about to become "another Cuba."

A few days after the discovery of the aborted coup and the beginning of the rebellion, twelve hundred U.S. Marines were dispatched with the declared purpose of protecting American lives. Soon, the entire Eighty-second Airborne Division was committed to the task of securing U.S. interests in the Dominican Republic; the American military presence then included some twenty thousand troops. In September 1965, a provisional government of anti-Bosch leaders was set up under Hector Garcia-Godoy. In presidential elections held in 1966, Bosch was defeated by Joaquin Balaguer, and the U.S. troops, as well as a smaller force sent by the Organization of American States, withdrew. Aside from the question of the propriety of intervening in another country's internal affairs, the U.S. objective—to prevent Bosch from assuming power—was achieved at moderate cost.

Grenada, 1983

Though Latin America and the Caribbean have always generated the greatest amount of containment activity, no president since Lyndon Johnson has been so agitated about leftist presence in the region as Ronald Reagan. A left-wing guerrilla movement in El Salvador led his administration to provide military and economic support to the Salvadoran government. A renewed surge of anti-Castro rhetoric, accompanied by vigorous economic and diplomatic pressure, brought U.S.-Cuban relations to their lowest point in almost two decades. But the administration was most disturbed by Nicaragua's Sandinista regime, which not only was Marxist but also was suspected of helping the Salvadoran rebels. Nicaragua was viewed as yet another Cuba, and in an effort to oust the Sandinistas, Washington organized and supported anti-Sandinista guerrillas, known as contras, many of whom had earlier been associated with former dictator Anastasio Somoza's ill-famed National Guard. Despite luke-warm congressional and public support, various forms of assistance were provided for harassment operations by the contras against the Nicaraguan government. The administration also established airstrips and other military facilities in neighboring Honduras. They were to serve as a staging platform from which an invasion of Nicaragua could be launched and as a base for large-scale military maneuvers designed to intimidate the Sandinistas.

The Reagan administration was also irritated by the Marxist, though not really anti-American, government of Prime Minister Maurice Bishop in Grenada, a tiny Caribbean island. U.S. officials had, for some time, been warning of Cuban influence in Grenada and of an unusually long runway on the island, which, they said, could be used for military purposes. In October 1983, a group of military rebels killed Bishop and two members of his cabinet and instituted a "revolutionary and military council" under the leadership of Gen. Hudson Austin, who was more of an avowed Marxist than his predecessor had been. Though many people found it difficult to get excited about the threat from a country of 120 square miles and just over 100,000 inhabitants, it was precisely the diminutive size of Grenada that made it seem to the administration like a good place in which to demonstrate its resolve in dealing with Marxists and the principle that, despite the reticence about armed interventions abroad that was a legacy of Vietnam, military force could still be effectively used in pursuit of external objectives. Without warning, a contingent of approximately six thousand Marines and airborne troops was dispatched to Grenada, ostensibly to "rescue" U.S. citizens there but actually to remove the new government. Somewhere between eight hundred and eleven hundred Cubans were "discovered" on the island when the U.S. troops landed; the majority were civilian construction workers, though several hundred appeared to be military personnel.

The Cubans held the U.S. troops off for several days, but the United States was soon in military control of Grenada. Members of the revolutionary government were arrested and elections were promised. International opinion, not only in the Third World but in most Western nations as well, was critical of the invasion as a blatant violation of international law, but U.S. public opinion was overwhelmingly supportive, and Washington viewed the operation as a great success. (Although no more than seven thousand troops had participated in the various phases of the operation, more than eight thousand medals were awarded to individuals who were involved in it.) In December 1984, thirteen months after the invasion, the New National Party, favored by the Reagan administration, swept to victory in the elections. Whatever else might be said about this intervention, it produced the results that the administration desired.

The Uses and Costs of Military Force

Radical critics of U.S. foreign policy generally assume that economic goals lie behind most activities abroad, particularly military interventions.[5] This argument may have had some merit when applied to armed interventions of an earlier era, but it is hard to see how economic motivations account, in any more or less direct fashion, for U.S. military activities in the Third World since World War II. It is difficult to find a compelling economic basis for the U.S. interventions in Lebanon in 1958 and 1983 or in the Dominican Republic in 1965, and virtually impossible to find one for the invasion of Grenada in 1983. (This is also true of the interventions in Korea and Vietnam, which will be considered later in this chapter.)

Political, not economic, objectives have for the most part motivated the use of military force by the United States in the developing regions, and these political objectives have almost invariably been associated with the Cold War. Democratic or not, acceptable regimes in the Third World have typically been anticommunist. For example, when discussing U.S. policy toward the right-wing Trujillo dictatorship in the Dominican Republic, President John F. Kennedy explained that "there are three possibilities in a descending order of preference: a decent democratic regime, a continuation of the Trujillo regime, or a Castro regime. We ought to aim at the first, but we really can't renounce the second until we are sure that we can avoid the third." [6]

This ranking, and the willingness it indicated to settle for considerably less than democratic regimes, suggests that rivalry with the Soviet Union and a desire to contain its expansion, rather than the attainment of positive ideological goals, have shaped U.S. policies in the developing areas. Containment implies that Soviet efforts to alter the international balance of power in its favor should be met by measured yet adequate counterforce. By being made to understand that its efforts at expansion were fruitless, or at least too costly, the Soviet Union would become a more tractable power to deal with.

Initially, the policy of containment was not addressed to the Third World, since Soviet pressure on Turkey toward the end of World War II, and its apparent support of the Communist side in the Greek civil war in the late 1940s, made the threat to the balance of power in Europe loom largest. In connection with the situation in Greece, President Harry S Truman announced in 1947 that "it must be the policy of the United States to support free peoples who are resisting attempted subjugation by armed minorities or by outside pressures." In this context, "armed minorities" meant leftists and "outside pressures" referred to the Soviet Union. Thus, a Soviet foray outside its recognized sphere of influence, or the emergence of a new Communist and potentially Soviet regime, would be resisted, through military power if necessary. The policy came to be known as the Truman Doctrine, and it was the first official formulation of the policy of containment.

The classical statement of the theory of containment was an article by George Kennan, published in 1947 under the pseudonym "X." [7] According to Kennan, a U.S. diplomat who had been stationed at the embassy in Moscow, Soviet policy was "a fluid stream which moves constantly, wherever it is permitted to move, toward a given goal. Its main concern is to make sure that it has filled every nook and cranny available to it in the basin of world power." Despite this belief, Kennan considered the Soviet Union to be a prudent world power and also a nation beset by a variety of internal weaknesses, which would not push its ambitions any further than external opposition allowed. Consequently, he said,

> The United States has it within its power to increase enormously the strains under which Soviet policy must operate, to force upon the Kremlin a far greater degree of moderation and circumspection than it has had to observe in recent years, and in this way to promote tendencies which must eventually find their outlet in either the break-up or the gradual mellowing of Soviet power.... In these circumstances, it is clear that the main element of any United States policy toward the Soviet Union must be that of a long-term vigilant containment of Russian expansive tendencies.... The Soviet pressure against the free institutions of the Western world is something that can be contained by the *adroit and vigilant application of counter-force at a series of constantly shifting geographical and political points, corresponding to the shifts and maneuvers of Soviet policy.* (Emphasis supplied.)

That, in essence, is the theory of containment: an application of counterpressure to restrain any expansion of Soviet influence. Faced with such counterpressure, the Soviet Union would scale down its international ambitions. Kennan's view of the instruments of containment included, as he later explained, psychological, political, economic, and military components.[8] Subsequent advocates of containment, however, have stressed the military dimension,[9] and the concept has provided the justification for most U.S. armed interventions abroad since 1947.

By the early 1960s, the Third World had emerged as the principal arena of U.S.-Soviet competition. A large number of former colonies had become independent nation states, and the United States realized that the Kremlin, which had previously paid little attention to the Third World, was now showing interest in these new nations. Stalin had considered them too insignificant to bother about, but Nikita Khrushchev, who became the Soviet leader after Stalin's death, was more aware of the geopolitical and psychological benefits of their friendship. The new Soviet leader professed enthusiasm for the international strivings of the emerging nations and proclaimed his support for "sacred wars of national liberation," by which he meant armed movements of anticolonial struggle with a leftist orientation.

Washington also supported emancipation from the colonial yoke, but it was concerned that the newly independent nations might gravitate toward Marxism and be receptive to Soviet blandishments or pressure. Already, a major war had been fought in Korea in the name of containment, and the policy demanded that, if necessary, additional measures be taken to halt the spread of Soviet influence beyond its East European buffer zone. U.S. anxieties were particularly aroused by the establishment of the Castro government in Cuba. In 1956, a handful of Cubans led by Fidel Castro organized an insurgency against the corrupt and dictatorial regime of Fulgencio Batista. On New Year's Day, 1959, Batista was overthrown; Castro took power and began restructuring Cuban society and government along socialist lines and adopting pro-Soviet positions. That so few men could have toppled a long-established dictatorship and should be making leftist and anti-American declarations less than one hundred miles from Florida seemed to underscore U.S. vulnerability. If its practical implications were modest, the psychological impact of Castro's victory was profound. Meanwhile, some U.S. leaders feared an expansion of Soviet influence in the Middle East as well, and civil war in the Congo led to the suspicion that Moscow's eye was on Africa, too.

When the Kennedy administration came into office, it decided to reinvigorate efforts at economic and military containment. President Kennedy believed that political extremism flourished in conditions of poverty and economic despair, and he felt that an expanded program of U.S. foreign aid would launch the new nations on the path toward economic development and political moderation and at the same time create bonds of gratitude with the United States. His administration's first substantial programs of foreign assistance were directed principally to Latin America, the area thought to be most vulnerable to Castro's influence. The new policy had a military side as well. Soviet support for "wars of national liberation" would be countered. If the Soviet Union furnished military aid to its friends, the United States would do the same for its own friends. If the Soviet Union sponsored armed subversion or outright aggression, the assistance would be of a more direct nature. A special interdepartmental task force, chaired by Robert Kennedy, the attorney general and the president's brother, was created to coordinate the national security establishment's response to such threats. The Defense Department created a Special Forces unit that was to be trained especially for counterinsurgency and counterguerrilla warfare. A Jungle Warfare School was established in the U.S.-controlled Panama Canal Zone to train Latin armies in antiguerrilla tactics. Military activities related to the Third World benefited from increased budgetary appropriations.

When the Kennedy presidency was terminated by an assassin's bullet in 1963, his successor, Lyndon Johnson, continued to follow the policy of containment with a military intervention in the Dominican Republic (discussed above) and an escalation of the war in Vietnam. But the policy was taking its toll. By the late 1960s, Americans were exhausted by the seemingly interminable war in Southeast Asia, the war-induced inflation was injuring the economy, confidence in the government had reached a nadir, and the nation's self-image had been badly battered. In Vietnam, armed force had not achieved its objectives and the costs had been much higher than anticipated. The desirability of military containment in the developing world was being reexamined. Eventually, Johnson's presidency ended in the Vietnamese mire. Richard Nixon became president in 1969, and four years later a cease-fire was signed.

Nixon's departure from office in 1974 ushered in several years of U.S. abstention from military intervention in the Third World. Gerald Ford, who was president from 1974 to 1977, ordered an armed rescue operation of the U.S. vessel *Mayagüez*, which had been seized by Cambodians, but the operation was of a very limited scope. Apart from the unsuccessful effort in 1979 to rescue the hostages being held in the U.S. embassy in Teheran, Iran, President Jimmy Carter also shunned the use of military force during his tenure.

But the disenchantment with military force turned out to be short-lived. It had dissipated by the late 1970s, as the result of two forces: the evidence of the Soviet Union's military activities in Africa and the return, especially after the humiliating hostage crisis in Iran, of militaristic sentiments. Many people in the United States came to believe that the country had let its guard down and that the Soviet Union had exploited the lapse, that the status of the United States as the world's greatest power was eroding, and that the rest of the world no longer looked up to the United States with awe and respect. President Reagan was elected on a platform not only of fiscal conservatism and free enterprise, but also of vigorous anticommunism and a call for renewed military boldness in world affairs.

One of the measures developed by President Reagan, though it had been initiated in the Carter administration, was the creation of a military unit designed specifically for Third World contingencies: the Rapid Deployment Force, later renamed the U.S. Central Command (CENTCOM). It involved troops from various existing marine, army, and naval units which, using rapid airlift and sealift facilities and prepositioned military materiel, would be deployed to an area such as the Persian Gulf to fend off threats to oil supplies, sea lanes, and other U.S. interests. A major U.S. military presence was also established in Honduras for possible military intervention in Central America. In addition, contingency plans were developed for "low-intensity" conflicts—

that is, operations of limited scope and specific goals, such as sabotage or the liberation of hostages taken abroad. The goal was to acquire a capacity for military activities short of all-out warfare; small-scale mobile units would apply the military scalpel of commando operations rather than the blunter tools of conventional warfare. Other units, such as the Army's Rangers, the Navy's SEALs (sea-air-land forces) and the counterterrorist Delta Force, were specially trained and equipped for this purpose. Thus, as détente collapsed and anticommunism once again became a dominant value in national life, military containment became, as it had been before, a cornerstone of U.S. foreign policy.

U.S. armed intervention abroad has been provoked not only by local Marxist movements whose presence has been associated with evidence of Soviet influence. As we have seen in the cases of Grenada, the Dominican Republic, and Lebanon in 1958, it has also occurred in the absence of any plausible evidence of Soviet or Communist activity. This suggests that there may be reasons for U.S. military activity in the Third World apart from containment. One of these reasons appears to be a concern with America's international *credibility* as a superpower.

The United States has traditionally sought to create an international image of itself which combines goodness and ferocity. It wants to be liked but also to inspire awe and fear. While this combination may be rooted in a culture that glorifies both virtue and force, the need to be feared has a more pragmatic basis as well. The United States has global interests not all of which could be defended simultaneously, since their scope vastly exceeds any conceivable military might that the nation could muster. Indeed, even many particular interests could be defended only at virtually prohibitive cost. It is therefore thought necessary to *deter* foreign threats by establishing the credibility of U.S. military power and of U.S. readiness to use it when necessary.

This seems to be the explanation, for example, of the U.S. invasion of Grenada. That tiny island could not possibly have been construed as a threat to the United States, but it did provide the U.S. government with a low-cost opportunity to demonstrate to the world that the nation was no longer traumatized by the memory of Vietnam and that military compellence was once again acceptable to both the government and the public. Six months before the invasion, Secretary of State Alexander Haig had expressed the Reagan administration's feeling that "we must demonstrate to everyone—the Russians, our allies, the Third World—that we can win, that we can be successful. We must move decisively and quickly turn things around in the world or be nibbled to death by the Soviets." [10]

Even in Vietnam, credibility was a major consideration. Assistant Secretary of Defense John McNaughton said that U.S. war aims there were "70 percent, to avoid undermining America's reputation as a guarantor; 20 percent, to keep South Vietnam out of Chinese hands; 10 percent, to permit the South Vietnamese people to enjoy a better, freer way of life." [11]

Has the use of military force for purposes of containment and credibility been worth the costs that resort to force inevitably entails? Leaving ideological predilections aside, the danger is that the ultimate level of military engagement, and consequently the magnitude of the costs, may come to significantly exceed the goals by which it had at first seemed justified. People, organizations, and nations often get themselves into more than they had bargained for, but the consequences of an escalating military involvement can be particularly pernicious. An application of modest, conventional military force in a regional conflict could lead to a direct clash between the superpowers and ultimately to total nuclear destruction (a contingency to be discussed in Chapter 11). In a less apocalyptic but still very unwelcome scenario, participation in what was intended to be a conflict of limited scope and duration could end up in a costly and bloody entanglement, one from which no easy exit can be found and which erodes national strength and morale far more than the initial objectives could have warranted. The U.S. interventions in Korea and Vietnam are vivid illustrations of this possibility.

The Dynamics of Escalating Involvement

Some of America's armed interventions have been brief and, by military standards, low cost. The 1958 invasion of Lebanon ended quickly and with minimal casualties, as did the 1965 intervention in the Dominican Republic and the 1983 invasion of Grenada. Though several hundred U.S. troops died in Beirut in 1983, this was the result of a terrorist attack on a military barracks rather than of battlefield operations, and U.S. involvement was terminated soon thereafter. It is not surprising that three of these four interventions were of short duration and involved limited casualties: in the first two instances, U.S. troops were never even confronted by organized enemy forces, and in the case of Grenada the U.S. preponderance in men and equipment was so overwhelming that a quick victory was inevitable.

Korea and Vietnam present quite another story. In both cases, an enemy had to be faced in direct combat, and hopes of easy victory were soon dashed. Tens of thousands of soldiers died and years passed before a way was found to extricate the United States from a conflict that bore but the most nebulous relation to initial political goals. Of the two interventions, Vietnam claimed more deaths and lasted more than twice as long. Vietnam is also instructive because, though the originally stated objective did not change, the level of military force devoted to achieving it was greatly increased. This is very different from the Korean case, in which General Douglas MacArthur's ambitions, which were initially endorsed by Washington, led him to constantly expand U.S. goals, which, in turn, led to further extensions of the conflict. Escalating conflict was thus driven by escalating objectives, but, as we shall see, this may be less dangerous than the case where, as in Vietnam, a nation loses control of its military engagements without a reassessment of goals.

Korea: The Pull of Expanding Goals

When President Truman decided to send U.S. troops to Korea under the banner of the United Nations, the aim was to repel the North Korean invasion and safeguard South Korea's independence. As pointed out in Chapter 4, this was quickly achieved. North Korea attacked on June 24; almost immediately, the UN Security Council voted for military resistance, and on June 27 Truman authorized General MacArthur to commit U.S. forces to this task. MacArthur advised that two divisions ought to suffice. By September, four divisions had been sent to South Korea and, on the fifteenth of that month, MacArthur executed a daring amphibious landing to the rear of the North Korean lines, at Inchon, on the west coast of the Korean peninsula just below the thirty-eighth parallel, which divided North and South (see Figure 10-1). The landing was successful and the North Korean troops were driven back over the thirty-eighth parallel. The purpose of the intervention had presumably been achieved, but MacArthur, with the president's approval, decided to pursue the North Koreans into their own territory. The goal of protecting the victims was replaced by that of punishing the invaders.

Despite China's stern warning that "the Chinese people [would] not stand idly by in this war of invasion," the first U.S. units crossed the thirty-eighth parallel on October 7, and within two days, Pyongyang, the North Korean capital, fell to MacArthur's troops. Emboldened by this success, the United States raised the goal another notch, to military victory over North Korea on its own territory, to be followed by removal of the Communist regime and the reunification of Korea on U.S. terms. Neither the president nor MacArthur took Beijing's warnings very seriously, but on October 26, Chinese troops launched a surprise attack on U.S. forces some fifty miles south of the Chinese border.

Although American losses were considerable, MacArthur insisted on pressing northward toward his next objective: the Yalu River, the border between China and North Korea. When the president expressed concern that this would provoke a major Chinese response, MacArthur assured him that the Chinese could deploy no more than 60,000 troops in North Korea; yet as he spoke, between 180,000 and 228,000 Chinese soldiers were crossing the Yalu. MacArthur argued, contrary to the opinion of the president and the Joint Chiefs of Staff, that the battle should be taken into China itself. This would surely have meant war between the two nations and could also have brought the Soviet Union into the fray. Nevertheless, MacArthur's goal now seemed to be invade China and destroy its Communist regime. He demanded that the administration take whatever measures were necessary to achieve this goal, "including the use of 20-30 atomic bombs against China, the laying down of a radioactive belt across North Korea to seal it from China and the use of half a million Chinese Nationalist troops." [12]

Figure 10-1 The Korean War, 1950-1953

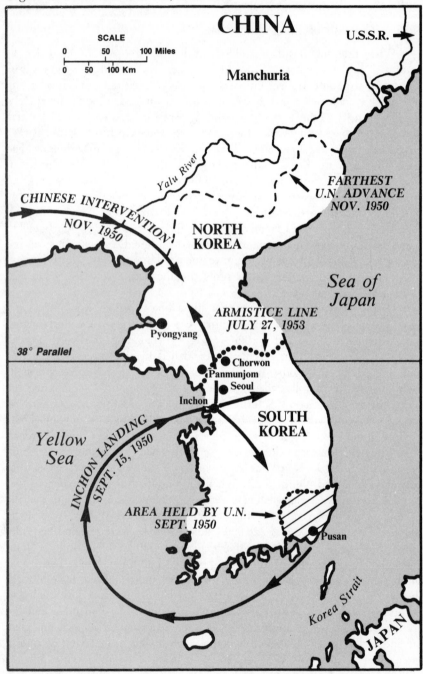

Source: Historical Maps on File (New York: Facts on File, 1983).

The White House and the Pentagon rejected these startling requests. Operational control of the war in North Korea was gradually shifted into the hands of Gen. Matthew Ridgway, and Truman began preparing a diplomatic initiative for cease-fire negotiations, together with proposals to discuss with China a variety of other problems in Asia and even an implicit offer to consider diplomatic recognition of the People's Republic. MacArthur was incensed at these preparations and, without authorization, delivered a public ultimatum of his own to China: he threatened total war if Beijing did not negotiate on Western terms, and he rejected the idea of linking the Korean issue to any other international questions. This was overt insubordination of a sort rarely witnessed in U.S. history; it left the president with virtually no choice but to fire MacArthur, which he did on April 11, 1951. After protracted cease-fire negotiations, the war ended in 1953 with North and South Korea once again divided at roughly the thirty-eighth parallel—a settlement that probably could have been reached in 1950 after the North Korean troops had been routed.

It was a dangerous episode, which almost brought a direct confrontation between the two superpowers. The reason that U.S. intervention assumed a scope far in excess of initial expectations was that the government had lost control over its goals. Yielding at first to the headiness induced by the early victories and then allowing some latitude to the ambitions of an overreaching general, the nation's political leadership failed for a while to keep in mind an appropriate relationship between goals and costs. Ultimately, though, MacArthur's recklessness was not shared by the White House or the Pentagon. Indeed, there were probably no decision makers in the administration who would have seriously considered an invasion of China or a nuclear attack upon that country.

The administration's sobriety and its willingness to dismiss MacArthur were expecially noteworthy because they ran counter to the prevailing public sentiment. Many people, including members of Congress, were captivated by the general's "John Wayne" image and were furious with the president for dismissing a man who, they thought, was so selflessly and resolutely determined to make the world safe for democracy, unlike the weak-kneed civilians in the government. MacArthur returned to a victory parade in his honor, then senator Richard Nixon denounced Truman's action as an "appeasement of Communism," and Sen. Joseph McCarthy called the president a "son-of-a-bitch." [13] When the general addressed a joint session of Congress, with a speech combining pathos and patriotism, senators and representatives openly wept; Rep. Dewey Short (D-Mo.) declared that "we saw a great hunk of God in the flesh, and we heard the voice of God." [14]

Vietnam: The Feat of Self-Ensnarement

U.S. involvement in Vietnam followed on the heels of France's defeat and expulsion from that country, its former colony. Despite significant U.S. military assistance to the French, amounting to $2.5 billion between 1950 and 1954,[15] the Viet Minh won a decisive victory at Dienbienphu in 1954, marking the end of the French presence in Southeast Asia. As we have seen, the Geneva Conference that followed divided the country into two parts: North Vietnam, under the Viet Minh led by Ho Chi Minh, a Communist and a nationalist, from the capital in Hanoi, and South Vietnam, under the pro-Western regime of Ngo Dinh Diem. U.S. support for the Diem government, in the form of both financial and military aid, began almost immediately, and a U.S. military advisory mission was sent to train and equip the South Vietnamese forces. But the government in Saigon, the South Vietnamese capital, was corrupt, intolerant, and repressive, and by the late 1950s, revolutionary violence, instigated by the Viet Minh's successors, the Viet Cong, and supported by North Vietnam, threatened the regime's survival.

In 1961, a Vietnam Task Force appointed by President Kennedy suggested that preparations be made for the possible use of U.S. forces in Vietnam. In May of that year, the size of the military advisory mission was increased from 700 to 1,650. But Viet Cong activity continued unabated, and in October, Gen. Maxwell Taylor and Assistant Secretary of State Walt W. Rostow went to South Vietnam to survey the situation. Upon returning, they urged that, in addition to various reforms by Saigon and more military assistance, 8,000 U.S. combat troops be sent to Vietnam. Undersecretary of State George Ball warned of the consequences of being drawn into Vietnam, and he predicted that the U.S. commitment could come to include 300,000 troops within five years. "George, you are crazier than hell," responded Kennedy,[16] but the president compromised by agreeing to send 15,000 advisers rather than 8,000 combat troops. By the time of Kennedy's death in 1963, the number of U.S. military advisers stood at 17,000. One of his aides reported subsequently that "the President told me that he had made up his mind that after his reelection he would take the risk of unpopularity and make a complete withdrawal of American forces from Vietnam."[17]

President Johnson's initial approach to the problems in Southeast Asia was cautious. In a 1964 speech, he declared that the war in South Vietnam was "first and foremost a contest to be won by the Government and people of that country for themselves."[18] At about the same time, he was ordering that contingency plans be made for taking the war to North Vietnam if necessary. In January 1964, the Joint Chiefs of Staff sent the president a memorandum urging an increased military commitment to Vietnam, especially in the form of aerial bombings of North Vietnam. The hope was to inflict sufficient damage on that country's industrial base to discourage it from assisting the insurgents in South Vietnam. In August 1964, the Gulf of Tonkin resolution gave the president virtually a blank check for further expansion of military activity in Vietnam (see Chapter 4). Again, and to no avail, Undersecretary Ball warned that once a tiger is mounted it becomes very difficult to dismount.[19] By March 1965, the number of U.S. military personnel in Vietnam had reached 27,000, and the number continued to grow. By June of that year, U.S. troops had actively joined battle with the Viet Cong. At approximately the same time, the president initiated Operation Rolling Thunder, the strategic bombing of industrial targets in North Vietnam (see Figure 10-2). To those members of Congress who were worried about this expanding commitment, Vice President Hubert Humphrey said that "there are people at State and the Pentagon who want to send 300,000 men out there. But the President will never get sucked into something like that." [20]

In July 1965, William Westmoreland, the U.S. commander in Vietnam, requested an additional 100,000 men; in November, 154,000 more; in December, 443,000, to be dispatched by the end of 1966. In January 1966, the figure was raised to 459,000, and in August to 542,588. To make these requests more palatable, and perhaps also because 1968 was a presidential election year, Westmoreland promised that the war would be over by the end of 1967. Meanwhile, the air war was escalating as well. Despite the CIA's finding that 80 percent of the bombing casualties in North Vietnam were civilians, Johnson ordered an increase in B-52 sorties, from sixty to eight hundred monthly.[21] By the end of 1967, more bombs had been dropped on North Vietnam than on the whole of Europe during World War II.

There was great suffering in South Vietnam, too. It is estimated that more than one-third of its population became refugees during the war, and vast areas of land in what was a peasant economy were made barren by defoliants sprayed from U.S. airplanes. One of the defoliant chemicals, Agent Orange, may have caused cancer and a variety of other illnesses in those exposed to it, including the U.S. troops. Yet there was little evidence that the war was being won. The South Vietnamese army was impotent, the Saigon government was corrupt and ineffective, and no honorable way out of the morass could be found. On January 31, 1968, the Communist forces launched the Tet offensive, during which the Viet Cong penetrated into every major South Vietnamese city, attacking even the U.S. embassy building in Saigon. Although the Communists suffered heavy losses, the offensive underscored U.S. military weakness. Despite three years of massive bombing, more than 500,000 troops, and extensive defoliation, the Viet Cong and the North Vietnamese demonstrated that they could strike almost at will. The effect on U.S. morale, both among the troops in Vietnam and among the public at home, went far beyond the offensive's military consequences.

The war had gone on much longer, and the extent of the involvement was much vaster, than the U.S. public had been led to expect, and, in addition, there was no sign of progress. Men and materiel had been poured into a remote country for elusive objectives. Moreover, occasional reports of atrocities committed by U.S. troops and of the effect of the bombings and the defoliation on the civilian population began to prey on the national conscience. The public had at first endorsed President Johnson's decision to send troops to Vietnam, but after Tet, a majority turned against the war. In March 1968, President Johnson announced a halt in the bombing and withdrew from the presidential race. Opposition was particularly vocal on college campuses; teach-ins and

Figure 10-2 North Vietnam and South Vietnam in 1965

demonstrations against the war were held at universities from Berkeley to Columbia. Public dissatisfaction with the nation's involvement in Vietnam became a major issue in the 1968 elections, and Sen. Eugene McCarthy, running in the Democratic primaries on an antiwar platform, began scoring unexpected victories. Other candidates for the presidency and Congress joined the opposition to the war. Although Vice President Humphrey received the Democratic party's nomination, he could not shed the stigma of his role in the Vietnam War. Richard Nixon was elected and came into office with a pledge of "peace with honor."

Negotiations among the parties to the conflict got under way soon after, but a peace agreement was not signed for several years. In the meantime, a new bombing campaign was launched against North Vietnam, and, in a major new escalatory move, Nixon ordered an incursion into Cambodia in April 1970 to destroy a suspected enemy sanctuary and supply depots. He assured the country that the action was necessary and that, since 1954, the United States had "respected scrupulously the neutrality of the Cambodian people." Three years later, it came to light that some 3,500 secret bombing raids against Cambodia had been undertaken in 1969 and 1970.[22]

Demonstrations against the war became even more vehement. Finally, in January 1973, negotiations between the Vietnamese parties and the United States were concluded. In 1975, the last American left Vietnam and a final North Vietnamese offensive brought about the fall of the Saigon regime and the reunification of the country under Hanoi's rule.

Kennedy, Johnson, and Nixon had all seemed confident of U.S. ability to bring the war to a quick and favorable conclusion, but each sank into the quagmire and committed the country to new levels of conflict in an effort to get out. Ultimately, the end was forced by a war-weary public, but why did it all happen in the first place? Why did a limited military activity, undertaken to achieve limited political goals, escalate to such an extraordinary level and last so long?

Daniel Ellsberg, a government official who had been involved in planning the intervention in Vietnam but who later became a critic of the war, has spoken of two sorts of explanations.[23] The first is the *quagmire* theory, defended by Arthur Schlesinger, Jr., President Kennedy's political adviser and an eminent historian. The second, favored by Ellsberg himself, is the theory of the *stalemate machine*. The gist of the quagmire theory is that the involvement was, in a sense, inadvertent. Guided by naive optimism, each administration honestly felt that every successive step would bring victory. As the nation sank deeper and deeper into the bog, it seemed that another hundred thousand troops, a few more billion dollars, an intensification of the bombing, was all that was needed to extricate it. By contrast, the theory of the stalemate machine rejects the notion that there was anything inadvertent about the ensnarement. Decisions to escalate were made, not because each step was thought to be the last one needed, or from a failure to anticipate the consequences, but because they were considered politically advantageous.

Afraid of charges from conservatives that they were "soft on communism," Kennedy and Johnson hoped to achieve at least a stalemate in Vietnam, so that Communist success in that part of the world could be postponed until after the next election, when their successor would have to face the prospect of "losing" Vietnam and of bearing the expected domestic political costs.

Another way of looking at the question is to distinguish among three kinds of forces that exerted pressure toward escalation. We may call these the logic of sunken costs, the logic of committed credibility, and the logic of domestic politics. The first two are more consistent with the quagmire model; the third corresponds better to the concept of a stalemate machine.

THE LOGIC OF SUNKEN COSTS. Governments, like people, generally strive for a reasonable balance between ends and means, between the anticipated benefits and the expected costs of an action. Occasionally, however, the disparity between the two becomes so great that the action seems irrational. There are probably few people in the United States who feel that, in retrospect, keeping the corrupt Saigon regime in power, or achieving whatever limited geopolitical goals may have been at stake, was worth more than 50,000 U.S. lives, a loss of national self-esteem, the alienation of international public opinion, and prolonged inflation with all of its economic and social consequences.

The problem, however, is that decisions are not always based on a straightforward calculation of costs and benefits. In the first place, costs cannot always be accurately predicted; certainly, the tenacity of the Viet Cong and North Vietnamese was not expected in Washington. More generally, decision makers look backward as often as forward. They have invested some amount of resources in a policy, and these *sunken costs* are regarded not merely as a liability to be balanced against the anticipated benefits of the policy, but also as something that has to be "redeemed." Hence, when the policy goals are not immediately achieved, more resources have to be invested, in order to prove that the decision to make the original investment was correct. In the case of Vietnam, this meant an intensification of the fighting, rather than the abandonment of an increasingly costly goal. Once several thousand lives had been lost, the government was unwilling to admit that the losses were in vain; they had to be justified by the attainment of a political goal—and the more lives and money were invested, the more difficult it became to withdraw without somehow redeeming the costs. If the government could have gone back in time and had the decision to make over, it might have decided against the intervention, but of course that was not possible. Instead, it felt compelled to press on with more troops, more bombs, more money, until national tolerance was strained beyond its limits.

THE LOGIC OF COMMITTED CREDIBILITY. A second force that moved the nation toward escalation was the view that, once a military commitment, no matter how ill-advised, has been made, it should be firmly pursued, since a decision to back down would lead other nations to doubt the country's reliability in similar situations in the future. As Sen. Richard Russell (D-Ga.) said in 1965:

It was a mistake to get involved [in Vietnam] in the first place; I have never been able to see any strategic, political, or economic advantage to be gained by our involvement. . . . [But] whether or not the initial decision was a mistake is now moot. The United States does have a commitment in South Vietnam. The flag is there. U.S. honor and prestige are there. And, most important of all, U.S. soldiers are there.[24]

In other words, if the United States did not push on, unfriendly nations might get the idea that it would not stick by its commitments, and they would not shrink from assaulting its interests in the future. They might come to believe that, if they weathered the initial costs of a conflict, U.S. resolve would eventually crumble, leaving them to pursue their objectionable activities. Not only might unfriendly nations make light of U.S. resolve, but so might U.S. allies. Consequently, they might seek accommodation with adversaries of the United States rather than count on its commitment to their defense. By this reasoning, credibility is strengthened by occasional military interventions and by a readiness to expand them when necessary. President Nixon, for example, explained his decision to extend the war to Cambodia in 1970 by the need to prove that the United States was "no pitiful, helpless giant."

Taken to its extreme, however, this logic of *committed credibility* may be self-defeating, for credibility can suffer just as much from evidence of a prolonged incapacity to win as from a premature withdrawal. Thus, the dilemma of effective choice is implicit here. The spectacle of the United States being held to a military stalemate did not strengthen its image as a nation to be feared. The more military resources were fruitlessly poured into Vietnam, the less formidable did U.S. military power seem. At some point, the hope that further escalation will produce victory is overcome by the fear that it will merely provide added proof of the limitations of armed force. At that point, credibility demands retrenchment or withdrawal, rather than escalation, but enormous costs may have been paid by then.

THE LOGIC OF DOMESTIC POLITICS. We have seen that foreign policy decisions are influenced as much by domestic politics as by international circumstances, and this was clearly the case in the Vietnam War. The right-wing assaults on President Truman for "losing China," and the memory of the McCarthyism of the early 1950s, has made many U.S. leaders fearful of charges of "softness on communism," appeasement, and the like. Even as intemperate a cold warrior as John Foster Dulles lived in constant apprehension of right-wing attacks, and President Truman's initial reluctance to rein in MacArthur was due to similar concerns. President Kennedy, as has been mentioned, wanted to wait for his second term, with its absence of reelection constraints, before withdrawing from Vietnam. Even President Nixon, who, by dint of a long history of anticommunist rhetoric, might have seemed immune to criticism from the right, was worried about the domestic political consequences of losing a war.

For President Johnson, the problem was compounded by his commitment to ambitious domestic welfare legislation under the rubric of his Great Society programs. He feared that if he "lost" the war in Vietnam, an accompanying loss of domestic political support would undermine those programs. At the same time, he was concerned that the cost of the war might itself deflect resources from his legislative plans. Still, Johnson's biographer says of him that "losing the Great Society was a terrible thought, but not so terrible as the thought of being responsible for America's losing a war to the Communists. Nothing could be possibly worse than that." [25]

Nevertheless, the terms of the logic of *domestic politics* are not invariable. Eventually, the domestic political costs of stubbornly pursuing a conflict can outweigh the political risks of pulling out, even without a victory. Those who will support any level of escalation and fighting of virtually any duration are a minority of the electorate. When U.S. troops are sent to foreign shores, the public almost always endorses the move at first, as an initial surge of patriotism sweeps the nation and the costs of the fighting are not yet evident. But as soldiers begin dying and the economic burden of the conflict becomes heavier, public approval starts dropping off. This clearly happened during the Vietnam War (see Figure 10-3). But by the time the majority had turned against the intervention, tens of thousands of lives had been lost and the national morale and the national economy had been badly damaged.

Conclusions

In recent decades, U.S. military interventions abroad have been guided by the goals of containing communism and establishing U.S. credibility as a country to be feared, a condition thought necessary to deter future assaults on the nation's interests. In some cases, these goals have been achieved at moderate cost, as in the Dominican Republic in 1965 and Grenada in 1983. In other cases, the costs were moderate but the achievements dubious, as in Lebanon in both 1958 and 1983. In yet a third set of cases, the costs were enormous and little was accomplished or, as in the Vietnam War, the effort was actually counterproductive.

The record therefore suggests that, while military force can sometimes serve foreign policy goals, its use can also impose enormous costs and sacrifices without corresponding benefits. When this occurs, it is because political goals and military commitments are not kept in proper balance. In the Korean case, escalating goals increased the scale of the engagement and threatened to pull the nation toward a major international confrontation. But Vietnam may be a more likely model of future interventions: a limited engagement for a limited goal escalating to the point of an immense commitment for the same limited goal. Intent on redeeming sunken costs, afraid of jeopardizing their credibility, and concerned with the domestic political costs of withdrawal, U.S. govern-

Figure 10-3   Public Attitude toward the Vietnam War

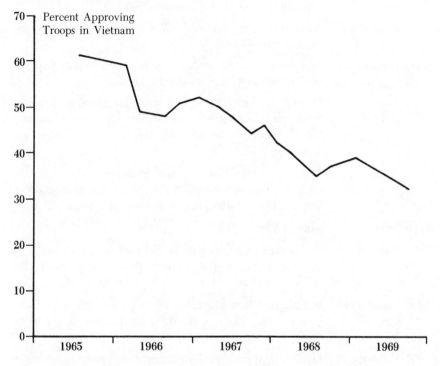

Source: From Hazel Erskine, "Is War a Mistake?" *Public Opinion Quarterly* 34, no. 1 (Spring 1970): 141-142.

ments could again take the country much further into a conflict than could be justified by the original objectives. In the areas of the Third World where future interventions seem most probable—Central America and the Persian Gulf—the likely opponents are deeply committed and well armed. In the absence of quick military victories, ample scope will be left for the three mechanisms described above to come into play, leading to a more costly engagement than had been anticipated. Finally, even a successful intervention would usually involve a political arrangement forcibly imposed upon another country, raising the dilemma of political principle.

Appendix: Major U.S. Military Interventions since World War II

1946 July-August   Naval units sent to Trieste in anticipation of an attack from Yugoslav and Soviet forces. After Army transport planes are shot down, reinforcements sent to Italy.

August	Naval task force dispatched to counter Soviet threat to Turkish control of the Bosporus Strait.
September	Aircraft carrier stationed off Greece when Communist takeover is feared.
1948 January	Marines sent to the Mediterranean as warning to Yugoslavia not to harass U.S. troops in Trieste.
July	During the Arab-Israeli War, consular guard is detached from the USS *Kearsarge* and sent to Jerusalem to protect the U.S. consulate general there; two Marines are wounded.
April	Marines sent to Nanking and Shanghai to protect U.S. diplomatic facilities and later to aid in the evacuation of U.S. nationals following Communist takeover of China.
1950 June	Korean War begins.
1954 July	Five aircraft carriers sent to the Tachen Islands north of Taiwan to evacuate U.S. and Taiwanese civilians and military personnel threatened by Chinese bombing.
1956 November	Marine battalion evacuates 1,500 persons, most of them U.S. citizens, from Alexandria, Egypt, during the Suez crisis.
1957 February	Marines stationed north of Sumatra to provide protection for U.S. citizens during revolt in Indonesia.
July	Four carriers sent to defend Taiwan during Chinese shelling of Quemoy.
1958 January	USS *Des Moines*, with one company of Marines on board, stationed off Venezuela as precaution during outbreak of violence in Caracas.
March	Marine forces deployed with the Seventh Fleet off Indonesia to protect U.S. citizens.
July	Soldiers and Marines sent to Lebanon to "assist Lebanon in preserving its independence."
1959 July	First U.S. soldiers killed in Vietnam. Lengthy involvement in Vietnam begins.
November	Marine force deployed to protect U.S. nationals during the Cuban revolution.
1961 November	Naval forces sent to the Dominican Republic to prevent members of the Trujillo family from seizing control of the government.

1962 May   Marine unit sent to Thailand to support the government against Communist threat.

    October   Naval vessels and Air Force bombers sent to challenge the Soviet introduction of missiles into the Caribbean to effect a "quarantine" of Cuba.

1963 May   Marine battalion is positioned off the coast of Haiti in the wake of domestic protest against the Duvalier regime and a threat of intervention by the Dominican Republic.

1964 May   Navy planes attack Pathet Lao strongholds in Laos; attacks continue until 1973.

    November   Transport aircraft in the Congo carry Belgian paratroopers in an operation to rescue civilians, including 60 U.S. nationals, held hostage by antigovernment rebels.

1965 April   Troops sent to Dominican Republic to quell revolt there.

1967 June   Sixth Fleet sent to eastern Mediterranean to warn Soviet Union against becoming involved in Arab-Israeli War.

    July   C-130 transport planes with crews sent to assist government of Congo in its struggle against white mercenaries and Katangese rebels.

1970 April   Troops and planes attack suspected Viet Cong sanctuaries in Cambodia.

1975 May   Navy, Marine, and Air Force units sent to rescue crew of 39 from U.S. vessel *Mayagüez*, which had been captured by Cambodians.

1980 April   Helicopter force makes unsuccessful effort to rescue U.S. hostages held in U.S. embassy in Teheran.

1982 July   Marine contingent sent to Beirut as part of the multilateral peace-keeping force; naval task force shells Moslem positions in support of Lebanese President Gemayel.

1983 October   Troops invade island of Grenada to remove U.S. students and depose leftist government.

1987 July   U.S. naval flotilla sent to Persian Gulf to offset Soviet naval presence and to protect Kuwait's oil tankers from hostile (mainly Iranian) attack.

Notes

1. Herbert K. Tillema, *Appeal to Force: American Military Intervention in the Era of Containment* (New York: Thomas Y. Crowell, 1973), appendix A; Barry M.

Blechman and Stephen S. Kaplan, *Force without War: U.S. Armed Forces As a Political Instrument* (Washington, D.C.: Brookings Institution, 1978), Chapter 2.

2. A good description of the situation in Lebanon at the time is Fahim I. Qubain, *Crisis in Lebanon* (Washington, D.C.: Middle East Institute, 1961).

3. U.S. Department of State, Bureau of Intelligence and Research, *World Strength of Communist Party Organizations*, Annual Report no. 10 (Washington, D.C., 1958), 47.

4. Radio-television message reproduced in *Department of State Bulletin*, August 4, 1958, 185.

5. See, for example, Michael Klare, *War without End: American Planning for the Next Vietnam* (New York: Alfred A. Knopf, 1972); Gabriel Kolko, *The Roots of American Foreign Policy* (Boston: Beacon, 1969); Harry Magdoff, *The Age of Imperialism* (New York: Monthly Review, 1969).

6. Quoted in Arthur Schlesinger, Jr., *A Thousand Days* (Boston: Houghton Mifflin, 1965), 769.

7. X, "The Sources of Soviet Conduct," *Foreign Affairs* 25 (1947): 566-582.

8. George Kennan, "Containment Then and Now," *Foreign Affairs* 65 (1987): 885-890.

9. The evolution of the strategies of containment is analyzed in John Lewis Gaddis, *Strategies of Containment* (New York: Oxford University Press, 1982).

10. Quoted in James A. Nathan and James K. Oliver, *United States Foreign Policy and World Order*, 3d ed. (Boston: Little, Brown, 1985), 450.

11. Quoted in Max Frankel, "The Lessons of Vietnam," *The Pentagon Papers* (New York: Quadrangle, 1971), 644.

12. Douglas MacArthur, "Reply to the Joint Chiefs of Staff, December 30, 1950," in Senate Committee on Armed Forces and Committee on Foreign Relations, *Hearings on the Military Situation in the Far East*, 82d Cong., 1951.

13. Quoted in John Spanier, *The Truman-MacArthur Controversy and the Korean War* (New York: W. W. Norton, 1965), 212.

14. Quoted in ibid., 226.

15. Robert Scigliano, *South Vietnam: Nation under Stress* (Boston: Houghton Mifflin, 1963), 174.

16. Quoted in David Halberstam, *The Best and the Brightest* (New York: Random House, 1972), 174.

17. Kenneth O'Donnell, "LBJ and the Kennedys," *Life*, August 7, 1970, 5.

18. Quoted in Wallace J. Thies, *When Governments Collide* (Berkeley and Los Angeles: University of California Press, 1980), 24.

19. George Ball, "A Light That Failed," *Atlantic Monthly*, July 1972, 41.

20. Quoted in Halberstam, *The Best and the Brightest*, 572.

21. Hedrick Smith, "Secretary MacNamara's Disenchantment: October 1966-May 1967," in *The Pentagon Papers*, 510.

22. William Shawcross, *Sideshow: Kissinger, Nixon, and the Destruction of Cambodia* (New York: Pocket Books, 1979).

23. Daniel Ellsberg, "The Quagmire Myth and the Stalemate Machine," *Public Policy* 19 (Spring 1971): 217-274.

24. Quoted in Leslie Gelb and Richard Betts, *The Irony of Vietnam: The System Worked* (Washington, D.C.: Brookings Institution, 1979), 216.

25. Doris Kearns, *Lyndon Johnson and the American Dream* (New York: Signet, 1976), 272.

War and Peace

Nuclear War:
Consequences and Causes

NO GREATER catastrophe could befall the United States, and the world, than nuclear war. Major disasters have befallen humankind since long before the nuclear bomb was invented—the bubonic plague that killed almost one-third of Europe's population in the fourteenth century, and the enormous human destruction of World War II—but nuclear war is different. Unlike the plague, it would most likely be a disaster produced by the deliberate actions of governments; unlike World War II, recovery would not be merely a matter of time and effort. If asked, almost everyone would probably express horror and revulsion at the thought of nuclear war, yet it probably occupies the thoughts of the average person little if at all. People worry about things they can assimilate, and these are, for the most part, the rather mundane matters of existence—losing a job, being disappointed in love, or falling ill. Massive annihilation of the sort that would result from nuclear war is too stupendous to be encompassed by the average person's emotional and intellectual equipment. Paradoxically, the greater the catastrophe, the less likely it is to generate public concern.

As political scientist Michael Mandelbaum has pointed out, the destruction caused in previous wars had a finite aspect to it. Though individuals might perish in the conflict, they could expect to endure in a symbolic sense since some of the things of value they had created (a business, a commodity, a work of art) or some of the people they had affected would survive; they thus would have immortality of a sort. "Death is not the end." But nuclear weapons, unlike the instruments of conventional warfare, have "the power to make everything into nothing," ending the possibility of even symbolic immortality.[1] Most people find this inconceivable, and consequently, the danger loses its meaning. This tendency is compounded by inurement: during the decades we have lived with it, the threat of nuclear warfare has become an everyday, and thus a trivialized, concern. It is difficult to be constantly on edge about a state of affairs that has become commonplace.

Nevertheless, the peril is real, and it is something students of U.S. foreign policy must come to intellectual grips with. At the very least, we should understand what the likely consequences of nuclear war would be and how it might occur.

Physical Effects of Nuclear Weapons

The destructiveness of nuclear war derives from the nature of nuclear weapons. Conventional chemical bombs, such as those used in World War II or in Vietnam, derive their energy from the rearranging of atoms *within* a molecule. Their explosive yield is usually expressed as the number of tons of TNT (trinitrotoluene, the chemical most often used) that the bomb contains. Fission, or atomic, bombs derive their destructive power from the energy released by the *splitting* of a nucleus of an atom of plutonium or uranium when it is struck by a neutron. The fission of a single nucleus releases about five million times as much energy as the explosion of a single molecule of TNT. The yield of atomic bombs is thus usually measured in kilotons—that is, thousands of tons of TNT equivalents. Fusion, or hydrogen, bombs derive their power from the *fusing* of nuclei of isotopes of hydrogen to form helium. A hydrogen bomb is about five times as powerful as an atomic bomb in terms of units of energy released per unit of starting weight, and its yield is often measured in megatons, or millions of tons of TNT equivalents.

Fission bombs were first tested by the United States in 1945 and dropped, that same year, on Hiroshima and Nagasaki in order to expedite Japan's surrender in World War II (and to impress the Soviet Union with America's might). The U.S.S.R. tested its first fission bomb in 1949. Fusion bombs were developed in 1952 by the United States and in 1953 by the Soviet Union. Much of the nuclear weaponry that is currently deployed by both countries involves a combination of fission and fusion principles, with the former usually serving as a "trigger" for the latter. Nuclear bombs marked a quantum leap in the levels of destruction that nations could wreak on one another. "Even a small nuclear weapon produces damage on an unimaginable scale. Instead of affecting city blocks as the large conventional weapon does, the nuclear weapon's damage is comparable to the scale of cities."[2]

The detonation of a nuclear weapon produces four kinds of physical consequences: a blast effect, a thermal effect, a radioactive effect, and an electromagnetic pulse. The first three could create destruction and suffering on an unparalleled scale; the fourth has significant implications for the escalation of nuclear war once it occurs.

The *blast effect* is the result of a wave of extremely high air pressure and winds, which demolishes almost everything in its path within a certain radius, vaporizing or leveling buildings and killing any human beings in the area. Destruction occurs both from the mechanical pressure of the blast itself or from the debris, such as pieces of stone and metal, that is hurled from destroyed objects. Some of the victims would die immediately, others after extensive hemorrhaging from their injuries. The chances of surviving the blast depend on one's distance from its center. In cases where multiple nuclear weapons were detonated over an area, the blast effect would be felt from several directions, and objects that could survive a single blast wave would have a much lower chance of withstanding the combination of blasts.

The *thermal effect* is the result of the enormous amount of heat produced by a nuclear explosion, which has been likened to the heat at the center of the sun. The most dramatic thermal effect is the *firestorm*. The nuclear blast creates massive quantities of burning debris, and the fires, by heating the air, produce a violent updraft. In turn, this updraft generates a powerful movement of air inward from the perimeter of the fire to replace the heated air, and this air movement causes the separate fires to coalesce into a single huge inferno. Thus, buildings and people that managed to escape the blast effect could be incinerated in the firestorm.

The *radiation effect* comes from an intense burst of radioactivity in the form of neutron and gamma rays. Acute doses of radiation produce various changes in the human blood system, especially a destruction of white blood cells and a breakdown of the organism's immunity. Victims of radiation become less able to resist the blast and thermal effects and the ever-present infectious agents. Over the longer term, exposure to radioactivity produces still other consequences, such as cancers of various organs and genetic damage, which can be passed on to the following generations. In addition, the detonation of a nuclear bomb produces a large amount of *radioactive fallout*. The nuclear blast throws up a large amount of dust and debris (forming a mushroom-shaped cloud), which absorbs the radioactivity and then moves into the upper atmosphere. The heavier particles fall to earth relatively quickly, depositing their radioactivity either directly on the surviving population or on the soil and any other material with which the survivors come into contact. The lighter particles drift into the stratosphere and remain there for months or even years before descending along with natural precipitation to the earth's surface, perhaps hundreds of miles away from the site of the explosion.

The *electromagnetic pulse* (EMP) is a surge of energy of a frequency close to that used for radio and television transmission. This pulse can damage electronic systems and communications equipment needed for the normal functioning of society, including the equipment needed for the conduct of the war. A physicist has described the effect this way:

> One large high-altitude explosion in the middle of the United States could bathe the country from coast to coast in an EMP that would be picked up by power lines, antennas, and the wires and circuits of all electronic equipment, damage the most delicate computers and electronic communi-

cation devices, and even disrupt the sturdiest electrical power generation and distribution system. It is quite likely that such an EMP would cause a total electric blackout and incapacitate the communications network of the United States.[3]

Even these physical effects of nuclear detonations, many thousands of which could occur over each superpower's territory in the event of a full-scale war, do not give a full accounting of the consequences of nuclear war.

Effects on the Society and Economy

On the basis of the experience of Hiroshima and Nagasaki, of various types of research, and of knowledge about the social impact of major nonnuclear disasters, a rough picture can be drawn of the world in the aftermath of a nuclear war.

Population Effects

A massive loss of lives would be the most direct and momentous consequence. Millions of people would perish from the blast and fires, and probably millions more would die later as a result of radiation-produced blood disease and cancer. Other millions would be permanently incapacitated with debilitating diseases, losses of limbs, or eyesight, or significant disfigurations. Even those who might be personally unscathed would suffer the loss of friends and loved ones and the horror of living with the physically ravaged survivors.

The precise number of casualties would of course depend on the magnitude of the nuclear exchange, as well as on such imponderable factors as wind directions. If there were to be a limited nuclear assault on the United States directed at major military facilities (such as ballistic missile silos and military airfields), but seeking to avoid population centers, it is estimated that between two million and twenty million Americans would be killed.[4] This wide range of estimates suggests the difficulty of accurately gauging the effects of nuclear war, but any figure within the range is nevertheless enormous. Two million is forty times greater than the total U.S. losses in Vietnam; twenty million approaches one-tenth of the nation's population. If we assume that there would be two injured persons for each fatality (and there could be many more than that), then the number of casualties would be between six million and sixty million. Even the lower of these figures would amount to the greatest disaster in the nation's history.

If there were to be a full-scale nuclear attack, designed to inflict maximum damage on the United States, fatality rates in urban areas would be between 50 and 80 percent of the population.[5] Between 20 and 30 percent of the population in these areas would sustain injuries, which means that the total casualty figure would range from 70 to 100 percent of the urban population. In rural areas, there would be fewer deaths but many radiation victims. It is estimated that, nationally, casualties would include at least one-third of the population, and possibly more.[6]

Of course, the number of deaths is hard to estimate, because of factors with which we have had no experience. For example, it is difficult to know how many of the injured could be effectively cared for. In peacetime, severe burns and torn limbs are treated in medical facilities and with a reasonable chance of success. But medical facilities would scarcely be adequate for the overwhelming number of victims of even a limited nuclear war. There would probably be between fifteen and thirty patients for each available hospital bed in the more seriously affected areas of the country. Fewer than one hundred hospitals in the entire country have facilities for specialized burn care, and there are only twelve burn-care centers, which provide treatment for still more difficult cases.[7] Thus, many injuries would probably go untreated, raising the death toll as well as increasing the amount of suffering.

But the situation might be much worse than even these figures suggest. Doctors and other medical personnel would be among the victims, and many medical facilities would be destroyed. The pharmaceutical industry would surely be seriously affected, so that there would be no medication for many injuries and diseases. Meanwhile, the injured would be vulnerable to a variety of infections, and even slight infections could be fatal, because the radiation-induced depression of white blood-cell levels would weaken the body's normal immunological defenses. Millions of people would die slow and painful deaths for which treatment was simply not available. And finally, there would be the long-term effects of cancers and genetic impairments. Clearly, the nation's population would be enormously depleted and physically debilitated for years and perhaps generations afterward.

Economic Effects

It has been estimated that, even in the event of an attack aimed only at military targets, about one-third of the country's manufacturing capacity would be destroyed.[8] Again, however, this does not tell the whole story, for the destruction of even a small proportion of manufacturing capacity would create bottlenecks that would ramify throughout the economy. Suppose, for example, that the industry producing bottle caps was destroyed—a small industry, accounting for but a tiny fraction of GNP and employment. Without bottle caps, there would be no point in producing bottles or, therefore, many of the beverages or medicines that are contained in bottles. In turn, retail outlets for bottled beverages (restaurants, bars, supermarkets) would lose business. Moreover, the trucking and other transportation companies that delivered the beverages would also be affected, and governments would be deprived of the tax revenues from the sale of beverages. The repercussions of this one small event would be virtually endless.

In the case of a full-scale nuclear war, both sides would try to devastate as much of the other's economy as possible. Critical industrial sectors such as petroleum refining and iron and steel production would be prime targets. Consequently, even if some portion of, say, the nation's automobile plants survived, they would have no more materials with which to work. The level of industrial activity could be set back by several centuries for both superpowers, and the survivors would have an extremely low standard of living.

Agriculture would suffer enormously as well. Some 60 percent of the hogs and 40 percent of the cattle in the United States, and between 45 percent and 80 percent of the nation's grain production, would be located in the states most seriously affected by even a limited nuclear attack.[9] Agricultural irrigation would suffer from the unavailability of petroleum, and substantial parts of the country could become arid as a result. The challenge of feeding the surviving population would be further compounded by disruptions in the country's food distribution system, as railways and roads were destroyed and because of fuel shortages. Not only would there be a severe economic depression, there would be widespread malnutrition and even starvation.

Environmental Effects

In 1984, a group of scientists published a study of the ecological effects of nuclear war in which they put forward the concept of a *nuclear winter*.[10] They contended that nuclear explosions, in addition to the effects already discussed, would produce a drop in global temperatures, large areas of darkness, a huge amount of toxic gases, and intense ultraviolet light.

This study traced the results of a combination of several of the effects of nuclear detonations, including some that had not been considered before. Extensive fires would generate great quantities of toxic gases and a black oily smoke that would rise into the lower atmosphere. At the same time, tremendous amounts of dust and soot would be propelled into the atmosphere by the nuclear blasts. The dust and soot would absorb a substantial portion of the sun's radiant energy, which, in turn, would lead to darkness and a significant cooling of the earth's surface. A prolonged period of cold would ensue. These effects would not be limited to the northern latitudes (where most of the actual nuclear detonations would presumably take place), since dust and soot would be carried into the Southern Hemisphere by atmospheric currents, bringing cold and darkness there as well. The detonations would also destroy a significant part of the stratospheric layer of ozone, and, since ozone absorbs much of the sun's ultraviolet radiation, the amount of the biologically dangerous ultraviolet light reaching the earth's surface would increase by several hundred percent. Ultraviolet light destroys the nucleic acids and proteins that are the fundamental building blocks of life on earth. Finally, as already mentioned, radioactive debris would cover large parts of the earth's surface, contaminating various forms of life.

The magnitude of these consequences can be indicated by a historical comparison. When the Tambora volcano erupted in Indonesia in 1815, the average global temperature fell by one degree Celsius because sunlight was obscured by the volcanic debris hurled into the atmosphere. Though this might seem like a trivial change, it led to temperatures such that the following year, as far away as Europe and America, became known as "the year without a summer." According to the nuclear winter hypothesis, a relatively "moderate" nuclear war, involving an exchange of 3,000 megatons, would produce enough cooling in the United States to freeze the ground to the depth of a meter, making agriculture impossible, reducing the supply of fresh water, and even complicating the burial of the dead. The darkness would disrupt the aquatic food chain. According to the authors of the study:

> Whether any people would be able to persist for long in the face of highly modified biological communities; novel climates; high levels of radiation; shattered agricultural, social and economic systems; extraordinary psychological stresses; and a host of other difficulties is open to question. It is clear that the ecosystem effects *alone* resulting from a large-scale thermonuclear war could be enough to destroy the current civilization of the Northern Hemisphere.[11]

Though the Department of Defense has accepted the possibility of a nuclear winter, other studies suggest more qualified or tentative conclusions.[12] While the evidence is not all in, a nuclear winter with all of its implications must be considered a possible consequence of a nuclear exchange.

Social and Political Effects

What we know about past disasters suggests that the human spirit and strength needed for reconstruction might well be absent in the wake of a nuclear war. A population afflicted by a large-scale disaster displays a tendency toward deadened emotions and an indifference to its social environment. When existence is marked by physical impairment, the threat of death through sickness or starvation, and widespread suffering, it is hard to generate the enthusiasm and vigor needed for major human endeavors. The fatigue born of suffering, the dread of death, and the associated helplessness and disorientation discourage great collective enterprises. Any effort that the human psyche and organism can muster under such conditions is more likely to be directed toward self-gratification. In Europe, the latter part of the plague-stricken fourteenth century was described as "a period of immorality and shockingly loose living."[13] Similarly, Thucydides records that, in the wake of a plague in Athens in the fifth century B.C., "people now began openly to venture on acts of self-indulgence which before then they used to keep dark."[14] The more tenuous survival appears, the more important does short-term pleasure become to those who are still in a position to enjoy it. For those who are not, a complete lack of emotion is likely to be the rule. In either case, the mood would not favor the extraordinary social effort that reconstruction would require.

In addition, social harmony would almost surely be undermined by a struggle for limited resources. History demonstrates that social and political cohesion is most easily achieved when the sum total of resources needed to satisfy human needs is a little less than the resources actually available. When the needs outstrip the resources, conflict over whatever is available ensues. This is what can be expected among the remnants of a society devastated by nuclear war. In the United States, survivors of the most seriously affected areas would presumably be evacuated, when possible, to the less seriously affected rural areas. But there, too, survival resources may be barely adequate. What is likely to follow is an unrestrained struggle over the meager resources for physical survival that are left. The struggle would be all the more vicious because the survivors would include relatively few of the more altruistic members of the prewar society. As a survivor of Hiroshima reported:

> In general, then, those who survived the atom bomb were the people who ignored their friends crying out . . . , or who shook off wounded neighbors who clung to them, pleading to be saved. . . . In short, those who survived the bomb were, if not merely lucky, in a greater or lesser degree selfish, self-centered, guided by instinct and not civilization . . . and we know it, we who have survived.[15]

Under such circumstances, any effort at rebuilding the ravaged civilization and society might be impossible without extensive coercion. Savage civil strife and lack of individual motivation could be dealt with only by making the punishments for noncooperation very severe—by relying on fear rather than enlightened self-interest to generate the human energies needed for the stupendous task. Harsh, dictatorial forms of political organization would seem to be a virtual necessity, even in the United States. Though the defense of democracy may have seemed to justify the moves that preceded the nuclear exchange, democracy could be buried forever in the rubble.

If this is the prospect of the aftermath of a nuclear war, it hardly seems possible that rational people would knowingly lead their countries toward it. However, it cannot be assumed that this ultimate catastrophe can never happen merely because it would be irrational. There are at least three paths that could lead to nuclear war between the two superpowers. The first is an accident or an unauthorized military action. The second begins in a crisis and proceeds to an effort to wipe out the other side's nuclear arsenal through a preemptive strike. The third is the escalation of what had been intended as a limited conventional conflict.

Nuclear War by Accident

A nuclear war could be touched off accidentally either by the malfunction of a strategic system, leading to an inadvertent nuclear launch or detonation, or by unauthorized action taken by a willful or deranged military commander. Neither contingency is likely, but neither can be dismissed as totally inconceivable.

System Failure

As we have been reminded by the accident at the Three Mile Island nuclear power plant in 1979, the explosion of the Challenger space shuttle with seven astronauts aboard in 1986, and the massive release of radioactivity at Chernobyl in the Soviet Union in 1986, there is no way of averting disasters with the products of man's ingenuity. Steps can be taken to reduce the probability of an accident, but the possibility of a malfunction can never be *totally* eliminated. It may be assumed that nuclear weapons are designed by responsible human beings operating within the bounds of scientific and political controls and that they have done what they can to prevent accidental launchings and detonations. Nevertheless, the historical record does not inspire complacency, for malfunctions (what the Pentagon calls "broken arrows") have occurred. Here is a partial list of such incidents.[16]

On March 11, 1958, a B-47 bomber accidentally dropped a nuclear weapon over Mars Bluff, South Carolina. The bomb's conventional explosive "trigger" was set off, producing a substantial crater, but no nuclear detonation followed.

On January 17, 1966, a B-52 bomber collided with a KC-135 refueling tanker over Palomares, Spain. Five crewmen died and four hydrogen bombs were dropped, causing some degree of radioactivity. The bombs were found only after an extensive search.

On January 21, 1968, in an attempted emergency landing at Thule Air Force Base in Greenland, a B-52 bomber crashed, leading to the detonation of the conventional-explosive components of all four of its nuclear bombs and creating an area of local plutonium contamination.

Other accidents have been even more ominous in their implications. On June 3 and again on June 6, 1980, the malfunctioning of a computer accessory (a forty-six-cent electronic chip) indicated to the U.S. early-warning system that a Soviet nuclear attack was under way. There was a flurry of consternation, but the problem was identified before a military response was made.[17] Seven months earlier, on November 9, 1979, a war-game tape simulating an attack by Soviet submarine-launched missiles was accidentally fed into the live system of the North American Air Defense Command in Colorado. Jet interceptors were scrambled, and missile bases put on alert for six minutes before the error was detected.[18]

These incidents illustrate the fallibility of the technical systems whose proper functioning may stand between peace and war. The greater the number of deployed weapons, and the more complex they and the associated systems become, the greater will be the risk of error and thus of catastrophe. As one scientist has said, "We have created a world in which perfection is required if a disaster beyond history is to be avoided." [19] It is sobering to reflect that we have become dependent on a quality that has never been achieved.

Unauthorized Action

Sole authority to use nuclear weapons is vested in the president as commander in chief. Because of the grave consequences of using them, an elaborate system has been put into place to try to ensure that they are in fact used only when the president has ordered it (see the box, "Emergency Action Conferences"). In the last analysis, however, a number of subordinate military officers actually execute the launch, and the question arises whether any of them could, *without* authorization, initiate a nuclear attack. In Stanley Kubrick's film *Dr. Strangelove*, a crazed general commanding a remote strategic bomber base decides on his own to order his aircraft, loaded with nuclear bombs, to attack the Soviet Union. Could something of this sort actually occur? The odds are that it could not happen, but it cannot be considered totally impossible. The danger seems least with land-based intercontinental ballistic missiles (ICBMs), slightly greater with strategic bombers, and somewhat more substantial with submarine-launched ballistic missiles (SLBMs).

ICBMs are typically designed to be launched in groups. To launch a set of ten ICBMs requires, upon receipt of a validated order from SAC, the synchronized action of four launch-control officers. These men are located in underground posts called capsules, two to a capsule. To effectuate a launch, both of the officers, seated at separate consoles in each capsule, must turn a key (similar to an automobile ignition key) at virtually the same instant. The distance between the two consoles is such that a single officer could not turn both keys at the same time. In order to guard against the possibility that one of the two might bully or cajole the other into joining him in an unauthorized launch, a similar two-key action must be performed at another, physically remote, capsule. The officers within the separate capsules cannot communicate with each other. Moreover, these launch-control officers are subjected to careful psychological screening before selection. We may assume that the Soviet Union has the same sort of procedures, though the information has not been made public. It is indeed hard to see how an unauthorized ICBM launch could occur with these precautions.

The procedure for bombers and missile-carrying submarines is slightly different. Because a bomber on an airfield or a submarine in port is vulnerable to destruction in an attack, most bombers are ordered into the air at the first warning, and most submarines spend much of their time under water, patrolling the oceans. Under these circumstances, bomber and submarine commanders are given somewhat more leeway for independent action than are ICBM launch-control officers. If NORAD detected evidence of a Soviet attack, all bombers on alert would be immediately scrambled into the air to avoid being destroyed on the ground, and they would proceed to predesignated targets. Before reaching enemy territory, they would pause and begin circling. If the National Military Command Center confirmed the attack, and if it had been decided to make a retaliatory response, the bombers included in the

Emergency Action Conferences

When the U.S. early-warning system detects a possible missile launch, four command posts—the North American Aerospace Defense Command (NORAD), the Strategic Air Command (SAC), the National Military Command Center (NMCC) at the Pentagon, and the alternate NMCC at Fort Ritchie, Maryland—begin formal evaluation procedures known as Emergency Action Conferences. Although the actual procedures for conducting these conferences are classified, the general sequence of events can be outlined.

If the system picks up an event that could threaten North America, the chief of NORAD calls a routine Missile Display Conference (MDC) to evaluate whether a threat exists. If there is no danger, the conference ends. If, however, a danger seems present a second MDC to evaluate possible threats is called, bringing senior Department of Defense officials into the assessment process. If the threat persists, additional senior personnel join a Threat Assessment Conference (TAC). Ultimately, if the threat appears real, the president is brought into the final Missile Attack Conference (MAC). The chart below details the Emergency Action Conferences the United States called between 1977 and 1984. According to unclassified information, a Missile Attack Conference has never occurred. Figures for the years prior to 1977 are, according to NORAD, "unavailable." The Reagan administration has classified the 1985 figures.

When asked about the substantial rise in the number of Missile Display Conferences in 1980 and 1982, NORAD officials attributed the increases to (a) the operational testing and evaluation of a Pave Paws phased-array radar and (b) two sets of revisions (by the Joint Chiefs of Staff) in the criteria for convening MDCs. As the system is upgraded with increasingly sensitive and redundant sensors, the number of detections (and routine MDCs) may continue to rise.

Year	Routine Missile Display Conferences (MDCs)	MDCs to Evaluate Possible Threats	Threat Assessment Conferences
1977	1,567	43	0
1978	1,009	70	2
1979	1,544	78	2
1980	3,815	149	2
1981	2,851	186	0
1982	3,716	218	0
1983	3,294	255	0
1984	2,988	153	0
1985 [a]	—	—	—

Source: "Accidental Nuclear War: A Rising Risk," *Defense Monitor* 15 (1986): 6.
[a] Numbers are no longer released by NORAD.

response would receive a "go code"—authenticated radio instructions authorizing them to proceed to their targets and deliver their payloads. The nuclear bombs they were carrying, which up to this point could not be detonated, would be made operational by the joint action of two crew members, the commander of the aircraft and the officer in charge of communications. The likelihood of action in the absence of a "go code" does not appear great, but the danger is higher than with ICBMs.

Submarines present an additional problem, because communication with a submerged vessel is very difficult to establish. (Research is being conducted on the use of laser beams for communicating with vessels when they are under water.) Consequently, wider autonomy is given to a submarine commander. Some observers have expressed the fear that, in an international crisis followed by an electronic blackout (perhaps because of an EMP), a submarine commander might assume that a nuclear war had begun and interpret that as an authorization to launch his considerable supply of missiles. According to a leading student of the intricacies of military command and control, the principal check on this possibility is "a* periodic signal indicating that headquarters was alive and functioning. This is sometimes called a 'fail deadly' command system, because a failure of headquarters to transmit the proper code at the proper time would be construed as turning over command authority to the armed unit." [20] Yet, because of the greater uncertainty and the difficulty of communication, a launch of nuclear weapons by a submarine commander is the most likely of the forms of unauthorized launch that have been discussed. None of them is very probable, and indeed, of the three paths to nuclear disaster, accidental or unauthorized initiation seems to be the least likely.

The Preemptive Strike

The image of nuclear war probably most firmly etched in the minds of Americans is that of an all-out Soviet surprise attack, a "bolt from the blue" announced by shrill warning sirens and obliterating much of the country in a convulsion of nuclear carnage. Soviet citizens are no doubt conditioned to fear a similar sort of attack from the United States. Actually, however, an obliterating first strike is not a very likely form of nuclear war. For it to be at all plausible, one would have to believe that one side would wantonly decide to incinerate the other and that, moreover, it thought it could do so with impunity. Neither assumption is credible or is likely to become credible in the future. Despite what the public imagination might conjure up, there are few responsible nuclear strategists, and few political and military leaders, who take this possibility seriously.

However, a *limited* first strike, designed to wipe out the other side's nuclear arsenal rather than its cities and population, is less implausible. During the late 1970s, proponents of a major U.S. strategic buildup warned of a "window of vulnerability," which could encourage a Soviet first strike against the U.S. ICBM force. The U.S.S.R., it was claimed, had been expanding the number of its own ICBMs and improving their accuracy. This, it was said, might lead Moscow to believe that, in a first or preemptive strike, it could wipe out all U.S. ICBMs, since these were immobile, ground-based missiles and thus "sitting ducks." It was further argued that the Soviet Union could do this by expending only a portion of its own land-based missiles. The United States would then be left with only its SLBMs. Since these were not very accurate, they could be used to destroy only large targets, such as cities, but the United States would shrink from doing that because it would mean the slaughter of millions of innocent civilians. The Soviet Union, on the other hand, would have no such qualms; having destroyed the missiles capable of retaliating against Soviet strategic targets, it would be able to coerce the United States into making various political concessions (withdrawing from Berlin, perhaps, or abandoning its commitment to Israel) by threatening a nuclear attack on U.S. cities.

This scenario was given great credence by advocates of stronger U.S. defenses, especially supporters of the MX, a large missile then in the planning stage that would carry ten highly accurate warheads and would supplement the chief U.S. ICBM, the Minuteman. Originally, the MX was to have been deployed in a mobile mode—for example, on rails—making it virtually invulnerable to preemptive destruction, and thus allowing the United States to retaliate with precision against Soviet strategic facilities and to destroy the weapons with which the Kremlin might otherwise extract concessions. The MX was to have closed the window of vulnerability.

Actually, the scenario was always rather far-fetched. It is very unlikely that the Soviet Union would hazard a first strike against U.S. ICBMs in the vague hope of gaining political advantage thereby. Moscow could not be entirely certain that the United States would not retaliate against Soviet civilians, and it is almost impossible to imagine what political benefits could even begin to outweigh the perils in the Kremlin's eyes of such a course of action. Furthermore, Soviet coercion of this sort would not even require the previous destruction of the U.S. ICBM force. As weapons specialist Richard Garwin told the Joint Congressional Committee on Defense Production in April 1976,

> The prelude is completely unnecessary. The Soviet Union could say, without destroying Minuteman, "Look here, Mr. President, surrender or we will destroy American cities." It wasn't necessary to destroy Minuteman in order to say that. The compelling nature of the argument would be just the same.[21]

It now appears that those who were issuing warnings about the danger of the window of vulnerability may have been less troubled by this specter than they were eager to have the MX built. Significantly, it has since been decided to acquire the missile but without deploying it in a mobile mode, meaning that it will be virtually as vulnerable as the older ICBMs—and once that decision was made, little more was heard about a preemptive Soviet attack.

Nevertheless, first strikes aimed at missile silos and airfields could occur, especially during a crisis, when each side might feel that the other was about to launch a preemptive assault. If the adversary did attack first, the victim's retaliatory weapons could be destroyed on the ground, leaving nothing to fight back with. The enemy could then continue the attack, or threaten to do so, with relative impunity. Thus, each side knows that, if it does not attack first, the other side might. Each side also knows that its adversary is reasoning in the same way, and that the longer it waits, the more likely it is to be the victim of a preemptive strike. These circumstances raise the possibility that one side or the other will initiate a nuclear attack. Even if neither the United States nor the Soviet Union desired nuclear war, both sides might deem it rational to launch an attack during such a crisis.

The condition in which a crisis could easily lead to nuclear war is called *crisis instability*. Conversely, the condition in which that is not likely is called *crisis stability*. Until the late 1970s, crisis stability was the rule between the two superpowers, because neither side thought it could preemptively destroy the other's retaliatory arsenal. There were two reasons for this. First, neither side had enough weapons for successful preemption. No single warhead can be assured of hitting its target, yet if a preemptive strike is to work, not many enemy missiles can be allowed to survive. Thus, more than one warhead must be aimed at each target. Moreover, the attacker could not afford to use all of his weapons in the first strike, for that would leave nothing for subsequent threats. Thus, the aggressor would have to possess, at the outset, a number of warheads significantly greater than the number of targets he wished to destroy. Secondly, land-based missiles are rather small targets, and they are protected by silos with very thick, blast-resistant walls of concrete. To be destroyed, they must be hit with great accuracy, and such accuracy had not yet been attained.

Since then, two developments have increased crisis instability. One of these was the introduction of multiple independently targetable reentry vehicles, or MIRVs, which are missiles that carry several warheads, each of which can be aimed at a different target. The MX is this kind of missile, as is the Soviet SS-18. Since each warhead can be targeted independently, a single MX or SS-18 could theoretically destroy ten separate enemy facilities, MIRVs were tested by the United States in 1968 and deployed in 1970 in the form of Minuteman III ICBMs. The Soviet Union tested them five years later and began deploying them in accelerated fashion in 1976. In 1969, the United States had 690 separate missiles, and, since each missile carried a single warhead, it had an identical number of warheads. The corresponding figure for the Soviet Union in that year was 1,176. By 1980, each country had only a few more missiles, but each had a total of about 7,000 warheads on their ICBMs and SLBMs as a result of MIRV programs (see Figure 11-1). The

Figure 11-1 MIRVs and the Growth of Nuclear Arsenals

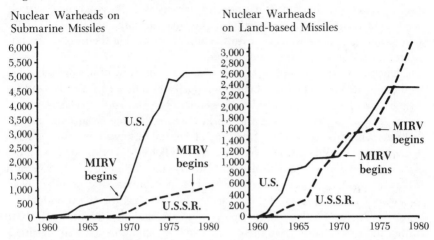

Nuclear Warheads on
Submarine Missiles

Nuclear Warheads
on Land-based Missiles

Source: U.S. Military Force—1980: An Evaluation (Washington, D.C.: Center for Defense Information, 1980), 24-25.

increased ratio of warheads to missiles made a successful first strike against ICBMs more likely than it had been before.

The other development was a great improvement in the accuracy with which the missiles could be delivered. A missile must be able to land close enough to a target silo for the crater created by the explosion to encompass the silo. The advances in accuracy during the 1970s were achieved by means of computerized guidance systems—complicated arrays of gyroscopes and accelerometers which, on the basis of computerized instructions, correct a missile's trajectory so as to keep it on a precise course toward its target. SLBMs have become more accurate as well, partly because satellite-based navigational techniques now enable a submarine's own location to be determined with great exactitude. In addition, there are now laser and infrared guidance devices by which missiles can receive signals from a synchronized transmitter that enable them to correct accumulated errors in flight, and so-called terrain-contour matching guidance systems, by which a computer on the missile compares actual position to the position preprogrammed on a map and makes the necessary corrections.

Each superpower now lives with the fact that the other's weapons are both accurate and numerous enough to make a preemptive nuclear attack during a crisis more feasible than it had been before. The only major strategic obstacle that remains to a preemptive first strike is the SLBM. Hidden in the enormous three-dimensional space of the world's oceans, submarines are "virtually impossible, at least with the current and foreseeable technical means at our disposal, to find and destroy." [22] Consequently, retaliation by SLBMs cannot now be prevented, and the number and accuracy of SLBMs are sufficient to ensure almost any amount of desired destruction. But this is not necessarily a permanent situation. Both superpowers are making large investments in the area of antisubmarine warfare, with the aim of improving their ability both to locate and to destroy enemy submarines.

The major way of locating a submarine is by the noise of its engines and of the human activities aboard, which can be picked up by a sufficiently sensitive system of acoustic sensors, called *hydrophones*. The United States has deployed a vast array of hydrophones in the world's oceans, but the oceans are so huge that one cannot be confident of hearing all the submarines they may contain. According to the physicist who has been quoted before, "Trying to detect a nuclear submarine somewhere in the Atlantic Ocean by listening for the sounds it makes is comparable to trying to find a person wearing wooden clogs somewhere in the streets of Los Angeles by listening for the sound of his steps."[23] On top of that, both superpowers are making intensive efforts to further reduce the noise from their submarines. Even if an enemy submarine is found, destroying it is very difficult. Unlike an ICBM, a submarine is a moving target, and it is, moreover, located under water, which makes it less vulnerable to detonations than an object located above ground. The superpowers have "attack submarines" designed to chase other submarines, but they must be able to catch up to their target and then protect themselves against the enemy's own attack submarines. It might be possible to destroy the target eventually, but probably not before the submarine launched its missiles.

Yet the military technology does have a way, through well-funded research and access to some of the best scientific and engineering talent, of developing capabilities that were once thought impossible. It is therefore reasonable to expect that the day will come when even this leg of the strategic triad will become vulnerable to preemptive destruction. Nuclear war would then be that much more likely.

Escalation from a Conventional War

War is rarely what its participants had intended it to be. Not only do nations often find themselves fighting when none had expected to, but the level of conflict typically exceeds anything they had planned on. International conflicts have certain dynamics of their own, and a nuclear war might occur as the final stage of what began as a limited conflict fought with nonnuclear weapons. Of the three paths to nuclear war, that of escalation from a conventional conflict appears to be the most likely.

History provides many examples of unanticipated escalation, but none quite as stark as World War I. The war was triggered in 1914 by the assassination of Archduke Franz Ferdinand of the Austro-Hungarian empire by a Serbian nationalist. However tragic on a personal level, this certainly was not a momentous international event. Nevertheless, and to the surprise of all parties, one reaction followed another, and the incident mushroomed into a global conflagration, involving not only all the major European countries but even nations as remote from Balkan politics as Australia and the United States. Indeed, few political leaders at the time were sure how it had all happened. Prince Bernhard von Bülow, who had been a chancellor of Germany before the war, is said to have asked his successor, "How did it happen?" "Ah, if only we knew," came the answer.[24]

When we look back on it, it is possible to understand the sequence of events. To begin with, the prevailing system of alliances meant that the great powers were obliged to come to the assistance of their allies if their own international credibility was to be maintained. Thus, Russia threw her military power and diplomatic support behind Serbia, Germany rushed to support Austria-Hungary, France came to Russia's aid, and so on. Next, it proved very hard to control the level of military commitment. Germany, fearing what France might do, felt it had to mount a major assault on that country, which it did through Belgium. Russia had considerable trouble implementing a state of partial mobilization and so undertook a full mobilization instead. Paranoia on all sides led to actions that were far more bellicose than the circumstances called for, and the participants regularly misinterpreted each other's intentions. Before the smoke had cleared, the entire continent was engulfed in history's deadliest war yet.

As the discussion in previous chapters has shown, concern with credibility of commitments, overreaction to the actions of others, paranoia, and misinterpretation have by no means disappeared from the world scene. Escalation from a relatively minor incident to a major conflict—today, to a nuclear war—must thus be considered a possibility. As an illustration, let us examine two areas where the superpowers might be propelled over the nuclear threshold.

In Central Europe

Europe is regarded by both superpowers as the biggest prize in the Cold War. It is politically, geostrategically, economically, and politically the area whose fate weighs most heavily in the East-West balance. Consequently, it is also the part of the world with the greatest concentration of soldiers and of both conventional and nuclear weapons. NATO alone has approximately 5,000 tactical (short-range) nuclear warheads there, and to these must be added those the United States would send to Europe in a crisis.[25]

The Soviet Union, which, from Napoleon to Hitler, has been subjected to invasions from the West, is obsessed with having secure defenses on its western borders. Although foreign invaders were always eventually repelled, they often managed to penetrate deeply into Russian territory, wreaking enormous destruction in their path. The U.S.S.R. has thus decided to establish defenses at forward positions, as far out from Soviet boundaries as possible. This is one reason why it has acquired control over a number of "buffer states" in Central

Europe. However, Moscow has not always found it easy to maintain control over these buffer states. Hungary was kept in the Soviet bloc only after a bloody invasion in 1956; Soviet troops moved into Czechoslovakia in 1968, when aspirations for independence became apparent; Poland's movement away from Soviet-style orthodoxy was prevented only by the imposition, with Moscow's prodding, of martial law in 1981. There is every reason to believe that similar problems will beset the Soviet empire in the future as well.

Suppose that frustration with the Soviet yoke becomes unbearable in Poland and that a mass revolt breaks out. It is not unreasonable to assume that many Czechs, who have not forgotten or forgiven the 1968 invasion, would emulate the Polish example. East Germany, which has some prewar demo-cratic traditions and no cultural identification with the Soviet Union, might follow in their footsteps. If so, West Germany might feel bound to assist its East German brethren, even if only with supplies, and the United States would be under great pressure to help in some way, too. In order to preclude West German assistance to East Germany, and to deal a preemptive blow to NATO's military forces, Moscow might then launch an invasion of West Germany.

Even before Soviet troops crossed the borders of West Germany from Czechoslovakia and East Germany (see Figure 11-3), the United States and its allies would presumably go into a state of high alert. What would happen to NATO's tactical nuclear weapons in such a situation? In peacetime, these weapons are under U.S. military control; their use must be approved by U.S. authorities. They are stored in special shelters called *igloos*, of which there are more than a hundred in Western Europe. But these could be destroyed by a nuclear or even a conventional attack. To prevent this, they might have to be dispersed and placed in the hands of the military officers—not necessarily U.S. officers—who would have operational control over their use in wartime. To avoid unauthorized discharge, they are protected by an electronic system called the Protective Action Link (PAL), which makes them unusable in peacetime. But in a state of high alert, the PAL codes would also have to be put in the hands of those exercising operational command over the weapons, for if one were to wait for actual fighting to begin, it might no longer be possible to trans-fer the codes, and the nuclear weapons would be unusable. At this point, the situation would be one of extreme tension, with several thousand nuclear weapons in the hands of hundreds of military commanders of various nationalities.

Assume now that the Soviet Union does launch a large-scale conventional attack on West Germany. Because of the substantial Soviet superiority in manpower and armored vehicles, NATO forces would be hard-pressed to repel the attack. In the initial phase of the offensive, Soviet forces could penetrate a hundred miles or so into West Germany (and possibly into Turkey as well, if southeastern Europe were involved in the fray). During combat of high intensity, command and control over military operations becomes extremely difficult, and individual military commanders are therefore given considerable autonomy. Battling a conventionally superior enemy, some officers will face the near certainty that their position will be overrun and their unit wiped out. They might feel that their responsibility requires them to do everything to save their troops—including the use of short-range nuclear missiles and nuclear artillery shells, even without authorization. The difficulty of maintaining absolute political and military control over every officer who has a finger on the nuclear trigger in wartime makes it possible, if not likely, that the nuclear threshold would be crossed in the early hours of combat.

Once even one or two nuclear weapons were used, subsequent escalation probably could not be prevented. In the first place, precise control of the level of nuclear violence would require smoothly and swiftly operating communication systems that would allow very specific orders to be sent to operational commanders. But, as already suggested, they are very unlikely to exist, because of the chaos of combat, the destruction of physical installations, and the breakdown of electronic equipment from EMP. Furthermore, under conditions of nuclear combat, response time would be reduced to a few minutes; reflex reactions, rather than considered decisions, would be the rule. Under the circumstances, it is easy to envision Central Europe becoming engulfed in a nuclear holocaust.

Moreover, destruction would probably not be limited to the European continent. Soviet cities, military facilities, and command centers are within range of U.S. strategic weapons and medium-range bombers stationed in Great Britain, and it might seem necessary to use them, if only to prevent reinforcements from being sent to the forces involved in the offensive. Retaliation against military or civilian targets within the United States might then seem justified from Moscow's perspective. Even before this entire sequence had run its course, the conditions would generate the kind of anxiety that could lead to a preemptive first strike by either superpower.

In the Middle East

The Middle East is one of the most war-prone areas of the world, and it is an area in which the interests of the superpowers run deep. The U.S. has major commitments to Israel, partly because of that country's position as the only Western-style democracy in the area and partly because of the demands of domestic politics. A portion of the oil consumed by Western Europe and Japan is imported from Middle Eastern countries and is shipped via the Persian Gulf, the Mediterranean Sea, and the Suez Canal, and the Soviet Union also conducts some maritime traffic in the Mediterranean. In addition, two NATO countries, Greece and Turkey, are located in the eastern Mediterranean, not far from the region where Arab-Israeli conflicts might occur.

Both superpowers furnish arms to their Middle Eastern clients and both maintain a large naval presence in the region, creating a risk that they might collide. The United States has access to military facilities in Egypt, while the Soviet Union has a military presence in Syria, where its troops man SAM-5 anti-aircraft missile sites. Both superpowers have brought nuclear as well as conventional weapons into the region. The United States has some three hundred nuclear warheads deployed in the Mediterranean on land-attack and antisubmarine weapons. The Soviet Mediterranean squadron carries, or has available, nuclear antiship cruise missiles and antisubmarine weapons (See Figure 11-2).[26]

Not only is the Eastern Mediterranean a powder keg of nuclear and conventional weapons, but it is also a politically volatile area, and its volatility is unlikely to decrease in the near future, for the causes of instability are numerous and deeply rooted. Aside from the protracted war between Iran and Iraq, the hostility between Israel and the Arab states does not seem to be moving toward a resolution. Some momentum was generated by the Camp David agreement (1979), and this did lead to Israel's withdrawal from the Egyptian territory of the Sinai Peninsula. But there is no indication of progress on other issues, such as the Golan Heights (which Israel captured from Syria in 1967) or, more fundamentally, the Palestinian problem. A conflict in the Middle East could spread in a variety of ways, one of which is the following.

Suppose Syria and Israel become drawn into combat in southern Lebanon, perhaps as a result of an Israeli decision to annex the former Jordanian territory of the West Bank, a Syrian attempt to retake the Golan Heights, or a

Figure 11-2 U.S. and Soviet Military Presence in the Eastern Mediterranean

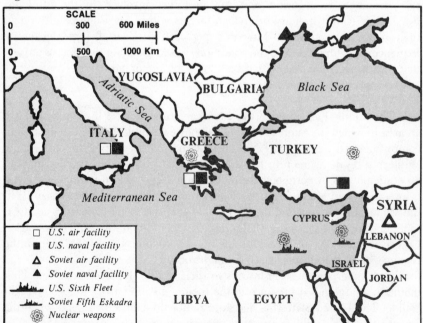

dispute over areas of control in Lebanon itself. The Israelis would rely heavily on their air force for reconnaissance, command, and control, as well as for actual combat, and so they would surely be concerned about the SAM-5 batteries in Syria. In the heat of the fighting, as military imperatives eclipsed political logic, Israel might decide to strike at the SAM-5 sites, despite the fact that they are manned by Soviet crews. The Israelis might count on self-restraint by the Kremlin, but they could be mistaken: the Soviet Union might feel that its influence in the Arab world and status as a superpower did not allow it to remain passive under these conditions. Soviet forces would probably not attack Israel directly, but large naval forces could be deployed off Lebanon and Israel, mock runs toward the shore could be staged, and amphibious exercises could be conducted.

The U.S. response would presumably be one of controlled reciprocity. A first move would be to augment the U.S. naval presence in the region. In addition, U.S. vessels might engage in maneuvers, interposing themselves between Soviet ships and the Israeli coastline where possible. A worldwide alert of U.S. forces would almost certainly be called.

Perhaps the confrontation would go no further than this, and a mutually face-saving de-escalation would be arranged. But it is also possible that the crisis could get out of control. As mentioned, both superpowers maintain a large naval presence in the area: on the one side, the U.S. Sixth Fleet, which includes, among other units, two aircraft-carrier groups and an amphibious task force, and, on the other side, the Soviet Mediterranean squadron, the Fifth Eskadra, which is drawn from the larger Black Sea Fleet. Because the Sixth Fleet is the much larger of the two forces, it could probably wipe out the Fifth Eskadra; moreover, its aircraft are capable of attacking the southwestern part of the U.S.S.R. The logical Soviet strategy would thus be to act preemptively to inflict maximal damage on the U.S. ships. As tensions mounted, Soviet vessels would move within range of the U.S. ships, ready to strike if hostilities broke out or seemed imminent. But U.S. command authorities would be loath to grant the Soviet Union an opportunity to make the first blow. Accordingly, each side would have a strong incentive to preempt the other, which makes for a very unstable situation. Even if neither side actually intended to fight, an accidental firing could occur.

At this point, the Soviet Union would almost surely wish to reinforce the Fifth Eskadra from the Black Sea Fleet, but the United States might try to prevent this by sealing off the Turkish straits through which the Russian ships would have to pass. Soviet ground forces might then move into Turkey, which would constitute an attack on a member of NATO. If the Soviet reinforcements did get through the Turkish straits, they would then have to pass through the Aegean Sea, which is guarded by Greece from bases on the numerous islands in the area. Thus, the Soviet Union might become involved in hostilities with another NATO member. Since both the Soviet and the U.S. ships are armed with nuclear weapons, the likelihood arises that they would be used. The fighting could easily spread to Central Europe, and both the United States and the Soviet Union might then call on their ICBMs, SLBMs, and long-range bombers. Moreover, as before, it must be expected that breakdowns in communications would make it difficult to control the level of violence. Once again, a local tinderbox would have sparked an all-out nuclear war through an unanticipated and virtually uncontrollable process of escalation.

Reducing the Risk of Nuclear War

A world with numerous nuclear weapons at the disposal of two nations that consider themselves bitter adversaries will always imply some risk of nuclear warfare. However, the risk can be reduced in a variety of ways. To some extent, the likelihood of war will be determined by the kinds of weapons the two sides possess, and the danger must thus be lessened through meaningful arms control, a process that will be discussed in Chapter 13. Aside from that, the United States and the Soviet Union can make nuclear war less likely in at least four ways: (1) by improving their diplomatic relations, (2) by developing better crisis-control mechanisms, (3) by establishing nuclear weapon-free zones, and (4) by maintaining submarine invulnerability.

The Task of Diplomacy

The most effective way of averting nuclear war is to reduce the level of tension between the superpowers. All three of the paths to war are more probable when relations are tense, suspicions acute, and rhetoric belligerent. Accidents are more likely to be interpreted as attacks, and crises of various sorts, including rival involvements in regional conflicts, are more likely to occur. Neither superpower can be expected to radically alter its views of its external interests, but the character of relations can be such as to avoid the types of situations which could propel the two nations over the nuclear precipice. This implies efforts of at least two kinds.

First of all, each side would have to refrain from activities and rhetoric that the other would view as provocative. On the whole, except in the late 1940s and early 1950s and during President Reagan's first term in office, both sides have tried to maintain a tone of civility, albeit chilly civility, in their relations. If this is to continue, both sides must resist the temptation to win increased domestic support by picking external quarrels. A measured tone and open channels of communication to the other side would have to be the rule for relations between the superpowers.

Secondly, each side would have to have an accurate idea of just where the other's most sensitive interests lie, to avoid provocations stemming from a lack of understanding of what is unacceptable to the other side. For example, North Korea's invasion of South Korea came six months after a declaration by Secretary of State Acheson that South Korea was not within the U.S. "defense perimeter." The North Koreans may thus have believed that South Korea's security was not of paramount importance to the United States. Similarly, the post-Vietnam sense of repugnance in the United States toward foreign intervention may have led Soviet leaders to believe that they could intervene in African affairs without concern for U.S. reaction. Their subsequent actions in Angola and the Horn of Africa were among the events that precipitated the collapse of détente. Ten years after the Cuban missile crisis, the major participants on the U.S. side reflected that,

> if we had done an earlier and stronger job of explaining our position on Soviet nuclear weapons in the Western Hemisphere, or if the Soviet government had more carefully assessed the evidence that did exist on this point, it is likely that the missiles would never have been sent to Cuba. The importance of accurate mutual assessment of interests between the two superpowers is evident and continuous.[27]

The suggestion has even been made that the United States and the Soviet Union draw up a "code of conduct," stating just what each side would and would not consider acceptable in the other side's activities, especially in the Third World. It would spell out the areas of the world where no interference would be brooked, and the activities that would be acceptable in areas where competition was unavoidable.[28] Clashes might still occur, but not because of a misinterpretation of what each side's interests were. Even if such a formal and detailed code of conduct proved unattainable, efforts at developing tacit rules of conduct would help avoid dangerous and unnecessary crises.

A Crisis Control Center

A major danger during crises is that, with nerves tense and reaction time short, one side might initiate conflict by wrongly assuming that an attack was imminent or already under way. At such times, it is crucial that the two sides communicate with each other, explain their actions, and allay unwarranted fears and suspicions. The importance of direct and rapid communication became especially clear at the time of the Cuban missile crisis, when the risk of war was great and it was imperative that neither side should cause the other to take precipitous action. One of the problems during the crisis was that the ordinary channels of diplomatic communication were too slow and cumbersome to permit the two sides to explain their positions to each other in a clear and timely fashion. Soon after the crisis, the United States and the Soviet Union established a direct and immediate communication link between the U.S. president and the Soviet leader—the so-called *hot line*.

Despite the way it is sometimes portrayed in the movies, the hot line is not a pair of red telephones. It is actually a set of teletype machines capable of printing in both Russian and English. (A telephone is not used because of fears that voice communication could lead to misunderstandings.) The original teletype connection was made by land and sea cable, but in 1971 satellite links were established (the cable was kept as a backup). In 1984, the hot line was further improved by adding the capability of transmitting pages of text, photographs, and graphic material (such as maps of respective military positions). It now connects military headquarters on both sides as well as the two national leaders.

The hot line has been used on several occasions and is universally regarded as a useful institution, but suggestions have been made for still better methods of crisis communication and management. One proposal, endorsed by a Senate resolution in June 1984, is that the two countries establish a joint *crisis control center*,[29] and an agreement to that effect was reached in 1987. Although the details are still unclear, the center will almost surely be staffed by U.S. and Soviet military officers and civilians and have responsibilities both during times of crisis and during placid times. Should a crisis break out, the center would presumably undertake to exchange and jointly interpret the military information required to ensure each side's understanding of the other's intentions and activities, thus reducing the scope for dangerous misunderstandings. The center's staff might also propose measures for reducing tensions and separating military forces if necessary. In normal times, the center's main task would be to anticipate possible dangers and misunderstandings and to develop procedures for resolving problems. This would reinforce established mechanisms for dealing with crises and help avoid wars due to accidents or the fear of preemptive first strikes. Moreover, the experience in operating a crisis control center might enhance mutual trust and spill over into other areas of diplomatic cooperation.

Nuclear Weapon-Free Zones

As pointed out earlier, during a regional conflict, as command and control become difficult and tactical nuclear weapons are dispersed, individual officers could be tempted to use them to protect their troops. But if nuclear arms are not used, the Soviet Union's conventional advantage might enable it to capture and destroy the weapons. NATO might thus be confronted with the choice between "using them and losing them." There would be very little time in which to make the decision and it might be the result of military reflexes rather than of a careful weighing of costs and benefits. George Ball, who was undersecretary of state at the time of the Cuban missile crisis, reported that he and other advisers of President Kennedy later concluded that, "had we determined our course of action within the first forty-eight hours after the missiles were discovered, we would almost certainly have made the wrong decision . . . with horrendous consequences." [30] Thus, sufficient time must be available to allow diplomacy to work before decisions on the use of nuclear weapons are made.

One way of providing that time is to establish a *nuclear weapon-free zone* (NWFZ) in the most dangerous regions. For example, an international group of statesmen has suggested that all nuclear weapons be withdrawn from a strip of 150 kilometers (about 90 miles) on each side of the line that separates NATO and Warsaw Pact forces—the border between West Germany on one side and East Germany and Czechoslovakia on the other (see Figure 11-3).[31] The absence of nuclear arms within this strip of land would reduce the incentive to use such weapons at the beginning of the conflict for fear that they would otherwise be captured, and it would also make it impossible for a beleaguered commander to use them on his own initiative. Furthermore, it would mean that a decision on whether or not to cross the nuclear threshold could be delayed by however long it might take to penetrate the 150-kilometer zone—several days, in all likelihood. Diplomacy would thus be given a chance, conventional defenses could be more fully mobilized, and nuclear war might be averted. An NWFZ has also been proposed for the Balkans, a zone which would include Turkey, Greece, Bulgaria, Romania, Yugoslavia, the Aegean Sea, and portions of the Adriatic Sea and the eastern Mediterranean.[32]

Thus far, however, neither superpower seems to be taking the idea of NWFZs seriously.

Figure 11-3 A Proposed Nuclear Weapon-Free Zone in Central Europe

☰ **Proposed 150 Km Nuclear Weapon-Free Zone**

Submarine Invulnerability

One of the reasons deterrence has worked so far is that, even if one side destroyed the other's ICBMs and bombers in a first strike, the victim could still deliver a devastating retaliatory blow with its submarine force. But there is a danger that the techniques of antisubmarine warfare (ASW) might remove this pillar of stability. The solution, it would seem, lies in a mutual agreement to abstain from ASW research and development, but this is probably unachievable. In the first place, such a ban would be almost totally unverifiable, since research and development could take place in countless enclosed laboratories and even some operational testing could be conducted in fresh-water bodies within a country's territory. Secondly, ASW technology is applicable to submarines equipped with conventional torpedoes as well, and neither side might wish to give up the nonstrategic functions of ASW.

A more feasible suggestion is to create *sanctuaries* for nuclear missile-bearing submarines: areas within which the instruments for submarine detection and tracking, as well as ASW weapons, could not be deployed.[33] This could be done either informally or formally. Informally, each side would focus its own ASW operations outside of the waters in which the other's submarines are kept on patrol. The United States, for example, has already practiced such restraint in the Barents Sea (in the U.S.S.R.'s northern waters) and the Sea of Okhotsk (between the eastern Soviet coast and Japan), where most of the Soviet Union's submarines are deployed. Moscow could reciprocate by keeping its own ASW capabilities out of waters contiguous to U.S. submarine bases.

More formally, both sides could agree to set aside certain tracts of the world's oceans for the exclusive use of their missile-bearing submarines. In the Soviet case, these might again be the Barents Sea and the Sea of Okhotsk, whereas for the United States the areas might be along its shores within the continental shelf. Neither side could deploy its ASW systems in the other's recognized sanctuaries, and even civilian vessels that might be used for surveillance could be kept out. Moreover, these areas would be large enough to make saturation attacks by ballistic missiles impossible. Although a formal agreement on sanctuaries would probably be more reliable, even an informal understanding might add another buffer between superpower crises and the temptation to launch a preemptive nuclear attack.

Conclusions

The consequences of a nuclear war would surely be more terrible than anything humanity has thus far experienced. Populations would be drastically depleted, economies would be destroyed, social fabrics would become unraveled, and coercive dictatorships might emerge even in societies that had previously been staunchly democratic. Yet the outbreak of nuclear war would not necessarily result from deliberate decisions. An accident in the form of an inadvertent launching or detonation, or an unauthorized action by a military commander in the field, could touch it off; it could result from the belief on one side or the other, during a crisis, that it must strike first; or it could come about by the escalation of a regional conflict.

The peril will always be with us. Nuclear weapons will probably never be entirely given up; and even if total disarmament were to be achieved, humanity will not forget how to make these weapons. There are ways of at least reducing the peril, especially through statesmanlike conduct on the part of the superpowers: refraining from belligerent rhetoric and provocative behavior, and gaining as lucid an understanding as possible of the other side's crucial interests and the limits of its forbearance. Beyond this, the possibility of averting nuclear war could be enhanced by such measures as the establishment of a crisis control center, the creation of nuclear weapon-free zones in volatile regions, and the setting aside of certain bodies of water as submarine sanctuaries.

Notes

1. Michael Mandelbaum, "The Bomb, Dread, and Eternity," *International Security* 5 (1980): 3-24.
2. Arthur M. Katz, *Life after Nuclear War* (Cambridge, Mass.: Ballinger, 1982), 27.
3. Kosta Tsipis, *Arsenal: Understanding Weapons in the Nuclear Age* (New York: Simon and Schuster, 1983), 60.
4. Office of Technology Assessment, *The Effects of Nuclear War* (Washington, D.C.: Government Printing Office, 1979).
5. Katz, *Life after Nuclear War*, 120.
6. Ibid., 59.
7. Ibid., 62.
8. Ibid., 48.
9. Ibid., 60.
10. Carl Sagan, "Nuclear War and Climatic Catastrophe," *Foreign Affairs* (Winter 1983/84): 255-293.
11. Ibid., 274.
12. Caspar W. Weinberger, *The Potential Effects of Nuclear War on the Climate* (report to Congress by the Department of Defense, March 1985); Stanley L. Thompson and Stephen H. Schneider, "Nuclear Winter Reappraised," *Foreign Affairs* (Summer 1986): 981-1005.
13. William L. Langer, "The Next Assignment," in *Psychoanalysis and History*, ed. Bruce Mazlish (Englewood Cliffs, N.J.: Prentice-Hall, 1963), 97.
14. Thucydides, *The Peloponnesian War* (Baltimore: Penguin, 1959), 155.
15. Quoted in Robert Jay Lifton, *Death in Life: Survivors of Hiroshima* (New York: Vintage, 1967), 20-21.
16. For details, see Louis René Beres, *Apocalypse: Nuclear Catastrophe in World Politics* (Chicago: University of Chicago Press, 1980), Chapter 1.
17. Richard Burt, "False Nuclear Alarms Spur Urgent Efforts to Find Flaws," *New York Times*, June 13, 1980.

18. A. O. Sulzberger, "Error Alerts U.S. Forces to a False Missile Alert," *New York Times*, November 11, 1979.
19. Lloyd J. Dumas, "Human Fallibility and Weapons," *Bulletin of the Atomic Scientists* 30 (1980): 18.
20. Paul Bracken, *The Command and Control of Nuclear Forces* (New Haven: Yale University Press), 229.
21. Quoted in Fred M. Kaplan, *Dubious Specter: A Second Look at the Soviet Threat* (Washington, D.C.: Transnational Institute, 1977), 19.
22. Tsipis, *Arsenal*, 123.
23. Ibid., 225.
24. Quoted in Ole R. Holsti, "Perception and Action in the 1914 Crisis," in *Quantitative International Politics*, ed. J. David Singer (New York: Free Press, 1966), 134.
25. Stockholm International Peace Research Institute, *World Armaments and Disarmament: SIPRI Yearbook, 1985* (London: Taylor and Francis, 1985), 51-52.
26. See Miroslav Nincic, *How War Might Spread to Europe* (London: Taylor and Francis, 1985), Chapter 2.
27. Dean Rusk et al., "Lessons of the Cuban Missile Crisis," *Time*, September 27, 1972, 85.
28. Arthur Macy Cox, *Russian Roulette: The Superpower Game* (New York: Times Books, 1982), Chapter 6.
29. This idea is developed in William L. Ury, *Beyond the Hotline: How We Can Prevent the Crisis That Might Bring on a Nuclear War* (Boston: Houghton Mifflin, 1985), Chapter 4.
30. Quoted in ibid., 37.
31. Independent Commission on Disarmament and Security Issues, *Common Security: A Blueprint for Survival* (New York: Simon and Schuster, 1982).
32. Donna J. Klick, "A Balkan Nuclear Weapon-Free Zone: Viability of the Regime and Implications for Crisis Management," *Journal of Peace Research* 24 (1987): 111-125.
33. Joel Wit, "Sanctuaries and Security: Suggestions for ASW Arms Control," *Arms Control Today* 10 (1980).

Weapons and Doctrines

An UNDERSTANDING OF U.S. foreign policy must include sound knowledge about strategic weapons—which are long-range nuclear weapons—and about the strategic balance between the United States and the Soviet Union, as well as the doctrines by which nuclear weapons have been justified. It also requires a recognition of the extent to which strategic doctrines are shaped by the state of weapons technology.

Trends in Weaponry

The nuclear arms race began with the detonation by the United States of the first atomic bomb in the summer of 1945. Although its development and use had momentous consequences for East-West relations and for national security, it was not immediately obvious that an arms race of such gigantic proportions was about to be launched. The Soviet Union did not then have a bomb of its own and was considered too economically backward and scientifically unsophisticated to engage the United States in a serious competition. Even when it did detonate an atomic bomb in 1949, it seemed unlikely that it could soon develop the capacity needed to deliver such weapons to targets in the United States. Furthermore, scientists initially doubted that enough uranium could be found to enable any country to build a large nuclear arsenal. In any event, the United States had just emerged from the costliest war it had ever fought, and there was little enthusiasm for shouldering the expense of vast new military programs.

Eventually, however, each of these constraints on an arms race gave way to the demands of accelerated military growth. The scarcity of uranium had been overcome by the end of Harry S Truman's presidency, and by 1953 the production rate of atomic bombs was triple its 1950 level. When Dwight D. Eisenhower came into office, one of his principal concerns was for the nation's economic strength, which he tended to equate with balanced budgets. Since military spending was a major contributor to budgetary deficits, he sought to restrain it. But as the Cold War gained momentum, and especially when the Soviet Union detonated its own hydrogen bomb, he yielded to pressures for renewed military growth. The deterioration of East-West relations, the conviction of many that the fate of the free world depended on a stern military posture, and a variety of domestic political and bureaucratic pressures opened the floodgates to increased armaments, and the Soviet Union responded in kind. The arms race was on. Apart from expanding defense budgets and the numerical growth of both nations' weapons, the military rivalry has been characterized by improvements in the design of nuclear bombs and the development of more efficient and more accurate ways of delivering warheads to their targets. Recently, the arms race has also taken both nations into space-based weaponry and the new types of technology that this implies.

If the fission bomb is viewed as a first-generation nuclear weapon, then the fusion bomb, as well as bombs incorporating a combination of fusion and fission principles, may be considered the second generation. Currently, a third generation is under development; these weapons do not incorporate any fundamentally new physical principles but are designed to produce more specific and discriminating effects than those which preceded them.[1] One such third-generation weapon is the *neutron* bomb, also known as the Enhanced Radiation Weapon. It is designed to limit blast and heat effects, while maximizing the amount of radiation, in the form of an intense burst of neutrons. It is thought that the neutron bomb would be particularly useful for stopping a Soviet assault through Central Europe. Such an attack would involve heavy use of tanks and armored personnel carriers in a densely populated part of the world. Efforts to destroy such formidable vehicles with first- or second-generation weapons would cause extensive collateral injury to civilians from the blast, thermal, and radioactive effects. The neutron bomb, on the other hand, would kill the tank crews by penetrating the tank armor with neutron radiation, while sparing the buildings and population in the vicinity. Opponents of the neutron bomb have argued that it would lower the threshold at which a conventional conflict would become nuclear and that subsequent escalation would be all but inevitable.

Another third-generation nuclear weapon currently under development is the EMP (electromagnetic pulse) bomb. Its purpose would be to generate the maximum EMP effect, even—or particularly—at the expense of other effects. It could be exploded within the atmosphere, over the opponent's rear echelons, in order to disrupt his command, control, and communications equipment, or it could be detonated above the atmosphere to impose similar damage over a wider area. One perceived benefit is that, since it might not be very lethal to the population, it could perhaps be used without provoking nuclear retaliation. Nevertheless, it appears that even such a bomb would cause many civilian injuries and considerable damage to civilian facilities, making it potentially as provocative as any other nuclear weapon.[2] Thus, the arms race has been partially driven by advances in nuclear weapon design, aimed at producing bombs custom-tailored for specific military purposes.

The second, and more widely publicized aspect of the arms race has been the search for improved delivery vehicles for the weapons. Nuclear bombs were initially carried by bombers with an intercontinental range or, in the case of the United States, on shorter-range bombers stationed at allied air bases located within striking distance of Soviet territory. The first major upgrading in delivery capability came with the introduction in the late 1950s of intercontinental ballistic missiles (ICBMs) that could travel at supersonic speeds; for a long time, both superpowers devoted great effort to improving their stocks of these missiles. At first they were based on and launched from the ground; later, they were also deployed on submarines, which made them much less vulnerable to attack. Another innovation in delivery has been the multiple independently targetable reentry vehicle (MIRV, see Chapter 11).

The first U.S. land-based missiles with intercontinental range were the Titan I and Titan II; these were followed by the Minuteman I, II, and III. The Minuteman II was the first ICBM to be MIRVed. The newest ground-launched missile to enter the U.S. arsenal is the MX, which carries ten warheads (compared to the three carried by the Minuteman III) and can be delivered with extreme accuracy. A projected addition would be the Midgetman, a smaller, very accurate single-warhead missile that could be mobile rather than deployed in a fixed position. The Soviet Union's major ICBM is the SS-18, which also carries ten warheads and was the first Soviet missile to attain a respectable level of accuracy. Several new land-based missiles (of which the SS-25 is particularly significant) have since been developed by the Soviet Union.

Another weapon, one in which the United States enjoys a commanding technological lead, is the *cruise missile:* a small self-propelled rocket that travels very close to the earth's surface, carrying a single conventional or nuclear warhead. Although it is subsonic, its advantage is that it can evade enemy radar because of its low flight path and small size. It is also much cheaper to produce than an ICBM. Cruise missiles can be launched from airplanes (ALCMs), from ships or submarines (SLCMs), or from the ground (GLCMs).

More recently, new long-range bombers are entering the superpowers' arsenals. The United States is currently deploying the B1-B, a supersonic bomber, and is working on a plane called the *stealth* bomber, incorporating technologies designed to make it nearly invisible to enemy radar. The Soviet Union is proceeding along similar lines.

In addition to qualitative changes in nuclear bombs and delivery vehicles, which involve the improvement of existing weapons rather than fundamental innovations, both the United States and the Soviet Union are also exploring completely new frontiers in military technology, especially in the area of space-based weaponry. A major impetus to this research was the discovery of *directed-energy beams*, which focus a very large amount of energy into a focused beam. One application is the *particle-beam* weapon, which generates a concentrated stream of atomic or subatomic particles accelerated to very intense energies. Another is the *laser-beam* weapon, which directs a beam of light or invisible radiation at a distant target at the speed of light. It is believed that laser-beam weapons could be used to destroy incoming enemy missiles, especially if they could be operated in outer space. The United States apparently intends to deploy space-based laser weapons in the 1990s. There is some disagreement on the best way to generate laser beams for military purposes, whether chemically or by a nuclear explosion. Another possibility is to place enormous mirrors in space that would focus and target laser beams generated on the ground.

Yet another exotic space-based system is the *rail gun*, a sort of slingshot powered by electromagnetic forces delivering small projectiles, guided by tiny sensors and thrusters, at such speed that they can destroy a missile in flight. As a Pentagon scientist observed: "You can try to run away from them, but there's no place to hide. They just keep seeking you out." [3]

These and other weapons are justified in terms of the Soviet Union's military capabilities and, more generally, in terms of prevailing strategic doctrines, which explain how and for what purposes they would be used.

The Strategic Balance

Perhaps the question most frequently asked concerning the arms race is, Who is ahead? Not only is it important from a security perspective, but it is also pregnant with domestic political implications. Candidates for office often seek political advantage by accusing the incumbents of allowing the Soviet Union to gain a military edge over the United States. Typically, the most ominous allegations concerning U.S. military weakness come from conservative groups and from the military establishment itself. These allegations are hard both to substantiate and to rebut. Beyond a certain level of strategic armament, claims of inferiority or superiority are quite relative, and by carefully selecting one's indicators of military strength, it is possible to make any case one desires. For example, during the late 1970s when a vehement national debate raged in the United States concerning the strategic balance, conservative groups launched public information campaigns warning of Soviet military superiority. In 1980, several campaigns for Senate seats revolved around issues of national defense, and Ronald Reagan's campaign for the presidency was largely based on charges that the administration of President Jimmy Carter had presided over a dangerous decline in America's strategic strength. But the data in Table 12-1 il-

Table 12-1 U.S. and Soviet Strategic Arsenals, 1979

	United States	*Soviet Union*
ICBMs	1,054	1,398
SLBMs	656	1,028
Long-range bombers	431	156
Nuclear warheads	9,318	6,000

Source: International Institute for Strategic Studies, *The Military Balance: 1979-1980* (London: IISS, 1980), 86-90.

lustrate the difficulties in comparing Soviet and U.S. nuclear strength. Even on the basis of so simple a numerical count as is presented in this table, it is possible to draw diametrically opposite conclusions. Alarmists could point to the fact that the Soviet Union had 2,582 delivery vehicles as opposed to only 2,141 for the United States. This was especially disturbing in view of the Soviet lead in the number of ICBMs, which would be the most effective weapons for a first strike. Accordingly, there was much talk of "Soviet military superiority" and of the irresponsibility of an administration that had allowed this asymmetry to develop. On the other hand, the United States had a lead of over 3,000 in the number of warheads. Its seeming inferiority in the number of delivery vehicles stemmed from the fact that it put more warheads on each missile—that is, it had taken the MIRV concept further than the Soviet Union. Hence, one could have argued that, since nuclear warheads and not missiles kill people and destroy industrial and military targets, the United States actually enjoyed nuclear superiority.

But it was not just the Soviet lead in missiles that caused dismay in some circles. Another measure of strategic capability is *throw-weight*, which is the total weight of the warheads, together with the "bus" that carries them, that a vehicle can lift into space. In other words, it is a measure of a missile's payload. Although the average throw-weight of U.S. missiles was 2,000 kilograms, compared to an average of 3,750 for the Soviet Union (see Table 12-2), we cannot infer that the Soviet missile force was the more powerful one. First, a missile's throw-weight only partially reflects its explosive yield, since bomb design often allows the same yield to be produced by warheads of different sizes, and U.S. scientists have been more successful than their Soviet counterparts in packing high yields into smaller bombs. Moreover, as was pointed out earlier, a warhead's ability to destroy its target, especially a relatively small military target, depends on its accuracy as well as its explosive force. In fact, accuracy is more heavily weighted than yield in calculations of a warhead's "kill probability" (the likelihood that it will destroy its target). Accuracy is expressed by a measure known as *circular error probable* (CEP), which is the diameter of a circle centered on the target within which half of the warheads can be expected to fall. The larger the CEP, the less accurate the weapon. As Table 12-2 shows, U.S. warheads are more accurate than those of the U.S.S.R.

Another consideration in evaluating the strategic balance is missile *survivability*—a missile's ability to avoid or withstand a hit by an enemy missile and thus be available for retaliation if needed. ICBMs, which are in known and fixed locations, are most vulnerable to preemptive attack; submarines are least vulnerable. Bombers are more or less vulnerable, depending on whether or not they are on alert and can take off before being hit. As Figure 12-1 shows, most of the Soviet Union's warheads have been on ICBMs, whereas most U.S. warheads have been carried on submarines or bombers, although the difference is somewhat less when considered in terms of the throw-weight megatonnage.

On the whole, it appears that the concerns about U.S. strategic inferiority have been overstated. Indeed, both the secretary of defense and the chairman of the Joint Chiefs of Staff have declared that there was no such inferiority. This does not mean that the Soviet Union has made no effort to increase its strategic power or that it cannot, in some ways, move ahead of the United States. The point, rather, is that, in assessing claims of inferiority or superiority, one should ascertain the basis for the claim, and what indicators of strategic strength were used or neglected. We must also keep in mind Henry Kissinger's admonition: "One of the questions we have to ask ourselves as a country is what in the name of God is strategic superiority? What is the significance of it politically, militarily, operationally at these levels of numbers? What do you do with it?" [4]

Strategic Doctrine

Development of a nuclear weapon is usually justified in terms of a *strategic doctrine*, which explains the objectives of nuclear force and the manner in which it might be used. Since its first detonation of an atomic bomb in 1945, the United States has espoused several, not always mutually compatible, strategic doctrines. Although it is sometimes not clear whether the doctrines actually guide the development and acquisition of the weapons or are designed as their rationalization, these doctrines are now an important subject of political debate.

In retrospect, it is surprising how little explicit political thinking went into the development of the atomic bomb. A consideration of the links between political goals and nuclear weapons may have seemed irrelevant, because the nation was at war and the Manhattan Project, which developed the atomic bomb, was thought of as ensuring U.S. victory. Despite Hitler's defeat, Japan seemed ready to pursue the war in the Pacific, and the nuclear weapon was

Table 12-2 Throw-Weight and Circular Error Probable (CEP) Accuracy of U.S. and Soviet ICBMs, 1979

	United States			Soviet Union		
ICBM type	Throw-weight (kilograms)	CEP (meters)	ICBM type	Throw-weight (kilograms)	CEP (meters)
Titan II	4,000	1,300	SS-9	7,300	1,150
Minuteman II	1,000	400	SS-11	1,000	1,400
Minuteman III	1,000	300	SS-13	500	1,300
			SS-17	3,200	450
			SS-18	7,300	450
			SS-19	3,200	375
Average[a]	2,000	667		3,750	854

Source: Stockholm International Peace Research Institute, *World Armaments and Disarmament: SIPRI Yearbook, 1980* (London: Taylor and Francis, 1980), xxxi.

[a] Not weighted by number of ICBMs of each type.

then designed to convince it of the futility of that venture. Although some argue that the same effect could have been achieved by an atomic detonation in the atmosphere and that the destruction of two cities was therefore unnecessary, nobody seriously questioned the bomb's value in terminating the war. But if this had been its sole objective, its mission would have ended with Japan's surrender. In fact, the Truman administration also had another objective: to impress Stalin with U.S. military power at a time when it was clear that the two nations would emerge as bitter postwar rivals.

In July 1945, at about the time the bomb was scheduled to be tested, Truman arrived in Potsdam for a meeting with Churchill and Stalin. The purpose of the meeting was to induce the Soviet dictator to join the war against Japan as soon as possible. However, when news of the successful test reached the president, he in effect stopped negotiating with Stalin. According to Churchill, "He told the Russians just where they could get off and generally bossed the whole meeting."[5] It was hoped not only that the atomic bomb would enable the Western allies to keep the Soviet Union out of the war in Asia and thus hold its postwar claims on China and Japan to a minimum but also that it could be used to reduce Moscow's demands in Eastern Europe.

The weapon's value appeared undiminished even after the postwar settlement had been reached. As the Cold War gained momentum, the idea of using the nuclear weapon against the Soviet Union itself was just below the surface of U.S. foreign and military policy. Many people in the United States, and not only those at the extreme right of the political spectrum or within the military establishment, were convinced that war with the U.S.S.R. was inevitable and that it was to be won with the help of the atomic bomb.

Figure 12-1   Distribution of U.S. and Soviet Nuclear Weapons, 1979

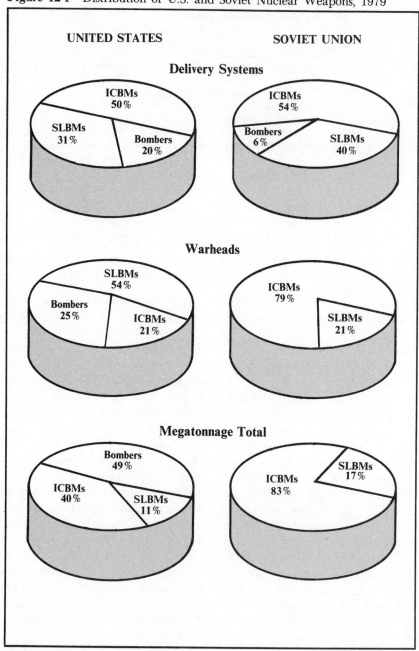

Source: Adapted from *World Armaments and Disarmament: SIPRI Yearbook, 1979* (London: Taylor and Francis, 1980).

Note: Totals may not add to 100 due to rounding.

The "Sunday Punch"

Most decisions on how and where the atomic bomb would be used were made by the nation's military leaders, especially by the Strategic Air Command (SAC) commander, rather than by civilian authorities. As early as 1946, the Air Force had drafted a war plan which proposed dropping a total of fifty nuclear bombs (virtually the entire inventory at that time) upon twenty Soviet cities. The exact circumstances that would call forth such an action were not spelled out, but the general idea was that the plan would be implemented if the Soviet Union invaded Western Europe. A few civilian consultants to the Air Force thought that cities and civilians should be spared—that only military targets should be destroyed; in other words, they argued for a *counterforce* doctrine (according to which military facilities would be the primary targets) rather than a *countervalue* doctrine (according to which populations and cities would be the primary targets). Military leaders were not persuaded. If war broke out, the U.S. nuclear arsenal would be used to wipe out Soviet industrial capacity, society, and war-making potential. The strategy came to be known as the "Sunday punch." [6] As the U.S. nuclear arsenal grew, the number of Soviet cities targeted for destruction grew as well: by 1955, SAC had plans to destroy at least three-quarters of the population in each of 118 Soviet cities in the event of war, as well as any targetable military facilities. The chief proponent of the notion of maximal possible destruction of the U.S.S.R. was Gen. Curtis Le May, who was SAC commander in 1948 and later was Air Force chief of staff. As a historian subsequently said, "To Le May, demolishing everything was how you win a war." [7]

When the Soviet Union acquired its own atomic bomb in 1949, the strategy required modification. A preemptive Soviet attack on the United States had become theoretically possible, and visions of such an attack loomed large in the minds of military planners. To prevent it, the Sunday Punch was to be administered at the first sign of a major Soviet military mobilization. In other words, SAC was considering a *first-use* strategy—one in which, under certain circumstances, the United States would use nuclear weapons before its adversaries did. The nation's civilian leadership does not seem to have been informed about these plans. Robert Sprague, a member of the Gaither Committee, a presidential panel examining defense policy, reported that, in a discussion with Le May, the latter volunteered that "if I see that the Russians are amassing their planes for an attack . . . I'm going to knock the shit out of them before they take off the ground."

"But General Le May," Sprague responded, "that's not national policy."

"I don't care," Le May replied, "It's my policy. That's what I'm going to do." [8]

Massive Retaliation

Though the concept of a nuclear assault against the Soviet Union had been part of the military's operational war plans since 1946, the conditions that would warrant such action were not articulated by the civilian leadership until several years later. Beginning in 1953, the Eisenhower administration moved toward a "new look" in military policy, involving a greater reliance on nuclear weapons. The United States was just emerging from the Korean War, which had been a draining national experience in terms of both lives and money. It left the president convinced that future costly entanglements in local conflicts were to be avoided, and it seemed that a good way of doing so was to threaten a nuclear attack in case of Soviet provocation. In addition, Eisenhower was a fiscal conservative, who worried about the damage that excessive military spending could have on the economy. In fact, a number of Republicans even argued that the arms race was probably a Communist plot to undermine the U.S. economy by forcing the country to undertake ruinous levels of military spending.

In October 1953, a National Security Council paper, NSC-162/2, defined the major challenge to national security policy as "meeting the Soviet threat" without "seriously weakening the U.S. economy or undermining our fundamental values and institutions."[9] In January 1954, in a speech to the Council on Foreign Relations, Secretary of State John Dulles declared that nuclear arms would henceforth be given a major emphasis in U.S. strategy. "The way to deter aggression," he said, "is for the free community to be willing and able to respond vigorously at places and with means of our choosing."[10] Thus, if the Soviet Union impinged on U.S. interests in one part of the world, the United States would not feel obliged to exert military counterpressure at the same place, as it had done in Korea. Rather, Dulles called for the "deterrent of massive retaliatory power"—that is, the nuclear bomb. This approach, which came to be known as the policy of *massive retaliation,* was generally interpreted to mean that, if the Soviet Union made a foray into some part of the world that the United States considered within its own sphere of interest, a large-scale nuclear attack against the Soviet Union would be the likely consequence (although other forms of retaliation were not necessarily excluded). As Eisenhower explained to selected members of Congress, the U.S. military strategy was "to blow hell out of them in a hurry if they start anything."[11]

If the doctrine of massive retaliation was motivated by fiscal frugality and by a desire to avoid protracted commitments of U.S. troops to local conflicts, it was made credible by the fact that the Soviet Union could not strike back with a massive counter-retaliation. The Soviet Union had both atomic and hydrogen weapons by this time, but it was not capable of delivering them to the United States. Since long-range missiles had not yet been developed, the bombs would have to be carried by airplanes, and, while neither superpower had a very good long-range bomber fleet, the United States was in a stronger position. At first, SAC's mainstays had been the B-29 bomber, with a range of 4,000 miles, and the B-50, with a somewhat longer range. Neither of these planes could reach the Soviet Union from U.S. territory, but they could be based in Western

Europe or refueled in the air. In 1949, a new long-range bomber was developed, the B-46; it was faster than the B-29 and the B-50 and therefore better able to penetrate Soviet air defenses, but it did not have an intercontinental range, either. In 1955, however, a year after the massive retaliation doctrine was proclaimed, the Air Force acquired the B-52, its first bomber capable of reaching the Soviet Union from the United States.

The first Soviet long-range bomber, the TU-4, was a copy of the B-29. In 1955, it was replaced by the Badger medium-range bomber, but this airplane could not undertake intercontinental missions, and the Soviet Union lacked both overseas bases close to U.S. territory and a capacity for in-flight refueling. Thus, initially at least, it seemed that the United States could attack the U.S.S.R. with impunity and that, realizing this, the Soviet Union would presumably avoid the kind of behavior that could unleash a nuclear strike. U.S. troops would thus not have to fight abroad and money could be saved by reducing expenditures for conventional forces. Political needs and military doctrine appeared finally to be wedded.

But the strategy was not attractive to everyone, and soon there were doubts about its credibility. On the one hand, the notion of a massive nuclear response for limited conventional provocations did not strike everyone as a believable threat, and if it was not believable, it might not deter Soviet interventions in parts of the world deemed important to U.S. interests. Moreover, it is a principle of Western society that punishment should be roughly proportionate to provocation, and this principle would be violated by massive retaliation. William Kaufmann, a defense analyst, argued that massive retaliation would be "out of character" and that it left the country with two equally unpalatable options:

> If the Communists should challenge our sincerity and they would have good reasons for daring to do so, we would either have to put up or shut up. If we put up, we would plunge into all the immeasurable horrors of atomic war. If we shut up, we would suffer a serious loss of prestige and damage our capacity to establish deterrents against further Communist expansion.[12]

Another problem was that the U.S. lead in nuclear delivery capability could not last forever. The doctrine's credibility became increasingly shaky as the Soviet Union began acquiring the capacity to respond with nuclear strikes of its own against the United States. The first evidence of its ability to do so came in 1956 and 1957, when the Bear and Bison bombers, with a range of more than 8,000 miles, entered the Soviet inventory. Although they were not produced in great numbers, they did give the U.S.S.R. a theoretical ability to deliver nuclear bombs to U.S. territory. Clearly, this made the threat of nuclear retaliation by the U.S. for Soviet moves implausible, since, presumably, the United States would not sacrifice its own cities for the sake of deterring aggression against other countries. The decisive blow was finally dealt to massive retaliation when the Soviet Union acquired a long-range missile capability.

In the summer of 1957, the United States had not yet flight-tested any ICBMs. The major reason for the lack of a sense of urgency was the perception of Soviet technological inferiority: surely a peasant nation would not be able to seriously challenge the United States to a missile race. This notion was so widely accepted that the first Soviet test of a long-range missile in August 1957 came as a jarring surprise, surpassed in impact only by the launching, just two months later, of Sputnik, the first artificial satellite. The U.S.S.R.'s ability to launch a satellite into orbit implied that it could also deliver a nuclear warhead from Soviet to U.S. territory. To many strategic thinkers, this meant the end of massive retaliation, for it suggested not only that the Soviets could counter-retaliate but also that, if they expected a nuclear attack from the United States, they might be tempted to launch a preemptive attack first, especially since the warning time of a nuclear strike dropped from approximately eight hours in the case of bombers to twenty-five minutes for missiles.

Military thinking is slow to evolve, in part because the interests of the several services often work against change, but a number of civilian thinkers and political leaders had been searching for a better strategy of deterrence. In 1960, however, the armed forces devised their first integrated plan for nuclear war, replacing the separate and overlapping plans of the separate services. It was called the Single Integrated Operational Plan, or SIOP, and President Eisenhower, who had qualms about massive retaliation and the prospect of civilian overkill, asked his science adviser to study it. He reported, to the president's amazement, that the plan had but a single option: an all-out strike with the entire U.S. arsenal against not only the Soviet Union but Eastern Europe and China as well, resulting in the probable death of some four hundred million people. A Soviet city about the size of Hiroshima was targeted with three one-megaton bombs and one four-megaton bomb. Hiroshima had been totally destroyed with a thirteen-kiloton bomb, yet the comparable Soviet city would receive more than five hundred times as much. Eisenhower admitted that these plans "frighten[ed] the devil out of me." But at that time he had only one more month left in office and it was left to the administration of John F. Kennedy to undertake a revision of massive retaliation.

Flexible Response and MAD

President Kennedy and his secretary of defense, Robert McNamara, began drafting new guidelines for the use of nuclear force as soon as they took office. The president wanted to have better choices than "put up or shut up"; he wanted to be able to make a range of nuclear responses, from limited tactical use to an all-out strategic assault. Nuclear weapons would be used only on military targets at first, holding a portion of the nuclear inventory in reserve for bargaining and leverage. Cities would be attacked only on the last rung of the escalatory ladder, one which it was hoped would never be reached. This strategy was attractive on both pragmatic and ethical grounds. It would mean that the slaughter of civilians could be avoided and that U.S. cities would be spared while the superpowers negotiated an end to nuclear hostilities. It was also a much more credible strategy, since the United States might be expected to sacrifice *military* facilities in an attempt to punish or repel Soviet aggression abroad, even though it might not be willing to have its population incinerated in the interests of deterrence. The new strategy thus involved preferential targeting of military objects (counterforce) and multiple options. It came to be known as the strategy of *flexible response*.

Enthusiasm for this strategy did not last very long. It was the object of two sorts of criticism. First, it was feared that it would make nuclear war more likely by making it appear more acceptable. The development of counterforce capabilities, by enabling both sides to launch a preemptive first strike, could also tempt either one to do so. Thus, from one point of view, flexible response seemed like an even more dangerous strategic doctrine than the one it had replaced. Second, it provided an enormous impetus to military spending and to the arms race. If the strategy calls for the destruction of military targets, then the number of weapons must exceed the number of targets. But the growth in weaponry would mean a further proliferation of targets, and so on. Thus, the strategy would surely accelerate the arms race. At this time, the nation was concerned with taking measures for counterinsurgency in the Third World as well as with nuclear deterrence, and the first steps were already being taken toward involvement in Vietnam. Many critics felt that the country could not afford the kind of all-out arms race that flexible response seemed to imply.

Faced with these difficulties, McNamara instructed his staff in January 1963 to discard the strategy that had just been developed, and the military was informed that it was no longer to be used as a rationale for new weapons requests. McNamara shifted his focus from fighting a nuclear war to deterrence and from a counterforce to a countervalue targeting doctrine (that is, one focused primarily on civilian targets). The major purpose of the U.S. nuclear arsenal was now to be to prevent Soviet nuclear assaults directed at the United States *itself*. This would be founded on the expectation that a retaliatory strike would follow a Soviet attack, and that the devastation to be expected would outweigh any advantage the Soviet Union could hope to gain through a first strike. This implied an ability and a willingness to deliver a countervalue blow against Soviet urban centers and economic facilities, and also an ability to weather a full-scale attack well enough to counter with a level of destruction unacceptable to the attacker. If this was to work, the survivability of a large enough portion of the U.S. delivery force had to be ensured, a need that encouraged the accelerated procurement of missile-launching submarines, because of their relative invulnerability. It also led to the hardening of ICBM silos with thick walls of concrete to make them more resistant to nuclear blasts in their vicinity.

The doctrine came to be known as that of *mutual assured destruction*, or MAD. The administration tried to make its premises as clear as possible. Not only was the function of a second strike explained, but also efforts were made to estimate what level of assured second-strike destruction would be unacceptable to Soviet leaders and to determine what would be required to inflict that level of damage after a first strike had been absorbed. In his last appearance before the House Armed Services Committee before leaving office, McNamara argued that devastation sufficient for deterrent purposes would mean the loss of at least one-quarter of the Soviet population and half of its industrial capacity—roughly twice the losses suffered by the Soviet Union during World War II. It was calculated that the amount of destructive power needed to achieve this was in the vicinity of four hundred "equivalent megatons." [13] Since U.S. strategic forces were based on the concept of a "triad" of land-based missiles, submarine-launched missiles, and bombers, it was proposed that *each* leg of the triad should have the ability to deliver the requisite amount of nuclear weaponry, in case the other two were destroyed.

The credibility of MAD resided in the fact that retaliation would follow an attack against the United States itself. Moreover, since the strategy implied abandoning the search for a counterforce capability, it would not provoke preemptive first strikes at times of crisis. Crisis stability would thus be greatly enhanced. Finally, since the weaponry needed to make the strategy work was finite and calculable, there would be much less reason to pursue a seemingly limitless arms race. Even then, the United States already had nuclear warheads in excess of those required by the strategy, and it seemed that the notion of "finite deterrence" would have a built-in bias toward arms control.

This was the first time that security was defined in terms of mutual vulnerability, and it was not a concept easy to explain to military officers or, for that matter, to the Soviet Union. For example, when it appeared that the Soviet Union was about to initiate a program of developing defenses against ballistic missiles, the United States argued that this could undermine the stability of deterrence by reducing Soviet vulnerability to a retaliatory second strike, but it was difficult to convince Soviet strategists that a defensive capacity could be destabilizing. Although there was much that was counterintuitive about MAD, it was at least as logical as the strategies that preceded (and succeeded) it. Nevertheless, it was not to endure. By the middle of the 1970s, the United States began moving back toward the counterforce doctrine which MAD had temporarily displaced.

Counterforce and Nuclear Warfighting

The swing away from countervalue and toward counterforce was partially the result of a rethinking of strategic assumptions and partially the outcome of the push of new military technologies and deteriorating U.S.-Soviet relations. Doctrinal dissatisfaction with MAD came from several sources. In the view of some critics, its reliance on a "balance of terror" was repulsive on ethical grounds.[14] Deterrence based on the massive destruction of civilian lives amounted, as Albert Wohlstetter, a leading strategic thinker, put it, to an attempt at making "murder respectable." [15] Should U.S. security be dependent on threats against innocent populations? Though proponents of MAD might argue that, paradoxically, it is exactly by such threats that nuclear war is averted, it was easy to find the strategy morally unattractive.

Other critics argued that the doctrine suffered from misplaced pretensions at scientific precision. The idea that Soviet aggression could be averted by threatening to wipe out some fixed proportion of its population and its economy seemed absurd to these critics. Did the figures imply that deterrence would fail if slightly less could be destroyed in a second strike? Moreover, how can it be determined what the U.S.S.R. is or is not capable of absorbing in war? McNamara's figures were not based on an objective appraisal of the suffering that the Soviet people could bear. Rather, the decision to consider the destruction imposed by four hundred equivalent megatons as sufficient for deterrence purposes appeared to be based on a more pragmatic consideration. It was indeed demonstrated that the choice of this figure grew out of calculations showing that beyond four hundred megatons the curve of destruction became increasingly flat—that is, any additional weapons delivered would destroy proportionately less and less of the U.S.S.R.'s population and industry.[16] Thus, the whole concept of MAD seemed to rest on a questionable foundation.

Most importantly from a strategic point of view, it was felt that MAD did not provide the United States with enough credible options in a confrontation with the Soviet Union. Like massive retaliation before it, MAD did not allow for responses to a number of strategic contingencies. It seemed capable of deterring only a full-scale Soviet nuclear attack against the United States, which was the least likely contingency. On the other hand, it was irrelevant to the task of deterring more limited and more likely provocations in other parts of the world.

A new element in the situation was that the United States appeared to have lost *escalation dominance* in Europe. Escalation dominance is the ability to respond to any level of an adversary's violence with violence just one notch greater. If the United States possessed this ability, it could theoretically deter Soviet aggression of just about any level, since it could nullify whatever advantage the Soviet Union hoped to acquire with that level of military activity by responding with slightly greater counterpressure. Escalation of the level of violence would be useless, because the same would be true at all rungs on the escalatory ladder. The loss of escalation dominance by the United States was attributed to the U.S.S.R.'s military buildup. The improved conventional forces confronting the United States and NATO meant that there was very little chance of fending off a non-nuclear Soviet attack without resorting to nuclear weapons. While the United States could perhaps have previously threatened to retaliate with U.S.-based strategic weapons in the event of conventional aggression, this was no longer credible, since the Soviet Union had, by the mid-1970s, acquired roughly strategic parity with the United States, and no one believed that U.S. cities would be sacrificed in the interests of allies.

The gap between provocation and response was thus too great for the retaliation to be believable. The United States did maintain tactical (shorter-range) nuclear weapons in Europe, but even these could no longer ensure escalation dominance, since the Soviet Union had increased and improved its theater-nuclear capabilities, especially with the deployment of the SS-20 intermediate-range missile. Thus, it was the Soviet Union which, in the eyes of some, was now in a position to exercise escalation dominance.

By the time President Gerald Ford came into office, alternatives to MAD were being actively sought. In 1974, Secretary of Defense James Schlesinger argued for a policy of "flexible targeting," reminiscent of McNamara's "flexible response." In his 1975 annual defense report, he called for an approach that would allow for "a series of measured responses to aggression which bear some relation to the provocation, have prospects of terminating hostilities before general war breaks out and leave some possibility for restoring deterrence." [17] The argument was not that MAD should be altogether abandoned, but that the range of available nuclear responses, and the weapons they implied, should be expanded. What was needed was the ability to conduct "limited" nuclear warfare, to target military installations and missile silos, and to limit collateral damage whenever possible and desired.

As mentioned before, the pressure for revision of strategic doctrine came both from the advent of new military technologies and from the deterioration of East-West relations. Strategic doctrine is not merely, perhaps not even mainly, guided by an objective appraisal of the demands of national security. Very often, the capabilities of the weapons devised by science and technology dictate what will be considered strategically desirable. For example, the U.S. lead in weapons and delivery systems had much to do with the emergence of massive retaliation, and the development of invulnerable submarine-launched missiles made mutual assured destruction seem like a good idea. The new military technologies that appeared in the 1970s could not be accommodated within the framework of MAD. The choice was between forsaking the new technologies and finding a new strategic doctrine that would offer a rationale for the new weapons. The choice was in favor of a new doctrine.

Among the new technological developments were MIRVs. Initially, MIRVs were justified by the apparent Soviet construction of a network of anti-ballistic missile (ABM) defenses that could, in principle, undermine MAD by making the U.S.S.R. safe from a devastating U.S. second strike. However, the prediction that the Soviet Union would soon have a substantial ABM system proved to be unfounded. In any case, the 1972 ABM treaty between the two nations limited ABM deployments to two sites (later reduced to a single site). Thus, if objective security needs stemming from MAD were the reason for having MIRVs, later developments should have led to their abandonment. Yet MIRV development moved ahead at full speed, leading to an ability to deliver several warheads to each Soviet missile silo. But this was a counterforce mission, quite irrelevant to MAD. If the program for MIRV development were to continue, a new doctrinal justification would have to be found.

When the Carter administration assumed office, the president reaffirmed his commitment to MAD, and Harold Brown, the new defense secretary, downplayed counterforce. However, the MX missile was entering an advanced stage of development, and a clamor arose for congressional funding; its substantial cost and the controversy surrounding the system meant that persuasive justifications for the weapon were needed. Another new missile, the Maneuverable Reentry Vehicle (MARV), with a variable postboost trajectory and increased accuracy was also being developed. The D-5 SLBM warhead, a counterforce weapon, was entering the testing stage, and new theater nuclear systems—mainly ultra-accurate Pershing 2 and cruise missiles—were scheduled for deployment in Europe. None of these weapons had any logical place in a doctrine that envisaged only the retaliatory destruction of large urban targets; if they were to be justified, a commitment to limited nuclear warfare and counterforce options was needed.

The cost of these new military programs was substantial, and it was obvious that they would undermine the process of arms control initiated by the two superpowers more than a decade previously. Had U.S.-Soviet relations retained the constructive tone of the late 1960s and early 1970s, it would have been very difficult to win approval for an acceleration of the arms race. But, as pointed out in earlier chapters, these were the years when the edifice of détente began to crumble. Indeed, by 1979, it had collapsed, and it was then easier to mobilize support for the new programs. The invasion of Afghanistan, it was argued, had demonstrated anew the Soviet peril. Since the end of the Vietnam War, public opinion had never been as receptive to increased military spending.

In July 1980, President Carter issued Presidential Directive 59, requiring that U.S. nuclear forces be able to undertake precise and limited strikes against military facilities in the Soviet Union. Assured destruction of cities was not abandoned, but the repertoire of possible actions was expanded to meet a greater variety of strategic contingencies and to reestablish U.S. escalation dominance.[18]

The counterforce approach was taken to even greater lengths in the Reagan administration. While the previous policy had been to acquire the ability to make measured responses to Soviet provocations and to limit escalation by a strategy of controlled reciprocity, the concept of fighting and "winning" nuclear wars was now broached. Some of this new thinking was incorporated into the five-year Defense Guidance Plan drawn up in 1982. This plan anticipated the possibility of a "protracted" nuclear or conventional conflict, in which the United States must "prevail" and "be able to seek earliest termination of hostilities on terms favorable to the United States."[19] This implied an ability both to impose modulated destruction on civilian populations and to destroy military targets, especially missiles in their hardened silos and military and political command posts (many of which were in underground locations). These capabilities were consistent with a striving for escalation dominance but they were also consistent with the pursuit of preemptive first-strike options. In any case, they seemed guided by the idea that the United States could and should seek to win a nuclear war in the event that deterrence failed.

This concept of nuclear warfighting was publicly set forth by Colin Gray, a nuclear strategist and consultant to the Reagan administration, in an article entitled "Victory Is Possible." [20] In it, he presented a "theory of victory" in nuclear war, which "would have to envisage the demise of the Soviet state." According to this article, "the United States may have no practical alternative to waging a nuclear war." Accordingly, the "United States should plan to defeat the Soviet Union and to do so at a cost that would not prohibit U.S. recovery [and it] should identify war aims that in the last resort would contemplate the destruction of Soviet political authority and the emergence of a postwar world compatible with Western values." This was a major new statement on the utility of nuclear weapons, and it did not go unchallenged.

The Critique of Counterforce

Advocates of the counterforce doctrine maintain that this approach will provide responses for a greater range of contingencies than MAD does, that it allows for less-than-total nuclear devastation in the event of war, that it restores escalation dominance to the United States, and, at least implicitly, that it makes a preemptive first strike against the Soviet Union feasible if circumstances should so require. Looming over all of these justifications is the belief that, if nuclear war does occur, the United States should be in a position to prevail without jeopardizing its existence as a functioning society. Its critics, on the other hand, maintain that the new approach makes nuclear war more likely and that concepts of limited nuclear warfare and escalation dominance bear no relation to what would happen should conflict actually occur. They doubt that nuclear conflict can be limited and that "victory" in a nuclear war has any meaning. The criticism is especially directed at two assumptions of counterforce doctrine: that the United States could control its own behavior in a nuclear war, and that Soviet behavior would conform to the ground rules established by the United States. In addition, critics point out that counterforce can lead to a virtually endless arms race between the superpowers.

THE ISSUE OF SELF-CONTROL. If nuclear war is to be carefully and selectively applied both to realize U.S. war aims and to ensure that destruction remains limited, the United States must be in a position to control the extent of its own military activity in the course of conflict. This in turn involves a number of requisites. First of all, the United States must know in advance how much destruction a weapon would cause. But not all the effects of nuclear weapons can be confidently anticipated. While it may be possible to have a rough estimate of the damage that would be produced by the blast effect, the effects of heat and radioactivity are much more difficult to gauge. The damage that would be caused by fire would depend on such variable conditions as wind and humidity, and the magnitude of the radioactive effect would depend on such imponderables as the dissipation of gamma radiation (which would also depend on meteorological conditions) and the amount of contaminated food that is ingested. But if the effects of nuclear weapons can only be roughly approximated, it is not clear how one could "fine-tune" their impact so as to modulate the amount of damage inflicted and thus to maintain controlled reciprocity.

Furthermore, the ability to orchestrate the nuclear conflict requires excellent command, control, and communication capabilities. Commanders must be able both to give precise orders to those who have operational control over the weapons and to get feedback on what has actually been done. But, as we have already seen, these capabilities cannot be assured in the course of conflict. Much of the hardware involved is vulnerable to physical destruction, and the EMP could wreak havoc with electronic communication equipment. If it is difficult both to give specific orders and to know what their effect has been, it may not be possible to place a ceiling on destruction and escalation.

Moreover, a belief in limited nuclear conflict seems inconsistent with what is known about the psychological dynamics that cause conflicts to escalate.[21] It may be possible to maintain an attitude of cool detachment toward the conflict in military gaming rooms, but it is much harder to do so when passions are unleashed in actual warfare. When cities and people are being incinerated in a nuclear fireball, the desire to punish the enemy could easily overwhelm the subtleties of controlled reciprocity.

THE ISSUE OF SOVIET BEHAVIOR. If nuclear war is to be kept limited so that it bears some relation to political goals and allows the United States to survive as a functioning society, the Soviet Union must be willing to exercise as much restraint as the United States. In other words, it should avoid escalation beyond the level chosen by the United States and should try to terminate the conflict before the destruction gets out of hand. Can it be counted upon to do this?

Unlike the case in the United States, not much has been published in the Soviet Union regarding strategic doctrine, so that Soviet thinking on the subject must be inferred from limited evidence. The evidence that is available suggests that many of the strategic niceties developed in the United States have found no place in Soviet thought. From the Soviet point of view, subtle nuances are not realistic in strategic doctrine. War must simply be fought as effectively as possible. The U.S.S.R. does assign a principally deterrent function to nuclear weapons, though not of the sort associated with MAD. In Moscow's view, deterrence is achieved not with a capacity for finite destruction in a second strike, but by a capacity to prevail in nuclear war. Such thinking would seem to resemble the counterforce doctrine, but there are important differences. There is little to suggest a Soviet belief in the feasibility of limited nuclear war. Each side would suffer unprecedented losses, but, if deterrence is to work, the United States should expect even greater losses than the Soviet Union, assuring the latter of at least a Pyrrhic victory. It therefore does not appear that Soviet strategists believe a nuclear war can be fine-tuned to serve finite political goals; escalation, in their view, would not result from a set of deliberate and controlled moves and countermoves. Moreover, Soviet military practice and deployments make it likely that a conflict would escalate rapidly even if the United States wanted to limit its intensity. In the event of conflict, the U.S.S.R. seems determined to take the initiative at the very outset and to remain on the offensive throughout. Soviet military and political leaders believe that the course of a conflict is often determined in its early hours or days, and that this is likely to be especially true of nuclear conflict. It is thus no more than wishful thinking to rely on a tacit understanding between adversaries on the desirability of mutual restraint.

The low probability that nuclear war could remain limited had led former secretary of defense McNamara, an early proponent of counterforce and flexible response, to state, two decades later, that "nuclear weapons serve no military purpose whatsoever. They are totally useless—except only to deter one's opponent from using them." [22] Critics of counterforce would agree.

COUNTERFORCE AND THE ARMS RACE.   Quite apart from any evaluation of the impact of the new strategic approach on deterrence and escalation, it does seem to provide fuel for the arms race. U.S. military spending never grew as rapidly in peacetime as it did since President Carter's Directive 59 and President Reagan's election legitimized this doctrine of the utility of nuclear weaponry. In order to be able to destroy a wide variety of military as well as civilian targets on the other side, one must acquire a very large number of weapons. But as the number of one's own military systems increases, the adversary has more targets that must be covered, leading him to expand his arsenal, which then gives the first party a larger number of military systems to destroy, and so on. Whereas MAD places a ceiling on necessary weaponry, a drive for boundless military growth is built into the very logic of counterforce. In fact, one could well imagine that this, even more than abstract strategic considerations, explains the enthusiastic support given by military establishments on both sides of the Cold War to the acquisition of nuclear warfighting capability. In pursuit of its organizational interests, the military continuously seeks new and more weapons and missions; consequently, it welcomes a strategic doctrine that justifies these pursuits. McNamara realized this, which partially accounted for his shift to MAD and countervalue targeting. Similar interests almost certainly shape Soviet military attitudes as well. Raymond Garthoff, a respected analyst of Soviet strategic policy, has reported a debate that took place in the Soviet military press. General Bochkarev, deputy commander of the General Staff Academy, attacked the position of those strategic theorists who maintained that nuclear war could not be won in any meaningful way, declaring that it implied that, in other words, the armed forces of the socialist state . . . will not be able to set for themselves the goal of defeating imperialism and the global nuclear war which it unleashes . . . and our military science should not even work out a strategy for the conduct of war . . . in this case, *the very call to raise the combat readiness of our armed forces and improve their capability to defeat any aggressor is senseless.*[23] (Emphasis added.)

As Garthoff observed, "It is clear what is troubling General Bochkarev. The entire rationale for supporting Soviet military efforts is seen as undermined." [24]

To sum up, counterforce does provide for a wide range of responses to aggression and is therefore more credible to an adversary than a doctrine that provides only a stark choice between nuclear inaction and mutual destruction. In principle, then, it establishes a link between nuclear weapons and political objectives. On the negative side, it seems to be founded on two very questionable assumptions: that nuclear conflict can really be limited and that it can provide a military victory worth having. There is also reason to fear that counterforce capabilities could provoke a preemptive first strike in a crisis. Finally, the logic of counterforce calls for a virtually endless arms race between the superpowers and, since that is incompatible with a relaxation of tensions, for a state of permanent hostility between them.

The Search for Strategic Defense

The history of strategic doctrine and the arms race has been characterized by a primacy of offensive military systems. At the level of weaponry, far more has been done to facilitate attack than to thwart it, and this has been reflected in doctrinal thinking. Attempts at developing workable ABM systems during the 1960s were a partial exception to this rule, but the systems were considered technically unworkable and were limited by the 1972 ABM treaty. Deterrence has thus relied on the threat of total or limited punishment rather than on the idea of making the aggressor's weapons ineffective. The focus has been on swords, not on shields. But strategic doctrine, as has been pointed out, is strongly influenced by military technology and by the weapons being sought. Since the late 1970s, several developments, especially in laser and particle-beam technology, have guided thinking in the direction of strategic defense.

In a speech delivered in March 1983, President Reagan surprised even his closest advisers by calling for a major national effort to develop a shield in space that would make nuclear weapons "impotent and obsolete." The idea, said the president, was to make the United States invulnerable to nuclear attack and, in the interests of world peace, to share the technology with the Soviet Union. The project, called the Strategic Defense Initiative (SDI) by the administration but popularly known as "Star Wars," came to be envisioned as one of the largest research projects of all time. It soon became clear that the goal of protecting the civilian population was unrealistic, since, even if the shield were but slightly porous, tens of millions of people would die.

Accordingly, the objective has since shifted to the defense of major military facilities (missile silos, submarine pens, and airfields) and military-political command posts. The program has generated an enormous amount of controversy, focused on its technical feasibility and its ultimate desirability.

It is certain that the task of identifying, tracking, and destroying thousands of enemy missiles almost simultaneously is extraordinarily difficult. It would require military technologies that could not be tested under wartime conditions and that rely on developments not yet within the grasp of science—if indeed they are even theoretically possible. An enormous burden would be placed on ABM missiles and on such esoterica as laser beams, giant orbiting mirrors, space-based rail guns, extremely complex computer hardware and software, and charged particle beams. Rail guns, for example, would use electromagnetic fields to launch "smart" (that is, guided) projectiles toward the enemy's missiles. X-ray lasers powered by nuclear detonations would fire X-ray beams at targets before consuming themselves in fireballs, while ground-based lasers would bounce their beams off orbiting mirrors. Space-based sensors would identify targets and help coordinate battle activities. Since even a modest rate of "leakage" through the defensive shield would mean millions of deaths, the system would consist of several layers, so that missiles slipping through one layer could still be destroyed as they attempted to pierce the next one.

Not everyone agrees that the necessary technology can be developed. Some doubt that the extremely complex computer system can be expected to work, since there would be no chance to debug it in the only relevant environment, that of actual wartime conditions. Finally, many are convinced that it would be relatively cheap and simple to devise countermeasures that would neutralize much of the system's effectiveness. For example, the incoming missiles could disperse chaff to confuse the sensors. Missiles and warheads could be given a mirrorlike coating that would reflect rather than absorb the laser beams. It might even be possible to detonate a nuclear weapon in space to create electromagnetic waves that would wreak havoc with the earth- and space-based electronic systems on which the defense depended. Some critics also believe that a defensive shield that could destroy enemy missiles could also destroy the enemy's defensive shield. If each side could destroy the other's defenses with its own prior to launching an attack, the net effect of the system would be zero.

At present, it is not yet clear whether advocates or opponents of Star Wars have correctly gauged its technological feasibility. As for the desirability of a defensive shield, it is certainly true that impregnable defenses, by rendering all military action ineffective, would serve the cause of peace. If the military instrument of foreign policy could be completely neutralized, governments would have to abandon aggressive designs and learn to manage their relations in peaceful ways. But if the prospect is for anything short of *total* defense by technologies available to *all* parties, its desirability becomes much more doubtful.

Suppose that a system capable of destroying the great majority—90 or 95 percent—of an aggressor's missiles can be developed. Even so, according to critics, a number of problems would have to be resolved, and a number of conditions met, before the program could be called an unambiguous step toward peace.

The major justification for the U.S. to acquire a defensive military system is that it would complicate the Soviet war planners' calculations, making a nuclear attack a risky venture from Moscow's point of view. Most importantly, a preemptive first strike against the United States would not be feasible, for some portion of U.S. ICBMs would survive the attack and be available for retaliation. As the head of the SDI program, Gen. James A. Abrahamson, put it, even an imperfect defense will "decrease the confidence of the Soviet attack planners that they can achieve their attack goals." [25] Or, as Kenneth Adelman, director of the Arms Control and Disarmament Agency in the Reagan administration, said, "The way to think about SDI is that you want to diminish any rational Soviet calculation that they can achieve their war objectives by going nuclear." [26] Accordingly, the benefits of SDI could extend to deterring limited attacks against European targets, for example. If so, the transition from conventional to nuclear combat would become less probable, and if it did occur, the United States would be in a better position to prevail. Thus, at various levels, SDI could make nuclear war less likely or at least more winnable. Under those circumstances, it would be well worth the effort required by the program.

Critics are not convinced. To begin with, it is not entirely certain that SDI would improve the security of Western Europe. It could conceivably protect key NATO targets, such as airfields and command centers, from Soviet missile attacks during the early stages of a European war. But, say the critics, there is a paradox here: By decreasing the role of nuclear weapons in a European conflict, defenses of this sort could once again make Europe "safe" for conventional conflict—and the U.S.S.R. is generally regarded as having an edge in conventional forces in this part of the world.

Secondly, it is doubtful that SDI would make a Soviet nuclear attack against the United States less likely merely by blunting a first strike. If there is to be a "Star Wars race," the Soviet Union, as well as the United States, will probably acquire missile defense technology. The consequence, as Congress's Office of Technology Assessment has observed, could be impaired, rather than improved, U.S. security.[27] Perhaps the U.S. SDI system would manage to destroy most of the Soviet missiles involved in an initial attack, but even a modest amount of penetration could mean that much of the nation's land-based retaliatory force would be wiped out. The United States would then be in a position to launch but a limited retaliation, and the Soviet defenses would have to deal with only a "ragged response." Thus, the U.S.S.R. could well conclude that it would come out ahead in any nuclear exchange it initiated. Deterrence would obviously suffer.

A particularly dangerous situation could arise if the SDI defense system itself was vulnerable to preemptive attack. Should this be the case, the temptation in a crisis would be to attack the system in order to make sure the adversary could not launch an attack from behind the defensive shield. This danger is magnified by the fact that space-based weapons capable of destroying an incoming missile would be even more capable of destroying enemy satellites, which would be, comparatively speaking, "sitting ducks" for such weapons. But satellites are needed to provide early warning of attacks, so their vulnerability would make both sides more "trigger-happy" than might otherwise be the case. First strikes could thus become even likelier in the future than they are now. As Representative Les Aspin, D-Wis., chairman of the House Armed Services Committee, has observed, "The real danger is that we will end up destroying the idea of deterrence without achieving the perfect world of defense." [28]

At least three things are apparent so far: (1) The nuclear arms race has taken both superpowers further down the path of military growth than either had initially anticipated. (2) U.S. (and possibly Soviet) thinking on nuclear weapons is determined not so much by objective thinking as by a desire to accommodate the new military systems yielded by technology. (3) Neither the United States nor the Soviet Union appears to be substantially more secure now than it was before the arms race began or during any of its subsequent stages. If there is to be likelihood of an end to this futility, the fundamental dynamics behind the arms race must be addressed. The following chapter will explore these dynamics and the steps that have thus far been taken toward arms control.

Notes

1. Kosta Tsipis, "Third-Generation Nuclear Weapons," in Stockholm International Peace Research Institute, *World Armaments and Disarmament: SIPRI Yearbook, 1985* (London: Taylor and Francis, 1985), 83-102.
2. Ibid., 101.
3. "Star Wars Research Forges Ahead," *New York Times*, February 5, 1985.
4. "Pentagon Rebuts Charges of U.S. Military Weakness," *Defense Monitor* 9 (1980): 7.
5. James A. Nathan and James K. Oliver, *United States Foreign Policy and World Order*, 3d ed. (Boston: Little, Brown, 1985), 39.
6. See Gregg Herken, *Counsels of War* (New York: Alfred A. Knopf, 1985), Chapter 9.
7. Fred Kaplan, *The Wizards of Armageddon* (New York: Simon and Schuster, 1983), 43.
8. Quoted in ibid., 134.
9. Quoted in Lawrence Freedman, *The Evolution of Nuclear Strategy* (New York: St. Martin's, 1981), 81.
10. John Foster Dulles, "The Evolution of Foreign Policy," speech delivered to the Council on Foreign Relations, January 12, 1954, in *Department of State Bulletin* 30 (January 25, 1954): 108.

11. Quoted in Herken, *Counsels of War*, 103.
12. William Kaufmann, *Military Policy and National Security* (Princeton: Princeton University Press, 1956), 25.
13. For a discussion of these figures and an explanation of "equivalent megatons," see Alan C. Enthoven and K. Wayne Smith, *How Much Is Enough? Shaping the Defense Program, 1961-1969* (New York: Harper and Row, 1971).
14. See, for example, Bruce M. Russett, "Assured Destruction of What? A Countercombatant Alternative to Nuclear Madness," *Public Policy* 22 (1974): 121-138.
15. Quoted in Freedman, *The Evolution of Nuclear Strategy*, 348.
16. Fred Kaplan, *Dubious Specter: A Second Look at the Soviet Threat* (Washington, D.C.: Transnational Institute, 1977), 33.
17. Quoted in Leon Sigal, "Rethinking the Unthinkable," *Foreign Policy* (Spring 1979): 37.
18. The Carter administration's movement from MAD to counterforce is traced in Jeffrey D. Porro, "Counterforce and the Defense Budget," *Arms Control Today*, February 1978.
19. "Pentagon Draws Up First Strategy for Fighting a Long Nuclear War," *New York Times*, May 30, 1982. See also "Aide Says U.S. Policy Is to 'Prevail' over Russia," *New York Times*, June 17, 1982.
20. Colin Gray and Keith Payne, "Victory Is Possible," *Foreign Policy* (Summer 1980): 56-91.
21. See Robert Jervis, *The Illogic of American Nuclear Strategy* (Ithaca, N.Y.: Cornell University Press, 1984).
22. Robert S. McNamara, "The Military Role of Nuclear Weapons," *Foreign Affairs* 62 (1983): 79.
23. Quoted in Raymond L. Garthoff, "Mutual Deterrence and Strategic Arms Limitation in Soviet Policy," *International Security* 3 (1978): 120.
24. Ibid.
25. "Star Wars Strategy: The Russian Response," *New York Times*, December 17, 1985.
26. "In Star Wars Debate, Tactical Issues Nearly Get Lost in the Shuffle," *Wall Street Journal*, October 15, 1985.
27. Office of Technology Assessment, *BMD Technologies* (Washington, D.C., 1985), Chapter 6.
28. "'Star Wars' Research Progresses: The Vision vs. the Reality," *New York Times*, December 15, 1985.

c h a p t e r   t h i r t e e n

Controlling the
Arms Race

ONE OF THE GREAT paradoxes of contemporary politics is the simultaneous professions of commitment to arms control and the modest record of achievement in this regard. With few exceptions (notably President Ronald Reagan's first term in office), every U.S. administration and every Soviet leadership group have declared that arms control was one of their highest priorities, and yet, until quite recently, little has been accomplished toward that end. Negotiations have occasionally taken place and agreements have sometimes been reached, but these attainments have usually been overshadowed by parallel military developments. For each agreement that seemed to promise future moderation, the arms race has typically taken several giant steps forward, crushing any hopes that may have been fleetingly entertained. Recent successes, such as the treaty on intermediate nuclear forces (INF) signed in 1987, should not obscure the danger that the arms race could simply go in other directions—for example, toward "Star Wars" programs. It is likely that for each hour of work devoted to arms control, thousands are devoted to perpetuating the military rivalry and magnifying its proportions. The budget of the U.S. Arms Control and Disarmament Agency is only a fraction of what is spent on military bands alone in the United States. But despite the frenetic arms race, few would seriously argue that either superpower enjoys more security now than it did several decades ago, when they possessed considerably fewer and less powerful weapons.

It may seem surprising that this inglorious record generated so little adverse reaction within either the United States or the Soviet Union. While the authoritarian nature of Soviet politics and the Soviet citizens' lack of sources of objective information may account for the popular apathy there, the low level of public concern in the United States is more mystifying. Perhaps part of the reason is that statesmen and military leaders have not seemed eager to enlighten the public on the problems of arms control; they appear content with the assumption that, lamentable though the arms race is, it is the natural outcome of the other side's baseness, ambitions, and aggressiveness.

Ultimately, the problem is that the forces driving military growth have been objectively more powerful than whatever forces were available to restrain it. Those interested in arms control have therefore faced a herculean task. In order to assess the chances of curbing the arms race, it will be necessary to examine the forces driving the superpowers' military rivalry. First, however, let us see just what has actually been achieved so far by way of arms control.

The Arms Control Record

First Sporadic Efforts

Unlike the aftermath of World War I, the end of World War II did not produce a sense of urgency about arms control. The experience of Nazi aggression suggested to many that postwar peace should be built on armed vigilance rather than on rapid disarmament, and the emergence of East-West hostility further decreased enthusiasm for arms control, especially as the Cold War reached its peak in the late 1940s and early 1950s. Even so, the belief that military growth should ultimately be checked was always in the minds of responsible U.S. political leaders; in particular, they were convinced that atomic weapons should not be allowed to proliferate uncontrollably.

One of the first significant arms control proposals in the postwar period was made by the United States, after it had acquired its first atomic weapons but before the Soviet Union had tested one of its own.[1] In 1946, a report by Secretary of State Dean Acheson and David Lilienthal, chairman of the Atomic Energy Commission, urged that nuclear energy should serve peaceful rather than military purposes and that an international authority should be given a monopoly over research and development on nuclear energy. A formal plan to this effect was conveyed to the United Nations by the noted financier and political adviser Bernard Baruch. This plan called for a halt to the production of atomic weapons and suggested that those already in existence should be destroyed. It also proposed that all available information regarding the production of atomic energy should be turned over to an International Atomic Development Authority, a body of the United Nations to be created for this purpose. However, the transfer of information to the UN agency would have to be preceded by an international agreement on safeguards and sanctions against violators who sought to misuse atomic energy for weapons development.

This was in many ways an enlightened and generous offer, since it meant that the United States would unilaterally have given up its atomic monopoly. Nevertheless, Moscow turned it down, apparently because it would have prevented the Soviet Union from acquiring the knowledge needed to make atomic bombs of its own, thus, in its eyes, freezing it in an inferior position. Also, the Kremlin was afraid that the inspection and control requirements would mean a breach in the Iron Curtain, which, obsessed with the fear of foreign espionage, it would not permit. Thus, the Baruch Plan came to naught, and with it went possibly the last chance to rid the world of atomic weapons. By the end of the decade, East-West relations had deteriorated badly: the Communist coup in Czechoslovakia, tension over Berlin, and then the Korean War created a climate that was inhospitable to any agreements with the Soviet Union.

In the mid-1950s, however, a slight thawing of the Cold War brought renewed interest in arms control. In March 1955, President Dwight D. Eisenhower appointed a special assistant for disarmament. He also proposed to the Soviet Union that, in the interests of reducing both sides' fear of a surprise attack, they should agree to open their territory to aerial inspection by the other side's planes. But because the Soviet Union is a closed society, the Kremlin judged that the United States would gain a lot more by inspecting Soviet territory than vice versa. In fact, the proposal was viewed as a thinly disguised effort to make an opening for espionage, and it was rejected.

During the 1950s, nuclear bombs were regularly being tested in the atmosphere, and there was considerable public concern about radioactive fallout. Fallout from the explosion of a fifteen-megaton bomb on Bikini Atoll contaminated a Japanese fishing boat. Scientists discovered increasing amounts of strontium-90 in the bones of children, and international pressure against nuclear testing grew steadily. In 1958, the Soviet Union declared that it was unilaterally discontinuing testing; soon thereafter, President Eisenhower announced that the United States was willing to negotiate a test-ban agreement. But the United States, fearing that the Soviet Union might cheat, insisted on stringent verification. In particular, the United States was concerned that the seismic sensors which were to be the main instruments for verifying compliance might not be able to distinguish between underground nuclear explosions and earthquakes. For this reason, Eisenhower was inclined to prefer a partial ban, covering only atmospheric nuclear explosions, which produce fallout and are easier to detect.

It seemed possible at this time that some sort of agreement could be reached, but an unfortunate incident scuttled hopes of progress. In 1960, a high-altitude U.S. spy plane, the U-2, was shot down over Soviet territory. Although Eisenhower claimed that the plane was merely gathering meteorological data, its espionage equipment survived the crash, as did its pilot. A U.S.-Soviet summit meeting that had been scheduled to take place at just about this time was canceled, and no further progress on arms control was made during the remainder of Eisenhower's administration. When President John F. Kennedy entered office, he showed some interest in pursuing the possibility of a test ban, but the problem of verification again blocked the way. The two sides could not agree on the number of on-site inspections needed to supplement the data provided by seismic equipment.

Although it could be said that both superpowers lacked a firm commitment to arms control at this time, the Cuban missile crisis of 1962 once more gave impetus to a search for common ground. The brief brush with nuclear disaster was a sobering experience. Both sides decided that they had to do better than in the past, and two agreements were reached not long afterward. One was the 1963 pact establishing the hot line between Moscow and Washington, which has already been discussed in Chapter 11. The other was the Partial Test Ban Treaty, also signed in 1963, which prohibited nuclear testing in the atmosphere, in outer space, or under water. Because of the verification problem, the treaty did not prohibit underground nuclear tests; thus, it allowed for the continued development of nuclear weapons but without the danger of radioactive fallout.

In 1968, the Nuclear Nonproliferation Treaty was signed. It barred the transfer of the technology for making nuclear weapons to any nations that had not already acquired it, and it imposed safeguards on nuclear power-generating equipment to ensure that it would not be used to fabricate fuel for bombs. The treaty has been signed by most of the world's nations and has contributed to slowing down the rate at which other nations were acquiring weapons of mass destruction, but it did nothing to limit U.S. or Soviet military developments.

The SALT I Agreements

The first negotiated ceilings on the strategic weapons of the two superpowers were the product of an extended series of negotiations known as the Strategic Arms Limitation Talks, or SALT.[2] These negotiations began in Helsinki in November 1969 and were held alternately thereafter in Helsinki and Vienna. A primary goal of the United States was to limit the number of Soviet land-based ICBMs. The Soviet Union was anxious to halt the MIRVing of U.S. missiles (it had not yet begun to place multiple warheads on its own missiles). The talks also dealt with ABM systems. Although neither side got all it wanted, two major agreements growing out of the SALT negotiations were signed in 1972: the Interim Offensive Arms Agreement and the ABM Treaty. In addition, an agreement was reached on modernizing the hot line, as was a vaguely stated accord on reducing the possibility of accidental nuclear war.

The *Interim Offensive Arms Agreement* prohibited both sides from beginning the construction of ICBM launchers after July 1, 1972. The effect was that the number of launchers on each side (whether operational or under construction) was frozen at current levels: 1,054 for the United States and 1,618 for the Soviet Union. The agreement allowed increases in the number of missile-carrying submarines (up to 44 for the Soviet Union and 62 for the United States) and in the number of missile-launching tubes that these submarines could have (710 for the Soviet Union and 950 for the United States), but only if any increases were offset by the dismantling or destruction of a corresponding number of older strategic ballistic-missile launchers. Launchers rather than the missiles themselves were made the object of the limitations because their numbers were considered to be more easily verifiable. No limits were placed on MIRVing or on missile accuracy.

Opposition to the treaty was voiced in the United States on the grounds that it granted the Soviet Union higher overall ceilings on strategic weapons launchers, but these numbers were misleading in several respects. First, the United States had nuclear-capable bombers based in Europe that could reach Soviet territory. Soviet proposals to include them in the overall ceiling were rejected. On the other hand, the United States successfully opposed Soviet efforts to place controls on MIRVs. The net result was that, despite the Soviet edge in launchers, the United States continued to have a considerable lead in warheads (3,550 to 2,090). Finally, some U.S. submarines were based in Spain and Scotland, which meant that they could easily reach battle stations within range of targets in the Soviet Union. Soviet submarines had no access to facilities in the vicinity of the United States and therefore would have to spend much more time simply getting to stations from which they could attack their targets. The complaint that the treaty gave strategic advantages to the Soviet Union is thus an example of something that was pointed out in Chapter 12: there are many ways of comparing strategic strength, and one's conclusions tend to reflect the biases one starts out with. If there were disappointing aspects of the SALT I agreement, they were that it called for not an actual *reduction* in either side's arsenal, but merely a ceiling on launchers that would maintain the status quo, and that it did nothing to limit the *qualitative* arms race—the development of ever more destructive weapons, through MIRVing, improved accuracy, and other changes.

The *ABM Treaty* dealt with defense rather than offense. The official rationale for this treaty, from the U.S. point of view, was connected to the MAD doctrine. If either side felt totally protected by its ABM system, it might be emboldened to launch an attack, thinking it could do so with relative impunity. However, the official rationale may have been less important than the fact that a truly effective ABM system was not considered technologically feasible at the time, for, had it been technologically feasible, pressures to deploy it would have been overwhelming and the ABM Treaty probably would not have been signed. By the terms of the agreement, both sides pledged to restrict their ABM deployments to two sites: one near a population center, the other protecting an ICBM site. Somewhat later, and in recognition of the fact that no workable system really existed, the number of ABM sites was limited to one. The United States constructed its single site at Grand Forks, North Dakota, but later abandoned it.

Thus, the treaty on offensive missiles did nothing to reduce their numbers, and the treaty on ABM defenses limited a system which neither side thought it could develop. Hence, their significance lay in what they seemed to portend rather than in what they actually attained. They suggested that there was a new spirit of cooperation between the two superpowers, raising hopes for future and perhaps more far-reaching agreements on strategic weapons.

The SALT II Treaty

Another round of negotiations, known as SALT II, began in 1972. The talks lasted seven years (more than twice as long as SALT I), a period marked by deteriorating U.S.-Soviet relations and a shift of U.S. public opinion toward a more harshly anti-Soviet sentiment. A considerable amount of opposition to the entire concept of arms control emerged, based on the beliefs that the Soviet Union invariably hoodwinked the United States and that the only reliable road to national security was successful military competition with the Soviet adversary. When a treaty was finally signed by President Jimmy Carter and Soviet leader Leonid Brezhnev in 1979,[3] opposition to the treaty within the Senate made it appear unlikely that it would obtain the two-thirds majority required for ratification. In any case, when the Soviet Union invaded Afghanistan in December 1979, the president withdrew the treaty from Senate consideration, and it has not been ratified.

The SALT II treaty dealt only with offensive arms and did so in considerably more detail than had SALT I. It set limits on total numbers of strategic nuclear weapons and delivery vehicles and sublimits on particular types. Thus, each side was permitted to have 2,250 strategic nuclear delivery vehicles; 1,320 launchers for MIRVed ICBMs and bombers carrying cruise missiles; 1,200 launchers for MIRVed missiles, whether ground-launched or submarine-launched; and 850 MIRVed ICBMs. The treaty also addressed the issue of qualitative improvements. It limited the number of warheads that could be mounted on a missile to the maximum number that that type of missile had been tested with. For ICBMs, this meant ten warheads; for SLBMs, eight. Considering that the largest Soviet ICBM, the SS-18, could theoretically have accommodated as many as forty warheads, that was a serious limitation. The treaty altogether banned certain new types of strategic systems—for example, missiles that differed by more than 5 percent in specified ways from existing missiles. To facilitate verification of compliance, the treaty obligated both sides to conduct all their strategic missile-testing on established test ranges, which were closely monitored by the other side's satellites, and it stated that neither side was to encode the stream of telemetric information (radio signals) that its missiles sent back during testing if that would hinder compliance monitoring by the other side. Since this telemetry provided information about a missile's performance characteristics, it could alert either side to violations by the other of the prohibitions against new missiles.

All in all, the SALT II treaty was the most comprehensive arms control agreement that the superpowers had reached. Unlike SALT I, it dealt with qualitative as well as quantitative issues, and it actually implied a slight reduction in the number of Soviet ICBMs. Although its ratification fell victim to Soviet behavior and the change in U.S. public opinion, it did have considerable effect on the subsequent course of the arms race and on the continuing debate over arms control.

After SALT

When President Reagan took office in 1981, his administration showed little interest in further arms control negotiations. Although the administration agreed to abide by SALT II temporarily, its attitude seemed to be that military superiority was the only sound basis for dealing with the Soviet Union. Thus, instead of beginning a new round of negotiations, the administration set out on the biggest peacetime military buildup in U.S. history. The argument was that a strong military position would make Moscow more forthcoming in any future negotiations, and if it failed to do so, the military strength could be used to the U.S. advantage. As Richard Garwin said of the nation's new leaders, "They believe we can't lose by pursuing this route because either we will be able to use it [militarily], or we will be able to use it politically to coerce them, or—if the Soviets manage to get this capability—they will destroy themselves economically." [4]

Apart from the overall political mood, a number of new strategic circumstances were complicating the outlook for arms control. To begin with, theater-nuclear (that is, intermediate-range) weapons deployed in Europe emerged as a thorny problem. Since 1977, the Soviet Union had been deploying its new SS-20 theater-nuclear missile in the European part of the U.S.S.R. This weapon embodied some major new features: a longer range, placing all of Europe within its reach; a mobile deployment mode, making it harder to locate and destroy; and an ability to carry three warheads. Concern with this new development led NATO to call for the deployment of U.S. Pershing 2 missiles in West Germany and ground-launched cruise missiles in several European countries. Thus, an entirely new category of nuclear weapons was added to the set of those that would have to be dealt with in efforts at arms control.

In addition, the decision of both the United States and the Soviet Union to embark on ambitious research programs designed to produce a "Star Wars" capability added another layer of problems for future negotiations. Probably because of its lag in the technology required for space-based weaponry, the U.S.S.R. has pressed strongly for an abandonment of the SDI, or for at least a promise not to carry it beyond the research stage, as a quid pro quo for concessions on existing forms of strategic weaponry. The Reagan administration vigorously has resisted any restrictions on its Star Wars programs.

After a two-year hiatus, the administration entered into two sets of negotiations with the Soviet Union in Geneva: one on strategic weapons, the other on theater-nuclear armaments. However, there was a widespread impression that the main purpose of these talks was to placate a public opinion which was becoming increasingly dissatisfied with the U.S. government's uncompromising posture. In fact, the initial proposals advanced by the United States appeared mainly designed to be rejected by the other side. The Soviet Union, for its part, seemed more interested in stirring up European public opinion against the plan to deploy the Pershing 2 and cruise missiles than in serious bargaining. Under these circumstances, no progress was made during President Reagan's first term in office. Indeed, when deployment of the Pershing 2 and cruise missiles began, the Soviet Union broke off the talks altogether.

However, soon after the beginning of President Reagan's second term, a renewed interest in arms control was evident. Apparently stung by criticism of his lack of interest in arms control, the president made overtures for a resumption of the Geneva talks. Moscow, which had failed to prevent deployment of the theater-nuclear weapons in Western Europe, returned to the bargaining table. The new round of talks seemed to be marked by a more serious spirit than that of the Reagan administration's first term.

The negotiations culminated in a U.S.-Soviet summit meeting in December 1987, at which a treaty was signed to remove all short- and medium-range missiles (both of which were considered theater-nuclear forces) from the European continent. For the Soviet Union, this meant the destruction of all its SS-20s, its older SS-4s, and two types of short-range missiles (300 to 600 miles). In return, the United States agreed to give up all of its ground-launched cruise missiles and Pershing 2s. For the first time in the history of superpower arms control, an entire category of nuclear weapons was to be eliminated. Unlike SALT I and SALT II, which involved only the *freezing* of arsenals at current levels, this was a case of arms *reduction*. Moreover, it reflected a significant change in the Soviet Union's attitudes toward arms control. Moscow agreed to give up a significantly larger number of theater-nuclear warheads than Washington (about 1,500 as opposed to about 350). Furthermore, and also for the first time, Soviet authorities agreed to extensive measures of on-site inspection to monitor compliance with the terms of the agreement. At the same summit meeting, the two sides also reached a tentative agreement to consider reducing the number of their strategic (long-range) warheads by at least 50 percent—a step that would have a far greater impact than the December 1987 treaty.

These new steps toward arms control inspired more optimism than most observers had felt for decades, but many years must pass before it will be known whether this optimism was justified. There is a danger that reductions in strategic and theater-nuclear forces may be compensated for by major strides in other areas: weapons for antisubmarine warfare, for example, or Star Wars systems. But it is impossible to judge the long-term prospects for arms control if the dynamics that drive the arms race are not understood. Some of these forces stem from the international system, and others are rooted in the superpowers' own societies.

The Dynamics of the Arms Race

Most people both in the United States and in the Soviet Union firmly believe that their own country's military forces are purely defensive. Their country must arm itself because the other side does as much; its military programs are regrettable but necessary, for their national security demands no less. The arms race is thus seen as a spiral of actions and reactions, with the rival performing the actions and one's own country the reactions. If this process is to be halted, the adversary must stop taking uncalled-for military initiatives, and one's own country can then be counted upon to follow suit. The forces that propel the arms race, however, are more complex than that.[5]

The Action-Reaction Thesis

A great deal of research, using sophisticated techniques, has gone into an exploring of the idea that the arms race is a sequence of moves and countermoves, in which both sides are locked and from which neither is willing to bow out for fear of the consequences.[6] The results of these studies have been surprisingly inconclusive. Although no one would seriously claim that Soviet military activity is irrelevant to the United States or vice versa, there is little evidence that the arms race is predictably interactive, that what each side does is invariably a response to some previous or current activity of the other side. It does not appear, for example, that the rates of U.S. and Soviet military spending can be predicted from the other's defense outlays. Even when spending only for strategic weapons is considered, the action-reaction thesis is not borne out.

On the contrary, both sides have embarked on military programs that had no convincing relation to any developments on the part of the adversary. For example, the Soviet acquisition of SS-20 missiles cannot be construed as a response to anything the United States had done or was planning at that time to do. Similarly, the U.S. development of cruise missiles, and for that matter the entire Star Wars program, cannot be plausibly linked to any prior Soviet activities. At first glance, military programs often seem to be related to the rival's activities, but more probing inquiry casts doubt on this relationship. The decision to MIRV is a case in point.

Upon the discovery in the early 1960s of a string of radars along the "Tallinn Line" on the western border of the Soviet Union, U.S. intelligence analysts speculated that the Soviet Union was well on its way toward developing an ABM system. In November 1964, a huge canister dubbed the "Galosh" and believed to contain an interceptor missile was displayed at a military parade in Moscow. In 1966, the Soviet Union began deploying a ring of these missiles around Moscow, a move that was interpreted in terms of deterrent logic: If an ABM system protecting Soviet cities from a retaliatory strike was deployed, a major constraint on a Soviet first strike would be removed and a central principle of deterrence would therefore be jeopardized.

The Pentagon and its supporters argued that the nation's security required an ability to penetrate Soviet defenses and that this could best be accomplished by placing several warheads on each U.S. missile. By thus MIRVing the missiles, it would be possible to overwhelm the Soviet ABM system, and deterrence would thus be preserved. The reasoning seemed convincing, and in 1970 the first U.S. MIRVed missiles became operational.

Certainly, this had the ingredients of action and reaction: the Soviet Union developed an ABM system capable of preventing U.S. retaliation, and the United States reacted with a logical counterweapon. However, the action-reaction explanation does not stand up to closer scrutiny.

Although the Soviet Union did begin deploying Galosh missiles around Moscow in 1966, the program slowed down the following year, and by 1969 only sixty-seven missiles had been deployed.[7] By the late 1960s, CIA experts seem to have concluded that the Tallinn radars were a defense against attack by strategic bombers and could not be used against missiles.[8] The justification for MIRVs as a necessary response to a Soviet move was thus no longer valid. Nevertheless, deployment of MIRVed Minuteman III missiles began in 1970, as a result of which the number of U.S. warheads reached 4,000 that year—an effort that is very hard to relate to any conceivable ABM deployment on the Soviet side. In 1972, the ABM treaty removed any vestige of the rationale for the MIRV program, yet the program continued apace for several years, apparently driven by a logic and momentum of its own.

The point should not be overstated. Any major military initiative by the Soviet Union will provoke a response from the United States (and vice versa), and neither Soviet nor U.S. defense expenditures would have attained their current levels if the other side did not exist. But action-reaction may not be at the core of the arms race. What appears to be the case is that a military move by one side is a *sufficient* but not a *necessary* cause for a response. In other words, the United States will always react to threatening Soviet moves, but it will also undertake actions of its own that the Soviet Union has done nothing to provoke. The same is true of the U.S.S.R. Thus, there must be other drives behind the arms race. These are, for the most part, located within each nation's society, and they are of four sorts: political, bureaucratic, economic, and technological.

The Political Reward Structure

The tenure of governments in the United States depends on popular approval, which can be jeopardized by charges of irresponsible political action. An important and recurring issue in U.S. politics is how to deal with the Soviet Union, and, in this respect, the government can err in either of two ways. On the one hand, it can be insufficiently attentive to national security because it *underestimates* the Soviet threat. On the other hand, it can be too prone to *overestimate* the danger from the Soviet Union and thus to take unnecessary and costly steps that further fuel the arms race. The political consequences of these two sorts of errors are likely to be very different.

If an incumbent administration is believed to have underestimated the Soviet threat, the repercussions are likely to be quite serious. The political opposition is likely to accuse it of irresponsibility, gullibility, and possibly even lack of patriotism. As the 1980 election may have demonstrated, the electoral consequences can be very unfavorable for a government thus accused. If, on the other hand, the administration is said to have overestimated the danger and perhaps undertaken needless military programs, the effects are likely to be milder. At worst, that segment of the public that is seriously concerned with arms control might feel indignant. But this is a relatively small proportion of the electorate, and its protests would probably be outweighed by the approval of those who feel that it is better to be too careful than not careful enough.

In recognition of this difference, political leaders are more inclined to overestimate than to underestimate the threat. Worst-case estimates of the foreign threat are thus likely to be the norm, and the arms race is stimulated independently of objective security needs.

Although the Kremlin plainly is not subject to electoral pressures, a rough analogy can probably be found in the structure of rewards and punishments in the Soviet Union. The chief difference is that Soviet decision makers are judged not by the general public but by their colleagues in the Politburo, and perhaps the Central Committee as well. But, as Malenkov's and Khrushchev's experience demonstrated, Soviet decision makers deemed guilty of underestimating U.S. military strength are apt to be treated more harshly than those who err by overestimating it.

Bureaucratic and Organizational Forces

It was pointed out in Chapter 5 that the interests of governmental organizations, especially the major bureaucracies, are important influences on foreign policy. This applies to defense policy as well. The people who staff the bureaucracies typically come to identify with the organization's interests, which are usually defined as appropriating the largest possible amount of budgetary resources and obtaining as many and as important policy missions as possible. When the interests of different bureaucracies clash, as they often do, policy is partially the result of the struggles between them. In this respect, it is significant that the biggest bureaucracy in the U.S. government, both in terms of manpower and share of the federal budget, is the Pentagon, and since it is so much more powerful than its bureaucratic rivals, it is more likely to get what it chooses to press for. Other bureaucracies related to national security, such as the Central Intelligence Agency, have interests which are more peripheral to the arms race, but they are nevertheless powerful actors within the governmental structure, and they are intensely concerned with national security. Consequently, organizational pressures embedded in the political system usually ensure that there will be a minimum degree of military growth, no matter what the national interest might require. These pressures operate through organizational routines as well as through interorganizational rivalries.

Most governmental bureaucracies are mammoth organizations. The burden of their bureaucratic weight, the complexity of their structure, and the rapidly changing nature of the world they must deal with lead them to make their tasks more manageable by adopting simple and routinized ways of handling their problems. One example is the budgeting process, which has been described as follows:

> Participants in budgeting deal with the overwhelming burdens by adopting aids to calculation. By far the most important aid to calculation is the incremental method. Budgets are almost never actively reviewed as a whole in the sense of considering at once the value of all existing programs as compared to all possible alternatives. Instead, this year's budget is based on last year's budget, with special attention given to a narrow range of increases or decreases.[9]

In the case of an organization like the Pentagon, and given the nature of political rewards and punishments discussed above, these increments are more likely to be upward than downward changes. This bureaucratic momentum is probably another of the reasons for military growth. The situation in the Soviet Union, where an even greater part of political life is conducted by bureaucratic organizations, must be very similar.

In addition to the struggle between the Pentagon and other bureaucracies, in which, as already discussed, the odds are in favor of the Pentagon, there is a parallel and perhaps even more important struggle *within* the Pentagon, and that is the rivalry among the armed services.[10] The attempts of the army, the navy, and the air force to match or outdo each other may account for some of the most pronounced surges in military growth. For example, the sudden increase in U.S. missile capability in the 1960s, even after it had become clear that the Soviet missile force already lagged considerably behind America's, may be partly explained by interservice competition for a role in long-range missile programs. After the Soviet Union's successful launchings of Sputnik I and Sputnik II, the air force was able to substantially increase its space-related activities, which included various missile and satellite projects. Not wishing to be outdone by a rival service, the navy acquired the Polaris missile and pressed for a navigational satellite known as Transit. Thereupon, the army lobbied for and got the Juno I intermediate-range missile system.

It seems that as soon as the possibility of adding a function, weapons system, or other program to the national military effort appears on the horizon, each service strives to garner as big an addition to its resources and roles as possible. The inevitable result is a particularly strong pressure for expansion, which leads to an even greater surge in the arms race than had previously been anticipated. Again, there is every reason to believe that this process works in a similar fashion in the Soviet Union.

The Economic Dimension

The economic role of military spending is related to the economic role of public spending generally, a role that was given prominence in Keynesian economic theory. Keynesian economics rejected the "classical" notions of the automatic adjustment of employment (through wage levels) and investment (through interest rates) to levels consistent with economic equilibrium. It argued, instead, that savings sometimes failed to translate into equivalent amounts of investment; business activity then fell short of an economy's productive capacity, and unemployment, decreased consumption, and recession or even depression might be the outcome. In such circumstances, government spending should supplement private investment and consumption to effectuate the necessary adjustment. Military spending can perform this function on a large scale. As a leading economist has pointed out, "If a large sector of the economy, supported by personal and corporate income taxation, is the fulcrum for the regulation of demand, plainly military expenditures are the pivot on which the fulcrum rests." [11]

Of course, military spending is not a necessary tool of economic policy, nor are governmental outlays the only way of propelling economic growth. Still, defense budgets are usually very expandable, and they are often politically more acceptable than public spending for civilian needs. Indeed, there is some evidence that, other things being equal, the rate of growth of military spending is likely to increase at times when private demand is sluggish and to retract in years when private demand is more vigorous. [12]

There is another twist to this. One of the most important determinants of the outcome of elections in the United States is the state of the economy. Incumbent senators, representatives, and presidents are more likely to be voted back into office if the economy is doing well than if it is not. [13] Moreover, it has been shown that incumbents make an especially great effort to generate economic growth in the year of a major election and during the year preceding it. They try to use the tools of economic policy at their disposal to affect the timing of economic cycles so that upswings occur when it is politically most beneficial to have them occur—a sort of "political business cycle." [14] This suggests that there may be a corresponding "military economic cycle." Research has shown that such cycles may indeed exist. [15] Although the idea may seem startling, it is worth invoking a recollection of Richard Nixon's. He reports that, while he was vice president, Arthur Burns, President Eisenhower's economic adviser, visited him and

> expressed great concern about the way the economy was then acting . . . Burns' conclusion was that unless some decisive governmental action were taken, and taken soon, we were heading for another dip, which would hit its low in October, just before the elections. He urged strongly that everything be done to avert this development. He urgently recommended that two steps be taken immediately: by loosening up credit and, where justifiable, by increasing spending for national security. [16]

Politics and economics never operate independently of each other, and this applies to the politics of defense spending as well.

The Drive of Technology

Many observers believe that the foundation of the arms race is to be found in the advances, often little noticed, in military-related research and development. Although this research may be too esoteric to seize the attention of the general public, it does arouse the interest of a variety of specialized lobbies that would benefit from having it applied to actual military systems. They include the scientists who participate in the research, the agencies and institutions that sponsor it, and private companies that anticipate lucrative contracts as producers of the new weapon or equipment. Whatever may be the military situation at the time, they begin to develop a strategic rationale for the innovation, perhaps declaring that it is absolutely essential to national security or that it is the answer to something that the Soviet Union might possess or be capable of possessing some day. The military itself soon joins the coalition (and internal rivalries may sharpen its interest), as do the political supporters of the military and a segment of public opinion. The arguments for deployment are developed and refined, and the burden of proving that the need does *not* exist will fall on the usually less well-organized opponents of military growth.

Again, the MIRV is a case in point. We have already seen that attempts to justify this development in terms of deterrent needs were unconvincing in light of the limited, and technically imperfect, Soviet ABM system. The decision to MIRV U.S. missiles was at least as much the result of a technological push. The capacity to deliver several warheads independently from the same missile requires a number of complicated maneuvers. Following the initial boost out of the atmosphere, a "bus" carrying several warheads must coast along a planned trajectory and eject a warhead at the appropriate moment. It must then adjust its trajectory and accelerate its pace toward a second target, to which it delivers another warhead, and the process is repeated until all the warheads carried by the missile have been fired.

The ability to execute this set of maneuvers was the outcome of several earlier projects, none of which had a MIRV system as its final goal. The first such project was the development, in 1960, of a missile named Able-Star, with a propulsion rocket that incorporated a restart and guidance capability; its purpose was to launch satellites rather than to deliver nuclear warheads. Three years later, the Agena rocket, capable of placing a pair of satellites into different orbits, was developed. Finally, an advanced postboost control system, Transtage, was created for use with the Titan III rocket. Like the Able-Star and the Agena, it was capable of coasting and restarting, but it could engage in even more complex maneuvers (as well as carry a larger payload). Its initial mission was to launch a series of defense satellites into different orbits. The requisites for a MIRV weapon were thus assembled from a series of programs that were unrelated to the objective of overwhelming an adversary's missile defenses.

As the technology took shape, a movement devoted to ensuring its eventual military application gathered momentum. Since a stronger rationale than the launching of multiple satellites seemed necessary, the concept and strategic justification for MIRV weaponry was articulated, first by participants in the research and development process. A number of private industrial companies and consulting firms soon joined in, and to these were added the powerful voices of the air force and navy leadership. The influence of this coalition was overwhelming, and in 1970, the first MIRVs were deployed. Their number continued to increase steadily, despite the subsequent treaties on ABM limitation. As an observer of the MIRV process has remarked, "Once the technology was developed MIRV assumed a momentum of its own; the chances of halting it were by then very slim." [17]

Military growth, then, includes far more than an attempt to match or to outdo the Soviet Union (although that is certainly part of it). It is, in addition, propelled by powerful political, bureaucratic, economic, and technological forces, all of which are woven into the fabric of U.S. society. It must be assumed that similarly powerful domestic forces fuel the Soviet Union's defense activities. Compared to these forces, those that press for arms limitation appear feeble indeed. The arms race does not rank high among the concerns that occupy the average person. The political reward structure discourages modest estimates of the Soviet threat, and there are no bureaucracies with a vested interest in arms control which enjoy power comparable to those with opposite interests. Although the economy almost certainly suffers in the long run from excessive military spending, the short-term employment effects of military production, and the often profitable contracts by which it is carried out, tend to suppress other concerns. And, finally, technology carries its own imperatives.

The Conditions for Arms Control

Despite the asymmetry between the forces promoting military growth and those opposing it, there are steps that can be taken to improve the outlook for arms control.

Creating a Favorable Climate

Mutual hostility and distrust are the major elements of U.S.-Soviet relations. Each side is convinced that the other harbors predatory intentions and fears being victimized if it were to let its guard down. As has been pointed out, these perceptions are grounded, from each side's point of view, in some historical fact. Moreover, the forces behind the hostility have become entrenched in the social, political, and economic institutions of the two societies. Hostility, in turn, affects the arms race in two ways: It furnishes convenient grounds for undertaking military activity in response to essentially domestic needs, and it provides a basis for interpreting such activity by the other side as a threat to national security. These two effects reinforce each other, but the mechanism can also be reversed: If domestic drives could be checked, the readiness to perceive the other side as threatening would decline.

There is, of course, nothing inevitable about hostility. Nations that once viewed each other as implacable foes have, at times, become friends and allies. France and Germany, which had fought against each other in three major wars in seventy years (the Franco-Prussian War, World War I, and World War II), came to be considered inevitable enemies—yet they are now two of Europe's closest friends. During the 1960s, China was regarded as an irrational and thoroughly hostile nation with which the United States might well have to do battle one day; but by the late 1970s, the two countries had virtually become allies. Two conditions have usually preceded such changes. First, there is sometimes a radical internal change within one of the two adversaries, leaving it to be regarded as a genuinely different nation by its rival; for example, this was the case with Germany after denazification and China in the post-Mao era. Second, the two countries have occasionally discovered a common enemy, one which has appeared as a greater menace to both of them than they are to each other, and the existence of this common threat has drawn them together. The Soviet Union has played that role both for France and Germany, on the one hand, and for the United States and China, on the other.

Nevertheless, it is unlikely that either of these two will apply to the United States and the Soviet Union. Neither country is likely to experience a major internal restructuring in the near future (although this may be ultimately inevitable for the Soviet Union), and it is implausible that a threatening common foe will emerge to draw the two superpowers together. Although it seems that some degree of antagonism will continue to characterize U.S.-Soviet relations, efforts should be made to curb this hostility so that it does not get out of hand and so that it does not provide a rationale for an uncontrollable arms race. Moreover, ways should be found of moving toward arms control despite the hostility, by maneuvering around it. Let us examine more closely the possibilities for *controlling* and *circumventing* hostility.

Psychologists who have studied the dynamics of threat perception and hostility reinforcement often agree that positive reinforcements are more effective in changing behavior than are negative sanctions. That is, rewards for "good" behavior are more likely to elicit desirable behavior than are punishments for "bad" behavior. The implication for U.S.-Soviet relations is that when the Soviet Union does something we approve of, every effort should be made to express our approval and to make an appropriate reward. Even if it is politically unavoidable that Soviet misbehavior will evoke some form of punishment from the United States, cooperation should be rewarded with at least as much zeal as misbehavior is punished. To interpret every instance of Soviet moderation as evidence of weakness, of an advantage for the United States that must be pressed, removes any incentive for future cooperative behavior, increases Moscow's threat perceptions, and ultimately exacerbates hostility even beyond its previous levels.

Another important step in controlling hostility is to avoid the tendency to allow attitudes and behavior toward the Soviet Union to be dictated by domestic political imperatives. Very often, when U.S. political leaders make a conciliatory move, they fear being accused of appeasement, insufficient vigilance, and failure to "stand up" to the Communists. Statesmanship requires that political leaders resist domestic political pressures when seeking a stable structure for peace and arms control. Moreover, as noted in Chapter 3, the U.S. public often approves of moves toward coexistence and away from confrontation.

But no matter how mature and enlightened political leadership may be, some degree of U.S.-Soviet hostility has to be expected for the foreseeable future. The challenge is to move toward arms control despite this persistent antagonism. In this regard, ways should be found to insulate arms control from other aspects of U.S.-Soviet relations. It is usually desirable to emphasize that, even when the United States feels obliged to show its disapproval of some Soviet action, it is still in the interests of the United States to refrain from undermining arms control. When the public has been angered by something the Soviet Union has done, a common reaction is to deny the desirability of talking to Moscow, the implication being that the United States is doing the Soviet Union a favor by negotiating for arms limitation and that the favor should be withdrawn when it misbehaves. But if the benefits of arms control are mutual—if both nations derive substantial benefits in terms of security and economic savings—then the interests of the United States are best served by continuing to move toward arms control, whatever the state of relations between the two countries.

Of course, this principle is easier to state than to act on, and domestic political pressures make it difficult to negotiate and sign agreements with the Soviet Union when it has just committed some outrageous act. Yet, on logical grounds at least, such a separation can be considered beneficial, and it must be stressed that statesmanship requires both a willingness and an ability to rise above short-term political calculations.

Controlling the Domestic Drives

The domestic pressures that work against arms control may be even more difficult to overcome than the antagonism that pits the superpowers against each other, and this applies to all four of these types of pressure—political rewards, bureaucratic interests, the economic functions of military growth, and technological drives.

The system of political rewards and punishments is an integral part of the structure of the political system, and any attempt at changing it has implications that go beyond the issue of arms control. Since the bias apparently operates in a similar fashion in the Soviet Union, it may be inseparable from the fact of being a superpower. If so, the problem may be intractable, and all that can be done at present is to recognize that it is a problem.

That it is difficult to resist the pressures of bureaucratic organizations may seem puzzling. After all, these organizations are part of the executive branch, which is hierarchically structured, and the political leadership at the top of this structure should be able to impose its policy. However, as was discussed in Chapter 5, these organizations are often impervious to "outside" efforts to move them, and they can sometimes even undermine established national policy. Particularly in foreign policy, this power and relative autonomy stem from the volume and complexity of the problems confronted, the specialized knowledge and skills required to deal with them, and the need for continuity and predictability of behavior. Here again, the situation is probably similar in the Soviet Union. As political scientist William Taubman has observed, "Soviet governmental behavior reflects not only the Politburo's deliberate political purpose but also the mode of operation of complex large-scale organizations that even a powerful central leadership cannot always and everywhere control." [18]

In the United States, the military bureaucracy is even able to evade the principle of civilian supremacy within the executive branch by winning over political allies in the legislative branch of government. Adam Yarmolinsky, a former Defense Department official, has described some of the methods that are used:

> The Pentagon takes a "carrot and stick" approach to Congress. The biggest contract awards have tended over the years to go to key members of the military committees, who in turn usually vote for the Pentagon's program. One former White House assistant said a special technique was employed by the services whenever the White House or the Secretary of Defense vetoed one of the service's favorite projects or wanted to buy something it did not want. "In this case," he said, "the service lines up a friendly Congressman to plant questions when the chief of staff of that service or another high-ranking officer appears on the Hill. The Congressman will ask the officer his 'professional' opinion on the weapons system, as opposed to the official Defense Department line." Then, he said, after the officer rendered his opinion, "the friendly faction of the committee has a field day criticizing the Secretary of Defense for not doing something the service chief thinks is in the national interest." [19]

It might be unwise for political leaders to constantly challenge the estimates that the armed services make of their own needs, but these leaders need to have the power to prevail when military appetites conflict with goals that are deemed to be in the national interest.

In devising ways to deal with the economic pressures for military growth, it must first be acknowledged that certain groups in the population would experience considerable, if only temporary, economic difficulties if these pressures were diminished. However desirable arms control may be on other grounds, it means that workers will lose defense-related jobs, companies will lose lucrative defense contracts, and congressional representatives in the affected districts may lose electoral support. Thus, effective arms control policy would have to include provisions for easing the transition from military to civilian production. These could include monetary compensation for lost income and assistance in acquiring new skills and in moving to new areas.

Furthermore, measures should be taken to make it easier for industries that have been heavily dependent on military contracts to move into other areas of economic activity. Different forms of contracts can be considered for firms that suffer a big drop in defense orders, and these should involve skills and expertise that are related to the firms' previous work for the military. The development of public transportation networks could, in some cases, provide a useful alternative source of activity; the further expansion of civilian space programs is another possibility. One interesting type of high-technology function, which a number of former defense contractors would be well suited to perform, involves the development and production of the ultrasophisticated equipment of arms control verification—the sensors, reconnaissance instruments, and decoding equipment for telemetric information that are essential to negotiated curbs on military growth and the need for which would increase with the progress of arms limitation.

The technological drives behind the arms race may be particularly difficult to control, because the scientific activities that yield new weapons do not necessarily originate as such. It is often hard to anticipate whether or how a given research program can be put to military purposes until it is well advanced, and by the time its military uses have become clear, the constellation of groups supporting it is often too powerful to be stopped. Moreover, since many technological innovations can serve both military and civilian needs—consider, among numerous examples, the internal combustion engine and the integrated circuit—unwanted applications can rarely be thwarted without jeopardizing desirable ones.

Nevertheless, there may be ways of checking the tendency of science and technology to spur military growth without undermining their ability to benefit society in other ways. In particular, it might be useful to pursue limitations on the testing of major military systems.[20] Testing is a crucial part of the research and development process that fuels the arms race; it provides validation of the proposed weapon by demonstrating that it is operationally workable. In the military area, this is usually the last step before a decision is taken to produce and deploy the new system. By the time the R&D process reaches this stage, the military applications of the innovation are quite evident; it merely remains to be demonstrated that it is operationally effective. Prior to the testing phase, on the other hand, the options may be relatively open. A civilian or military use of the discovery might be possible, and if a military application seems likely, it may be desirable or undesirable. Also, before the phase of actual testing, the forces promoting the new military system may not yet be so mobilized as to be politically unstoppable. Thus, by limiting the testing of certain systems, it may be possible to close the gate on unwelcome military applications.

Although the superpowers have discussed restrictions on the actual detonation of nuclear weapons, such talks have not usually involved a broader conception of limitations, such as limitations on the flight-testing of strategic missiles or of space-based weaponry. Without the necessary foundation of political will, it would not be possible to negotiate and implement meaningful testing innovations, but by doing so, a major step could be taken toward reasserting control over technological dynamics which have tended, partly by their own imperatives, to determine the nation's political and strategic options.

To sum up, the arms race is not simply a competition between two adversaries which could come to a halt if either of them exercised self-restraint. Although it is partly an interactive process, military growth has more complex sources, some of them intrinsic to the nature of the superpowers' societies. In turn, the arms race affects the tone of superpower relations, their strategic doctrines, and even the likelihood of global nuclear destruction. These factors, even aside from the economic burden it places on both societies, make the arms race perhaps the single most important problem which the superpowers face. Merely to dismiss it as the result of the other side's baseness and aggressiveness provides no useful insights or guidelines for solutions. Arms control policy must take U.S.-Soviet relations into account but it cannot be limited to bilateral issues. It would be useful to detach arms-limitation negotiations from other aspects of U.S.-Soviet relations and from domestic political demands. Effective arms control must also address the political, bureaucratic, economic, and technological roots of the arms race. This is a formidable agenda, but the stakes are immense.

Appendix: Principal Arms Control Agreements Signed by the United States

1925   Geneva Protocol: Prohibits the use of poison-gas and bacteriological weapons.

1959   Antarctic Treaty: Internationalizes and demilitarizes the Antarctic continent and provides that it shall be used for peaceful purposes only.

1963   "Hot Line" Agreement: Establishes a direct link, by teleprinter and telegraph, between the White House and the Kremlin for immediate communication during crises.

Partial Test-Ban Treaty: Signatory nations agree not to conduct nuclear tests in the atmosphere, in outer space, and under water.

1967   Outer Space Treaty: Prohibits the deployment of weapons of mass destruction in outer space and limits the use of the moon and other celestial bodies exclusively to peaceful purposes.

Latin American Nuclear-Free Zone Treaty: Establishes Latin America as a region in which no nuclear weapons will be deployed.

1968   Nonproliferation Treaty: Seeks to prevent spread of nuclear weapons to nations not already possessing them; introduces safeguards against international spread of technology for making nuclear weapons.

1971   Seabed Arms Control Treaty: Prohibits emplacement of nuclear weapons on the ocean floor.

"Accident Measures" Agreement: The United States and the Soviet Union agree to improve arrangements for guarding against unauthorized or accidental use of nuclear weapons and to immediately notify each other in case of such use.

"Hot Line" Modernization Agreement: Improves the existing hot-line link by the addition of two satellite communication circuits.

1972   Biological Weapons Convention: Prohibits deployment, production, acquisition, and stockpiling of biological weapons.

SALT I ABM Treaty: Restricts the superpowers to two ABM deployment sites each and prohibits sea-based, air-based, and space-based ABM systems.

SALT I Interim Offensive Arms Agreement: Limits number of U.S. and Soviet ICBM and SLBM launchers.

1973   Prevention of Nuclear War Agreement: Commits the United States and the Soviet Union to avoid situations that might lead to nuclear conflict and to consult with each other if such a risk should arise.

1974   ABM Protocol: Further restricts ABM deployment by limiting each side to one ABM site.

Threshold Test Ban Treaty:° Prohibits underground nuclear weapons tests with a yield exceeding 150 kilotons.

1976   Peaceful Nuclear Explosions Treaty:° Prohibits underground nuclear explosions for peaceful purposes of a yield exceeding 150 kilotons.

1977   Environmental Modification Convention: Prohibits military or other hostile use of environmental modification techniques.

1979   SALT II Treaty:° Limits the United States and the Soviet Union to 2,250 strategic nuclear delivery vehicles, with sublimits on various types of missiles and launchers; places qualitative restrictions on strategic-weapon innovations.

1987   INF Treaty: Obligates the United States and the Soviet Union to remove all theater-nuclear weapons from Europe.

° Treaty was signed but not ratified by the United States.

Notes

1. A good historical overview of the early postwar attempts at superpower arms control is provided in John H. Barton and Lawrence D. Weiler, *International Arms Control: Issues and Agreements* (Stanford: Stanford University Press, 1976).
2. The SALT negotiations are vividly chronicled in John Newhouse, *Cold Dawn: The Story of SALT* (New York: Holt, Rinehart and Winston, 1973).
3. A good narrative of the SALT II talks is provided in Strobe Talbott, *Endgame: The Inside Story of SALT II* (New York: Harper and Row, 1979).
4. Garwin is quoted in Gregg Herken, *Counsels of War* (New York: Alfred Knopf, 1985), 318.
5. The following section is based on Miroslav Nincic, *The Arms Race: The Political Economy of Military Growth* (New York: Praeger, 1982).
6. See, for example, Nancy Lipton and Leonard S. Rodberg, "The Missile Race: The Contest with Ourselves," in *The Pentagon Watchers*, ed. Leonard S. Rodberg and Derek Shearer (New York: Doubleday, 1970), 36-61; A. F. K. Organski and Jacek Kugler, *The War Ledger* (Chicago: University of Chicago Press, 1980); Albert Wohlstetter, "Is There a Strategic Arms Race?" *Foreign Policy* (Summer 1974): 3-21.
7. Nincic, *The Arms Race*, 17.
8. Ibid.
9. Otto A. Davis, M. A. H. Dempster, and Aaron Wildavsky, "A Theory of the Budgetary Process," *American Political Science Review* 60 (1966): 529.
10. On this subject, see Samuel Huntington, *The Common Defense* (New York: Columbia University Press, 1961).
11. John Kenneth Galbraith, *The New Industrial State* (New York: Penguin, 1967), 235.
12. Miroslav Nincic and Thomas Cusack, "The Political Economy of U.S. Military Spending," *Journal of Peace Research* 10 (1979): 101-115.
13. See, for example, Gerald Kramer, "Short-Term Fluctuations in U.S. Voting Behavior, 1896-1964," *American Political Science Review* 65 (1971): 131-143, and Edward Tufte, "The Determinants of the Outcome of Mid-Term Congressional Elections," *American Political Science Review* 69 (1975): 812-826.
14. The classic work on this topic is Edward Tufte, *The Political Control of the Economy* (Princeton: Princeton University Press, 1978).
15. Nincic and Cusack, "The Political Economy of U.S. Military Spending."
16. Richard M. Nixon, *Six Crises* (New York: Doubleday, 1962), 309.
17. Herbert York, "Multiple Warhead Missiles," in *Progress in Arms Control?*, ed. Bruce M. Russett and Bruce G. Blair (San Francisco: W. H. Freeman, 1979), 6.
18. William Taubman, "The Change to Change in Communist Systems: Modernization, Post-Modernization, and Soviet Politics," in *Soviet Politics and Society in the 1970s*, ed. Henry W. Morton and Rudolf L. Tokes (New York: Free Press, 1974).
19. Adam Yarmolinsky, *The Military Establishment: Its Impact on American Society* (New York: Harper and Row, 1971), 41-42.
20. This is further developed in Martin B. Einhorn, Gordon L. Kane, and Miroslav Nincic, "Strategic Arms Control through Test Restraints," *International Security* 8 (1983-1984): 108-151.

National Prosperity
and
International Welfare

chapter   fourteen

Economic Relations
in the Developed World

MAINTAINING COOPERATION with other Western industrialized countries (including Japan) is vitally important to U.S. foreign policy. They are the nation's principal friends, to which it is linked by shared interests that go beyond common security needs. The industrialized democracies are, above all, linked by a common belief in core political values, which include representative government, open elections, and guaranteed civil liberties. These countries support one another by mutual example and provide proof, on a large geographical scale, that democracy is a workable political arrangement. In addition, these are societies whose prosperity depends on their economic cooperation: it is inconceivable that the West would be nearly as wealthy as it is today without the benefits of open commerce among its members.

Despite these strong ties, there are several areas of discord between the industrialized democracies. As was pointed out in Chapter 9, they have somewhat different views about the proper methods of dealing with the Soviet Union. For example, the nations of Western Europe are less willing to rely as much on military solutions to East-West problems; they are more inclined to favor diplomatic means of dealing with Moscow and to believe in the benefits of economic leverage over the Soviet Union as well as in arms control. Thus, the European members of NATO strongly opposed the Reagan administration's decision in May 1986 to abandon the SALT II treaty. On the other hand, where their security interests are most directly involved (as with regard to nuclear weapons in Europe), they are often less enthusiastic about arms control than is the United States.

The United States and its allies also tend to squabble over their respective contributions to the common defense and over their economic relations. Of these issues, it is probably the last mentioned, particularly trade relations, that most rankles the U.S. public and that represents the greatest threat to Western solidarity. For these reasons, and because economic issues have a number of special features, this chapter is devoted to these problems.

It is important to emphasize that political and economic issues are inseparable. Economics deals with the creation and distribution of wealth, politics with the exercise and distribution of power—but plainly, wealth and power have very much to do with each other. Political systems create a context within which economic activity is pursued; economic systems shape the contours of political relations and institutions. The distribution of wealth often determines the distribution of power, and vice versa. Economic conflicts frequently lead to political conflicts, and economic interdependence tends to strengthen political friendships. These general truths are particularly applicable to relations within the Western industrialized world, whose overall solidarity will very much depend on how its economic controversies are handled.

The Advantages of Free Trade

There is widespread agreement today that free trade is the ideal form of international economic relations, but that has not always been so. On the contrary: During the great portion of the history of economic thought, protectionism has been favored over free trade. Between the fifteenth and eighteenth centuries, both on the European continent and in England, this preference was reflected in the doctrine of *mercantilism*. The doctrine was tightly entwined with the political order of the era: the establishment of centralized monarchies from out of the loosely structured feudal arrangements of the Middle Ages, and the rise of nation states whose power was manifested in overseas expansion. According to mercantilism, political power ultimately depended on economic wealth, and economic wealth was measured in terms of the possession of precious metals, mainly gold. Gold, in turn, was acquired by having a surplus in the nation's balance of trade, because international payments were made in gold, so that a country that exported more than it imported would receive more gold than it paid out. Accordingly, the key to power and wealth was to promote one's own exports at the expense of those of other countries and to discourage imports. This implied that international economic relations were inherently conflictual: one side's surplus was another's deficit, and mercantilist policies thus came to be called "beggar-thy-neighbor" policies. International political relations were frequently the victim.

By the end of the eighteenth century, mercantilism had come to be recognized as self-defeating. The case against it was made by some of the greatest figures in the history of social thought. One of them, David Hume (1711-1776), argued that if a favorable balance of trade did lead to an influx of gold, this would have the effect of driving up the prices of a country's products (since gold was money, an increased supply of which fuels inflation). As these prices rose, other countries would be less willing to buy the products, and exports would therefore decrease. Soon afterward, Adam Smith made a compelling argument for the benefits of unrestricted commerce in his famous work, *The Wealth of Nations* (1776). Finally, David Ricardo (1772-1823), the founder of international trade theory, demonstrated that if all nations specialized in producing that which they could make most efficiently, exporting their surpluses and importing from others the products that could be made more efficiently elsewhere (the theory of *comparative advantage*), the wealth of all the trading partners would increase. The logic was persuasive, and *free trade* came to be accepted by Western nations as the most desirable economic relationship. The theory has undergone numerous revisions and refinements, but few today would contend that nations would not, in general, be more prosperous by allowing a free flow of exports and imports.

The political arguments in favor of free trade are as strong as the economic ones. As was also pointed out in Chapter 9, countries that are economically interdependent tend not to allow their relations to deteriorate too far, for they have too much to lose thereby. One of the most stable regions of peace in history is constituted currently by the nations of the OECD, consisting of Western industrialized nations that are heavily dependent on each other for trade and investment. Even such long-standing international rivalries as that between France and Germany have been buried in recent decades partly as a result of economic cooperation.

The case for free trade is greatly reinforced by the memory of the most recent period of its absence. After World War I, most Western industrialized nations experienced a surge of economic growth, which was largely attributed to the unfettered operation of market mechanisms both within and between these nations. Economies grew, living standards rose, and a kind of social euphoria swept through the West, expressed in the United States by the phrase "the roaring twenties." When the bubble burst, beginning with the stock market crash in October 1929, the shock and disillusionment were profound. The crash was followed by the Great Depression, which started in the United States and ultimately spread throughout the industrialized world. The U.S. national product dropped by nearly one-half, banks failed, and unemployment was as high as one-third of the labor force. The situation in Western Europe was even more dire. In Germany, a country especially hard hit by the Depression and the accompanying drastic decline in international trade, Adolf Hitler was brought to power by a public desperate for any solution to the economic morass (see Chapter 7).

As national income fell and joblessness soared, the natural reflex was to try to keep out imported goods that competed with domestic products. It seemed wrong to allow foreign producers to sell their goods at the expense of domestic producers and at the expense of the home country's workers who made those goods. In the United States, the Smoot-Hawley Act of 1930 erected the highest tariff barriers the country had ever had. Economic nationalism and cutthroat protectionism became the norms of international relations. One economist has described the situation this way:

> Exports were forced; imports were curtailed. All the weapons of commercial warfare were brought into play: currencies were depreciated, exports were subsidized, tariffs raised, exchanges controlled, quotas imposed, and discrimination practiced through preferential systems and barter deals. Each nation sought to sell much and buy little.[1]

Yet these very measures exacerbated each nation's predicament. As protectionism spread, the fruits of free trade disappeared. Quotas were met with quotas and tariffs with tariffs. When one trading partner depreciated its currency, to discourage imports by making them more expensive, the others typically did the same. Soon, no nation was selling much abroad, and without international markets, the Western nations found themselves deprived of one of the main pillars of their past economic success. The worse conditions became, the more intense was the pressure for ever more stringent protectionism. Thus, a collapse of economic solidarity and cooperation went hand in hand with the rise of nazism and fascism, and the world marched toward its second major war in the century.

The Economic Order after World War II

The need for cooperation and economic coordination among the Western industrialized nations was realized as soon as World War II ended. It was generally acknowledged that the economic collapse of the 1930s had provided a fertile breeding ground for totalitarian movements of the right. Fascism had, in fact, been enthusiastically accepted by many people desperate for a solution to their economic predicament, and there was now the further fear that domestic Communist movements, many of which had distinguished themselves during the war, would turn any new economic troubles to their own ends. Thus, it was a matter of internal political, as well as economic, necessity that all should be done to ensure postwar prosperity.

Moreover, there was the fact of the rapidly developing Cold War between East and West. The wartime alliance between the Soviet Union and the Western allies had never been a very smooth relationship, and barely had victory been assured than the Cold War became the dominant fact of international life (see Chapter 2). As fear of the Soviet Union increased, the conviction grew that only an economically strong West could stand up to a Soviet military threat. To the extent that prosperity and unfettered trade were regarded as inseparable, economic and political goals were also firmly linked.

If these goals were to be achieved, certain changes would have to be made in international economic relations. Barriers to trade, whether in the form of tariffs or quotas on foreign imports, would have to be reduced or removed. New monetary arrangements would also be necessary, since protectionism could be pursued through monetary policies as well as direct restrictions on trade. When one nation buys goods from another, it must usually pay for these goods in that other nation's currency (since this is obviously what the sellers of the goods use for their own purposes). This foreign currency must be purchased with the currency of the buying nation, and its price is given by the exchange rate between the two. If one nation's currency is expensive relative to that of another, then the second will have to pay relatively high prices when it imports goods from the first, and consequently it will buy less. If, conversely, the first country's currency is relatively cheap, its exports are likely to increase. Because of this, a country will sometimes depreciate its currency relative to that of its trading partners, in an effort to increase its exports, decrease its imports, and improve its balance of payments and (at least temporarily) its domestic welfare. But other nations would probably not accept this passively; instead, they would depreciate their own currencies in retaliation, and so on, in a vicious circle— which is exactly what happened after World War I. Thus, monetary relationships can endanger free trade as much as tariffs and quotas can.

A reformed economic order was instituted by two major agreements: the General Agreement on Tariffs and Trade (GATT), signed in Geneva in 1947, and the Bretton Woods agreement, signed in 1944 at the New Hampshire resort by whose name it is known. The former dealt with matters of trade, the latter with international monetary arrangements.

The major thrust of GATT was to establish an open and nondiscriminatory trading order. It prohibited the use of quotas and other quantitative restrictions on imports, except under very exceptional circumstances. It also provided for a gradual reduction in tariff barriers between GATT signatories through successive multilateral negotiations. Perhaps most importantly, it stipulated that tariff reductions should be applied in accordance with the "most-favored-nation" principle, which obligated each signatory to accord to all GATT members tariff rates no less favorable than those applied to the similar products of any one signatory nation. Thus, GATT amounted to a commercial code of free and nondiscriminatory trade which introduced "a form of permanent international oversight and accountability for commercial policies that, prior to its existence, were viewed as exclusively national prerogatives." [2]

The major aim of the Bretton Woods agreement was to avoid competitive currency devaluations by establishing a system of fixed exchange rates between the currencies of the member nations. In order to keep the relative values of national currencies stable, a common measure of their value would have to be employed, and it was decided that the parity of currencies would be established in terms of gold. Each nation's currency would be valued according to the amount of gold it could be exchanged for, and this valuation was to be fixed and subject to only minor changes. The resulting stability and predictability of exchange rates were expected to facilitate free trade. To oversee these arrangements and enforce the rules, an International Monetary Fund (IMF) was created. Exchange-rate adjustments could occur only when deemed absolutely necessary to a country's balance of payments, and only with IMF approval. If a balance-of-payments problem should arise for a member of the system, its first step would be to turn to the IMF for credits to finance a temporary disequilibrium. Another institution created at Bretton Woods was the International Bank for Reconstruction and Development (known as the World Bank), whose function was to provide loans for postwar economic recovery, so that a vigorous international economic order could be built quickly. Thus, and largely under U.S. leadership, an institutional framework for recovery, growth, and free trade was erected. The difficulties of the interwar period had been identified and, it was thought, resolved.

However, the problems of the international economy seem to have been underestimated, and the benefits of recovery were elusive at first. On the one hand, the economic devastation wrought by World War II was enormous. Much of Western Europe's productive capacity had been destroyed, and the cost of reconstruction was even greater than anticipated. Moreover, the European nations had rather small domestic markets and therefore needed international trade in order to grow; but since the consequences of the war were felt by virtually the whole continent, and since these countries were traditionally each other's major trading partners, their export markets had disappeared. Neither the resources of the IMF nor those of the World Bank were adequate to meet existing needs.

There was another obstacle to implementation of the new international financial order. A major premise of the order was that national currencies be convertible into gold. This assumed that sufficient gold would be in the hands of each of the nations concerned, and that was not the case. Partly because of its favorable balance-of-trade position and partly because of gold transfers during the war, the United States held approximately two-thirds of the world's total gold currency supply, while most other countries had insufficient amounts.[3]

The new agreements were thus not enough, in and of themselves, to launch postwar economic recovery. The United States, as the only Western nation to have emerged economically strengthened from the war, was called on to play an even larger role. To deal with the problem of inadequate gold reserves, the role that gold was originally to have had was assigned to the U.S. dollar. Instead of a gold-exchange standard, the industrialized nations moved to a *dollar* standard, which was feasible since the dollar itself was directly convertible into gold (at thirty-five dollars an ounce). It was, for all practical purposes, as "good as gold." Thus, countries could measure the respective values of their currencies in terms of their exchange rate with the dollar. Moreover, as the dollar came to be accepted as the Western world's currency, nations would want it both for purposes of trade and as an internationally acceptable reserve of wealth. They would therefore not be inclined to demand conversion of all of their dollar holdings into gold, and the United States would not have to fear significant downward pressures on its currency. In many ways, therefore, a solution to the scarcity of gold seemed to have been found.

Another problem was that dollars were not widely enough available. This problem was solved in two ways. Ordinarily, other nations could have earned dollars by exporting more to the United States than they imported from it, but given the state of most European economies at the time, this was not a realistic expectation unless special provisions were made. What was required was that the European countries be allowed to engage in a certain amount of protectionism. Though this was contrary to the free-trade premise of the new order, it was considered a necessary and temporary evil if rapid recovery was to be ensured. Thus, the United States not only tolerated, but actually supported, a modicum of discriminatory trade practices directed against itself.

Secondly, the United States took unilateral measures to inject dollars into the international system. Mostly, this took the form of foreign aid, through such vehicles as the Marshall Plan (named for the secretary of state who proposed it) and a variety of bilateral aid programs. Between 1948 and 1952, the United States gave sixteen West European nations some $17 billion in outright grants. Furthermore, Washington was anxious to reconstruct Western military power as a defense against a possible Soviet threat. Military assistance programs, as well as the dollar spending by U.S. forces stationed in Europe, also contributed to the outflow of dollars and to the provision of liquidity for the postwar international economic system.

Thus, through the exercise of U.S. leadership, which recognized the connection between the nation's economic and political goals, the dollar became the new international currency, and, by extension, the United States became the world's central banker. Gradually, impediments to free trade were reduced or removed. Among the clearest manifestations of the determination to create a system of free international commerce were the successive rounds of tariff-reduction negotiations sponsored by GATT. These culminated, in 1967, in the so-called Kennedy Round agreements, which included a broad reduction of the tariffs on nonagricultural goods among GATT members. Trade between Western nations more than doubled during the 1960s.[4] In the United States, which remained much less dependent on foreign trade than most other industrialized countries, the share of exports in GNP rose from 4.4 percent to 6.8 percent.[5]

The Emergence of Neomercantilism

The new system seemed, then, to have been successfully launched. Indeed, the reconstruction of both Western Europe and Japan exceeded most expectations. With their technological know-how and strong motivation, their recovery achieved considerable momentum, and by the 1960s, Europe—with a "miraculous sprint in productivity growth"[6]—emerged as a major economic competitor to the United States. Several years later, Japan became a rival to both. The recovery of the European nations was also facilitated by the formation of the

European Economic Community (EEC), which provided them with an expanded local market and the basis for an efficient international division of labor. In 1971, for the first time in the twentieth century, the United States had a balance-of-trade deficit, one which has been steadily growing ever since.

The position of unrivaled economic leader, which the United States had come to take for granted, was being increasingly challenged. This was not only because of the resurgence of Europe and Japan, but also because of shortcomings in U.S. economic performance. The United States had become less competitive in several ways. First, a large part of its economic growth has always been due to the superior productivity of U.S. labor, which means that it took fewer work-hours to produce a given product in the United States than it did abroad. But by the mid-1960s, productivity was growing more rapidly in Japan and in a number of European countries than in the United States.

Secondly, the U.S. economy became afflicted with considerable inflation, largely because of the Vietnam War. The military involvement in Southeast Asia was extremely expensive, but because the war did not enjoy much domestic support, President Lyndon B. Johnson was loath to finance it with higher taxes. Rather, he attempted to do so by borrowing, and the resulting budgetary deficit unleashed inflationary pressures which the economy had to live with for the next fifteen years. Inflation tends to make a country's goods more expensive abroad and foreign goods less expensive at home. The effects were an increase in the balance-of-payments deficit and rising unemployment.

Yet a third explanation for the deteriorating economic position of the United States was found in the multinational corporation. The rapid growth of Western European and other nations led to numerous and profitable investment opportunities abroad, opportunities of which many U.S. corporations availed themselves. In some cases, foreign investment was motivated by a desire to take advantage of cheaper foreign labor, and in other instances it was prompted by the existence of affluent foreign markets to which goods produced by U.S. corporations could be sold. If these corporations or their subsidiaries produced the goods in the country in which they were sold, the corporations could avoid tariff barriers and so be in a better position to penetrate the foreign market. But goods produced abroad for sale abroad added nothing to U.S. exports, while goods made in a foreign country for reexport to the United States increased U.S. imports. For both reasons, the U.S. balance of payments, and the employment of its workers, suffered.[7]

The growing U.S. deficit and the loss of economic dominance has had consequences both on the nation's relations with its allies and on domestic attitudes toward free trade. In the aftermath of World War II, the dependence of the industrial democracies on U.S. military support, exports, and aid was evident and widely accepted. But by the 1960s, their economies had recovered and they were major exporters in their own right. Consequently, their need for U.S. dollars decreased. Imports from the United States were a less important presence on their markets, and as their own exports entered U.S. and international markets, more dollars were being earned. The postwar dollar shortage was turning into a dollar glut, to the disadvantage of holders of dollar reserves. An implicit understanding that U.S. friends would not present their surplus dollars for conversion made these countries, for all practical purposes, unwilling creditors. And as they found themselves holding dollars whose value, due to inflation, was falling, they were "importing" the economic problems of the United States. The United States wanted its friends to revalue their currencies upward, thus making their exports less competitive, but this they were understandably reluctant to do.

Moreover, as Europe's economic dependence on the United States diminished, its willingness to follow the U.S. lead in foreign policy waned as well. Especially with the détente of the 1960s and 1970s, it was less inclined than the United States to continue giving security issues as important a position as they had had since the end of the war. This meant that another bond among the Western nations had weakened.

Within the United States, inflation and the balance-of-payments deficit were reflected in slackening rates of domestic growth and in rising unemployment, both of which had become, by the time the administration of President Richard M. Nixon assumed office, major political issues. The Johnson administration ultimately felt compelled to deal with the inflationary pressures it had created by a combination of tax surcharges and restrictive monetary policies, but by the end of the decade the problems had still not receded. The next administration was tempted to devalue the dollar, to discourage imports and promote exports, but this would have been contrary to the Bretton Woods agreement, which the United States itself had promoted. Meanwhile, policies designed to curb inflation were increasing unemployment and jeopardizing economic expansion. By 1970, the country was in the throes of a recession. Unemployment reached 6 percent and real GNP shrank by approximately $3.5 billion. The political consequences were inescapable: that year, the Republican party experienced serious reverses in congressional and state elections.

The pressure to seek a solution in protectionist measures became stronger and stronger. Foreigners, concerned with the value of the dollars they found themselves saddled with, were increasingly presenting their holdings for conversion into gold. By the late summer of 1971, the U.S. gold stock had declined to 10 billion dollars, and there were 80 billion of dollar holdings that could be presented for conversion. On August 15, 1971, without consulting other countries and in defiance of Bretton Woods, President Nixon declared that henceforth the dollar would no longer be convertible into gold. In the future, its value was to "float" to whatever level international market forces pushed it. Concurrently, and possibly in violation of the GATT agreement, Nixon imposed a 10 percent surcharge on imports into the United States.[8] The postwar international economic order was dealt a staggering blow by the nation that had been its chief architect.

Neomercantilism and Politics

The integrity of even the best-conceived economic order is inevitably subordinated to the existing structure of political interests: When political expediency so dictates, economic principles are often abandoned. As one observer has remarked about the end of the dollar's convertibility: "Nixon's political survival seemed in flat contradiction to the requirements of the Bretton Woods monetary regime. Rather than continue the recession to save the dollar, Nixon let the dollar depreciate to save his Administration." [9]

In other words, a purely economic logic, operating independently of the political realm, may be unworkable in the context of practical politics. In any case, the West seems to be reverting to the policy of subordinating economic requirements to political interests, which was identified above as mercantilism. It is now known as *neomercantilism*, and as before, it leads to a variety of economic inefficiencies and problems.

International trade and capital movements affect a variety of vested interests within the societies of the trading partners, and professional lobbyists and practicing politicians mobilize to shape commercial policies accordingly. For example, in Chapter 6 it was pointed out that both labor and business groups lobby against competing foreign imports and that they are frequently successful in this endeavor. Adam Smith and David·Ricardo may have believed that a national economy should be unaffected by anything outside the marketplace, but that was expecting too much. In a democracy, foreign economic policy is unavoidably the outcome of a process of political bargaining, in which groups representing a variety of interests compete in promoting their own policy preferences. For example, automobile makers, who benefit from access to cheap foreign steel, may clash with domestic steel makers, who want to exclude foreign steel; exporters may want more public resources used to build up external markets, whereas advocates of domestic welfare programs may want more resources to be devoted to expansion of those programs. The outcome of such disputes is determined by the relative power of the groups involved.

Foreign economic policy is influenced by international as well as domestic political forces. The decision by the United States to promote the postwar international economic order and the recovery of Western Europe and Japan was dictated by Cold War considerations at least as much as by purely economic concerns. Likewise, Europe's readiness to challenge U.S. economic leadership and to treat its own GATT obligations in a rather cavalier fashion had much to do with the perception of a lessening Soviet threat and with a decreased reliance on the U.S. security shield. This raises the possibility that, as economic rivalry becomes more intense, the fundamental political bonds within the Western industrialized world may recede into the background, or even that the economic realm may itself become an area of political conflict. As one economist and policy maker has warned:

When trade relations sour, they infect other areas of policy, even "high policy," via domestic political attitudes and pressures. As public antagonism in the arena of trade mounts, it erodes the president's freedom to pursue constructive actions toward other countries in other arenas as well as trade.[10]

In any case, mutual recriminations became common by the early 1970s. Most of the accusations that the trade rivals leveled against each other did have some basis. For example, one U.S. complaint against the EEC concerned the Common Agricultural Policy (CAP), which protected European agricultural goods (see Chapter 9). The revenues derived from these levies were used to subsidize agricultural exports from the Common Market countries to other countries whose markets, in the absence of these subsidies, they would have been unable to penetrate. This was clearly a discriminatory form of protection, and it created particular problems for the United States, where farm groups resented being kept out of European markets. However, the CAP had been established at the insistence of President Charles de Gaulle of France, who had to deal with powerful and well-organized agricultural interests in his own country.

Similarly, the United States found cause for irritation with Japan. During the 1960s, Japan's share of world exports virtually doubled, from 3.2 to 6.2 percent, and by 1970, when the United States was heading toward its first balance-of-trade deficit in decades, Japan's exports were growing at an annual rate of 20 percent.[11] But this performance owed much to neomercantilist practices: severe import restrictions, aggressive export subsidies, and resolute limits on foreign investment. In addition, the Japanese maintained a substantially undervalued yen as a tool of economic protectionism. The anger that these policies provoked in the United States was reflected in threats in the Senate's refusal in 1971 to ratify a treaty reverting to Japan jurisdiction over the island of Okinawa, which the United States had appropriated for its military purposes after World War II.

When taken to task for flaunting the GATT rules, the European nations retorted that the United States had also been guilty, albeit in more subtle ways, of violating free-trade principles. A major charge against the United States involved its policy of seeking "voluntary export restraints" on goods that threatened domestic producers, a policy that at the very least violated the spirit of GATT. In 1962, the United States had organized a series of multilateral talks leading to the Long-Term Cotton Textile Agreement, which discouraged textile exports to the U.S. market and which was updated, in 1974, as the Multi-Fiber Agreement. Similar agreements proliferated in the 1970s and included "voluntary" restrictions on exports to the United States of steel, electronic equipment, footwear, and other goods. In addition, legislation in the United States, notably the Trade Reform Act of 1974, made it easier than before for U.S. industries to claim injury from foreign competition and to use the courts to force the government to impose tariffs and countervailing duties on imports.

Although new rounds of negotiations were undertaken in the hope of avoiding further obstacles to free trade, they no longer had the kind of support that they had had in the 1960s. The Tokyo Round, begun in 1973 and concluded in 1979, did lead to some reductions in tariffs on manufactured goods. But in general the agreements were more notable for their emphasis on nontariff barriers (NTBs), such as sanitary and public-health restrictions on imports, government procurement policies that discourage the use of foreign goods, and environmental regulations that penalize imports. The Tokyo Round, though it did not do much to eliminate NTBs, did codify a set of rules to govern their use—for example, in deciding which sorts of NTBs imposed by one country would be considered fair retaliation for those imposed by another country. Obviously, this was very different from the Kennedy Round of the previous decade.

By the mid-1970s, the decline of U.S. industrial production had reached alarming proportions. A nation that had dominated the world automobile market was finding that foreigners were buying fewer and fewer of its cars while its own citizens were showing an increasing preference for Japanese (and, to a lesser extent, European) automobiles. A nation whose industrial strength had been largely based on steel production now found that it was among the least efficient steel producers in the developed world; less expensive steel products from abroad were flooding the U.S. market, while the country's traditional steel-producing areas were experiencing economic decay and high rates of unemployment. Textile makers in New England migrated to the South in search of cheaper labor to better confront foreign competition, often leaving economic desolation in their wake, and yet the textile industry remained moribund. Japanese electronics invaded the U.S. market, and Japanese producers mounted challenges to their U.S. counterparts even in areas of high technology that had previously been considered the exclusive preserve of the United States.

The economic arguments for free trade now had a more hollow ring. While it could be demonstrated that, in the long run, everyone benefited from free trade, that theoretical abstraction might not be persuasive to the mayor of a town that had recently lost its main industry, or to a worker whose skills were no longer needed, or to a representative whose district was depressed by unemployment. From a political point of view, there was more to be gained by criticizing Japan and by demanding that the jobs of U.S. citizens be protected than by praising free trade. To be sure, there were those whose economic interests were more hurt than helped by protection. Pressures to protect the textile industry have been opposed by the Retail Industry Trade Action Coalition, which represents chain stores that sell many imported products, and shoe producers' efforts to obtain trade relief have been opposed by retailers who sell foreign-made shoes. Nevertheless, interests supporting free trade have been, in the United States at least, overpowered by those clamoring for protection.

The fact remains that free trade does have its victims. If goods are to be produced by countries that have the greatest comparative advantage in their production, then the less efficient producers in other countries must be nudged aside in the process. If the winners were more powerful than the losers in each of the trading partners, there would be no political problem, but this generally is not the case. So long as the United States enjoyed undisputed leadership in most economic sectors, and had the political power to match, it could ensure that the rules of free trade would be widely accepted (even if it had to grant occasional exemptions from their application). But once the largest of the trading partners seemed to have at least as many domestic losers as winners, the system was imperiled.

The situation has not been improving in recent years. In 1985, the U.S. trade deficit reached an all-time high of $150 billion, and neomercantilist sentiments became stronger than ever. By the mid-1980s, it could be accurately observed that "such ferocious demands for protection have not been heard since the 1930s." [12] In May 1986, Congress overwhelmingly adopted a revision of existing trade laws. One of its main thrusts was to reduce the president's latitude in deciding how to respond to instances of damaging competition from abroad, virtually requiring that stern measures, such as import quotas, be taken to deal with foreign competition. The president described the bill as an "openly and rankly political document," and he declared that this "anti-trade bill, this protectionist legislation would have our nation violate the most basic tenets of free and fair international trade." [13] Secretary of the Treasury James Baker declared that "we are facing a trade war with the EEC." [14] Nevertheless, the political imperatives were apparently irresistible for most members of Congress, who, as one lawmaker pointed out, voted for the bill "to solve a political problem back home." [15]

Thus, economic rivalry and trade wars are a two-sided problem. On the one hand, there are domestic interests that suffer when the barriers to trade are lowered, and it is politically difficult to refuse to help them by providing some protection from foreign competition. On the other hand, such protection means that consumers are deprived of the range of choices they might otherwise have and that they pay more for what they buy, and it also means that producers who rely on raw materials or components produced abroad will be placed at a disadvantage. Moreover, the incentives for innovation and greater productivity are weakened in the absence of competitive pressures. This became quite apparent when some U.S. producers were given "temporary" protection from foreign imports until they could recover their ability to compete. When, for example, Washington extracted "voluntary" export restraints from the Japanese car industry, U.S. auto manufacturers failed to take full advantage of this reprieve by improving the quality of their products or lowering prices.

The solidarity of the Western alliance is also impaired when its members engage in trade wars among themselves, and its ability to fashion creative and constructive responses to the challenges it faces is correspondingly diminished. All of this generates a dilemma of effective choice, and we must ask how it can be dealt with.

Dealing with Neomercantilism

One approach might be to assume that the drive for protectionism cannot be stopped and that the appropriate recourse is to strengthen cooperation in noneconomic areas so as to render them less vulnerable to "contamination" from economic rivalries. This means that as economic cooperation becomes shakier, extra efforts should be devoted to resolving other, more tractable, problems. These could include attempts to coordinate policies on East-West relations, to develop a consensus on the proper mix of military and nonmilitary instruments of Western security, and to reach agreement on the sharing of NATO's burdens. Desirable as all of this may be, it is unrealistic to think that the repercussions of trade wars can be contained indefinitely. Sooner or later, the economic problems will have to be dealt with if the cohesion of the West is to be maintained.

The erosion of the competitive edge of the United States has had at least as much to do with economic trends within the country as with the economically predatory attitudes of others. Some observers have blamed America's economic sluggishness on the decline of the work ethic, a supposed phenomenon that conservatives frequently associate with excessive welfare spending and a correspondingly decreased incentive to work on the part of those who benefit from society's largess.[16] But this explanation fails to account for the fact that the principal competitors of the United States typically have even higher levels of welfare spending. Moreover, one could argue, as Lester Thurow does, that "both our experience and foreign experience demonstrate that there is no conflict between social expenditures or government intervention and economic success. Indeed, the lack of investment planning, worker participation, and social spending may be a cause of our poor performance." [17]

Although the United States is still a leader in economic productivity, its lead has been declining. From 1948 to 1968, output per hour worked in the United States increased at an average annual rate of 3.2 percent. Between 1968 and 1973, this rate was 1.9 percent, and between 1973 and 1979 it was 0.7 percent. By the end of the 1970s and into the early 1980s, productivity actually fell. The decline was especially significant in such key manufacturing industries as motors and generators, steel, and aluminum. Meanwhile, productivity was growing in Japan and Germany. In 1950, the average productivity of Japanese workers was only 16 percent of U.S. workers'; by 1973, it was 55 percent, and by 1979, it was 66 percent. The German worker produced 40 percent as much as the U.S. worker in 1950, but 74 percent in 1973 and 88 percent in 1979.[18]

During the decade of the 1970s, the United States lost 23 percent of its share of the world market, a share which had already declined by 16 percent during the 1960s. U.S. manufacturers' share of their domestic market fell as well.[19] The problem has been most evident in steel, automobiles, and textiles, but the aircraft and plastic industries have also been losing ground. Consumer electronics have been especially hard hit. In 1960, about 95 percent of radios and television sets sold in the United States were made domestically. By 1980, imports had captured half the U.S. market. In fact, the United States no longer makes radios at all, black-and-white television sets are almost all made abroad, and domestic color-television production subsists only behind the barrier of "voluntary" export restraints.

One explanation for these changes holds that they are attributable to the changing structure of the U.S. economy. At the beginning of the century, the typical worker was engaged in agricultural production, but during the first half of the century, there was a substantial movement of labor out of agriculture into industry. Since productivity increased more rapidly in industry than it did in agriculture, productivity in the economy as a whole rose as a result of that movement. More recently, however, the movement has been out of industry and into the service sector, where productivity grows less rapidly or not at all. It is difficult for lawyers, teachers, or waiters to increase their "productivity" very rapidly, and this change may consequently account for some of the decline in U.S. economic performance. But since other developed countries have gone through the same kind of change, this cannot be the entire explanation.

Another proposed explanation is that levels of investment in the U.S. economy are lower than in the economies of its principal competitors.[20] Productivity is critically dependent on investment in capital equipment, and the United States may not have been investing enough. Although investment in the United States amounted to approximately 10 percent of GNP in 1980, the comparable figure for Germany was 15 percent, and for Japan, 20 percent. Thus, while the U.S. steel industry went on using traditional open-hearth furnaces, competitors invested in more efficient oxygenation and continuous casting and were thereby able to produce steel more efficiently. To a significant extent, the U.S. steel industry was using its profits to acquire businesses in other sectors of the economy rather than to acquire modern equipment.[21] By 1980, steel operations accounted for only 11 percent of the operating income of the U.S. Steel Company; the rest came from chemicals, utilities, manufacturing, transportation, and resource development.[22]

This problem of underinvestment has led to calls for a national *industrial policy*. The concept of industrial policy is rather amorphous. In its essentials, however, it involves a program of cooperation between business and government to steer industry toward those activities in which it is likely to have the greatest comparative advantage and away from those sectors where it does not. Interest in industrial policy was aroused by the belief that Japan, the most vigorous and successful rival of the United States, owed much of its success to its adoption of a form of economic guidance through state-business cooperation.

The Japanese institution which is primarily responsible for industrial policy is the Ministry of International Trade and Industry (MITI).[23] Its main role is to promote investments in new and promising economic sectors and, by the same token, to encourage business to disinvest from what it believes to be declining industries. These two aspects of industrial policy are equally important, for the average productivity of an economy is affected by the productivity of both its worst and its best sectors, and as much of an improvement can be obtained by pulling out of low-productivity sectors as by moving into high-productivity sectors. Moreover, disinvestment from declining sectors releases the funds needed to move into activities with a more promising future. MITI helps arrange funding for new companies, directs money toward high-technology areas, and studies and disseminates information about industrial and economic trends. Through MITI, the Japanese government can also arrange for favorable tax treatment, encourage mergers and cartels, and promote research and development.

Partly because of this example, a number of economists have suggested that the road back to international economic leadership for the United States lies in the adoption of a national industrial policy. Not everyone agrees, however. Conservatives object that this would lead to "socialistic" government intervention in the economy; they advocate tax reduction and the free market as the cure for the country's economic ills. Others point out that tax reductions have in fact been enacted but have not had very much of a stimulative effect on investment or productivity. Critics on the left are concerned that a national industrial policy might lead to large-scale plant closings and relocations, the effects of which would be borne by the working class.[24] They would prefer more strenuous efforts to save the "sunset" industries than to promote the "sunrise" sectors. Proponents of industrial policy fear that this would lead to a kind of "lemon socialism," designed to save failing economic enterprises at public expense (as was often the case in Great Britain).

A leading proponent of a national industrial policy has been Felix Rohatyn, the investment banker who designed the plan to save New York City from bankruptcy in the late 1970s. Rohatyn has advocated the creation of a quasi-governmental Reconstruction Finance Corporation, modeled after the agency of that name created in 1933 to help deal with the Great Depression. Its purpose would be to identify industries that were worth encouraging or, in certain instances, worth subsidizing.[25] Lester Thurow is another proponent of industrial policy. Lamenting the fact that "disinvestment is what our economy does worst," [26] he points out that

> eliminating a low-productivity plant raises productivity just as much as opening a high-productivity plant. But doing so takes fewer resources. Large investments are not necessary. To close a low-productivity plant also makes it

possible to move the workers and capital that have been tied up in this activity into new, high-technology, activities. With more men and investment funds, new activities can grow more rapidly. Paradoxically, the essence of investment is disinvestment.[27]

Thurow has proposed the creation of public/private "corporate investment committees," which would be responsible for redirecting investment flows from declining toward rising industries. These committees would serve as "public investment banks," to promote investment in industries whose payoffs might not be immediate enough to interest private financial companies.[28] Such public investment banks could also help restructure ailing industries by insisting on certain conditions (for example, increased investment) that private banks are usually unwilling to demand. He also advocates various fiscal reforms designed to promote research and development and accelerated innovation.

While industrial policy would probably be welcomed by the emerging sectors of the economy, which would be its principal beneficiaries, it is likely to be resisted by the "sunset" sectors that could be its victims—and declining industries tend to be politically more powerful than emerging ones. The old industries are more labor intensive than the newer ones, which means that there is a large constituency, including organized labor, to defend them. Moreover, cities and even entire regions have been dependent on such declining industrial sectors as steel, coal, and textiles. By comparison, the emerging industries, almost by definition, employ fewer people and have less well-established lobbies. Thus, the nation's political structure militates, at the very outset, against a national industrial policy of the sort that has been described.

This chapter has described the economic sources of frictions within the Western alliance. To a certain extent, trade rivalries are inevitable as the gap between economic partners narrows. While free trade does benefit most members of the system in the long run, in anything less than the long run the most powerful of the partners reaps most of the benefits by winning out in the competition both in its domestic market and in the international market, while the weaker partners experience the pains. But as long as the partners are grossly unequal in power, the strongest is in a position to impose free trade on the others. That was the state of affairs in the years following World War II.

But as Western Europe and Japan began catching up to the United States, and as the perceived need for U.S. security assistance declined, international receptivity to free trade waned. At the same time, as the U.S. position became less clearly dominant, free trade appeared as less of an economic boon to U.S. producers, many of whom decided that it was easier to seek protection against imports than to take the steps necessary to deal with their foreign rivals. Declining industries, many labor unions (some of which had previously been vocal champions of free trade), and numerous political leaders in search of issues joined the protectionist bandwagon. This drive toward neomercantilism is dangerous both to national prosperity and to international security. Perhaps what economic historian Charles Kindleberger referred to as "the mercantilist instinct which seems to be inbred in human nature"[29] comes to the surface when gaps between partners begin to shrink. Yet it is politically necessary to avoid the excesses of neomercantilism, and the best way may be to resolve the domestic economic weaknesses which are, to a very large extent, responsible for the current state of affairs.

Notes

1. Clair Wilcox, *A Charter for World Trade* (New York: Macmillan, 1949), 8.
2. David H. Blake and Robert S. Walters, *The Politics of Global Economic Relations* (Englewood Cliffs, N.J.: Prentice-Hall, 1976), 13.
3. Ibid., 49.
4. United Nations Conference on Trade and Development, *Review of International Trade and Development, 1970* (New York: United Nations, 1970), 45.
5. Organization for Economic Cooperation and Development, *Policy Perspective for International Trade and Economic Relations*, report of the High-Level Group on Trade and Related Problems of the Secretary General of the Organization for Economic Corporation and Development (Paris: OECD, 1972), 18.
6. Paul A. Samuelson, *Economics*, 10th ed. (New York: McGraw-Hill, 1976), 713.
7. Robert Gilpin, *U.S. Power and the Multinational Corporation* (New York: Basic Books, 1975). For a different perspective, see Raymond Vernon, *Storm over Multinationals: The Real Issues* (Cambridge: Harvard University Press, 1977).
8. To place this decision in context, see Susan Strange, "The Politics of International Currencies," *World Politics* 23 (1971): 215-231.
9. David Calleo, *The Imperious Economy* (Cambridge: Harvard University Press, 1982), 29.
10. Richard N. Cooper, "Trade Policy Is Foreign Policy," in *A Reordered World*, ed. Richard N. Cooper (Washington, D.C.: Potomac Associates, 1973), 57.
11. *United States International Economic Policy in an Interdependent World*, report to the president submitted by the Commission on International Trade and Investment Policy (July 1971), 351.
12. I. M. Destler, "Protecting Congress or Protecting Trade," *Foreign Policy* (Spring 1986): 101.
13. "House 295 to 115 Votes to Tighten Trade Regulation," *New York Times*, May 23, 1986.
14. "Protectionism Rides Again," *Business Week*, May 5, 1986, 25.
15. "House 295 to 115 Votes to Tighten Trade Regulation."
16. See, for example, George Gilder, *Wealth and Poverty* (New York: Basic Books, 1981).
17. Lester C. Thurow, *The Zero-Sum Society* (New York: Basic Books, 1980), 8.
18. "Stunted Growth in Productivity," *Business Week*, June 30, 1980, 65; *Economic Report of the President, 1986* (Washington, D.C.: Government Printing Office, 1986), 251.
19. "A Drastic New Loss of Competitive Edge," *Business Week*, June 30, 1980, 59.
20. Robert Heilbroner and Lester C. Thurow, *Economics Explained* (Englewood Cliffs, N.J.: Prentice-Hall, 1982), Chapter 14.
21. Barry Bluestone and Bennett Harrison, *The De-Industrialization of America* (New York: Basic Books, 1982), 198.
22. Robert Reich, "Making Industrial Policy," *Foreign Policy* (Spring 1982): 859.
23. The role of MITI is described in Ezra Vogel, *Japan As Number One* (New York: Harper and Row, 1979).

24. For example, Bluestone and Harrison, *The De-Industrialization of America*, esp. Chapter 13.
25. Felix Rohatyn, "Reconstructing America," *New York Review of Books*, February 5, 1981.
26. Thurow, *The Zero-Sum Society*, 77.
27. Ibid., 81.
28. Lester C. Thurow, *The Zero-Sum Solution* (New York: Simon and Schuster, 1985), esp. Chapter 9.
29. Charles P. Kindleberger, *Power and Money* (New York: Basic Books, 1970), 117.

Problems of
Third World Development

IN STRICTLY NUMERICAL terms, the United States, and indeed the entire industrialized portion of the world, is a rather small part of the international community. The United States, wealthy and powerful though it is, constitutes less than 5 percent of the global population; the developed nations of the OECD and the COMECON together account for no more than 25 percent. The majority of the world's people live in what are called (often euphemistically) the developing nations. For the most part, these are countries characterized by squalor, malnutrition, short life expectancy, and scant hope for the future.

Comparisons between industrialized and developing nations are usually made in terms of such standard measures of prosperity as annual GNP per capita, where the range is from $14,110 for the United States to $130 for Bangladesh (see Table 15-1). But the differences are just as huge on such other quality-of-life indicators as life expectancy, infant mortality, and nutrition. While life expectancy is 50 years in Bangladesh, and 56 years in Saudi Arabia, it is above 70 in virtually every industrialized nation. While more than 80 out of every 1,000 babies born in Zambia die before they attain their first birthday, the figure is around 10 for France and the United States and only 7 for Japan. In Bangladesh, a person may be considered fortunate to consume over 2,000 calories a day; in the developed countries, it often requires self-discipline to avoid exceeding 3,500. In Thailand, some 7,000 people must compete for the attention of each physician; in the United States and Hungary, there is a doctor for every 400 people.

Many of the developing countries, in addition to their staggering economic difficulties, are only a few decades old and are still striving for a sense of pride and identity. Their fervent nationalism and frequent anti-Western

Table 15-1 Quality-of-Life Indicators for Ten Countries, 1983

Country	Annual GNP per capita (dollars)	Life expectancy (years)	Infant mortality[a]	Per capita daily consumption (calories)	Population per physician (thousands)
Bangladesh	130	50	132	1,922	8.0
Zambia	580	51	81	2,054	7.7
Thailand	820	63	50	2,296	7.1
Colombia	1,430	64	53	2,551	1.7
Hungary	2,150	70	19	3,520	0.4
Yugoslavia	2,570	69	32	3,642	0.6
Japan	10,120	77	7	2,891	0.8
France	10,500	75	9	3,572	0.6
Saudi Arabia	12,230	56	29	3,111	1.7
United States	14,110	75	11	3,616	0.4

Source: World Bank, *World Development Report, 1985* (New York: Oxford University Press, 1985).

[a] Number of deaths during first year per 1,000 live births.

sentiment must be seen in the context of their colonial history (see Chapter 2). Although the United States has generally supported the process of decolonization, its policies in the Third World have been more heavily influenced by its own ideological and geostrategic objectives than by the desires of the developing nations, and it is this fact above all that defines relations between the United States and the developing countries and that imparts to these relations many dilemmas of effective choice.

As pointed out previously, U.S. political leaders (like their Soviet counterparts) tend to perceive the Third World primarily as a set of countries to be recruited for the East-West struggle and as a source of military bases and geostrategic staging areas. But this is not the way in which most developing countries conceive of their international role. Diplomatic and security issues which seem paramount to the United States are far less important to the developing nations than their poverty and their struggle to join the ranks of affluent countries. For them, it is often not the division of the world into a political East and West that is the dominant fact of international relations, but the division of the world into an affluent North and a destitute South. This does not mean that economics is all that matters for the developing nations, but it does imply that it is what matters most to them in their dealings with rich societies in general and the United States in particular.

From the U.S. point of view, the economic instruments of foreign policy are considered means of achieving political and security objectives. For the developing nations, more advantageous economic relations and accelerated growth are the primary goals, although political and security inducements may be used as instruments in their pursuit. Thus, what the North treats as ends, the South often treats as means, and vice versa. Although U.S. foreign policy has generally regarded the development of poor nations as incidental to political objectives, the perceived relation of ends and means has undergone several changes. Different administrations have had different ideas about how economic aid and development would promote U.S. foreign policy goals, and these views have also shifted with swings in public opinion.

Generally speaking, and admittedly with some oversimplification, the conservative position has been that economic aid (often in association with military assistance) should lead directly to an increase in the developing nations' support for U.S. foreign policy goals, by virtue of both the dependence and the gratitude that it would generate. Liberals, on the other hand, have tended to view aid as a foundation for economic growth, which, in turn, would decrease social instability, improve the outlook for democratic development, and thus create a world of like-minded nations supportive of U.S. diplomatic positions. Typically, too, liberals have assigned a more important place to the developing nations in U.S. foreign policy than have conservatives. Thus, a survey of the place of economic development in U.S. foreign policy is to some extent a history of the alternation and evolution of these conceptions.

The Postwar Years

After the end of World War II, the developing world was low on the U.S. list of foreign policy priorities. The Cold War congealed in Central Europe, with strains over Poland, Czechoslovakia, and the two Germanys, and it was assumed that, if the superpowers were to collide, the clash would take place in Europe. Moreover, both superpowers felt, as to a large extent they still do, that control of the Eurasian land mass was the key to global dominance and that their efforts should be devoted mainly to winning the competition for Europe. Thus, the developing world played little part in the international power equations on which the superpowers' foreign policy was predicated.

To the extent that U.S. policy makers did concern themselves with the economic plight of the Third World, they tended to think that the solution did not lie with the developed nations. The generally conservative perspective of the postwar years was that a nation's poverty was essentially its own problem, to be dealt with by its own efforts. The credo was one of self-help, not of international beneficence. If the industrialized nations did have a role to play, it was through the private, not the public, sector. Consequently, it was up to the developing countries to encourage private business rather than seek largess from foreign governments. In particular, they should do what they could to attract investment in their economies—for example, by liberalizing trade and by promoting a favorable business climate (above all, by forswearing national-ization of private enterprise).

By the late 1940s, however, and especially at the beginning of the 1950s, there was a change of perception in Washington. U.S.-Soviet relations had entered a period of intense hostility, and both superpowers were bent on pursuing the Cold War within an ever-larger geostrategic arena. Moreover, a desire to enlarge the repertoire of foreign policy instruments engendered increasing interest in economic tools, and foreign aid came to be recognized as a way of exerting diplomatic influence. In 1950, the International Develop-ment Act proclaimed that it was "the policy of the United States to aid the ef-forts of the peoples of economically underdeveloped areas to develop their resources and improve their living conditions." [1] But words preceded deeds, and very little assistance was actually forthcoming. A proposal for a Special United Nations Fund for Economic Development was made at about this time, but it met with opposition from many developed countries, including the United States. Although a modest amount of foreign aid was appropriated, it had a significant military component and was preferentially directed toward nations thought to be of primary geopolitical significance for Cold War purposes—namely, those bordering on the Soviet Union or China. Thus, though foreign assistance became an instrument of foreign policy, it was still very sparingly used.

It should also be pointed out that direct aid was probably not the major preoccupation of the nations seeking foreign economic help. They were eager, rather, to expand their exports to the industrialized countries in order to acquire the resources needed to finance their growth. Toward this end, what they wanted above all was access to the markets of the developed world. This could have been provided, but there was a problem: GATT demanded reciprocity in the granting of trading privileges, and this the less developed countries (LDCs) did not feel that they were in a position to grant.

It was pointed out in Chapter 14 that the argument for free trade is based on the theory of comparative advantage. However, free trade is not necessarily an optimal arrangement, even among countries with different comparative advantages, if they are at very different levels of economic development. If one country is industrialized and rich while another is underdeveloped and poor, the latter often cannot compete with the former even if it has a long-term com-parative advantage in the production of the good in question. The situation may be compared to that of a talented and promising but very young boxer who is prematurely forced to compete with professionals. This is known as the "infant industry" argument. It is based on the fact that producers in an LDC are not yet able to exploit their comparative advantage, and may never be able to do so if they must immediately face competition from a more powerful economy. Thus, a certain measure of temporary protection is sometimes warranted to allow an industry to get on its feet. In other words, a poor country may occasionally be justified in seeking preferential treatment in international trade without having to reciprocate with trading concessions of its own.

The infant industry argument was not readily acceptable in the practical politics of the postwar years. The only principle around which an international consensus could be generated at that time was the principle of nondiscriminatory free trade. The requests of developing nations for preferential treatment violated that principle and therefore were not given serious consideration. As far as U.S. policy makers were concerned, if a case could be made for external assistance at all, direct grants would be less costly than trade concessions and would be a more flexible tool of diplomatic influence, since they could be increased or decreased in accordance with the recipient's behavior.

Around the mid-1950s, however, there was another change. After Josef Stalin's death in 1953, the Soviet Union was discovering the significance of the Third World to its own foreign policy calculations, and it embarked on a modest foreign aid program, directed largely toward Asia and the Middle East. In 1958, the U.S. Development Loan Fund was established with an appropriation of $300 million, and by 1961 its allocation had doubled to $600 million.[2] In 1956, with U.S. encouragement, the World Bank established a subsidiary named the International Finance Corporation, whose purpose was to make loans for private investment without the government guarantees that were required for normal World Bank loans. In 1960, again at U.S. initiative, the International Development Association, another institution affiliated with the World Bank, was created; its mission was to make "soft" loans on especially easy terms for economic development. In 1961, the Agency for International Development (AID) was established to administer U.S. unilateral aid programs. Thus, the United States had begun to take a leadership role in the promotion of international assistance to the Third World. At the same time, the rationale for foreign aid became somewhat more sophisticated than it had been earlier.

"All Good Things Go Together"

While the initial political justification for foreign aid was that countries that were economically beholden to the United States were likely to support its international positions, policy makers now also took account of the anticipated domestic effects of economic assistance. It was no longer merely a matter of "buying" support outright but of shaping societies and political systems in a way that would make their political interests more compatible with those of the United States. Poverty, so the reasoning went, bred dissatisfaction, social instability, and political radicalism. Under such conditions, Marxist and Soviet influences could take root, and U.S. interests would be undermined. To the extent that foreign aid promoted development, it would also create a context favorable to democratic political evolution and, by extension, to sympathy with the United States. Two influential authors pointed out that foreign aid would "help the societies of the world develop in ways that will not menace our security—either as a result of their own internal dynamics or because they are weak enough to be used as tools by others." [3]

The belief that foreign aid could be used to promote support for U.S. policies via democratic development was especially pronounced in the liberal ethos of John F. Kennedy's presidency. Policy makers in the Kennedy administration took the position that self-sustained economic development must be preceded by a "takeoff" phase, which many LDCs could not hope to complete without some Western assistance. Development in Third World countries would bring not only political democracy but also the emergence of an economically secure middle class, on the analogy of nineteenth-century Europe. This has been called the "all-good-things-go-together" view of the world.[4] It was reflected in the AID *Program Guidance Manual*, which stated that AID's purpose was to promote the development "of a community of free nations cooperating on matters of mutual concern, basing their political systems on consent and progressing in economic welfare and social justice. Such a world offers the best prospect of security and peace for the United States." [5]

One of the most ambitious endeavors of the Kennedy administration was the Alliance for Progress, conceived of as the most substantial aid program since the Marshall Plan. It focused specifically on Latin America, a region of particular foreign policy concern to Washington at that time. The preamble to the charter of the Alliance, and the president's Declaration to the Peoples of the Americas, specified such objectives as "personal liberty," "representative democracy," and "democratic institutions." Between 1961 and 1969, $4.8 billion was provided by the United States to Latin America under the aegis of this program. In 1961, the Peace Corps was also established. In the aggregate, U.S. foreign aid to the LDCs increased from $2 billion in 1957 to $3.7 billion in 1963.[6]

The reasoning behind the program of economic assistance to developing countries was as follows: In order for its economy to grow, a nation must invest in new productive facilities. Normally, this is accomplished through the savings of its people—that is, resources are diverted from current consumption into investment. But a poor nation is one in which people are living on the margin of subsistence, and consequently cannot afford to reduce their consumption to any meaningful extent. Foreign aid would therefore replace domestic savings as the basis for economic growth.

The belief in the economic and political foundations of foreign aid was maintained throughout most of the 1960s. Although academics occasionally questioned the premise that economic growth and democracy necessarily went hand in hand,[7] U.S. policy makers in both the Kennedy and the Johnson administrations seemed convinced that aid could in fact serve foreign policy purposes. Eventually, however, the commitment to economic assistance waned. In 1972, U.S. aid to the Third World amounted to $3.35 billion, which was not only less than the figure for 1963 but represented even more of a decline when inflation is taken into account. In 1962, aid amounted to approximately 0.5 percent of U.S. GNP; by 1972, it had decreased to 0.3 percent. By this measure, the United States dropped from third to twelfth place among the Western industrialized nations in the amount of foreign economic assistance it was rendering.[8]

The move away from economic aid can be traced primarily to two factors. In the first place, it was less and less evident that foreign assistance was stimulating economic development. A few countries, such as South Korea and Taiwan, had managed to attain a respectable rate of growth that was to some extent due to foreign aid, but these were exceptional cases, and, in any event, they had received truly massive amounts of assistance. Lesser amounts of aid did not seem to be adequate to the task. Meanwhile, countries such as Mexico and Thailand were industrializing with only minimal amounts of external assistance. Finally, and contrary to expectations, the gap between rich and poor countries was not narrowing; if anything, it was widening, and foreign aid did not appear to be making much of a difference. If foreign aid could not ensure economic growth, it could not, by extension, be expected to lead to the sort of social and political development that was its ultimate objective.

The expectation that assistance to the Third World would have the same effects as the Marshall Plan had on Western Europe overlooked some important differences. The funds provided to Europe had merely to reactivate an economic and technological base that had already been established, and social and political democracy were also already firmly rooted in the European nations.

The second reason that support for foreign economic aid declined was the growing doubt that political support could be obtained in exchange for economic favors. Anti-American sentiment, a lack of support for U.S. actions like the intervention in Vietnam, and votes against U.S. positions at the United Nations all suggested that recipients of aid were not always properly grateful. In addition, the experience of Vietnam—the costs, frustrations, and cynicism which that misadventure spawned—led to a reassessment of the value of the country's involvement in the developing regions. Even many liberals in Congress who had been enthusiastic supporters of foreign aid came to see it as a first step toward unwelcome involvement in the affairs of other countries. Finally, in the late 1960s, the United States and the Soviet Union entered upon the period of increased cooperation and decreased tension known as détente. Consequently, and for the time being at least, Cold War competition in remote regions lost some of its urgency to both superpowers, and the economic instruments of this competition became less important as well.

Assertiveness of the Third World

If economic aid to the developing world lost much of its appeal during the 1970s, more general issues of economic development did not fade in importance. In fact, they clamored for solutions with greater force than ever. Two developments in particular led to renewed concern with North-South economic relations.

One was a surge of Third World economic activism that began in the early 1970s. The signal event was the sudden, and very substantial, increase in the price of oil brought about by the petroleum-producing developing nations. Oil is obviously vital to the economic well-being of developed countries. It is their primary source of industrial energy and their major fuel for heating and transportation. Since most plastic and other synthetic materials are oil-based, petroleum is also a vital raw material for advanced economies. In fact, it can be argued that oil is the most essential primary commodity in modern societies. Virtually all industrialized countries are importers of petroleum; the United States, although less externally dependent than many other countries, nevertheless imported approximately 40 percent of its oil in the early 1970s.

In 1960, the major Arab oil-producing nations, and several other Third World nations, formed the Organization of Petroleum Exporting Countries (OPEC). (Its members were Algeria, Ecuador, Gabon, Indonesia, Iran, Iraq, Kuwait, Libya, Nigeria, Qatar, Saudi Arabia, United Arab Emirates, and Venezuela.) The organization's primary purpose was to help its members coordinate their policies, especially in dealing with the giant oil multinationals such as Exxon, Gulf, and Royal Dutch-Shell. The organization was not especially active during the first years of its existence, but it began flexing its muscles in the early 1970s. To some extent, it was emboldened by the Libyan government's decision in 1970 to demand a greater share of the profits realized by the oil companies operating on its territory. Negotiations stalled, and as a warning that it was serious, the Libyan government moved to nationalize Occidental Petroleum, a relatively small company. Alarmed by this display of resolve, the other multinationals capitulated to Libya's demands.

Following the Libyan example, OPEC as a whole demanded an increase in oil prices and raised taxes on foreign oil-producing companies. In 1971, most of its demands were met; the price of oil increased by 27 percent (from $1.80 to $2.29 per barrel) and government royalties and taxes from oil increased by 10 percent. In 1972, the price of Persian Gulf oil rose another 8 percent, and talks began on the progressive nationalization of the oil companies, as well. In 1973, a major event stiffened OPEC's determination to use its newly discovered power. On October 6, the fourth Arab-Israeli war broke out, and in accordance with its long-standing policy, the United States threw its support behind Israel. In retaliation, the Arab members of OPEC declared an oil embargo against the United States. In addition, and partly as a way to bolster Arab strength, these nations declared another oil price increase. By January 1, 1974, the price of Persian Gulf oil had climbed to $11.95 per barrel, a more than fivefold increase since 1971.

The U.S. economy reeled under the impact. Inflation, which had been launched by Vietnam-related expenditures, was given further momentum, and the economy entered a recession. This led to a novel economic condition that came to be called *stagflation* (a combination of stagnation and inflation). Many feared that worse was to come. Not only was there a chance that oil prices would continue to rise, but the prices of other raw materials produced by the Third World might do so as well. OPEC's power flowed from its character as a *cartel*—that is, an organization capable of restricting a product's or commodity's supply. In an influential article published in 1973, C. Fred Bergsten, a member of National Security Council staff, warned of the possibility of other cartels in copper, tin, bauxite, natural rubber, and coffee.[9] This could place serious strains on the developed nations and disrupt international money markets. Furthermore, developing nations could exert considerable power over U.S. foreign investment (which at the time exceeded $23 billion in the developing world), perhaps engaging in massive confiscations and thereby damaging the U.S. balance of payments. Bergsten attributed these possibilities not to any intrinsic hostility of Third World countries toward the United States, but rather to their search for economic strength in a world unwilling to help them achieve their developmental goals. He lamented that the United States "regards developing countries . . . solely as pawns on the chessboard of global power politics."

> The United States is the least responsive to Third World needs of any industrialized country at this time. U.S. help is small in quantity and getting smaller. It quality is declining. It often runs directly counter to the central objectives of the LDCs. . . . It lags far behind the policies of Europe and Japan.[10]

Accordingly, there were calls for a more forthcoming U.S. attitude toward the economic needs of poor nations, but now with a new twist. No longer was it argued that U.S. aid was needed for diplomatic and Cold War goals; rather, it was now considered necessary if the Third World was not to exercise its capacity to hurt the United States economically.

Dependency Theory

The other reason for the greater attention paid to North-South relations in the 1970s was the growing conviction that the rich countries of the Northern Hemisphere were largely responsible for the economic predicament of the developing nations. This belief was articulated in a body of theory known as *dependency theory*, which was elaborated mainly by European and Latin American economists and political scientists. Although several variants of the theory emerged, there have been a number of core concepts and beliefs.[11] The central idea of dependency theory is that the South has been linked to the North by a relationship in which the prosperity of the latter has been contingent on the poverty of the former. In other words, poor countries are poor because rich nations are rich, and vice versa. Dependent nations are *peripheral* nations; those upon which they are dependent are the nations of the *center*. The foundations of their relationship were laid during the period of colonialism, but developed countries which were never actually colonial powers also participated in the exploitation of the peripheral nations, and the exploitation has persisted beyond the demise of formal colonialism.

Not everyone within poor nations has suffered, according to the dependency theorists. The maintenance of the status of dependency has been possible only because certain privileged strata within the dependent societies were co-opted by the nations of the center and made their partners in the exploitation of the periphery. These could be commodity-exporting interests (for example, mine or plantation owners) or those sharing in the benefits of manufacturing facilities set up by center nations within peripheral societies. Since their favored position depends on maintaining their society in a subordinate position, they must ensure a system of domestic stratification in which they are dominant. Thus, the inegalitarian and often exploitative nature of Third World societies is also a product of their dependence on the center. The two specific relations between center and periphery that are seen as most responsible for the poverty of the Third World are those of trade and investment.

One of the main obstacles to economic development, in the eyes of many dependency theorists, is the structure of international trade. The problem is that a history of colonialism and inequality has relegated many societies of the periphery to the role of exporters of primary commodities (minerals and foodstuffs) to the rich countries, from which they import processed goods—both consumer products (such as radios and sewing machines) and capital goods (such as tractors and machinery). But the prices of primary commodities tend not to increase as rapidly as prices of processed goods. Thus, the Third World's *terms of trade* (the ratio of the prices of what they sell abroad to the prices of what they purchase from other countries) are constantly declining, and the peripheral nations must export more and more to buy the finished goods that their development would require. As a result, their development proceeds at a very slow pace or is altogether frustrated.

Moreover, according to one variant of dependency theory, the damaging effects of this pattern are not limited to adverse trends in the terms of trade. When a country imports raw materials and processes them into finished goods, it stimulates its own technology and improves its economic know-how, and it then benefits from a number of spillover effects. For example, a country that imports steel and other raw materials to produce tractors will learn, in the process, to produce other things as well (for example, trucks or tanks). Its people will acquire technical skills which will feed upon themselves, and they will learn to organize society in ways that maximize its growth possibilities. On the other hand, a country that imports a finished good can learn only how to use it, which produces far fewer beneficial spillovers than learning how to produce it.[12]

Another problem with being an exporter of raw materials comes from the typically large and abrupt swings in the prices of primary commodities. Although the reasons for this are quite complex, these swings are of a much greater amplitude than those that characterize the prices of most manufactured goods. Because of this volatility, the economies of many Third World countries follow a "boom and bust" cycle, a problem that is all the more serious because exports of a single raw material (or at most two or three) usually account for a very large proportion of their GNP, so that they have nothing with which to offset a loss resulting from a drop in the price of one commodity. Not only is this economically debilitating, but it also strains the social and political fabric of many developing countries.

The other basis of Third World poverty, according to dependency theory, is investment. This may take the form of a transfer of capital from center to periphery, for the purpose of putting it to work in the latter for the benefit of the former, or the acquisition of existing productive facilities—plants or even entire companies—in developing societies by corporations in rich nations. The major vehicle of foreign investment is the multinational corporation (MNC), and the country with the most and biggest MNCs is the United States. Because of the sheer economic power of these companies, it is inevitable that they should produce far-reaching effects on the countries in which they operate. Their presence therefore provokes strong political responses, and they merit closer examination.

U.S. multinationals have gone abroad for a variety of reasons. One of the first was the need to gain access to raw materials; thus, there are multinationals engaged in the extraction of foreign oil (Exxon), aluminum (Alcoa), and copper (Anaconda), and in the growing of fruit (United Brands). Another reason, which has been more important in recent decades, has been a desire to benefit from cheaper foreign labor. Lower living standards and the absence of powerful trade unions in the LDCs have often meant that industries, especially those that are labor-intensive, could reduce their costs of operations substantially by transferring some of their operations abroad. This cost reduction was compounded by the less stringent regulation (for example, regarding pollution control) which most Third World countries imposed on firms operating on their territory. Finally, multinationals sometimes go abroad to be close to a foreign market to which they had previously been exporters. By establishing themselves as local producers, they avoid transportation costs and, even more importantly, the tariff barriers that would otherwise impede their access to the foreign markets. Market considerations are important chiefly to MNCs that sell to other developed nations (particularly Canada and Western European countries), because they have large numbers of relatively affluent consumers. However, several developing countries with a large middle class (such as, for example, Argentina and Brazil) are attractive for the same reason.

The effects of MNCs on the host countries are a matter of considerable controversy. While there are those who argue that MNCs make a vital contribution to economic and social development, others maintain that they have debilitating consequences for developing nations. One charge is that they take more out of the country than they put into it. In its simplest form, the criticism is that MNCs engaged in the extraction of minerals are "stealing" the nation's natural resources. Some observers, on the basis of a broader and more sophisticated analysis of MNC operations, have declared that the profits repatriated from the host country sometimes exceed the amount invested in the local economy. Moreover, it is said, this is exacerbated by the fact that not even all of an MNC's investment represents an actual addition to the host country's resources. Often, multinationals borrow the money they invest from financial institutions in the host country. Conversely, repatriated profits do not include everything that is taken out of the host country; one must also consider such less visible transfers as patent fees, royalties, and other payments charged by the parent company to the local subsidiary.

Most importantly perhaps, MNCs are accused of distorting the economic and social development of the host country. The firms often exist in a sort of enclave, with very few beneficial links to the rest of the local economy or society. They produce with technologies stemming from, and geared to the needs of, affluent countries, and these technologies are not necessarily applicable to the conditions and needs of a developing country. They are too sophisticated and expensive to be useful in an economy that has barely begun to mechanize. Moreover, the goods themselves are primarily intended for the markets of developed countries and may be irrelevant to the needs of the developing host country—for example, electric rather than manual sewing machines, or tractors with elaborate functions and capabilities. If the products can be consumed locally, it is only by an affluent elite. In many cases, foreign capital is attracted to the more advanced and dynamic sectors of the local economy, further widening the gap between the sectors of the host-country economy.

Thus, both trade and investment relationships between North and South have come under criticism from dependency theorists. In both cases, the bulk of the benefits are said to be garnered by the developed country, while most of the costs are borne by the developing nation, thus perpetuating the chasm between rich and poor countries. Since the United States is the world's largest trader and the home of some of the most powerful MNCs, it has been the target of most of the criticism. It should be noted that some of the most vociferous critics of the U.S. impact on Third World economic development have come from the developed world, including some from the United States itself. Thus, the credibility of the criticism is enhanced by the fact that it does not come only from developing countries. These criticisms have prompted proposals to remedy the Third World's economic plight, but the outlook is not encouraging.

The NIEO

Rumblings within the Third World about the state of North-South economic relations had been audible for several years, mainly within the context of the United Nations Conference on Trade and Development (UNCTAD). This organization was established in the mid-1960s and soon became the principal institutional setting for international bargaining on matters of trade and aid. The Third World nations within UNCTAD, initially known as the Group of 77 (membership has since increased considerably), drew up a set of specific demands in 1974 which they presented at a special session of the UN General Assembly. Their proposals called for the establishment of a New International Economic Order (NIEO), touching on many aspects of the relations between rich and poor nations, though the emphasis was on aid and trade.

Aid-related provisions of the NIEO included requests that developed countries set aside 0.7 percent of their GNP for foreign assistance; that they increase the funds for dealing with food and energy emergencies in Third World countries; and that there be a renegotiation of the Third World's outstanding foreign debt, which, largely as a result of rising oil prices and the failure of other commodity cartels, had been expanding greatly. In addition, the developing countries sought a larger voice in how the aid allocated by international organizations would be used and distributed. Decision-making power in the World Bank and the IMF was weighted according to a country's financial contribution, which meant that decisions had to have the approval of the United States and a few other industrialized nations. The Third World countries wanted a revision of the voting rules that would give them more power.

However, most of the demands included in the NIEO concerned trade. Exports accounted for approximately 80 percent of the inflow of foreign resources into the Third World, so improving the prospects for exports was a more pressing issue than increasing foreign assistance. A number of proposals were made toward this end.

First, the LDCs sought easier access to the markets of the developed nations. Their own markets were often too small to allow for manufacturing at competitive economies of scale, and the only substantial markets for finished goods were those of the rich countries. Moreover, unless LDCs entered the international division of labor as something other than exporters of minerals and foodstuffs, they could never hope to fully participate in the benefits of development. The obstacle to easier access to the markets of the developed countries was that the rules of international trade normally require that all preferences be reciprocal; favors in terms of tariffs and other regulations for a country's exports had to be met with similar favors on the part of the exporting country. But this the Third World found unacceptable. Since developing countries were economically weak, they felt it necessary to protect their fledgling producers against competition from producers in countries with strong economies. In their view, they could not be expected to reciprocate tariff reductions granted by developed nations. What they wanted, rather, was preferential treatment for their exports, or what was known as a *generalized system of preferences*.

The LDCs also wanted help in resolving the problem of the volatility of their export prices. Unless something was done to mitigate the wide fluctuations in the prices of Third World products, the LDCs could not plan for development; long-term investment strategies cannot be implemented unless future earnings can be anticipated with some confidence. One proposal called for *indexing* (linking) the prices of primary commodities to those of manufactured products. The former prices would then vary no more than the latter and would also rise by the same amount over the long run. This proposal was summarily rejected by the United States and other developed countries. Another proposal was for *long-term multilateral contracts*, whereby importing nations would agree to buy specified quantities of a commodity at a specified price. Still another was for the establishment of *buffer stocks* for certain commodities, which would allow price fluctuations to be controlled by purchases for and sales from a central stock. When a price experienced strong downward pressures, the commodity would be purchased and added to the central stock, thus reducing its supply and preventing its price from falling; when a price increase was in the offing, the commodity would be sold from the buffer stock, increasing the supply and holding the price down. This would be administered in an Integrated Program for Commodities, financed mainly by the North and covering a number of internationally traded commodities.

Other provisions of the NIEO included access to the technology of rich countries and more host-country control over MNCs, along with a code of conduct to make multinationals more responsive to the economic and social needs of the developing nations in which they functioned.

The NIEO proposals were vigorously promoted by Third World countries, and many hoped that they would provide the foundation for more equitable relations between rich and poor countries. But the response from the North was unenthusiastic. The proposals found some endorsement, mainly among intellectuals and journalists, but very little governmental sympathy or support. The aid target of 0.7 percent of GNP was not met except by a few relatively small developed nations—Denmark, Norway, Sweden, and the Netherlands. U.S. aid, on the other hand, never went above 0.3 percent of GNP.[13] Since the United States has the largest GNP in the world, its failure to meet the target has been especially disappointing to the framers of the NIEO.

The situation with regard to trade has not been much better. The European Common Market did take some relatively generous steps to improve Third World export earnings. It adopted what came to be known as the Stabex system (for *stab*ilization of *ex*port earnings), whereby it undertook to compensate, with increased financial assistance, a number of LDCs when their export earnings fell below a certain baseline. The same European countries agreed to grant various forms of preferences to LDCs covered by Stabex. However, the U.S. government has not followed the European lead and has been generally less forthcoming on matters of trade.

It did set up a system of preferences, but the system was subject to a variety of restrictions that seriously limited its benefits to developing nations. Some goods produced by developing countries were granted preferential treatment, but this applied only to imports below certain quantitative limits; above these limits, full tariffs continued to be applied. Moreover, the preferences did not cover goods that the United States itself made, even if Third World nations had a comparative advantage in their production. Finally, leather products, textiles, and similar goods making up a large part of the LDCs' exports of processed goods were not given meaningful preferences. With the U.S. textile industry in trouble and defended by powerful unions, no U.S. government wished to pay the domestic political costs of allowing foreign producers free access to the nation's markets. Free trade could not be allowed to stand in the path of votes from U.S. textile producers.

Plans to control fluctuations in the prices of primary commodities have also made little headway. In 1979, a number of industrialized countries agreed to establish a Common Fund, whose purpose would be to finance price-stabilization schemes under an arrangement called the Integrated Program for Commodities. This included the creation of buffer stocks (in tin, for example); the establishment of export quotas, as a way of managing the supplies (and hence the prices) of certain commodities; and multilateral contracts for the purchase of commodities at prices that would be fixed for a certain period of time. However, the execution of these plans has foundered on the unwillingness of the developed countries, including the United States, to contribute the resources needed to finance them.

From the developing nations' perspective, the only commodity-price policy not requiring the cooperation of the developed countries would have been cartelization along OPEC lines. If successful, such cartels could have substantially boosted export prices and provided participating nations with the resources needed to finance their development plans. The idea did of course occur to many LDCs but, unfortunately for them, cartels do not usually work.

By the early 1980s, it became apparent that even OPEC had lost much of its vitality. Oil prices began dropping and OPEC was in disarray. As this experience demonstrated, there are several significant obstacles to successful cartelization. The essence of a cartel is to collectively restrict supply and thus pump up the price of the good in question. But as the price increases, each member is tempted to cheat and to supply more than the cartel allows in order to make a large profit at the higher price. Others then follow suit, and soon the increased supply deflates the price. Success, therefore, tends to breed failure. Another obstacle is that a cartelized good must meet some very important need; if it does not, the price increase will be met by decreased demand, and the producers will have gained nothing. While oil certainly meets that condition, other products that were the chief exports of some LDCs—for example, cocoa and bananas—did not. In addition, there must be no adequate substitute for the good; otherwise, consumption would shift toward a substitute as the price of the original good increased. But there are not many goods without at least one reasonably adequate substitute: tea can replace coffee, scrap metal can often be used in place of tin, synthetic rubber can serve much the same purpose as natural rubber. Thus, neither the hopes of the Third World nor the fears of the developed countries that were awakened by the initial success of OPEC were borne out by subsequent events.

In sum, the lot of LDCs has not improved appreciably since the NIEO proposals were made. The steps that the Third World could have taken have proven ineffective, and the cooperation from the North that the poor countries had hoped for has not materialized. Once again, since the United States is the richest and most influential of the industrialized nations, and has also been one of the countries least receptive to Third World economic demands, it has been the target of much of the bitterness that the failure of the NIEO generated.

U.S. Economic Interests in the Third World

The relations of the United States with the Third World have come full circle since the end of the war. During the 1950s, what little interest there was in the developing nations was associated with their role in the geopolitical tug of war between the two superpowers. Under President Kennedy and President Johnson, the Cold War continued to dominate U.S. concern with the developing nations, but in a more sophisticated way; the strategy was to establish the economic conditions within which democracy, and thus pro-Western attitudes, might flourish. In the 1970s, North-South issues became important in their own right, rather than as an appendage of Cold War objectives, because of the fear of potential Third World cartel power and also by virtue of an occasional pang of conscience for the plight of the world's poor. But the 1980s resemble in many ways the 1950s: The primary significance of the Third World once again derives from its role in the superpower rivalry. Foreign aid to LDCs has gone mostly to those in which the United States had a stake rooted in that rivalry, or else to those whose economic collapse would have had serious consequences for the U.S. economy (for example, because they owed large debts to U.S. banks). Beyond that, the Reagan administration has tended to limit its activism in the economies of the Third World to calls for greater latitude for free-market forces (since the state plays a large role in the economies of most LDCs). On the issue of greatest concern to the Third World, promotion of its economic development, very little has been achieved, and that will continue to mar U.S. relations with the developing regions.

The lack of interest in the Third World on the part of the United States can ultimately be traced to the belief that the poorer nations of the world have little impact on U.S. national interests. This, however, is a misconception. The developing countries constitute the vast majority of the world's nations and contain the majority of the world's population. This has a number of important economic implications. The Third World represents a very large market for U.S. exports. For at least the past decade, more than one-third of all U.S. exports have gone to the developing countries.[14] An even larger proportion of exports of manufactured goods, representing the more dynamic sectors of the U.S. economy, goes to the Third World.

It must also be remembered that the main justification for international trade is that countries have different comparative advantages, permitting certain nations to buy that which they cannot most efficiently produce themselves and sell that which others are not as well equipped to make. In this regard, it has been correctly pointed out that, "because of the great discrepancy in comparative advantage, U.S. trade with developing nations probably creates more economic gains than trade with developed countries. The latter tend to exchange similar products." [15]

Thus, and contrary to what many seem to believe, trade with the Third World produces as many significant benefits for the United States as it does for the developing nation. In particular, it should be understood that one industrial job in six within the U.S. economy has, in recent years, depended on exports to the Third World.[16] There would be a socially and politically explosive rise in U.S. unemployment if developing world markets were to disappear. The political consequences would probably be more profound than those which an opening of U.S. markets to imports from developing countries would produce.

In addition, the United States is dependent for much of its critical raw materials on nations in Africa (for example, Zimbabwe for chromium, southern Africa for a number of strategic metals), Latin America (for example, Chile for copper), and Asia (for example, Malaysia for tin). Finally, the economies of certain Third World nations can affect the United States in special ways. For example, the economic collapse of the Third World debtor nations could imperil the U.S. banking system, and a depression in Mexico could lead to massive migration—much of it illegal—into Texas and California, placing a severe economic burden on the affected areas.

It is therefore a mistake to consider the Third World as a meaningful part of the international system only in connection with the Cold War. Such a perception can only alienate the developing countries—and help perpetuate the U.S.-Soviet rivalry as well. The developing nations do affect U.S. interests, especially its economic interests, quite outside of the East-West context.

In the mid-1980s, the developing regions accounted for approximately three quarters of a global population rapidly approaching five billion people. By most responsible estimates the world's population will climb to over six billion by the end of the twentieth century, and at that time, the Third World's population will account for some 80 percent of the total. By the end of the twenty-first century, the earth's population may stabilize at approximately eleven billion people, and close to 90 percent will be living in what is now the developing world.[17] So large a proportion of the world's population is bound to affect, perhaps to determine, the course of international affairs, even assuming that the developed world is spared nuclear devastation. It would be well to lay the foundations now for what may be a vastly altered international system. It is a matter not only of sparing the United States the long-term consequences of the bitterness of the majority of mankind, but also of providing it with the opportunity to derive the maximum economic and political benefits from a more forthcoming policy toward the Third World. This does not imply that the United States, or even the industrialized world as a whole, should consider itself wholly or principally accountable for the poverty of developing nations. At least some of the responsibility lies within these countries themselves. Bureaucratic inefficiency, imprudent economic policies, corruption, and local conflicts have hampered their growth. Nevertheless, the developed countries, which collectively control the bulk of the earth's wealth, technology, and economic power, cannot escape shouldering some of the burden for improving conditions in the Third World, out of self-interest if not out of altruism.

Notes

1. Quoted in Göran Ohlin, *Foreign Aid Policies Reconsidered* (Paris: Organization for Economic Cooperation and Development, 1966), 16.
2. David A. Baldwin, *Economic Development and American Foreign Policy, 1943-1962* (Chicago: University of Chicago Press, 1966), 204.
3. Max F. Millikan and Walt W. Rostow, *A Proposal: Key to an Effective Foreign Policy* (New York: Harper and Brothers, 1957), 39.
4. Richard Packenham, *Liberal America and the Third World* (Princeton: Princeton University Press, 1973).
5. U.S. Agency for International Development, *Program Guidance Manual*, August 1, 1963 (Washington, D.C.), 1.
6. Organization for Economic Cooperation and Development, *Flow of Financial Resources to Less-Developed Countries, 1956-1963* (Paris: OECD, 1964), 19.
7. For example, Samuel P. Huntington, *Political Order in Changing Societies* (New Haven: Yale University Press, 1968), 5-7.
8. Organization for Economic Cooperation and Development, *Development Cooperation, 1973 Review* (Paris: OECD, 1973).
9. C. Fred Bergsten, "The Threat from the Third World," in *A Reordered World*, ed. Richard N. Cooper (Washington, D.C.: Potomac Associates, 1973), 103-122 (originally published in *Foreign Policy* [Summer 1973]).
10. Ibid., 105.
11. Among the most important works in the literature of dependency theory are Samir Amin, *Accumulation on a World Scale*, 2 vols. (New York: Monthly Review Press, 1974); André G. Frank, *On Capitalist Underdevelopment* (Bombay: Oxford University Press, 1975); Johan Galtung, "A Structural Theory of Imperialism," *Journal of Peace Research* 8 (1971): 81-117; Stephen Hymer, "The Multinational

Corporation and the Law of Unequal Development," in *Economics and World Order*, ed. Jagdish Bhagwati (New York: Free Press, 1972), 214-236; Theotonio dos Santos, "The Structure of Dependence," *American Economic Review* 60 (1970): 231-236.

12. Galtung, "Structural Theory of Imperialism," *Journal of Peace Research* 8 (1971): 81-117.

13. U.S. Department of Commerce, Bureau of the Census, *Statistical Abstract of the United States, 1986* (Washington, D.C.: Government Printing Office, 1985).

14. Ibid.

15. John W. Sewell and John A. Mathieson, *The Third World: Exploring U.S. Interests* (New York: Foreign Policy Association, 1982), 11.

16. Brandt Commission, *Common Crisis: North-South Cooperation for World Recovery* (Cambridge: MIT Press, 1983), 27.

17. Robert S. McNamara, "The Population Problem," *Foreign Affairs* 62 (1984): 1113.

section six

Conclusions

Looking Back
and Looking Ahead

THE ATTAINMENT OF important national goals depends on an effective foreign policy, making foreign policy a crucial part of national political life. But the challenges facing U.S. foreign policy are difficult, the means of pursuing external objectives are imperfect, and no simple formulas can encompass so complex a policy arena. Nevertheless, the principles and the evidence that have been discussed here suggest certain broad conclusions. These will be recapitulated, and we will examine their implications for U.S. foreign policy and world politics.

Foreign Policy and Democracy

The United States, as a nation with extensive external needs and demands, must have the ability to deal with its international environment in a flexible and effective manner. At the same time, its behavior abroad bears on fundamental national values, and foreign policy is not the only facet of the country's existence. Accordingly, we must ask whether the goals of U.S. foreign policy can coexist with political ideals—whether, in particular, external pursuits might not occasionally clash with democratic values and practices. The question jointly addresses the dilemmas of aggregation and political principle.

Policy making in a democracy must have three principal attributes. (1) It should be based directly or indirectly on the policy preferences of the public. This does not mean that policy should be dictated by public-opinion polls; it means, rather, that the public should affect major decisions through its electoral choices. The public's representatives—in the case of the United States, the members of the Senate and the House of Representatives—should have adequate input into foreign policy decisions, at least to the extent provided for by the Constitution. (2) There should be definite constraints on the power of those who are entrusted with the management of the nation's affairs, and these limits should operate even when policy does not contradict the will of the majority. This in turn implies two things: (a) that the principle of checks and balances should ensure that no branch of government wields a share of power in excess of its constitutional prerogative, and (b) that where policy flows from the pressure of organized private interests, a plurality of private interests should ensure that narrow parochial interests do not impose their will on the nation. (3) No matter how democratically a decision has been made, it cannot be allowed to violate a core set of rights and liberties, whether these are embodied in the Constitution or in generally accepted norms of democratic practice. How compatible has the conduct of U.S. foreign policy been with these principles?

Role of the Public and Congress

A number of observers have expressed concern that the U.S. public is in no position to influence the conduct of external affairs. The public, they say, is both too ignorant of the issues and too emotionally volatile to provide useful input into foreign policy. The discussion in Chapter 3 suggested that this was partially, but only partially, true. Most U.S. voters are indeed surprisingly ignorant of the issues of foreign policy, and they usually take notice only when international affairs affect their pocketbook or in the extreme case when military actions or very high political stakes are involved. But, as we have seen, this does not disqualify the public from having a foreign policy function. Governmental accountability can exist even if most citizens do not have a full understanding of the issues involved. As long as voters know what they want in foreign policy and can tell whether the government is providing it, they can play their role by reelecting or defeating political leaders on the basis of the leaders' performance. For example, voters may not know much about the intricacies of economic policy, but they may know that they dislike inflation, they can recognize inflation when it occurs, and they can react accordingly at the next election. Similar statements could be made about international confrontations, arms reduction, and other issues in international relations. A person who is totally apathetic could not play even this limited role in policy making, but that is too harsh a description of the average U.S. voter.

It is also probably true that the public is not as intemperate and volatile in its foreign policy moods as some observers have suggested. In fact, it has at times demonstrated more circumspection, especially on military issues, than have its leaders. Thus, while the public's role in the conduct of external affairs will necessarily remain limited to making judgments about its elected officials every few years, there is no reason why its preferences in foreign policy should be disregarded.

A review of recent U.S. history showed three phases in the participation of elected representatives in foreign policy decision making. During the first phase, covering the decades preceding full-scale military involvement in Vietnam, Congress was loath to involve itself in external affairs or to challenge the decisions made by the president and his administration. It was virtually obsequious toward the executive branch and abstained from playing a meaningful foreign policy role. Its passive and uncritical acquiescence to the interventions in Korea and, at first, in Vietnam clearly illustrated its attitude.

Beginning in the late 1960s, the legislators shook off their reticence, and a new congressional disposition emerged. The conflict in Vietnam played a catalytic role. As it escalated and as its high costs became more apparent, members of Congress became increasingly aware of the dangers of allowing the executive branch a free hand in foreign affairs, especially where possible military involvements were concerned. The fact that both the Johnson and the Nixon administrations had deceived the nation about the circumstances of the U.S. military presence in Southeast Asia, and the public outrage that ensued, emboldened Congress to assume a more activist role in foreign affairs. The strongest indication of the changed outlook was the passage, in 1973, of the War Powers Act, which significantly restricted the president's ability to commit U.S. troops to foreign conflicts. Congressional oversight of covert activities abroad was also strengthened. With the Arms Export Control Act of 1976, Congress also established a measure of legislative control over arms transfers abroad. The Case Act of 1972 limited the executive branch's ability to bypass, via executive agreements, congressional control over international treaties. Dismayed by the repressive political practices of some of the nation's Third World allies, Congress restricted the flow of economic and military assistance to governments that systematically violated basic human rights. It also demonstrated an increasing willingness to reject presidential foreign policy appointees of whom it disapproved.

Subsequently, some people began to feel that the pendulum had swung too far in the opposite direction and that the president's ability to conduct a flexible and effective foreign policy was being unreasonably hampered by congressional restrictions. The dangers of legislative meddling, they feared, had come to outweigh the perils of unconstrained presidential power. Nevertheless, Congress seems unwilling to return to the role of a passive spectator where foreign affairs are concerned. If the executive branch departs from guidelines that Congress deems appropriate, Congress will exercise its constitutional prerogatives. However, legislators have many political concerns that are unrelated to foreign policy, and their resources for monitoring the minutiae of external affairs are limited. Thus, Congress does not feel impelled to exercise the full range of its powers on a continuous basis or to involve itself in the daily details of international relations. It has limited its role to preventing egregious departures from basic goals and accepted methods. This seems like a reasonable position and one that is compatible both with the principles of democratic control and with the need for effective executive management of foreign policy.

Thus far, the conduct of foreign policy in the United States does not seem to be drastically out of line with basic principles of democratic policy making. Contrary to what is sometimes thought, the public is not irrelevant to the process, and Congress does participate in what is probably the most appropriate way. Thus, the first of the three democratic principles (direct or indirect public participation) appears to be in reasonable harmony with the making of external policy. Nor does congressional involvement in international affairs represent much of a hindrance to flexible and dynamic external policy. In any case, a lesser congressional role would probably place more power in the hands of the executive branch than would be compatible with democratic principles and would provide real potential for abuses of the sort witnessed during the Vietnam War. One such abuse may be a disregard for certain basic liberties. The Nixon administration's program of spying on U.S. citizens who opposed the Vietnam War effort, President Lyndon B. Johnson's lies regarding the nature and circumstances of the nation's military involvement, and the "misinformation" campaigns directed toward the press during the Reagan administration (even if meant theoretically to confuse the country's adversaries) show that vigilance is still needed to ensure that democratic practices are followed in the execution of foreign policy.

The Bureaucracy and Private Power

The reassertion of congressional control over the executive branch in matters of foreign policy is relevant also to the second principle of democratic policy making—that there should be limits to the power of any one branch of government and of any single private group—but there is more to the problem than that. In particular, questions have been raised about the influence of the governmental bureaucracies and of powerful organized private interests that are not effectively countered by other private organizations or by public authority.

Much of what emerges as national policy is the product of the routines, preferences, and intramural wranglings of the foreign policy bureaucracy. These often invisible forces tend to escape legislative control and, to a large extent, presidential control as well. The precise effects of this phenomenon, which is inherent in the nature of large organizations, are not well understood. The bureaucracy's major influence lies not in its ability to undertake significant policy initiatives, but in its tendency to promote policies that enhance its own missions and resources, with little or no regard for their bearing on the interests of the nation as a whole. In addition, there is the danger that bureaucratic agencies whose work requires a degree of secrecy will operate entirely outside the purview of meaningful political control. Fears that this would be (or had been) the case with the CIA led to the initiation of congressional oversight of covert activities. More recently, it has come to light that the staff of the National Security Council negotiated with Iran on trading arms for hostages, in clear contravention of official policy, and that proceeds from arms sales to Iran were used to fund activities of the Nicaraguan contras, in apparent violation of existing legislation—yet President Reagan was said to have been totally unaware that this was being done. There are not many cases of this kind, but the violence they do to democratic practices is obvious.

As for private interests, certain segments of the business community and of organized labor, as well as a number of ethnic lobbies, sometimes seem to have a substantial impact on foreign policy. Acting occasionally in concert with parts of the executive or legislative branches, they seek to shape policy in a direction consonant with their own interests rather than with those of the nation as a whole. It would not be accurate to say that private lobbies dominate foreign policy, but their relative power sometimes exceeds the portion of the overall societal interests they represent.

The conclusion thus far is that, while there has not been a total incompatibility between the requisites of democracy and the requirements of effective foreign policy, the two occasionally have an uneasy relationship. The problems have not reached such proportions that either democracy or effective policy is threatened, but the possibility cannot be ignored. In this regard, neither the dilemma of aggregation nor the dilemma of political principle has been fully resolved.

Security, Peace, and Military Force

East-West Hostility

An understanding of the sources of hostility and confrontation provides the foundation for effective policies of peace and security. In the case of the U.S.-Soviet relationship, the explanations that serve as the basis for official policy are surprisingly superficial. We saw that enmity between nations usually stems from two kinds of causes: a primary complex of circumstances that initiate the rivalry and the secondary conditions that reinforce it. At some point, however, the initiating causes may fade away and the animosity may be perpetuated by the secondary causes alone.

In the case of the United States and the Soviet Union, it proved difficult to identify objective conflicts of interest that might be the primary cause of the hostility. Neither territorial nor economic competition seems to be involved. Ideological contention is clearly not irrelevant, but its effect has probably been exaggerated. The Soviet Union would almost certainly prefer a world of nations after its own image, but it seems unwilling to undertake major risks to achieve such a world. Moreover, the pursuit of radical political change within developing nations seems less important to the Kremlin than its more pragmatic foreign policy goals. Indeed, both superpowers have demonstrated considerable capacity to get along with nations that have political values antithetical to their own when it appears to be to their diplomatic or security advantage to do so.

It appears, then, that internal drives may be largely responsible for the state of superpower relations. For example, the domestic legitimacy of the Soviet regime may be partly contingent on its ability to inspire fear and respect abroad, particularly since the regime's performance in domestic areas, such as the economy, has not been especially impressive. Bureaucratic politics and organizational momentum also influence the course of Soviet behavior. In the United States, the power of the national-security bureaucracies probably establishes a limit beyond which improvements in superpower relations cannot go, at least in the short run. In this respect, it is probably fair to say that the national-security establishments of the two superpowers are each other's implicit allies. Nikita Khrushchev once told Norman Cousins, the author and publisher: "The generals need each other. [The arms race] is the best way they have of strengthening their positions and making themselves important." When Cousins relayed this observation to President John F. Kennedy, the latter agreed.[1]

Much of the hostility between the two countries is rooted in fundamental dissimilarities—cultural, political, and economic. However, these dissimilarities would not give rise to animosity were it not that both nations believe that their own values have universal applicability, so that the rival's very existence and claims represent a challenge to each side's pretensions. The psychological mechanism that seeks to establish cognitive consistency then reinforces mutual dislike and distrust: If the other side stands for so much that is contrary to our own values, it is satisfying to believe that its international behavior is contrary to our interests. Consequently, we respond to the other side in a hostile manner, thus confirming the other side's worst suspicions and creating a self-perpetuating cycle of hostility and distrust.

If the tension in U.S.-Soviet relations arose from objectively competing interests, it could be relieved by a compromise of some sort or by one side's abandonment of that which is incompatible with the other's interest. But if it is accepted that much of the tension grows out of drives internal to the two societies, reinforced by their dissimilarities and by the psychological consequences of those dissimilarities, then a solution is much harder to envisage and would probably be extremely difficult to implement. None of this implies that there is no way out of the morass of superpower rivalry, but it does suggest that a substantial amount of political will and great reserves of patience would be required. While working to improve superpower relations over the long term, a number of immediate challenges must be met. The most pressing tasks are to decrease the likelihood of nuclear conflict, to achieve meaningful arms control, and to restrict the use of military force in the pursuit of Cold War advantages in the developing world.

The Threat of Nuclear War

Most people are not thrown into a permanent state of anxiety by the specter of nuclear war. Partly, this is because we have become inured to the danger by having been exposed to it for so long (many of us for our entire life-